MASTERS OF THE MIDDLE WATERS

MASTERS *of the* MIDDLE WATERS

Indian Nations and Colonial Ambitions along the Mississippi

JACOB F. LEE

THE BELKNAP PRESS OF
HARVARD UNIVERSITY PRESS

Cambridge, Massachusetts
London, England
2019

Second printing

Library of Congress Cataloging-in-Publication Data

Names: Lee, Jacob F., author.
Title: Masters of the middle waters : Indian nations and colonial ambitions
    along the Mississippi / Jacob F. Lee.
Description: Cambridge, Massachusetts : The Belknap Press of Harvard
    University Press, 2019. | Includes bibliographical references and index.
Identifiers: LCCN 2018039441 | ISBN 9780674987678 (cloth)
Subjects: LCSH: Indians of North America—Mississippi River Valley—Politics
    and government. | Indians of North America—Mississippi River
    Valley—History. | Indians of North America—Kinship—Mississippi River
    Valley. | Illinois Indians—History. | Illinois Indians—Politics and
    government. | Indians, Treatment of—Mississippi River Valley. |
    Mississippi River Valley—History. | Europe—Colonies—America—History.
Classification: LCC E78.M75 L44 2019 | DDC 977 / .01—dc23
    LC record available at https://lccn.loc.gov/2018039441

To my family

CONTENTS

MASTERS OF THE MIDDLE WATERS

Introduction

Cities of the Living, Cities of the Dead

In 1836, an American traveler named Edmund Flagg stood on the crest of a Mississippian Indian mound in the northern suburbs of St. Louis. The scene overwhelmed him. "There are few more delightful views in the vicinity of St. Louis of a fine evening," Flagg wrote, "than that commanded by the summit of the 'Big Mound.'" From his vantage point, he watched the broad Mississippi River cut through its wooded valley, and he could hear it crashing against the limestone cliffs that lifted the city above the river's rushing waters. Flagg's gaze followed the river's current from north to south. On its banks, he observed engineers contemplating how to ensure deep water at the St. Louis docks, and southward, he noted the richness of the landscape and the "delightful villas and country seats" that punctuated the forests on the city's outskirts. Beholding "the empire valley of the West," Flagg predicted that the region and its seemingly inexhaustible soil would soon become "the garden of North America."[1]

As Flagg envisioned the future of the midcontinent, he also tried to make sense of its past. Like most Americans, Flagg believed the continent's history began when European colonists arrived on its shores. But as he wandered through the ancient metropolis of Cahokia and its western suburbs in St. Louis, Flagg confronted the remnants of monumental architecture that predated the presence of Europeans in the region by more than half a millennium. Moreover, he understood that Cahokia's planners had weighed the same factors as had the founders of St. Louis. As Cahokians built their city,

1

Fig. I.1 St. Louis as seen from the east bank of the Mississippi. The Big Mound appears on the far right.

they had capitalized on the spot's location near the intersection of multiple rivers and on the region's verdant landscape. "It is evident from these monuments of a former generation," Flagg wrote of the mounds, "that the natural advantages of the site upon which St. Louis now stands were not unappreciated long before it was pressed by the first European footstep."[2]

For Flagg, the ruins, remnants of some great civilization long since dead, raised more questions than they answered. He did not know that, around AD 1050, Mississippian Indians had erected the city and, from it, ruled the midcontinent for two centuries. Nor did he have any understanding of the four hundred years of migration, warfare, diplomacy, and trade that followed the demise of the mound builders and predated European colonization. From atop the mound, Flagg asked, "What vicissitudes and revolutions have, in the lapse of centuries, rolled like successive waves over the plains at its base?" Flagg looked over "the cities of the dead . . . side by side with the cities of the living," pondering his question and finding no satisfactory answers. He recognized that the past of Cahokia and the future of St. Louis intersected under his feet, but he could not fit the pieces together into a coherent story, beyond the usual nineteenth-century platitudes about the "onward march of civilization."[3]

Flagg did not know it, but the fall of Cahokia and the rise of the United States bookended a tumultuous era in the long history of Middle America. This book uncovers that story and, in doing so, offers a new history of colonial North America. In the centuries between the collapse of Cahokia and the U.S. conquest, power flowed through the kinship-based alliances and social networks that shaped travel and communication along the many rivers of the midcontinent. Because most economic, military, and political activity in Middle America took place along the region's waterways, commanding those conduits allowed Native peoples and Europeans to vie for status, influence, and wealth.

Empires exist to dominate. They assert paramount sovereignty over vast regions to extract wealth and resources. Yet, in practice, imperial domination can be fragile, as it often rests on alliances with local people. In Middle America, where many powers struggled for authority, alliances became the key to projecting power in an uncertain environment. And those partnerships depended on kinship ties. As a result, successful alliances were rooted in reciprocity. Allies joined forces for mutual benefit, and kinship ensured that interests remained entangled. Empires, nations, and individuals could attract allies without kinship, but those tenuous relations depended even more heavily on outsiders demonstrating their political, economic, or military value to the peoples who ruled the midcontinent.[4]

Indians and colonists alike organized society around kinship—both familial and fictive—and they understood that the bonds of kinship reinforced alliances between individuals and between polities. In the midcontinent, ambitious people depended on marriage and ritual adoption to build the personal connections that fueled their endeavors. Consequently, early American empires operated as a series of overlapping familial, economic, and diplomatic networks. Those networks permeated empires and extended beyond their borders, and kin ties pulled in multiple directions. The bonds that linked the desires of colonists to the interests of the empire weakened the further one ventured from the seat of power, because traders, officials, and others became enmeshed in new networks. Put another way, colonists' primary loyalties were often to their families and their local communities. Officials struggled to link the ambitions of the colonists of the midcontinent to the needs of the empire. By embedding intertwined Native and imperial histories in the social and physical geography of the midcontinent, this book reveals the power of personal relationships embedded in a complex, dynamic environment to shape the course of empires.[5]

Between the fall of Cahokia and the rise of the United States, waves of Native peoples, missionaries, traders, settlers, and imperialists attempted to remake the Mississippi valley to suit their interests. In each instance, the past influenced the new regime. The French empire appended itself to the Native political landscape of the midcontinent, and its efforts to control the region hinged on established relationships between Indian nations as much as on interactions between those nations and the French. When Spain and Great Britain replaced France in the 1760s, they discovered that the actions and policies of their predecessors had forged a political landscape that needed to be navigated as carefully as the rivers of the physical landscape. At the turn of the nineteenth century, Americans believed that the United States and its experiment in republicanism stood apart from its Indian and imperial predecessors. But as much as they pretended otherwise, Americans built their empire atop the remnants of French, British, and Spanish colonies on a continent still largely dominated by Native peoples. The legacies of those preceding centuries inscribed an indelible mark on the future of an emerging American empire.[6]

≈ Too often, historians establish a false dichotomy between Native peoples who built societies around kinship and Europeans who focused on race. In early America, both Indians and Europeans organized society primarily through kinship. As they differentiated between family and strangers, they divided their worlds into three realms: the household; the community; and the outside world.[7] When navigating the boundary between the community and the outside world, all relied on notions of kinship to decide how to engage with foreigners.

Kinship—familial and fictive—united individuals into households and communities. The household formed the primary building block of society. In Illinois society, for example, as among many of the midcontinent's Native peoples, family members, including parents, children, and grandchildren, lived together across generations in a longhouse of two dozen or so relatives. Europeans, by contrast, typically lived in single-family households, which newlyweds formed at the time of their marriage. Extended kinship ties linked them to parents, grandparents, aunts, uncles, and cousins in their towns and hamlets and occasionally in the world beyond the city limits. Like their Indian counterparts, Europeans called on relatives for aid and support, and they used personal relationships to acquire influence and wealth.[8]

Beyond the household, fictive kinship bonds of culture, politics, class, and religion forged lineages into larger communities. Although dispersed from what is now Iowa to present-day Arkansas, the eleven divisions of the Illinois composed a single nation, united by kinship, language, ceremony, and commerce. The same was true for Osages, Miamis, and other nations that maintained distinct villages separated by many miles. Likewise, the French, as children of their king and the Catholic God, shared common bonds that united them into larger political and religious communities. Similar ties linked British and Spanish subjects into coherent communities. And so, Indians and Europeans in the midcontinent encountered one another as representatives of nations and empires as well as individuals.

Over centuries of migration, trade, and war, Middle Americans repeatedly encountered newcomers, and kinship provided a framework for understanding people who looked, spoke, and dressed differently. In North America and in Europe, individuals without kinship ties were strangers and potential enemies. When Indians and Europeans met foreigners, they assessed the benefits of incorporating those newcomers into their communities. When desirable, they integrated strangers into their families and nations through ritual adoption, marriage, or both. In other instances, they excluded them.

Rituals became crucial tools to build connections with valuable allies beyond the boundaries of the community and, in effect, to expand those borders. In the midcontinent, Indians used the calumet ceremony to adopt outsiders and build alliances between nations. By the middle of the seventeenth century, some 300 years after its introduction, the calumet—a pipe with a decorated stem—had spread throughout Middle America, and each nation in the region adopted the ritual as its own. As Indian leaders encountered outsiders, they greeted them with a calumet and, through an elaborate ceremony, converted enemies and strangers into allies and kin. Europeans brought their own rites. As they established outposts in North America, colonists performed an array of rituals—speeches, parades, planting crosses and other objects—which ostensibly transformed foreign lands into the holdings of their kings. On an interpersonal level, missionaries baptized Indians to establish a shared identity as the children of God.[9]

Indians and colonists used marriage to build and reinforce relations across political and cultural boundaries and to incorporate outsiders into households and, by extension, the community at large. Marriage played a central role in forging diplomatic and economic alliances. Men and women bound together these networks. By the middle of the seventeenth century, Illinois Indians had employed marriage and ceremonies to forge alliances with many nations throughout the Mississippi River valley. Illinois women married men from the Miami, Kickapoo, Osage, Quapaw, and other nations to strengthen ties between those polities. At the end of the next century, Osage leaders brokered marriages between their female relatives and francophone traders to facilitate commerce and increase their authority within their nations and abroad. In Europe, families used marriage to build economic and political alliances. When colonists journeyed across the Atlantic Ocean, they applied their understandings of kinship and community to the peoples they encountered in North America. Fur traders married into Native communities, and through those unions, they gained access to furs while their in-laws enjoyed a direct source of European goods. Missionaries in Middle America depended on marriage between Indian women and French men to build the pious nuclear families they believed defined Christian society.[10]

Kinship linked individuals and communities, but it excluded outsiders as much as it included relatives. Indians drew sharp distinctions between their clans, towns, and nations, on one hand, and outsiders, on the other. Many Indian nations referred to themselves as "the people," "the real people," "the men," or other names that bestowed superior status on themselves and demeaned outsiders as lesser beings, sometimes less than human. In other instances, names reflected commonalities or differences between nations. The name "Illinois" originated among the closely related Miamis, who noted their kinship with their western neighbors, who could "speak the regular way." Those within the household or community united together in a common identity that excluded foreigners, who spoke different languages, held different beliefs, and bore different appearances—usually in dress and hairstyle, more than skin color. Outsiders had no rights, and they could be killed or enslaved without fear of retribution, except from the victim's kin in some distant nation.[11]

At the same time, Native peoples believed they could transform outsiders and incorporate them into their nations. The treatment of captives offers one of the clearest examples of how Native peoples remade outsiders into community members. Illinois, Osages, Chickasaws, and the other nations of the midcontinent adopted captured enemies to replace deceased loved ones. Upon returning from battle, captors selected captives for adoption. They usually chose women and children. Adult men trained as warriors posed too great a danger to incorporate into the community. Townspeople sent the adoptees through the gantlet, stripped them of their clothing, cut their hair, and placed them with families that had lost members. Over time, as adoptees learned their new community's language and expected social behaviors, they became fully integrated as community members.[12]

Likewise, until the early nineteenth century, most European theorists believed that differences between themselves and Indians stemmed from environmental and cultural, rather than biological, factors. As Europeans encountered Indians, they fit them into their theories about the earth and its inhabitants, and they posited that all shared a common ancestor in Noah, the ark builder of the Abrahamic tradition. In other words, kinship united them, even as differences in physical appearance and culture made them distinct. To be sure, Europeans believed that they possessed superior cultures to the peoples they encountered in North America, but they also believed that by altering the behavior of Native peoples, they could incorporate them into the "civilized" world. From French imperialists and Jesuits in the 1600s to the proponents of U.S. "civilization" policy late in the following century, secular and religious officials believed that education and religious conversion could transform Native peoples.[13]

During the early nineteenth century, however, Europeans and Euro-Americans contracted the borders of kinship. Race became the primary criterion for establishing the parameters of acceptable interaction between different groups. Beginning in the late 1700s and gaining acceptance in the early 1800s, new theories posited that the creator had formed the peoples of the earth at different times and that Europeans, Indians, and Africans did not share a common ancestor. Having never been connected to Indians and Africans through familial ties, Europeans concluded that such relationships were unnatural. Moreover, they decided that they were destined to rule North America, while Africans and Indians would serve and disappear, respectively.[14]

U.S. imperialists were not the first outsiders to bring restrictive ideas about kinship and race to the midcontinent, but they were the first empire to wield the power needed to implement their vision of an ethnically and racially homogeneous society. During the early 1700s, French officials banned intermarriage between French colonists and Native peoples because they thought Indian spouses lured French men into Indian Country, where they became ungovernable. Yet, beyond a few towns in the Illinois Country, the French lacked the influence to halt French-Indian marriage, which continued largely unabated. From 1763 to 1765, the Ottawa war leader Pontiac and the Delaware prophet Neolin preached a pan-Indian message that promoted a unified Native identity in opposition to European colonists. However, Pontiac's supporters rallied around him because of his many kinship ties to the nations of Middle America, not because of his rhetoric. The number of American colonists immigrating to the region gave the United States power un-matched by earlier empires, and their growing authority forced francophone midwesterners to ally either with the United States or with Native peoples. Most chose the United States. As Americans remade the midcontinent, they upended 150 years of interaction between Indians and Europeans even while they relied on kinship with francophone Louisianans as a foundation of their trans-Mississippi empire.

≈   Centered on the site of the ancient city of Cahokia, where Edmund Flagg surveyed the landscape in the 1830s, the midcontinent is a region de-fined by rivers. North America's major rivers—the Illinois, Mississippi, Missouri, Ohio, Tennessee, and Wabash—all meet within less than 200 miles of one another. Those waterways affected daily life, imperial ambitions, trade, and war. Rivers served as avenues of colonial expansion. Conversely, the vulnerability of river travelers offered opportunities for those who wished to halt commerce or invasion. For centuries, numerous Indian nations, Eu-ropeans empires, and individuals struggled for power and wealth and fought to limit the authority of others. Because rivers were central to so many as-pects of Native and colonial life in the midcontinent, they were often the front lines of these contests.[15]

Waterways linked regions too often seen as discrete—the South, the Great Plains, and the Great Lakes—in a shared history. In turn, those connections shaped large expanses of North America as ripples from the midcontinent spread in all directions. In the borderlands of the central Mississippi River valley, rivers joined disparate and distant groups of Indians and Europeans in an interwoven social landscape of movement and interaction. Under-standing the midcontinent as a point of convergence for diverse peoples re-orients Native and imperial histories away from artificial lines of demarca-tion dictated by colonial claims or imagined by outsiders. The social geography of the midcontinent was a network of alliances and rivalries that sprawled across the region's waterways. Three Indian nations—Illinois, Chickasaws, and Osages—controlled much of the midcontinent into the early nineteenth century. The middle waters connected them in a unified history that crossed linguistic, cultural, and environmental borders. Interactions between those three nations and between them and Europeans—sometimes peaceful, sometimes not—altered the course of history for all in Middle America, and events in the midcontinent reverberated throughout eastern North America and across the Atlantic.[16]

Beyond the simple facts of river-based travel and communication, under-standings of the landscape changed depending on who viewed the region, how they perceived the environment around them, and what they hoped to accomplish there. During the seventeenth century, Illinois Indians took con-trol of the central Mississippi River valley by seizing important crossings and confluences. In command of choke points, Illinois built commercial and political alliances with neighboring nations. Soon, they controlled the trade in slaves, furs, and European goods between the western Great Lakes, eastern Great Plains, and lower Mississippi valley. Illinois power stemmed from their ability to travel unhindered from Lake Superior to present-day Arkansas and from Lake Michigan west onto the Plains.[17]

Beginning in the early eighteenth century, imperialists saw the Missis-sippi and its tributaries differently: as passageways, links between their col-onies in the interior of the continent and European markets. In the midcon-tinent, it was easier to stop travelers than to ensure safe passage, and Indian nations who could halt canoes and convoys—or protect them for the right price—became the most important allies to aspirational European empires. During the first half of the 1700s, France needed access to the Mississippi, Illinois, and Wabash Rivers to supply the Illinois Country from Louisiana and Canada and to communicate between the Gulf Coast and the St. Law-rence valley. After 1765, Great Britain relied on the Ohio—not the Illinois and the Wabash—to reach the midcontinent and on the Mississippi to re-turn to the Atlantic seaboard. At the same time, Spain, with its colonial ad-ministrators based in New Orleans, depended on safe travel on the lower Mississippi to govern St. Louis and the rest of Upper Louisiana. For more than a century, Europeans could not run or, in some cases, even reach their colonies in Middle America without the aid of Native peoples.

Even groups that traveled predominantly by foot or horseback used their command of waterways to become formidable powers, and their relationship to water shaped their identities. The Osage Nation, based west of the Mississippi, rose to prominence as equestrians. Yet rivers play a central role in Osage history. Long ago, when Sky People, Land People, and Water People joined together, they called themselves *Ni-u-kon-ska*, Children of the Middle Waters. Their name symbolized "the universe of sky and earth and land and water." It also reflected their understanding of the geography of Middle America and their place in it. Likewise, Omahas and Quapaws took names that reflected their location in relation to related nations, including Osages. The name "Omaha" *(umáha)* means "upstream people," indicating their presence farther up the Missouri, while "Quapaw" *(okáxpa)* denotes "down-stream people," referring to their place at the confluence of the Arkansas and Mississippi Rivers. Long after the Children of the Middle Waters became known as *Wazhazhe (wažáže)*, which French colonists heard as "Osage," they ruled the rivers that linked the midcontinent and the Great Plains. They blocked dangerous traffic, detained intruders, and thwarted invasion. Into the early nineteenth century, Osages controlled the middle waters, especially the lower Missouri and its tributaries, and dominated Indian and European neighbors alike.[18]

In the late 1700s and early 1800s, the United States followed in the footsteps of its imperial predecessors, recognizing the importance of western rivers in linking its trans-Appalachian colonies to markets on the Atlantic coast and in Europe. Without safe passage on the Mississippi River, Ohio valley colonists could not transport their produce to New Orleans, the entrepôt for all trade west of the Appalachians. As the U.S. empire began spreading west, American officials acquired use rights from Spain, which claimed the west bank of the Mississippi, and bought or seized lands along the Ohio and Mississippi from Native peoples.[19] In 1803, the United States purchased all of Louisiana including the Mississippi. West of the great river, the United States continued to push rivals away from important waterways. Beginning with the Lewis and Clark Expedition of 1804–1806, the Missouri River became the primary avenue of American movement into the Far West, and the empire secured the river starting with an 1808 treaty by which Osages ceded all of their lands along the lower Missouri. As Americans invaded farther up the Missouri, Arkansas, Red, and other rivers, they replayed these negotiations over use and control of waterways.

Across centuries, rivers remained the central feature of the midwestern geographic landscape and a key to shaping its social landscape. Individuals, nations, and empires all recognized the necessity of controlling the rivers or, at least, maintaining access to them. Those who amassed wealth and influence invariably succeeded in harnessing the potential of waterways, using them to construct networks of kinship and other diplomatic ties, while those who did not often misread the landscape or stumbled in their efforts to rule it.

≈ In 1836, as Edmund Flagg gazed out across St. Louis and the Mississippi River, he witnessed the remade North American midcontinent and heard echoes from a deep past. The rivers remained, running toward New

Orleans and the Gulf and carrying American produce to market, but the United States had splintered the social networks that had once dominated trade and diplomacy in Middle America. Driven by ideas of racial supremacy and a belief in its destiny to span the continent, the United States had enacted an aggressive policy of colonization in the midcontinent, and unlike under previous empires, colonists poured into the region and spearheaded conquest. In 1804, about 10,000 Euro-Americans lived in Missouri. In 1830, Missouri's population stood at 140,000. A decade later, more than 380,000 Americans lived within the state's borders.[20]

Having conquered Middle America, the United States and its colonists drove out or oppressed all those they considered unfit to be Americans. A circumscribed understanding of kinship lay at the core of this exclusionary and eliminationist impulse. Hardened theories about innate differences between races replaced earlier ideas about the mutability of appearance and culture. Americans in the Midwest still depended on kinship to explain their relationships to people around them, but they demarcated stricter boundaries between the community and the outside world. The United States created a new kind of empire. Officials and colonists deemed Indians permanent outsiders doomed to extinction, to "vanish" in the language of the day, not potential members of the community.

As Flagg described the mounds and their builders, he captured American sentiments toward all Indians, not just the long-deceased residents of Cahokia: "the far traveller, as he wanders through this Western Valley, may linger around these aged piles and meditate upon a power departed, a race obliterated, an influence swept from the earth for ever."[21] Still, despite the rhetoric of American imperialists and colonists, mirrored in Flagg's musings, the United States dispossessed Native peoples but did not destroy them. Forced out of their homelands, Native peoples moved west to Indian Territory, where they rebuilt their nations and used old alliances as the framework for new associations on the eastern Plains. Indians adapted to the pressures of U.S. colonialism by drawing on the power of kinship networks that dated back to the precolonial era.

Midwesterners often preferred to look toward the future rather than the past. Yet, all around them, reminders of the midcontinent's deep history endured. Although worn by erosion and damaged by farmers and relic hunters, Cahokia's mounds loomed over the landscape as a symbol of ancient Indian power. The francophone elite of St. Louis bore witness to the persistent influence of French culture in the midcontinent. Through it all ran the rivers.

Just as they connected disparate provinces of North America, those water-ways linked Middle America's history and its future. As long as Americans depended on the rivers to transport people and goods, they participated in an ongoing history of Middle America that was deeper and more complex than they understood or wanted to acknowledge.

CHAPTER ONE

In Cahokia's Wake

Three villages sat on the rich flatlands overlooking the Des Moines River, a few miles above where its waters met the southward rush of the powerful Mississippi. The 300 longhouses of Peouarea and two other towns stretched along the river's south bank on a vast tallgrass prairie broken occasionally by stands of maple, walnut, and cedar trees. Upward of 8,000 Illinois Indians moved through the town streets, tended cornfields, and ventured out to look for game or gather supplies. A few weeks earlier, only a small population of guards and farmers inhabited the rush-covered lodges. They protected the year's fledging corn crop while the rest of the townspeople stalked bison on the grasslands to the west. Now, well into *anaahkapi kiiri-hswa* (the month when the corncob appears), the hunters had returned. The towns bustled with activity. Some Peoria women prepared the spoils of the expedition, scraping bison hides and smoking meat from as many as 2,000 animals. Others nurtured the corn, ensuring the roots remained covered with soil and inspecting the ears for worms. They welcomed the steady rains that fell as the cool spring gave way to a warm, humid summer. Soon, the first harvest would begin. Meanwhile, men hunted and fished in the forests that punctuated the prairies and lined the waterways. Before long, they would leave town again, this time heading north to Green Bay, where they would sell enslaved Indians and bison hides to their Miami and Ottawa allies. On their return, they would bring iron axes and knives, copper kettles, porcelain beads, cloth blankets, firearms, and other goods that traveled

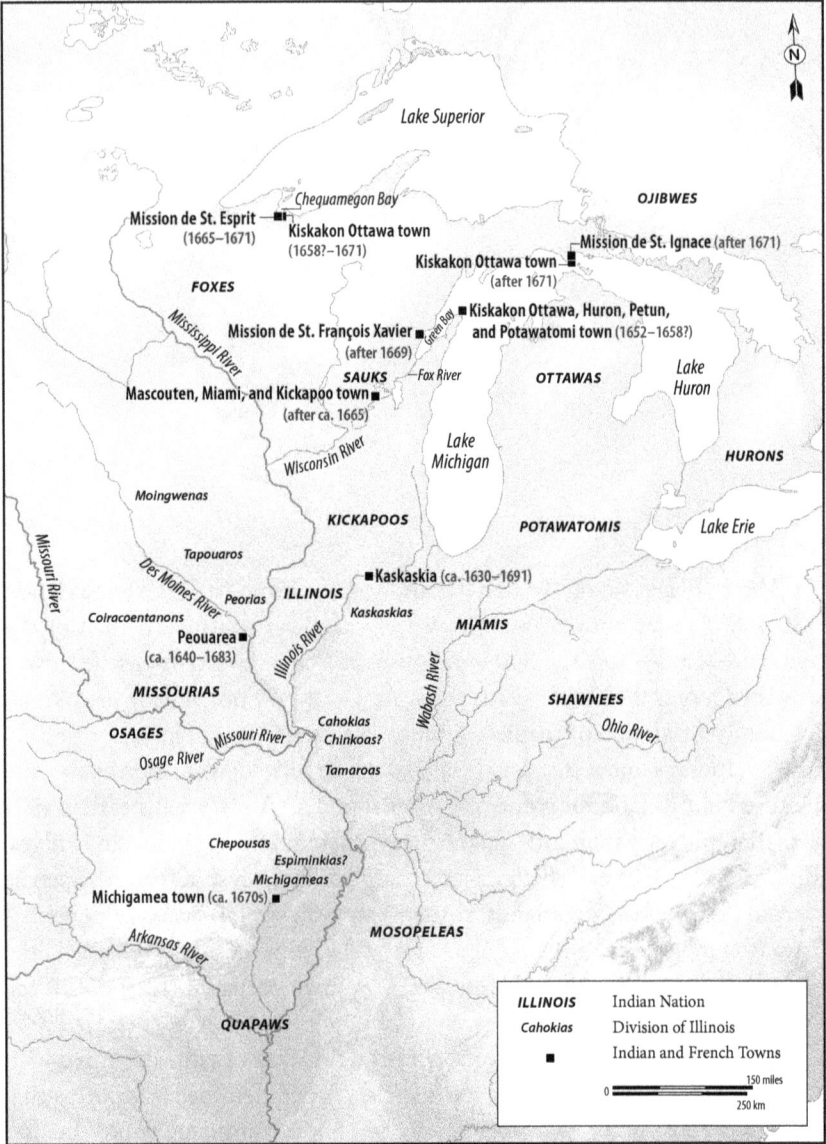

Map 1 The Illinois Country, ca. 1673.

from Europe to the Great Lakes in French ships and Ottawa canoes. But that was in the weeks to come. For now, life centered on the work to be done at home.[1]

Shouts startled the Peorias. They looked up from their work and filed out of their longhouses, searching for the source of the noise. The voices sounded close. Scanning the prairie, they spotted two strangers standing in the tall-grass near the edge of town. Any trepidation the Peorias felt disappeared when they noticed the distinctive black gown worn by one of the two men. It marked him as a friend. Black-clad Jesuit priests lived among Ottawas and Miamis, and Illinois traders and diplomats spoke to them each autumn during their sojourn to the Great Lakes. Some, maybe many, Peorias had seen Europeans on previous occasions. But none of the foreigners had ever ventured into the Illinois Country. Four old men carrying two calumets—highly decorated, ceremonial pipes used to greet visitors—ventured out to meet the newcomers.[2]

The two foreigners had traveled hundreds of miles to visit the Peorias and the rest of the Illinois Nation. Along with five companions, they had paddled their canoes down the waterways that linked Lake Michigan to the Mississippi River and found their way through swamps, marshes, and lakes that obscured the route. By the time they passed the confluence of the Des Moines and Mississippi Rivers on June 25, 1673, they had not laid eyes on another human in more than two weeks. One recalled, "we knew whither not we were going, for we had proceeded over one Hundred leagues without discovering anything except animals and birds." Later that day, just down-stream from the mouth of the Des Moines, they spotted a trail leading away from the west bank of the Mississippi. Following the footpath, the Black Robe and his companion feared who they might meet at the end of their walk. The priest later wrote that such an "investigation [was] a rather haz-ardous one for two men who exposed themselves, alone, to the mercy of a barbarous and Unknown people."[3] Far from discovering danger, the two so-journers received a warm welcome from the four elders who approached them.

Standing before the Illinois men, one of the strangers identified himself in a shared language. He was Father Jacques Marquette. Thirty-five years old, Marquette had devoted more than half of his life to serving God. Don-ning the black robes of the Jesuit order as a teenager, he spent a dozen years studying, teaching, and praying in French universities and monasteries. From a young age, he craved the adventure of North America with its unconverted masses and, should it come, the glory of martyrdom. After arriving in New France in September 1666, the zeal that drove the Jesuit to leave Europe pushed him to venture beyond the limited boundaries of French North America. Marquette spent the next six years learning half a dozen Native languages and traveling from the small outposts of Quebec and Montreal to the westernmost Jesuit missions in the Great Lakes. Stationed at Sault Ste. Marie, Chequamegon Bay, and Michilimackinac between 1668 and 1673, Marquette collected stories and rumors about lands along a great river to the west and the Indian nations that populated its banks. Marquette hungered for new converts, and the nations along the Mississippi River offered an opportunity. Beginning in 1669, Marquette and the fur trader Louis Jolliet planned an expedition that would take them west to the Mississippi and south to anticipated riches in furs and souls. The ambitions of the Jesuit and the trader converged with the dreams of French officials, who chased two legends: the gold mines of the kingdom of Quivira and a water route to China. In the spring of 1673, Jolliet arrived at Marquette's mission to the Ottawas at Michilimackinac with word that the colonial government had approved their proposal. He and Marquette prepared to travel west.[4]

Leaving Michilimackinac on May 17, Marquette, Jolliet, and five companions had little idea of what they would find in the "Unknown countries" beyond Green Bay, the last outpost of the Jesuit mission system. Over the next four months, they encountered nations and lands that French colonists knew only through tales of distant wars and disjointed accounts of a river that went somewhere, maybe to the Pacific Ocean. Before this voyage, the French had, at best, four decades of conflicting knowledge about the Illinois and their homelands. In 1634, the explorer Jean Nicolet reported that the "Eriniouai" lived in some unspecified location west of the Menominees and Ho-Chunks of Green Bay. As Jesuit missionaries moved farther into the Great Lakes, they learned more and more about the people called "Irinons," "Linioueks," "Alimoueks," and other variations. But the reports were haphazard and contradictory. The Illinois lived somewhere in the West. Maybe they numbered sixty towns. Maybe it was ten. In 1658, a Jesuit placed the Illinois population at over 100,000. A little more than a decade later, one Jesuit on Lake Superior reported 2,000 Illinois to the south, while another at the same mission estimated four times as many. One missionary stated that "continual wars" reduced the Illinois to two towns, but three years later, they were living in "five large Villages." In short, the priests had little reliable information about the Illinois and their neighbors. The Catholic friars based their reports on incomplete accounts provided by a range of people with competing motives and agendas, and they must have had difficulty separating good intelligence from bad. Even if their information had been accurate, the Jesuits could be careless in their estimates, as one father recognized in 1671 when he noted that, because the French had met the Illinois first, they applied that name to all the nations of the central Mississippi valley.[5] As Marquette headed west, he could not have felt confident in his knowledge of the people he would meet.

For Peorias, Marquette and Jolliet represented direct access to French traders and a chance to cut out Ottawa and Miami middlemen. Peorias did not know the specific origins of these two strangers, but they could have guessed much about them and their voyage. Peoria traders and diplomats knew the best routes between their town and the missions of the Black Robes on the western Great Lakes. Some of these Illinois may have even chatted with Marquette a few years earlier at Mission St. Esprit on Lake Superior. Moreover, by 1673, Illinois associated the French with the metal, porcelain, and cloth goods they acquired on the Great Lakes. The presence of those items in Peouarea comforted Marquette. He noted that he felt safe when offered the calumet: "much more so when I saw them Clad in Cloth, for I judged that they were our allies."[6]

The arrival of Marquette and Jolliet in the midcontinent in the summer of 1673 was one in a series of encounters between newcomers and locals stretching back thousands of years. Between the collapse of Cahokia in the thirteenth century and the invasion by the Illinois 300 years later, the American midcontinent experienced a period of profound political, economic, and social upheaval. Cahokia's demise was but one part of the turmoil that swept the Mississippi valley. In the century or so after Cahokia fell, the region's other chiefdoms collapsed, and new peoples arrived from the north and east and challenged dwindling Mississippian power. Oneota peoples drove rivals out of prime locations, built alliances, and formed sprawling trade networks that carried goods hundreds, if not thousands, of miles through the interior of the continent. By 1400, Oneotas controlled the waterways and trade routes between the central Great Plains and the western Great Lakes.

In the early 1600s, as Illinois Indians remade Middle America, they employed strategies that would have been familiar to many of their predecessors. They recognized the power that came from controlling waterways and river travel. And they built kinship-based alliances that linked their towns to trading partners in the western Great Lakes, the Great Plains, and the lower Mississippi valley. In the decades that followed their entry into the Mississippi valley, Illinois established towns at important river crossings and confluences. With this strategy, they exerted influence over a region that extended well beyond the confines of their towns. Meanwhile, they used their alliances with neighboring nations to safeguard their own trade routes across the midcontinent. Through blood and fire, captives and calumets, the Illinois became masters of the middle waters.

≈ Near the beginning of the last millennium, long before the Illinois Nation mastered Middle America, a metropolis emerged near the confluence of the Mississippi, Missouri, and Illinois Rivers. In this land of rich, black soil, later called the American Bottom, Cahokia rose from scattered farming communities to become the largest city north of Mexico. Fueled by a warming climate and a subsequent agricultural revolution, Cahokians used intensive corn agriculture to feed thousands of residents. In time, it became the largest of the Mississippian chiefdoms that stretched across much of the present-day U.S. South and along the Mississippi from the Gulf to what is now Wisconsin. Although politically distinct, these communities shared cultural and agricultural practices, most notably their construction of imposing flattop mounds and their dependence on corn. At the city's height, Cahokia and its suburbs housed as many as 20,000 people and encompassed 120 earthen mounds, some of which represented the greatest monumental architecture in North America. The rivers of the American Bottom connected Cahokia to people and natural resources across much of eastern North America, bringing exotic shells, stones, and metals into the hands of the city's elite. As it became the most powerful polity in the region, the lords of Cahokia—a paramount chief and his extended family—conquered neighboring peoples and settled them on fertile farmlands on the edge of the city. These upland vassals provided agricultural surpluses and craft goods that fed the city and perpetuated the rule of urban elites. Laborers also ventured into the Ozark Mountains, returning with much-needed minerals, stone, and wood. As the city's status grew, Cahokians ventured up the Illinois and Mississippi Rivers, carrying their practices far to the north.[7]

Soon after Cahokia's ascent in the eleventh century, immigrants from the city brought Mississippian culture to the central Illinois valley. At the confluence of the Spoon and Illinois Rivers, southwest of present-day Peoria, these newcomers led the building of ceremonial mounds and the creation of a new political order centered on a hereditary chief. The arrival of Mississippians inaugurated centuries of conflict over the Illinois River, which linked Lake Michigan to the Mississippi River. The region provided rich resources, including fertile farmland for the maize-dependent Mississippians and an array of wild plants, game animals, and fish. This natural diversity stemmed from the presence of several habitats—woodland, riverine, and prairie—along and near the Illinois River. Such advantages made the region attractive. But competition for those varied resources led to conflict between Mississippians and other residents of the Illinois River valley.[8] Between 1050 and 1425, Indians moved in and out of the Illinois valley, interacting with other newcomers and established residents alike. No single type of interaction defined relations between the region's polities. Warfare could be brutal and devastating, but alliances created peace and prompted trade. Interactions with the natural world followed a more uniform pattern. Unless outside threats compelled considering defense first, Native peoples built their towns at places that allowed them to control rivals' movement and offered a diversity of natural resources for subsistence. In each instance of migration, alliance, and warfare, Native peoples made conscious decisions about how best to preserve and increase their power and wealth.

While the residents of Spoon River welcomed Cahokian influence, about seventy miles farther upstream, near present-day Joliet, locals responded to the intrusion, not by joining the Cahokians but instead by banding together against them. These divisions reflected much-older rivalries, as the buffer zone between Spoon River and the upper Illinois settlements predated Mississippian intrusion by centuries. As peoples known to archaeologists as the Langford and Fisher traditions joined forces to stave off the Mississippians, they settled along the upper Illinois and its tributaries and claimed two strategically significant confluences. From south to north, the first was at the Starved Rock rapids, near the confluence of the Fox and Illinois Rivers. The second was at the meeting of the Des Plaines and Kankakee Rivers, the source of the Illinois. From those spots, the Langford and Fisher people could limit further Mississippian incursion up the Illinois into the southern Lake Michigan basin. A well-established buffer zone between the Spoon River and upper Illinois peoples limited initial interaction between the Mississippians and their opponents. Then, from 1148 to 1248, droughts desiccated the Midwest. During that century, one drought spanned sixty years, while another lasted two decades.[9] These droughts hastened the collapse of Cahokia, which became all but deserted by 1350. The dry years also wrought

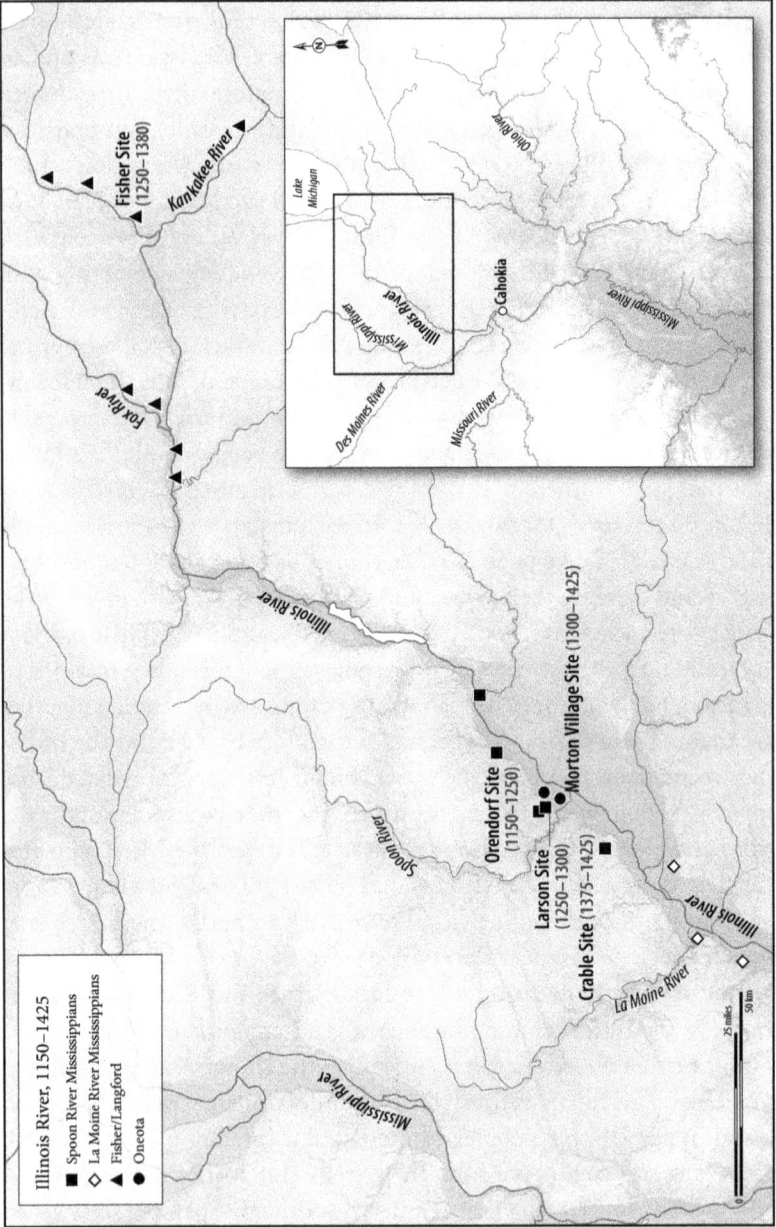

Map 2 Illinois River, 1150–1425.

20

havoc on the peoples of the Illinois valley. Without ample rain, poor corn crops produced hunger and desperation. Spoon River and upper Illinois peoples probably ventured farther and farther into the buffer zone looking for game, risking violence to stave off starvation. As rival populations struggled for resources and survival, warfare consumed the region.

Raids and ambushes punctuated by large-scale attacks defined warfare in the Illinois valley. Most victims died as individuals or in small groups, rather than in massacres. Yet, over time, casualties mounted, and entire communities suffered. At the Spoon River Orendorf village, more than 15 percent of all adults died at the hands of enemies or survived being wounded or scalped. Most of the victims ventured too far from town or went out in numbers too small to dissuade attacks. Large-scale assaults—or, perhaps more accurately, successful large-scale assaults—probably happened only once a generation. But, on occasions when raiders carried out bolder attacks, they could devastate a community. A mass grave at Orendorf held the remains of at least fifteen men, women, and children, possibly victims of a single battle.[10]

Violence pushed Spoon River Mississippians into fortified towns, where living conditions deteriorated. Around 1200, the 400 or so residents of Orendorf abandoned the town and built a new, stockaded village a short distance away. Over time, more people flocked to the community, seeking strength in numbers and protection behind the walls. The town twice expanded its stockade to accommodate newcomers. The walls kept out invaders but restricted residents, who no longer felt safe hunting and gathering outside the village. Residents consumed fewer of the wild plants, fruits, and nuts they previously collected on the outskirts of town. Instead, their dependence on corn soared. Even in the best of times, Orendorf Mississippians consumed enormous amounts of corn, and after they moved to the fortified town, maize provided as much as 70 percent of their diet. Consequently, many suffered from malnutrition and anemia. Confined in tight living quarters, communicable diseases such as tuberculosis swept through the population. Young women were particularly susceptible to infection during pregnancy and childbirth. High rates of female mortality reduced population levels and strained subsistence, as women provided the bulk of agricultural labor.[11]

In the middle of the thirteenth century, attackers dealt Orendorf a deathblow when they broke through the stockade and burned the town. Only a large army, probably gathered from multiple towns, could have achieved such an overwhelming victory against a walled settlement. Perhaps upper Illinois peoples determined to end the Mississippian threat once and for all. As the homes of the Mississippians burned, they recognized their untenable position at Orendorf and retreated about twenty-five miles southward, where they regrouped at another fortified town, the Larson site.[12]

Upper Illinois peoples also suffered great losses during their thirteenth-century war with the Mississippian newcomers. Although representing distinct groups, Langford and Fisher peoples united for mutual defense at a dozen or more large towns, notably the Fisher site near the Des Plaines and the Kankakee Rivers. Residents of the Fisher site suffered intense fighting from about 1225 to 1300. As at Orendorf, most victims at Fisher died during skirmishes and ambushes that inflicted low numbers of casualties. But, toward the end of the thirteenth century, an enemy force destroyed the town in a final, devastating blow. Attackers routed the village and killed at least forty men, women, and children. Some of the dead showed signs of being killed while retreating. At the end of the fighting, the victors burned the abandoned village. When the coast was clear, refugees returned to bury the dead. The aftermath was gruesome. The survivors found victims as young as nine months. Multiple corpses had been scalped and mutilated. They buried their relatives in a mass grave, and when their work was complete, they set off to join kin and allies in nearby towns.[13]

The destruction of the Fisher village weakened the upper Illinois peoples, but they recovered by calling on neighboring towns for aid and reinforcement. Even after the devastation at Fisher, the upper Illinois towns wielded enough military might to strike the Spoon River Mississippians. Perhaps the defeat convinced them that Spoon River Mississippians still posed too great a threat. Around 1300, rival forces drove the Mississippians from Larson. Enemies burned portions of the town during battle, or Larson residents destroyed the town as they evacuated. In either case, the defeated Mississippians again followed the Illinois River farther south.[14]

In the central and upper Illinois valley, these wars ended around 1300. Having vanquished the Spoon River Mississippians, residents of the upper Illinois valley dispersed into smaller communities, a sign that defense was no longer the preeminent concern. To the south, though, new conflicts loomed. As Spoon River Mississippians retreated downstream, they entered the territory of a rival chiefdom on the La Moine River. At the same time, Chiwere Siouan-speaking newcomers—groups archaeologists call Oneota—moved southward from present-day Wisconsin and made their homes close to the abandoned Mississippian towns on Spoon River. Their motivations for this migration are unclear. Possibly they moved south as invaders, intending to drive the weakened Mississippians from the region. More likely, Spoon River Mississippians invited them to settle nearby and ally with them. After catastrophic defeats such as those suffered at Orendorf and Larson, Spoon River Mississippians needed assistance. Settling only twenty miles north of the new homes of the Spoon River people, the northern newcomers probably arrived as welcome allies rather than as aggressors.[15]

These newcomers to the Illinois valley participated in a much-larger wave of migration and upheaval that accompanied the decline of Mississippian power. Beginning in the 1200s, the Chiwere Siouan ancestors of Ho-Chunk, Ioway, Missouria, and Otoe peoples became the most powerful polities in the Midwest. Their emergence is shrouded in debate and uncertainty. Oral histories recall that Oneotas entered the upper Midwest from north of the Great Lakes. Other evidence points toward an older homeland also to the east but farther south, possibly in or near the Ohio River valley. Regardless of their origins, by the end of the first millennium AD, they lived in the upper Mississippi valley as clans in a single tribe. About 900 years ago, according to Ho-Chunk traditions, food resources dwindled in the western Great Lakes, and Oneotas migrated south and west looking for new homes. As they moved, the clans separated into distinct nations. The first to leave the group, Ho-Chunks stopped at a large lake, now called Lake Winnebago, drawn by the supply of fish. In later centuries, they spread out along Green Bay and the eastern shore of Lake Michigan. The remaining Oneotas headed west to the Mississippi River. They probably struck the great river near Lake Pepin, Minnesota. Ioways stayed near the upper Mississippi and made homes along the river and its tributaries between Lake Pepin and Rock River in present-day Illinois. Missourias and Otoes continued south and established a village on the lower Missouri River, near the confluence of the Missouri and Grand Rivers. A conflict between the two groups resulted in Otoes moving upstream. They spent a long time, years or maybe decades, traveling through the lower Missouri valley before settling on the Platte River in present-day Nebraska.[16]

The interactions between Oneota newcomers and Illinois valley Mississippians offer a glimpse into the diverse outcomes, peaceful and violent, of this migration. As Oneotas moved into the homelands of the Spoon River Mississippians, they settled at Morton village, which occupied a ridge just north of the confluence of the Illinois and Spoon Rivers, while a smaller town sat a short distance up the Illinois. Across the Spoon River, Mississippians lived at the Crable site, a bluff-top village overlooking the Illinois valley.

Oneotas and Spoon River Mississippians intermarried and exchanged traditions and technology. All the while, they fought a brutal war with a nearby foe, probably the rival La Moine Mississippians. Cultural exchange and marriage, killing and captivity all accompanied the Oneota migration into the Illinois valley.[17]

The Oneota–Spoon River alliance operated like many alliances in precolonial North America. Members of the two groups intermarried, and family relations provided a foundation for political and economic cooperation. To renew and reinforce the alliance, Oneotas and Spoon River Mississippians periodically came together to perform public rituals, such as feasting and gift giving. In public spaces at Morton village, Oneota and Mississippian leaders exchanged food and goods made from rare materials acquired from hundreds of miles away.[18] These exchanges demonstrated each group's wealth and power and, thus, its value as an ally. Rituals also established a continual reciprocity between the two groups. Through the power of kin ties and periodic reminders of the material value of cooperation, Oneotas and Spoon River Mississippians crossed linguistic and ethnic boundaries to form a lasting alliance.

Over decades of marriage, trade, and coresidence, Oneota and Mississippian material culture and social practices began to share similarities where few had previously existed. Mississippian and Oneota ceramics featured notable differences in shape and decoration, but at Morton and Crable, households often included both. At Crable, Oneota women made between 10 and 15 percent of the pottery, while Mississippians produced approximately the same percentage of the ceramics at Morton. Over time, potters in both towns created hybrid ceramics, such as Mississippian plates and effigy bowls with Oneota decorations. Architectural styles also changed as the two groups borrowed from each other. Across the Midwest, most Oneotas lived in oblong longhouses. At Morton village, by contrast, Mississippian influence appears in the presence of square or rectangular buildings. The burials at the Crable and Morton villages indicate further cultural exchange. As at many Mississippian cemeteries in the Illinois valley, earlier burials at Crable face south or southwest. That orientation carried spiritual importance, which remains mysterious. Yet later burials show an Oneota influence. Like the graves of Morton villagers, they were oriented around local topography rather than cardinal directions.[19]

Despite the Oneota–Spoon River alliance, warfare consumed the Oneotas' early years in the Illinois valley. While Crable villagers suffered attacks as well, the residents at Morton bore the brunt of the violence. At least one-third of adults buried at the Morton town cemetery died from battle wounds. Much of this violence was opportunistic. Oneota subsistence relied on seasonal hunting, gathering, and farming. Both men and women helped feed their families and communities, and during these violent years, they put themselves in danger to protect their loved ones. Most children, not yet old enough to hunt or gather, escaped the violence. Raiders could anticipate when women would leave town to gather hickory nuts or men would pursue deer. Lurking out of sight of the town, they attacked those they found alone or in small groups. They then scalped, decapitated, or otherwise mutilated the dead and returned home carrying trophies of their victories.[20]

As the war escalated, Oneota villagers suffered in ways familiar to the ancestors of their Spoon River allies. When they first moved into the Illinois River valley, Oneotas exploited all of the food options available to them. They raised corn, beans, and squash; gathered nuts, seeds, berries, and plants; and hunted deer, elk, fish, turkeys, water fowl, and turtles. The lower population density of unfortified villages limited the spread of disease, and healthy diets allowed many to survive tuberculosis or other ailments. On average, they lived several years longer than Spoon River Mississippians. Notably, Oneota women survived their childbearing years in much greater numbers than did their Mississippian counterparts. In the Oneotas' last years at Morton, the threats that waited beyond the tree line kept Morton villagers close to town, where they could draw only on a limited range of foods. Their diet centered on corn from the town's fields, turtles and fishes from nearby sloughs and lakes, and the occasional deer or elk.[21] After attackers burned Morton village, Oneotas relocated to a fortified village, and some joined the Mississippians at Crable.

La Moine River Mississippians seem to have been the aggressors in these conflicts. Much like their Spoon River neighbors, La Moine River Mississippians appeared in the eleventh century, emerging from a combination of local populations and immigrants bringing Cahokian influences. By the fourteenth century, their shared origin mattered little as climate change and migration provoked conflict. As Spoon River Mississippians and Oneotas allied against them, La Moine Mississippians gathered into a handful of easily defended bluff-top villages south of the La Moine River. From there, they could strike their upstream rivals.[22]

By 1425, endemic warfare in the Illinois valley convinced Mississippians and Oneotas alike to abandon the region. The fate of the river valley's residents is unknown. Perhaps La Moine Mississippians moved west to the Mississippi River. Spoon River Mississippians and at least some Oneotas may have moved south to the mouth of the Wabash River. There, they merged with their former trading partners from the Mississippian chiefdom at Angel Mounds and created a new confederacy known to archaeologists as Caborn-Welborn. Caborn-Welborn material culture shows a heavy Mississippian influence augmented by northern, Oneota culture. The migrants, regardless of where they chose to settle, deemed the central Illinois valley too dangerous, despite the rich natural resources it offered for hunters, gatherers, and farmers. The region remained uninhabited for the better part of two centuries.[23]

The history of Oneota migration, warfare, and alliance in the central Illinois valley composed one part of a much-larger story of Oneota expansion during the thirteenth and fourteenth centuries. By the mid-1300s, Oneota peoples settled in what is now Wisconsin, Michigan, Minnesota, Illinois, Indiana, Missouri, Iowa, Kansas, Nebraska, and the Dakotas. In the face of Oneota expansion, Mississippians retreated southward, midwesterners went east toward the Fort Ancient towns of present-day Ohio, and the ancestors of Great Plains nations such as the Arikaras moved farther northward into the Dakotas. No individual, council, or town orchestrated Oneota expansion. Oneota groups probably supported one another through trade and alliance, but each group possessed its own motivation for moving into new territory. The onset of the Little Ice Age, a 550-year era of global cooling and unpredictable climate starting circa 1300, may have shortened the growing season in the upper Mississippi valley and motivated residents to move south and west. Local conditions determined the response to Oneota expansion, but across the midcontinent, violence accompanied their migrations. Some Oneotas may have been invited to relocate, but as in the Illinois valley, that did not preclude war. Others simply drove out earlier occupants. Regardless of the variations in experience, the effect was the same. Mississippian influence waned in the Midwest as Oneotas became the dominant people in the region.[24]

The initial expansion of Oneota peoples onto the eastern Plains brought with it a prolonged period of alliance building, negotiation, and cultural exchange. Oneota peoples probably moved onto the Plains in search of larger bison herds, which were present only in small numbers east of the Mississippi. As Oneota peoples invaded the Great Plains in the thirteenth and fourteenth centuries, they encountered Caddoan-speaking ancestors of

Pawnees and Arikaras. Initial Oneota forays into Caddoan lands seem to have produced a similar combination of violence, avoidance, and diplomacy as their arrival in the Illinois River valley. In general, Caddoan peoples retreated up the Missouri River to clustered, fortified villages, but at some towns in present-day western Iowa and eastern Nebraska, Oneotas and Caddoans interacted peacefully. They exchanged goods and ideas, including pottery and housing styles.[25]

The most important exchange between Caddoan and Oneota peoples was the calumet ceremony. Although pipes and ritual smoking had existed in Native North America for thousands of years, the calumet ceremony became Middle America's most important method of creating allies, adopting strangers, and reinforcing trade and diplomacy. The ceremony probably developed in Caddoan communities during the last half of the 1200s, around the same time Oneotas entered the central Missouri valley. Whether these developments are related is unclear, but the timing suggests that as Caddoan peoples moved within the central Plains, they adopted novel ceremonies to create peaceful relations with new neighbors. Believed to be a gift from the Sun, the calumet conferred the power of the spirits on agreements of peace or declarations of war. Breaking such an accord was, in the words of a later French observer, "a crime which cannot be pardoned."[26]

Although the calumet served many purposes, it primarily converted strangers into fictive kin, making it particularly important in relations between Indian nations. Each nation attached its own motifs and interpretations to the calumet, but the principal form of the ritual remained intact. Through the Oneota alliance, the calumet became the most important cross-cultural ritual in Middle America by the end of the fifteenth century. Within 300 years of its introduction, the calumet spread through the plains, prairies, and woodlands of the Arkansas, Illinois, Missouri, Mississippi, and Ohio River valleys and the western Great Lakes. Archaeologists have uncovered Oneota-style pipes at Caddoan, Mississippian, Iroquoian, and Fort Ancient sites from present-day South Dakota to western New York, from central Minnesota to central Alabama.[27] All the while, Oneota peoples solidified their control over the region's trade networks, a process that began with their rapid territorial expansion in the wake of Cahokia's collapse.

Beginning in the late fourteenth century, Oneotas maintained their power through a new strategy that centered on controlling movement with large towns at key points along the region's rivers and trails. As with the cause of

Fig. 1.1 The Great Captain of the Illinois holding a calumet.

their expansion, the motivation is unclear, but their approach is obvious. By 1400, they pulled back from the frontiers and abandoned huge swaths of the midcontinent. They converged in large, fortified villages at strategically significant points across the Midwest and created buffer zones between themselves and their enemies. The easternmost group, ancestors of the Ho-Chunks, settled along the western and southern shores of Lake Michigan. Missouria Indians controlled much of the lower Missouri River valley and its tributaries, while Ioways and Otoes maintained towns at key river crossings and confluences on the Mississippi River in present-day Iowa, Illinois, and Wisconsin. By claiming strategic locations—choke points—in the Mississippi and Missouri River valleys, Oneotas used geography to their military and economic advantage, much as Cahokians had done in earlier centuries. Although they lacked the rigid hierarchy and centralization of Mississippian chiefdoms, they maintained connections through trade and political alliances.[28] The Oneota alliance controlled movement from east to west, north to south, along the rivers and overland trails of the midcontinent and dominated the Midwest from Lake Michigan to the Great Plains, from Minnesota to central Missouri.

At confluences, crossings, and other choke points, Oneota peoples developed a series of regional trade hubs on the eastern Plains, stretching from present-day central Missouri to far northwestern Iowa. On the lower Missouri River, Missouria Indians commanded trade from their expansive town, known to archaeologists as the Utz site. Covering more than 300 acres, this town became a hub of exchange, and networks of diplomats and traders returned to the site with exotic goods from throughout North America. They carried striking black-on-white Pueblo pottery and turquoise out of the deserts of the Southwest. Shells from the Tennessee River valley and Gulf Coast became ornaments, as did copper from the upper Midwest. Craftspeople turned northern Great Plains catlinite, also called red pipestone, into sacred objects such as calumets. In proto-Ioway settlements in what is now southeastern Iowa, archaeologists have recovered pottery and copper pendants similar to those used by Fort Ancient peoples and assorted raw materials from present-day Illinois, Minnesota, Missouri, North Dakota, Tennessee, and Wisconsin. At the Blood Run site in present-day northwestern Iowa, Oneota peoples acquired similar arrays of shell, metal, ceramic, and stone items. They also mined catlinite for pipes and ceremonial objects and produced tools from bison bones, the two principal trade goods of western Oneota peoples.[29]

Kinship furthered alliance building and trade. During this era, Oneota peoples shifted from patrilocal to matrilocal residence patterns, as female-headed kin groups moved into larger, multifamily longhouses. Oneota matrilocality may have increased trade among Siouan peoples in the Mississippi valley, as men and women from one village likely found partners from another. After marriage, men would move to the homes of their wives but maintained links to their old towns, easing exchange between groups.[30]

The patterns of alliance building and cultural exchange continued as a second wave of western migration occurred around the turn of the sixteenth century. At that moment, Dhegiha Sioux groups—ancestors of Osages, Kaws, Omahas, and Poncas—joined Chiwere-speaking Oneotas on the eastern Plains, while Quapaws, another Dhegihan group, settled farther south at the mouth of the Arkansas River. The Dhegiha and Chiwere branches of the Siouan language family divided centuries earlier, maybe as long ago as AD 600. The origins of the Dhegiha Sioux, like their distant Chiwere relatives, are uncertain but lay somewhere in the Ohio valley. Dhegiha material cultural and oral tradition reveal an array of Mississippian, Oneota, and Algonquian influences, indicating the Caborn-Welborn confederacy or, further back, Cahokia as possible ancestors.[31]

Sometime around the turn of the sixteenth century, Dhegiha Sioux moved down the Ohio River toward its mouth. At the confluence, they separated. Different storytellers offer various explanations for the Dhegiha dispersal. In one account, a storm blew the Quapaws off course as they crossed the Mississippi. In another, Dhegihas used a vine to cross the fog-covered river, but it snapped before the Quapaws could cross. Unable to see the far bank through the mists, they mistakenly believed their relatives had headed south, and they turned in that direction, hoping to catch up to them. Regardless of what happened at the Mississippi, the Quapaws settled at the mouth of the Arkansas River and became a separate nation, "the downstream people." The rest of the Dhegihas traveled up the Missouri River. Osages split off at the mouth of the Osage River. Kaws continued on into what is currently Kansas, and Omahas and Poncas followed the great river until they reached their future home, the Blood Run site on the current boundary line of Iowa and South Dakota. This migration occurred over an extended period of time. Omahas and Poncas reached Blood Run early in the 1500s, but Quapaws established themselves near the mouth of the Arkansas River much later, long after Hernando de Soto passed through the region in the early 1540s. Osages and Kaws divided later as well, probably sometime around 1675.[32]

During these centuries, Osages, Kaws, Omahas, and Poncas adopted Oneota technologies, customs, and ideas over a lengthy period of alliance and close habitation. At Blood Run, Omahas and Poncas created ceramics similar to Oneota styles, while extensive trade networks brought pottery acquired from Caddoan speakers to the west and Ioways to the east. Osages and Kaws are harder to locate during this era, although some evidence suggests they lived with Missouria Indians at the Utz site. In the late nineteenth century, Osages and Kaws stated that they had been "one people, inhabiting an extensive peninsula, on the Missouri River," before continuing their move west. That description, albeit vague, suggests geography similar to the location of Utz, which is surrounded on three sides by a dramatic bend in the Missouri. Perhaps they also adopted Oneota pottery styles, making them difficult to identify in the archaeological record. In contrast to these northern Dhegiha groups, Quapaws on the Arkansas River produced pottery and other goods that had more in common with midwestern styles, perhaps suggesting the form and decoration of other Dhegihan ceramics before their westward migration.[33]

Yet, for all of the utility of ceramics, tools, and other items, the adoption of the calumet ceremony was the most important adaptation of Dhegiha migrants. From the Blood Run site, Omahas and Poncas could access, and perhaps even control, one of the few sources of catlinite available to Oneota peoples. That red pipestone soon proliferated in Oneota trade networks and hubs, becoming one of the most important pieces of evidence of Oneota presence or influence. As the calumet ceremony spread, it too underwent changes and adaptations. Some societies constructed their pipes from local materials, rather than using Oneota catlinite. Sometimes they imitated the red color with local stone. Sometimes they used other material altogether, perhaps reflecting some cultural significance unknowable through artifacts alone. Each nation added its own decorations to the pipe stems that held the stone bowl. Yet, even with these adaptations, it retained its importance as an alliance-building ritual. No later than the middle of the seventeenth century, the calumet ceremony extended from present-day New York to the Southwest, from the northern Great Plains to the lower Mississippi River valley.[34]

≈   In the late afternoon or early evening after arriving in Peouarea, Marquette and Jolliet sat on reed mats alongside the Great Captain of the Illinois, a man of great power and influence, probably the chief, or *akima*, of

his nation. Shaded from the summer sun, the three men watched a performance of the calumet ceremony. Tobacco smoke wafted over them, and
drumming filled their ears. Propelled by the rhythm of the drums, a head
dancer circled the open area in the middle of the mats, carrying the decorated calumet. The dancer invited warriors to join him in the ritual, and one
by one, they entered the circle, where the two men mimed the warrior's past
victories in battle. At the end of the reenactment, the dancer held the calumet high and narrated the warrior's feats. In Marquette's words, the dancer
"recounts the battles at which [the warrior] has been present, the victories
that he has won, the names of the Nations, the places, and the Captives whom
he has made." After receiving a gift, the warrior stepped aside, making way
for the next man. Such a ceremony could last for hours, as all of a town's
warriors performed their duty in recounting their exploits. Given that
Peouarea's total population exceeded 8,000, Marquette and Jolliet may
have spent a long while observing the calumet ceremony.[35]

The parade of warriors served not just to bolster the reputation of individuals but also to present the Illinois as a powerful nation deserving of respect from the French newcomers. The ceremony told of the Illinois conquest of Middle America. During the early seventeenth century, when Illinois
arrived in the Mississippi valley—probably from present-day Ohio—they
were newcomers, buffalo hunters and aspiring traders who sought better
opportunities in the West. Fifty years later, as they informed Marquette,
they stood as the most powerful nation in the region. They controlled the
vital waterways that linked the Great Lakes to the Great Plains. They governed the trade of furs, slaves, and European goods between those two regions. This expansion was reenacted in the ceremony that Marquette and
Jolliet observed. Older Illinois warriors told of their fights against Ho-Chunk
Indians near present-day Chicago or ancestral Ioways, whom the Illinois
had driven out of the area around Peouarea. Younger warriors boasted of
more recent journeys west and south to capture enemies, whom they traded
to allied nations on Lakes Michigan and Superior. Through actions and
words, the Illinois told the French that they dominated the heart of the
Mississippi valley.

Illinois combined warfare, diplomacy, and marriage to destroy and remake
the region's political and economic networks, putting themselves at the center
of exchange and trade. They used military might to seize possession of natural
resources and strategic, riverine locations. Illinois also merged alliances old
and new to create a diverse exchange network that pervaded the central

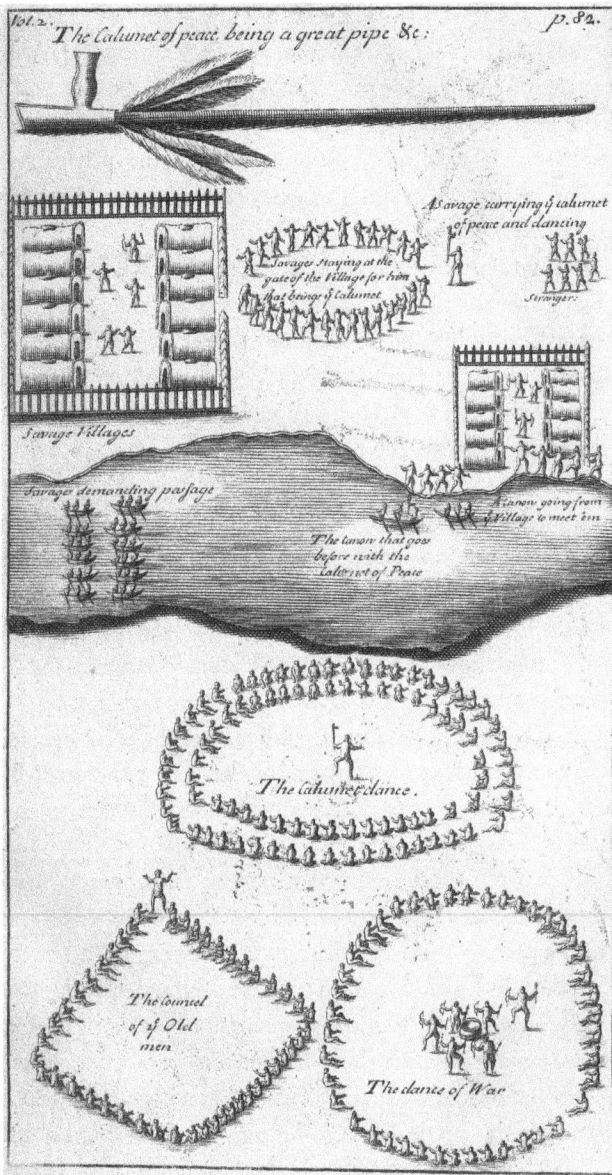

Fig. 1.2 On land and water, travelers presented a calumet to friends and strangers as a sign of peace. The calumet ceremony also served as a method of ritually adopting foreigners and making them kin.

Mississippi valley. They cultivated relationships with key trading partners, often using marriage to seal agreements, and they adopted the calumet ceremony, recognizing its growing power in Middle America. In half a century, the Illinois emerged as political and economic leaders in the Mississippi valley, but their methods and strategies for gaining power centered on building alliances and controlling rivers, much like the Mississippian and Oneota peoples who preceded them.

A speaker of half a dozen Algonquian languages, Marquette understood enough to recognize the content of the ceremony but failed to grasp that the included history lesson highlighted Illinois power. He thought it little more than "the diversion of a Ball or a Comedy." Compounding this limited comprehension, Marquette, Jolliet, and subsequent French colonists arrived in the Mississippi valley with their own understanding of North American history. The specter of the Iroquois clouded their vision of the Great Lakes and the lands to the west. Beginning in the late 1640s, French missionaries witnessed firsthand the violence and destruction that Iroquois inflicted on the Eries, Neutrals, Petuns, Wendats (also called Wyandots or Hurons), and others on Lakes Ontario and Erie. During these wars, the Iroquois killed eight Jesuits. The memory of those martyrs loomed large in the missionary consciousness for decades afterward. As Jesuits traveled among the western nations, they believed they entered a political world that resembled the one to the east. Their own fear of the Iroquois led them to perceive a similar anxiety among all the peoples they met and blinded them to the political realities of the Mississippi valley.[36]

Through the turn of the seventeenth century, the Oneota alliance maintained its preeminence, but a century or less before Marquette and Jolliet stumbled up the path to Peouarea, Illinois Indians began moving west from their country south of Lake Erie. Their precise origins are unknown, but they may have been related to the Whittlesey peoples of present-day northeastern Ohio or shared ancestors with the Fort Ancient peoples who lived on the Ohio River in what is now southern Ohio and northern Kentucky. As in the Mississippi valley, the Little Ice Age brought severe droughts and endangered agricultural production south of Lake Erie.[37] Facing a dwindling food base at home, Illinois moved west to seize better environmental, political, and economic opportunities.

Illinois only needed to look to their southern neighbors, the Fort Ancient people, to see the power brought by trade across eastern North America. During the sixteenth century, Fort Ancient peoples linked Oneotas in present-day Iowa, Mississippian chiefdoms on the lower Mississippi River, and Iroquois in the Northeast, creating a network that moved prestige goods and rituals, such as the calumet, thousands of miles. In earlier centuries, Fort Ancient people frequently interacted with Siouan peoples south of Lake Michigan, but those connections faltered in the fifteenth century.[38] Illinois likely identified a niche for themselves in resurrecting trade relations with a group that had disappeared from existing Fort Ancient networks.

Like the Fort Ancient people, Illinois power stemmed in part from their access to valuable and exotic items sourced from across the continent, but Illinois also dealt in new prestige goods that were foreign to North America. Around 1500 but possibly earlier, fishermen from across western Europe began to exploit the wealth of fish and whales available off the coast of Newfoundland. Within half a century, hundreds of Basque, English, French, Portuguese, and Spanish boats made the voyage every year. From their earliest arrivals, these seamen traded metal, glass, and cloth goods to Indigenous peoples, who integrated them into existing customs and patterns of exchange. Beginning in the mid-1500s, *entradas* led by Hernando de Soto and Francisco Coronado into the South and Great Plains, respectively, and the establishment of short-lived European colonies on the Atlantic coast later in the century introduced similar goods into Native trade networks. Passed from one polity to another, often in the forging of alliances, these goods soon traveled through much of eastern North America, reaching the Midwest in small quantities by the middle of the sixteenth century. With access to European goods, Illinois held an economic advantage over nations to the west, who sought the power transmitted by these objects but lacked another source for them. No later than the 1660s, steel blades and firearms gave Illinois a military advantage as well.[39]

At the same time, Illinois saw an opportunity to exploit the growing bison herds of the Midwest. Large numbers of bison arrived in the midcontinent in the fifteenth or sixteenth century. The arid Great Plains bore the brunt of Little Ice Age droughts, and bison sought refuge in the prairies of the Mississippi valley. Oneota peoples integrated the shaggy beasts into their hunting cycles. At the turn of the seventeenth century, as the Illinois looked for new opportunities to the west, they learned about the massive bison herds and sought to reap the benefits for themselves.[40]

Heading west from Lake Erie, the Illinois first encountered ancestral Ho-Chunks living on the southern end of Lake Michigan in a group of villages in and around present-day Chicago. Beginning in the early decades of the seventeenth century, European goods appeared in proto-Ho-Chunk towns, usually in connection with the arrival of Illinois traders. Within a decade or two, relations between Illinois and Ho-Chunks turned hostile. Ho-Chunks warred with Ottawas and Wendats, who controlled the increasingly impor-tant trade between the western Great Lakes and the French in the St. Law-rence valley. In 1634, Samuel de Champlain sent Jean Nicolet to broker a peace between these groups. Nicolet, taking his place in a long line of overconfi-dent French diplomats, reported success in his negotiations, when in reality he had been treated with respect by Ho-Chunks and then promptly ignored following his departure. Probably not long after Nicolet left Lake Michigan, Ho-Chunks received Ottawa envoys, whom they killed. War continued.[41]

Seeing an opportunity to build alliances and gain diplomatic influence, Illinois attempted to end the conflict between Ottawas and Wendats to the east and the Indians of southern Lake Michigan. Doing so would have placed them in the advantageous role of intermediaries between the growing power of Ottawas and Ho-Chunks, who commanded the headwaters of water routes west. However, such an endeavor included great risk as well. In an age when torturing captives satiated grief for dead relatives, a party of strangers entering a foreign village might meet an agonizing demise. When 500 Il-linois arrived at a Ho-Chunk village, carrying gifts and seeking diplomacy, Ho-Chunks greeted them, built a lodge, and prepared a feast. As the Illinois ate, Ho-Chunks avenged their casualties in the war. They sliced the Illinois' bowstrings and "massacred them, not sparing one man." Later that night, according to Ho-Chunk oral tradition, a lone owl appeared at their village. Landing on the top of the lodge that hosted the massacre, the owl hooted, "The [Ho-Chunks] will have bad luck."[42] Expecting retribution, Ho-Chunks fled their village, likely heading north to join their relatives in present-day Wisconsin. Not long after, other Illinois came looking for their missing relatives and found only abandoned cabins and piles of bones.

The killing of the Illinois diplomats assuaged the spirits of the Ho-Chunk dead, but it also unleashed the wrath of a new enemy. For a year, Illinois mourned their losses and rallied their allies, who pledged their assistance in revenge. At the end of their mourning, joined by "all the nations," Illinois marched on the Ho-Chunks. They found the entire Ho-Chunk village on a winter hunt and stalked them through the woods, turning the hunters into the hunted. Following the Ho-Chunks back to their settlement, the Illinois and their allies assaulted the Ho-Chunk town. Already weakened by an un-known epidemic disease that "turned their bodies yellow," Ho-Chunks offered little resistance to the onslaught. The Illinois laid waste to the Ho-Chunks, killing nearly all of the men and taking the women and children captive. French and Ho-Chunk accounts depict near-total destruction. Jesuits reported that either one man or a few men, badly wounded, escaped the fighting and found refuge among the sole Ho-Chunk ally, the Menominees. Ho-Chunks, however, recounted that the Illinois had killed all of the adult men, and as they began to slay the boys, one Ho-Chunk woman saved her son, when she tied back his penis so he could pass as a girl.[43] The boy escaped execution and became the progenitor of all later Ho-Chunks. The surviving Ho-Chunk men and women—those whom Illinois did not keep as captives—reconstituted the nation as French traders and missionaries found it when they reached the shores of Green Bay later in the seventeenth century.

Illinois quickly adapted to changing political and economic conditions. By the end of the 1630s, they had moved west to the Mississippi River, where they forced Oneota relatives of the Ho-Chunks from a town at the Des Moines Rapids, a cataract and crossing on the Mississippi between its confluences with the Iowa and Des Moines Rivers. Given the reported epidemic among Ho-Chunks, disease may have struck Ioways as well. However, disease alone was not enough to produce the depopulation Ioways suffered. Only when combined with malnutrition, warfare, or other aggravating factors did disease unleash the cataclysmic effects that could convince a community to relocate hundreds of miles away. Unfortunately for Ioways, multiple hardships hit their communities in short order. During the late sixteenth century, before Illinois expansion, a "megadrought," more severe than the Dust Bowl of the 1930s, hit the Midwest and brought all the maladies associated with water shortages and crop failures. Disease, drought, and finally Illinois attacks drove Ioways away from the Mississippi and pushed them far to the west. Ioways settled at and near the Blood Run site in northwestern Iowa, a place of great economic and spiritual power due to its close proximity to two sources of catlinite, the red stone used to make pipe bowls for calumets and other ceremonial items. At their new homes, they engaged in a program of mound building that was unprecedented among Oneota peoples. This may have been an effort at cultural revitalization and renewal, as the process of mound building echoed Ioway creation stories.[44]

With Ho-Chunks devastated and Ioways retreating to the northwest, the Illinois became the dominant power on southern Lake Michigan, the Illinois River, and a key stretch of the Mississippi River from the Wisconsin

River to present-day Arkansas. In the seventeenth century, the Illinois Nation comprised at least thirteen distinct divisions: Amenakoas, Cahokias, Chepoussas, Chinkoas, Coiracoentanons, Espiminkias, Kaskaskias, Michigameas, Moingwenas, Ooukas, Peorias, Tamaroas, and Tapouaros. Although these groups spread across a vast geographic area, each maintained linguistic, cultural, economic, and political ties with the rest.[45]

Kinship also created ties between distant Illinois towns. It is possible that each Illinois village represented an exogamous, patrilineal clan or lineage. In that instance, a woman from one village would marry a man from another, and she would reside among his family. Another and probably more likely scenario is that the clans dispersed through multiple villages, giving members of the clans relatives in different locales in the Illinois Country beyond those acquired through marriage.[46] In either case, kinship ties connected the individual towns.

The village served as the primary political unit among the Illinois, and while each Illinois village possessed its own peace chief, the nation as a whole probably had a head chief, usually drawn from the Kaskaskias. These chiefs possessed noncoercive power that stemmed from personal accomplishments rather than heredity, although it is possible that lineage once played a larger role in the selection of leaders. Additionally, each village may have performed a unique duty at Illinois rituals, creating spiritual connections among the groups.[47]

As the Illinois spread through the central Mississippi valley, each division established a town at a key location in the Illinois exchange network. About ninety miles from the southern tip of Lake Michigan, where the Des Plaines and Kankakee Rivers join to form the Illinois River, Kaskaskias, sometimes considered the paramount Illinois group, established their eponymous town. The Illinois River valley had seen little activity since the Mississippians and Oneota abandoned it 200 years earlier. Illinois faced little difficulty in claiming the river's course from its headwaters to its mouth at the Mississippi. Leaving Kaskaskias at the northeastern edge of the Illinois Country, Tamaroas and Cahokias traveled south to the American Bottom. Chepoussas and Michigameas relocated farther south into present-day Arkansas. To the north, at the confluence of the Des Moines and Mississippi Rivers in what is now the northeastern corner of Missouri, Peorias established the town that Marquette and Jolliet visited in 1673. Tapouaros may have also lived there or nearby, while Coiracoentanons and the Moingwenas pushed up the Des Moines River. For the others, geographic information is sparse or nonexistent. By the 1670s, the Illinois had spread out in an arc from the southern tip of Lake Michigan, west to the Mississippi River, and south to the Arkansas River. In this pattern, they controlled the major trade routes running between the western Great Lakes, the Great Plains, and the lower Mississippi River valley.[48]

Illinois recognized the great spiritual and practical power of the region's waterways. Rivers, lakes, and other bodies of water served as borders between This World and the Underworld, the home of the Underwater Panther and a place symbolizing both disorder and fertility. The Underwater Panther embodied the dangers of river travel. It ambushed unwitting travelers, sometimes snatching them off riverbanks. Indians inscribed these beliefs on the landscape. On the Mississippi, shortly above its confluence with the Illinois River, the Piasa, a cliff drawing of the Underwater Panther, warned travelers of approaching rapids, a water feature thought to be the home of the water monster. To avoid such attacks, Illinois and other midcontinent Indians offered gifts and sang songs to the Underwater Panther and other mighty beings, hoping to buy safe passage. Allying with the forces of the Underworld could be risky but not as dangerous as ignoring their power.[49]

Illinois also recognized the practical benefits of controlling the region's rivers. As Illinois taught French missionaries their language around the turn of the eighteenth century, they included phrases such as *nikipalihka siipiiwi*, which Jesuits translated to mean "I barricade the river to defeat the enemy, await him there." *Nintetah8reg8* translated as "people do not want me to cross, people are denying me passage in a canoe."[50] (In their writings, Jesuits borrowed the character *8* from the Latin combination of the letters *o* and *u*, and like *ou* in French, *8* is pronounced either as *oo*, as in *vous*, or *w* as in *oui*.)[51] The vulnerabilities of river travelers presented opportunities to those who could take advantage of their weakness. Whether in spiritual or practical terms, the Illinois seized every occasion to harness the power of the rivers.

≈   At the end of the calumet ceremony, the Great Captain presented the pipe to Marquette and Jolliet "as a token of the everlasting peace" between the Illinois and the French. Marquette recognized the performance and the gift of the pipe as honors. As the priest knew, Indians employed the calumet "to put an end to Their disputes, to strengthen Their alliances, and to speak to Strangers." However, Marquette appears not to have realized that the ceremony functioned as an adoption ritual. As a Great Lakes trader noted, in performing the calumet ceremony for a visitor, Indian leaders "render him . . . a son of the tribe, and naturalize him as such."[52] On that day in June 1673, the Illinois converted Marquette and Jolliet from strangers to members of the nation and forged a bond between themselves and the French empire.

As adoption followed mock battle in the calumet ceremony, alliance building followed conquest in the Illinois Country. By the time Marquette and Jolliet set foot in Peouarea, Illinois were practiced at the rituals of peace. Ruling the rivers and footpaths that connected disparate regions of the mid-continent only mattered if Illinois could build the alliances necessary to obtain desirable goods and put the waterways to use. Between 1630 and 1670, Illinois created a wide network of alliance and trade, employing three strategies for alliance building that were common in Native North America: real kinship, fictive kinship, and gift giving.

Intermarriage formed real kinship ties. A daughter or sister of a prominent man of one nation would marry an important man of another nation and would then live with her new husband and his people. Women served a crucial role in these marital exchanges, because the Illinois and their allies practiced patrilineal social organization. In patrilineal societies, lineage follows the father. Thus, while men who married into patrilineal nations retained their relatives from their natal communities, they had no kin beyond their wives in their spouse's community. Without adoption or an alteration of social norms, those men were marginal in their wives' nations. Likewise, their children lacked clan affiliations or extended families. These marriages had less diplomatic or economic value than those in which women married into patrilineal societies, because children were woven into their father's kinship networks. Wives served as cultural brokers, and over time, her children reinforced that connection. Limited evidence reduces the visibility of marriages between Indian nations, especially in the precontact era, but scattered records hint at their prevalence. At the turn of the eighteenth century, at least one Michigamea woman lived among the Michigameas' trading partners, the Quapaws. Close Illinois kinship ties with Osages, Missourias, Miamis, and Ottawas, to name a few, in the eighteenth century suggest that better documentation would reveal marriages linking the Illinois and their allies in the 1600s.[53]

In Illinois society, men oversaw courtship and marriage arrangements, and it is likely that diplomatic marriages followed similar protocols. To maintain decorum and female chastity, men and women rarely interacted while courting. An Illinois man informed his father of his intention to marry a woman. While the son was away from town, either on a hunt or for war, his father sent a present to the brother of his son's proposed wife. If the woman had no brother, her father headed negotiations. The man's father would offer "five or six kettles, two or three guns, some skins of stags, bucks, or beavers, some flat sides of buffalo, some cloth, and sometimes a slave, if he has one."[54] The suitor's father then requested an alliance with the woman's family. If the woman's brother deemed the offer worthy of consideration, he counseled with his parents or extended family.[55] If the family accepted the offer, they sent their own presents to the suitor. If not, the family returned the original gifts, indicating that they declined the marriage proposal. Sometimes, this was the final word, but other times, it signaled a demand for a richer offering of presents. If the would-be groom's family upped their offer, the woman's relatives reconsidered. When they accepted the proposal, the woman usually joined her husband in his family's longhouse.[56]

Patrilineality limited the ability of nations to incorporate male outsiders through marriage, but ceremonies created fictive kinship ties. Illinois circumvented the limits of lineage through the calumet ceremony and other rituals, which they used to adopt foreigners, usually prominent men.[57] Such rituals linked the two parties in bonds of mutual obligation, much like actual kinship, and they reinforced old relations or formed the basis of new alliances in the absence of marriage.

Finally, gift giving, especially of captives, sealed these agreements. The gift of humans demonstrated the power and generosity of the giver. The giver not only possessed the military strength to seize captives but also valued the recipient highly enough to part with such a valuable commodity. Moreover, the giver often referred to the captive as "my son" or "my flesh," imbuing the offering with symbolic kinship. At the same time, many of the Illinois' trading partners spoke mutually unintelligible languages, and captives who spoke multiple languages could serve as interpreters, further strengthening the alliance. A few years before Marquette's journey down the Mississippi, he informed his superiors about a Kiskakon Ottawa whom he had nursed back from the verge of death. In gratitude, the Kiskakon man presented Marquette with a slave, who, in turn, an Illinois ally had given to him a short time previously. Marquette then employed the slave as a tutor in the Illinois language as he prepared for his 1673 voyage.[58]

In a few short decades, using rituals that created real and fictive kinship ties, the Illinois Nation became the central node of an elaborate network of alliance and exchange. By the second half of the 1600s, Illinois authority extended through much of the central Mississippi valley, and their behavior demonstrated their confidence in their power. Illinois maintained an annual subsistence cycle in which they abandoned their villages and cornfields during May and June to hunt bison in the West. Life depended on productive corn crops, yet Illinois left their towns lightly guarded, doubting that their enemies would or could destroy their fields. Further revealing the extent of Illinois influence, travelers employed the Illinois language as a lingua franca. Groups as diverse as the Sioux, Senecas, Foxes, Missourias, and Quapaws could communicate in Illinois. If in doubt about whom they encountered in the woods or on a river, they hailed in Illinois, expecting that their message would be understood by whoever lurked out of sight.[59]

Throughout Marquette and Jolliet's voyage, they traveled through a region dominated by the Illinois and their allies. In May 1673, the two men departed from Michilimackinac, the home of the Kiskakon Ottawas, the Illinois' closest friends in the North. Together with Wendats, Ottawas provided Illinois traders with the French-made goods they transported to their allies to the south and west. By the time Illinois, Wendats, and Ottawas joined forces in their wars against the Ho-Chunks, Wendats and Ottawas had traded with the French for two decades. In 1611, Wendats formed a trade alliance with Samuel de Champlain's Quebec, and by 1615, Ottawas had opened their own direct line to French trade goods, in addition to their exchange with the Wendats. Together, Wendats and Ottawas were the earliest source of French goods in the western Great Lakes. The Wendat trade network stretched from Lake Ontario to the western shores of Lake Michigan, ending with the Ho-Chunks. When the Illinois replaced the Ho-Chunks on southern Lake Michigan in the 1630s, they secured access to French trade goods.[60]

In these early years, French goods probably entered the Illinois Country only in small quantities, and by the time they reached midcontinent, they were probably in poor condition. When Ottawas traded with allies to the north, they brought "old knives, blunted awls, wretched nets, and kettles used until they were past service." Newly acquired goods they kept for themselves. Still, the French would buy any beaver pelt, and even "worn-out beaver robes" fetched a healthy return in knives, hatchets, and guns. The farther a beaver pelt traveled from its point of origin, the more value it gathered. The same was true of French goods. At the end of the Wendat and Ottawa trade networks, Illinois held an advantage over their western neighbors, but they paid a premium for European manufactures. Over time, they would seek better sources of these goods.[61]

Beginning in 1648, marauders from the Five Nations of the Iroquois League briefly upended these trade networks. Iroquois forces drove Wendats, Petuns, and Kiskakon Ottawas from their homelands on Lakes Ontario and Erie and eastern Lake Huron. They left behind them burned villages, the bones of their ancestors, and relatives who were now held captive in Iroquoia. The destruction of the Iroquois' initial campaigns seemed to foretell an easy triumph for the Five Nations, and the one-sided victories of these early years have colored accounts of the wars, which often overstate both the geographical reach of Iroquois armies and their successes. Other than the vanquished Eries and Neutrals, the dispersed Wendats, Petuns, and Kiskakon Ottawas suffered the worst of the Iroquois attacks, but they soon recovered. They drew on their western alliances and regrouped on Lakes Michigan and Superior. The winter of 1652–1653 found those nations planning counterattacks. Soon, they retaliated against the Iroquois, destroying invading armies and launching punitive expeditions into the heart of Iroquoia. By the early 1660s, the western alliance stood as an equal rival to the Five Nations.[62]

Beyond the eastern Great Lakes, most nations escaped the violence of invasion. During the 1650s, Illinois, for example, lived well past the reach of all but the most daring Iroquois armies. The one documented battle between Illinois and Iroquois from this era occurred in 1655. That year, Iroquois warriors appeared in the far western Great Lakes, seeking their Anishinaabeg enemies. One force headed to the north, where it met defeat at the hands of the Anishinaabeg. The main body of Iroquois continued west and "found themselves among the buffaloes." Nearly out of food, they discovered a small Illinois town, which they attacked. The survivors called for nearby allies. "Assembling all their warriors," a French trader later reported, they "made a hasty march, surprised the enemy, and utterly defeated them in battle." Only a "very few" Iroquois lived to return home.[63]

Regardless of the devastation of the early Iroquois attacks, Ottawas, Wendats, and others resumed their trade with the St. Lawrence valley no later than 1654. Now that they embarked from new homes in the western Great Lakes, that trip was more onerous. It took twelve weeks to paddle canoes from Michilimackinac to Montreal, even longer from Chequamegon Bay. They had to navigate open lakes and turbulent rivers and carry canoes and cargo across some thirty portages. But skilled Ottawa boatmen were up to the task, and they soon returned to the west with the trade goods that were much desired by their allies. The westward movement of Kiskakon Ottawas and other traders brought those goods all that much closer to the Mississippi valley and the Illinois Nation.[64]

In this changing political world, Illinois maintained especially close relationships with two groups in the western Great Lakes: the Miami Nation and the Kiskakon clan of the Ottawas. The Illinois-Kiskakon alliance had developed recently, but the Illinois connection with Miamis was rooted in a much older history. Until shortly before their contact with the French in the seventeenth century, Illinois and Miamis constituted a single nation. Illinois and Miamis probably divided around the time that Illinois began their expansion into the Mississippi valley. According to Miami oral history, Kaskaskias split from Miamis, and in turn, Peorias separated from Kaskaskias. During the 1650s, both Miamis and Kiskakons lived on Green Bay, and a group of Illinois Indians temporarily relocated there, probably as part of a seasonal migration, to live closer to their trading partners. With *voyageurs* operating in a combined Wendat, Petun, and Potawatomi village nearby, Illinois and their allies had a ready source of European goods, which they then funneled south to towns on the Mississippi. Illinois continued to make regular trips to Green Bay during the 1660s. In 1672, Jesuits reported "twenty cabins" of Illinois, possibly a combined group of Kaskaskias, Moingwenas, and Peorias, residing with Miamis near Green Bay.[65]

By the middle of the 1600s, the Illinois-Kiskakon alliance played an integral role in the success of the Illinois exchange network, although that relationship only dated back two or three decades. Their connection was so strong that Illinois referred to all Ottawas as *kiscak8a*. Each time the Kiskakons moved between the 1650s and the 1670s, Illinois soon arrived to trade. That fact held true even when Kiskakons moved farther away from the Illinois Nation. During the 1660s, Illinois at Peouarea, rather than rely solely on their Miami allies at Green Bay, traveled a much greater distance, about 500 miles, to the new Kiskakon town at Chequamegon Bay. On western Lake Superior, they traded slaves and furs to Kiskakons for "hatchets and kettles, guns, and other articles that they need."[66]

The slaves whom Illinois traded and presented to Kiskakons came from the plains and prairies in the West, beyond Peouarea and the other Illinois villages on the Des Moines and Missouri Rivers. By the end of the seventeenth century, French colonists referred to all Indian slaves as *panis*, but the slaves exchanged in Native and French settlements originated in diverse communities, most of them not associated with the Pawnee Nation, as it was known in the eighteenth century. Illinois warriors acquired these human commodities from a variety of communities. In 1673, Peorias told Marquette that they raided nations that lived far enough to the south and the west that they were ignorant of European firearms. Peorias used guns, Marquette wrote, "especially to inspire, through their noise and smoke, terror in their Enemies." In 1682, Michigameas presented to the French explorer René-Robert Cavelier, Sieur de La Salle, a *panis* slave, who was likely a Wichita Indian from southwest of the Missouri River. Around the same time, Illinois began taking captives among Chickasaw Indians in present-day northeastern Mississippi.[67] In general, Illinois established trade relations with their neighbors and warred against those nations at a greater distance. Such a strategy kept trade routes safe, while ensuring that the Illinois acquired captives for diplomatic and economic exchange.

The growing trade in Indian slaves depended as much on exchange as on warfare. When Illinois exchanged captives with their friends, they received people who had sometimes been traded three or four times before reaching them, much like the glass and metal goods moving in the other direction. For example, the Wichita boy given to La Salle in 1682 had been taken by Skiri Pawnees, who lost him to Osage raiders. Osages traded him to Missourias, who passed him to Michigameas.[68] As Illinois people traded with nations to their south and west, they in part maintained ties that they had forged long before when living south of Lake Erie, but they also created new alliances with nations that had lived in the West for centuries.

On the lower Missouri River, Illinois maintained regular trade with Missourias, who had lived in present-day central Missouri since at least the mid-1400s, and Osages, who had only recently migrated westward from the Ohio valley. Missourias were Chiwere speakers like Ioways and Ho-Chunks, whom the Illinois dispossessed and destroyed, but Illinois sought a trade alliance with Missourias. Perhaps the explanation lies in the far-ranging trade network that Missourias had forged from the Utz village near the confluence of the Grand and Missouri Rivers. Soon after Peorias established Peouarea, they began to exchange slaves and European goods with the Missourias along an ancient trade route that linked the Des Moines–Mississippi confluence with the lower Missouri River.[69]

Among the Dhegiha Sioux, Osages and Quapaws became the Illinois' most important allies and trading partners. Farther from the eyes of the French traders, officials, and missionaries who documented the Illinois' trade with Ottawas and Miamis, relations between the Illinois, Osages, and Quapaws are more difficult to detail beyond broad outlines. Illinois people, probably Cahokias and Tamaroas at the mouth of the Missouri as well as Peorias, carried on a regular trade with Osages beginning sometime in the mid- or late seventeenth century. Osages probably provided bison robes that they took on the Plains, augmenting the rewards of the Illinois' own annual bison hunts. The Osages' most important contribution to the Illinois trade came in the form of slaves they captured from their Caddo and Pawnee enemies to the west and southwest. In turn, Illinois provided kettles, hatchets, knives, awls, beads, and other goods they acquired from their allies on Lakes Michigan and Superior. At times, relations between Illinois and Osages turned sour, but these short-lived conflicts must have stemmed from minor squabbles. By the early 1680s, Illinois trusted Osages to the point that they sought refuge among Osages after Iroquois warriors attacked the principal Kaskaskia town on the Illinois River.[70]

The southernmost member of the Illinois alliance, the Quapaws of the Arkansas River, served as their closest friends downstream from the Illinois Country. Like Illinois, Quapaws recognized the power of the region's rivers, and after their migration out of the Ohio valley, they established several towns near the confluence of the Arkansas and Mississippi Rivers. Their position allowed them to move easily north, south, or west and to prevent others from traveling on those waterways. Illinois had known of the peoples of the Arkansas valley long before they and Quapaws moved west. In 1680, Illinois elders still spoke with familiarity of long-gone Tunica and Caddo chiefdoms that Hernando de Soto's expedition encountered there in 1541. Any relationship that Illinois had with those chiefdoms must not have been particularly friendly, as Illinois remained close with Quapaws after they drove Tunicas out of the lower Arkansas valley. By 1673, Michigameas followed centuries of travelers south on the Natchitoches Trace from the midcontinent to present-day Arkansas and established a town halfway between the Quapaw Nation and the American Bottom. At their town, Michigameas traded axes, knives, beads, brass tinklers and points, and other items for captives, skins, horses, and decorative ceramics that Quapaws obtained farther west and south. Before winter set in, the Michigameas returned to the American Bottom, where they met Tamaroas and Cahokias, who brought them more trade goods and carried the valuables from the Arkansas valley north to French or Indian trading partners. Sometimes Quapaws joined them on their trip home. In 1680, La Salle reported that some Quapaws lived among their allies in the Illinois Country.[71] Through marriage, trade, and cohabitation, Illinois cemented their alliance with Quapaws and connected the Arkansas valley to markets hundreds of miles to the north.

From north to south, Illinois allied with Ottawas, Miamis, Osages, and Quapaws against western nations such as Wichitas, Caddos, and Pawnees. Illinois controlled the crossings and confluences of the central Mississippi River, and they constructed an exchange network that linked the Great Lakes, the lower Mississippi valley, and the Plains. Ottawas and, to a lesser extent, Miamis brought French goods into the western Great Lakes, where Illinois traded for them using furs, skins, and slaves that they, Osages, and Quapaws collected farther west. At the center of that network, Illinois commanded the middle waters and influenced political and economic activity throughout the region. When Marquette and Jolliet arrived in Middle America in 1673, they entered a world dominated by an alliance network built and maintained by the Illinois, a world made up of interconnecting rivers and kinship networks that crisscrossed the social and geographic landscape of the region.

≈   Upon Marquette and Jolliet's return to the Great Lakes, Claude Dablon, the head Jesuit in New France, praised the men for possessing "the Courage to dread nothing where everything is to be Feared." Going to the Mississippi and back, the explorers had covered nearly 3,000 miles and "passed through a thousand dangers." Dablon and other French observers looked beyond Quebec and Montreal and saw only chaos. Ignorance and prejudice prevented them from recognizing the well-ordered social and political world constructed by Illinois and their allies. At no point in Marquette and Jolliet's expedition did they reach a place that was unfamiliar to the Illinois diplomats, warriors, and traders who linked Ottawas, Quapaws, and the many nations in between. In fact, on the return trip, a slave whom the Great Captain of the Illinois gave to Marquette at Peouarea took the explorers on a shortcut up the Illinois River to Lake Michigan, saving the party hundreds of miles and many days of travel.[72]

By 1673, centuries of migration, warfare, and social upheaval had given way to a few decades of calm, but that would change again soon. Quapaws recognized that the entry of French traders and friars into the Mississippi valley threatened to upend Illinois hegemony over the region. Despite close relations, Illinois refused to trade guns to their western partners, preferring to keep that advantage for themselves. With direct access to French firearms, Quapaws could hold off the eastern Indians who had begun to encroach on their eastern frontier. Marquette and Jolliet met some of these newcomers during their voyage. South of the Ohio River, the travelers encountered a well-armed nation, maybe Ofos or Chickasaws but unnamed in Marquette's account. Comparing them to the Indians he knew, Marquette reported that they tattooed their bodies like Iroquois, and the women dressed similarly to Wendats. Most importantly for the political dynamics of the Mississippi valley, they traded with Europeans in the East.[73] Others would soon join this new wave of invaders, all looking for greater power along the mighty river. Longtime residents began to seek out new partnerships that were meant to improve their position in the regional hierarchy of trade and warfare. Once again, the Illinois and their allies had to adjust to an evolving political world. As they met French and Indian newcomers, they employed strategies of warfare and diplomacy that they had honed over centuries.

CHAPTER TWO

Conversions

S tripped of her jacket, stockings, shoes, and "petty ornaments," the teenage girl hid in the grass on the riverbank outside Kaskaskia. Enraged by her refusal to marry a French trader, her father, Chief Rouensa, had taken her clothes, all except "what covered her," and banished her from their longhouse. Rouensa wanted the wedding because it would strengthen his family and his nation's alliance with Michel Accault, one of the region's most prominent fur traders. Accault arrived in the Illinois Country in 1680, part of René-Robert Cavelier de La Salle's expedition into the western Great Lakes and down the Illinois River. Early in his years in the Illinois Country, he had become "well-enough educated" in the languages of the region's Native peoples. He "knew all their customs and was loved by many of these peoples." Now, thirteen years later, he had become a partner in the fur monopoly of La Salle's successors.[1] The marriage between the seventeen-year-old Marie Rouensa and the nearly fifty-year-old Accault would cement Chief Rouensa's access to European goods and reinforce his power in Kaskaskia and the Illinois Nation as a whole. But his daughter rejected custom and the husband that he had chosen for her.

Ashamed and afraid, Marie waited on the water's edge, until a sympathetic passerby tossed her his jerkin. She "at once came to the chapel," where she confided in the Jesuit priest Jacques Gravier. Since 1689, Gravier had worked in the Illinois Country, struggling to win converts to Catholicism. For four years, he had little success in his mission beyond a small cadre of young women, including Marie. Raised in a patriarchal society that proscribed women's influence and authority, these women found possibility in Catholicism, which venerated the Virgin Mary and other female saints. Marie referenced her faith in her rejection of Accault, explaining that "she did not wish to marry" because "she had already given all her heart to God, and did not wish to share it." Marie found Accault an especially undesirable partner, as he was a lapsed Catholic "famous in this *Ilinois* country for all his debaucheries" and had stoked hostility toward Gravier and other missionaries.[2]

After days of conflict in Kaskaskia, Marie reached an epiphany. She would use her marriage to Accault to bring others to Catholicism, starting with the French trader and her parents. Gravier supported Marie's decision, encouraging her "to do precisely whatever God inspired her, without fearing anything." Calling her parents and Accault to the chapel, Marie informed them that she agreed to the marriage, but only if all three embraced Catholicism, a condition they accepted. Her father "informed all the chiefs of the villages, by considerable presents, that he was about to be allied with a Frenchman."[3]

After the marriage ceremony, Accault and the Rouensa family followed through on their promises to Marie. According to Gravier, Accault became "the first conquest [Marie] made for God." Accault confided in the priest, "I am ashamed that a savage child, who has but recently been instructed, should know more than I who have been born and brought up in Christianity." He swore "to lead a good life in the future." Chief Rouensa and his wife sponsored gender-segregated feasts during which they pleaded with the townspeople to join them in "happiness" and "salvation." Their public baptisms demonstrated their commitment to the new faith. Yet Gravier reported that Chief Rouensa's alliance with Accault failed to produce the political and economic benefits Rouensa desired. Accault's newfound zealotry "made him odious to every one." For his part, Rouensa found that "the French who had displayed the greatest friendship toward him would not even look at him since he was a christian."[4]

The conflict over the marriage of Marie Rouensa and Michel Accault hinged on the question of who would dictate the terms of conversion. Would Chief Rouensa, through his daughter, bring a French trader into his family and profit from such an alliance? Or would Marie, backed by Gravier, transform her family and her nation by subsuming them into the Catholic Church? In the decades following Marquette and Jolliet's journey through the Illinois Country, these contests over power defined interactions between

Native peoples and the French. Marriage often played a key role in shaping those relationships.

Superficially, missionaries and traders had much in common as French sojourners in unfamiliar lands. In practice, though, the two groups found themselves at odds more often than not. Following the example of Marquette, Jesuit priests such as Gravier and their counterparts and rivals from the Séminaire des Missions Étrangères (Seminary of Foreign Missions) entered the Illinois Country to convert the Illinois to Catholicism. At the same time, roving traders paddled their canoes through the Great Lakes and into the Illinois and Wabash River valleys, seeking furs and wealth. Missionaries such as Gravier believed that the traders such as Accault inhibited the religious education of Native peoples, encouraging debauchery and licentiousness that hampered the building of Catholic nuclear families. By contrast, licensed fur traders, called *voyageurs*, and their illegal counterparts, *coureurs de bois*, entered the midcontinent keenly aware that the surest route to finding trading partners was to adapt to Indian customs. If they married Native women, traders did so *à la façon du pays* (in the custom of the country)—on Indian terms and beyond the reach of the Catholic Church. *Voyageurs*, then, believed that missionaries hindered their economic activities. Missionaries, in turn, regarded most traders as depraved and irreligious men. In sum, missionaries and *voyageurs* came to Middle America with competing goals. Their objectives put them in conflict with one another and with imperial officials in Quebec, New Orleans, and Paris.

During the seventeenth and early eighteenth centuries, the question of intermarriage spurred debates among secular and religious officials about the future of New France and the appropriate method of building productive colonies. Imperialist proponents of intermarriage joined missionaries in advocating it as a way of "civilizing" or "Frenchifying" Native peoples. Others denounced the corrupting influence of cross-cultural marriage, particularly the country marriages of the western *voyageurs*. Critics often highlighted French men who joined Native communities, claiming that their Indian wives had lured them away from the French colonies.

In reality, both supporters and opponents of French-Indian intermarriage were correct. Rates of intermarriage and the function of French-Indian marriages varied greatly in colonial Louisiana.[5] Even within a single Indian nation, the nature of intermarriage changed depending on the marriage's purpose (trade or religious conversion) and the couple's residence (an Indian town or a French hamlet). Intermarriage brought Kaskaskia Indians closer to the missionaries' ideal of a Catholic, agrarian community. Yet, for most other divisions of the Illinois, the marriage of Illinois women to French men incorporated French traders into Illinois communities. Cahokias and Peorias, especially, resisted conversion to Catholicism. Jesuits and traders alike developed intimate connections with Native peoples, often in defiance of imperial decree. Kinship relations defined these separate spaces, and diverse ambitions shaped the multiethnic communities of the midcontinent.

≈   After paddling hundreds of miles through the Mississippi valley and Great Lakes, Marquette and Jolliet returned to an empire uncertain that it should colonize the midcontinent. The risks of a far-flung empire concerned Louis XIV and his advisers. The 1674 census of Canada showed a decline in the colony's population. The incredulous king insisted that "whoever made up those returns committed a very great error, as the country contained, ten years ago, more people than at present." Regardless, Canada's small population made the crown hesitant to add new colonies in the Mississippi valley. Louis wrote to the expansionist governor of New France, Louis de Buade de Frontenac, "it is much better to occupy less territory and to people it thoroughly, than to spread one self out more, and to have feeble colonies which can be easily destroyed by any sort of accident." The crown denied Jolliet's request to establish a new post in the Illinois Country. As Louis's adviser Jean-Baptiste Colbert explained, "it is necessary to multiply the *habitants* of Canada before thinking of other lands."[6]

Throughout the late 1600s and early 1700s, the king struggled to establish policies that would maximize profits from the colony, mostly derived from the fur trade, while minimizing the risks posed by *voyageurs* and *coureurs de bois*. Officials accused the men of the woods of creating "infinite disorders and abominations." In 1685, the king complained that the West attracted so many "that the settlements have been abandoned, and the land, not being cultivated, has returned to the same condition in which it was before it had been cleared." Even more troubling, the presence of *coureurs de bois* in Indian Country sparked violence. War was expensive and threatened New France's weak colonies. As a result, the crown imposed a variety of policies to curb "disorder" in the West. At times, the empire issued small numbers of licenses or altogether forbade traders from entering the Great Lakes.[7] As a result of this fickle imperial policy, the midcontinent's colonies emerged in a haphazard manner, driven mostly by missionaries and adventurers who often skirted the line between legal and illegal enterprise.

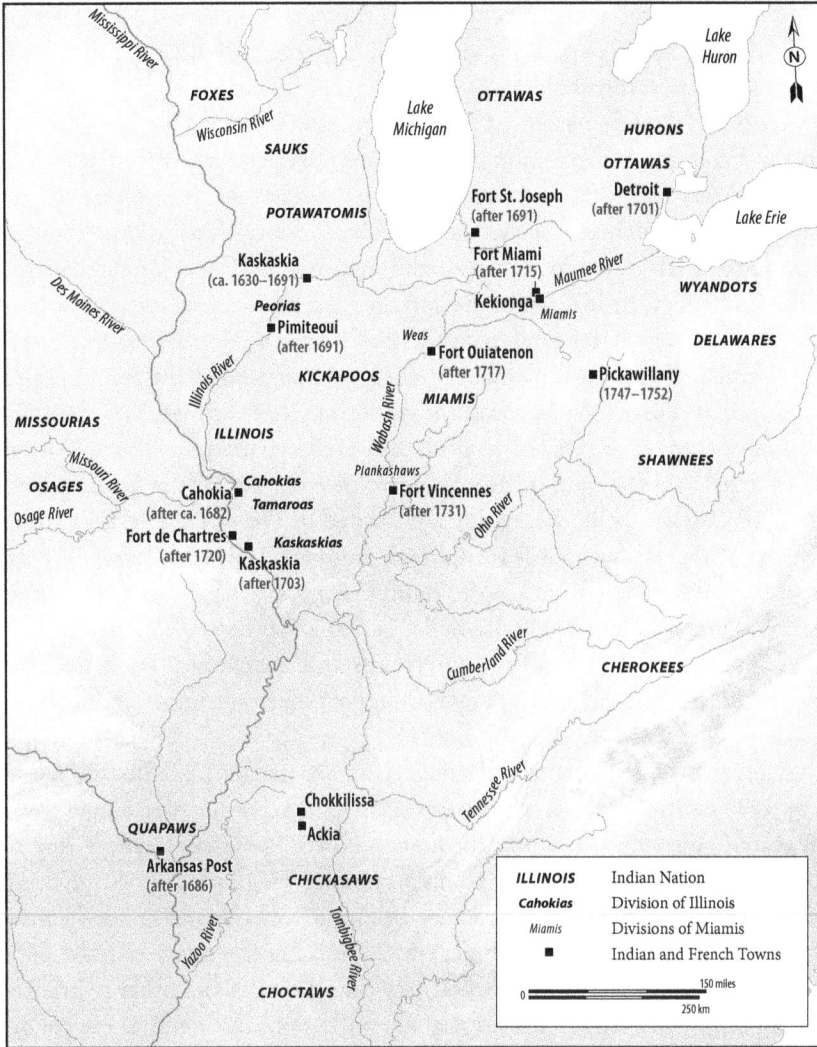

Map 3 The North American midcontinent, 1680–1754.

While Louis and Colbert fretted over the dangers of colonizing the midcontinent, they learned that the distance between Paris and Quebec imposed barriers to imperial control of New France. Governor Frontenac defied the king's orders to limit French colonization to the St. Lawrence valley. In official dispatches, he compared *coureurs de bois* to "the bandits of Naples, and the buccaneers of St. Domingue." In practice, he protected them when they were captured.[8] Louis condemned Frontenac's behavior, but the governor's double-dealing was part of a much larger scheme to expand the fur trade and enrich himself and his allies.

Louis and Colbert permitted two exceptions to their prohibitions on travel to the West. If an expedition might locate a warm-water port that would make Quebec accessible year-round or if it would cut off a rival empire's threat to the French colonies, they would allow it. Those two conditions provided Frontenac with cover to send expeditions into the Great Lakes and the Illinois Country. In 1673, he built a fort, bearing his name, at the point where the St. Lawrence River flows out of Lake Ontario. He explained to a suspicious Colbert that his diplomacy at the post had gained the friendship of the Iroquois—especially Senecas, the westernmost of the Five Nations—and curbed the ambitions of the English and Dutch traders at Albany. Moreover, it reduced the motivation of *coureurs de bois* to enter the Great Lakes, because Ottawas and other nations, protected by the fort, could bring their furs to Montreal without fear of attack from the Iroquois. The next year, Frontenac encouraged the king to hand over control of the fort to Frontenac's friend and political ally La Salle, "a man of spirit and intelligence and the most capable . . . for all the enterprises and discoveries that one would entrust to him."[9] The king approved the governor's recommendation, emboldening him and his coconspirators.

After two years of lucrative trade at Fort Frontenac, La Salle traveled to France to petition the crown for permission to travel to the Mississippi River in search of a year-round port for French North America. In the spring of 1678, Louis and Colbert approved his proposal, giving him five years to make the journey and construct forts where he chose. La Salle was to conduct the voyage at his own expense. Under no circumstances was he to trade with Ottawas or any other nation "who carry their Beavers and other peltries to Montreal."[10] The crown trusted that La Salle would abide by these conditions, but it had no way to compel compliance.

As La Salle undertook his western endeavor, he relied not only on the friendship of New France's governor but also on a set of trusted lieutenants. François Dauphin de La Forest had worked alongside La Salle since 1675, serving as a second in command at Fort Frontenac. Henri de Tonty was a newer addition to La Salle's circle. Then in his late twenties, Tonty had already made a name for himself, "having been eight years in French service, by land and by sea." He served on galleys and warships on the Mediterranean and then fought in Sicily, where an explosion from a grenade cost him his right hand. His metal prosthesis earned him the nickname "Iron Hand" from In-dians of the midcontinent. In 1678, when he failed to secure a spot at the court of Louis XIV, powerful friends introduced him to La Salle, whom he accom-panied to New France.[11] In the coming years, La Salle depended on La Forest and Tonty to continue his endeavors in the Great Lakes and Illinois Country as he traveled across North America and tended to affairs in Europe.

When La Salle ventured down the Illinois River in the winter of 1679–1680, Illinois Indians recognized the dangers and opportunities he repre-sented. La Salle carried hatchets and knives with him as gifts. He promised that other French colonists would soon arrive with an array of trade goods. La Salle wanted to build a trading post, Fort Crèvecoeur, near their village of Pimiteoui. Illinois leaders balked. The proposed fort threatened to upend their control over commercial networks running between the Great Lakes and the Great Plains. La Salle warned that if the Illinois refused his request, he might instead build his outpost in the Osage Nation. To prevent that, they agreed that La Salle could build the fort near their village.[12]

La Salle's arrival, as Illinois anticipated, upset the political world of Middle America. For decades, Illinois warriors, traders, and diplomats traveled be-tween the Great Plains and Lakes Michigan and Superior. Beginning in 1680, thanks in no small part to La Salle's actions, they faced a rising Iro-quois threat from the East. Illinois had known the Iroquois since at least 1655, when they "utterly defeated" an invading Iroquois army. In late 1677 or 1678, Illinois forces again beat back Iroquois raiders. Then, La Salle set forth into the midcontinent. Before he left, he met with Iroquois diplomats, probably Senecas, and informed them of his plans. He would head westward, seeking a route between Europe and Iroquoia, superior to the St. Lawrence River and its rapids. Success would allow him to provide merchandise to the Iroquois "at a better price."[13]

When La Salle sailed away from Niagara carrying a cargo of trade goods, Iroquois knew that he would encounter their enemies on his journey, a risk they could not bear. A few years earlier, a Seneca chief had complained, "every day [the French] make new discoveries, and enter nations which have ever been hostile to us." Condemning the governor for his new alliances in the West, the chief proclaimed, "He threatens to bring desolation on our land."[14] La Salle's dealings with western nations posed an existential threat to the Senecas.

Seneca leaders were right to fear the consequences of La Salle's expedi-tion. In the year after leaving Fort Frontenac, La Salle built Fort Crèvecoeur near the Illinois village at Pimiteoui. He then sent Tonty back upstream to Starved Rock to build another outpost a short distance from the Illinois town of Kaskaskia. La Salle promised he would furnish the Illinois with "arms and ammunition." He stipulated that they could not "employ them against the nations who live under the protection of the King," but no Frenchman could enforce such a demand. So began a robust trade in beaver pelts. Within nine months, he had acquired some 20,000 livres worth of skins, nearly triple the value of the trade merchandise he carried into the Illinois Country. (It is easiest to establish the value of a livre on the basis of what it could purchase. In Quebec, the most desirable beaver pelts, called *castor gras,* sold for five and a half livres. One *castor gras* could purchase about two and a half pounds of glass beads or fifty metal arrowheads.)[15]

La Salle arrived in the Illinois Country at a moment of consolidation for the powerful Illinois Nation. Starting no later than early 1675, more and more Illinois moved from Peouarea and other towns on the Mississippi River to the central Illinois River valley. By 1680, most divisions of the Illinois Nation along with contingents of allied Miamis, Shawnees, Missourias, and others occupied a string of villages from Starved Rock to Pimiteoui. Near Starved Rock, Kaskaskia (or the Grand Village of the Illinois, as the French called it) housed so many people that, in 1677, a Jesuit remarked, "One cannot well satisfy himself as to the number of people who Compose that village." It was easier instead to count the 351 lodges they occupied. Three years later, the town had grown to 460 lodges. As many as 8,000 people probably lived in the Grand Village, making it the largest town in a group of settlements numbering 20,000 people.[16]

Beginning in 1680, Iroquois armies entered the Illinois Country to destroy their enemies and remove the threat of a strengthened French-Illinois alliance. In September of that year, as Tonty constructed the second fort at Starved Rock, 600 Seneca and Onondaga warriors appeared. Since the beginning of the year, La Salle had returned to Fort Frontenac, and nearly all of the men attached to the party had deserted with any valuables they could carry. They left Tonty, two Recollect missionaries, and three other men "stripped of everything and at the mercy of the Indians."[17] La Salle's departure and the desertions, combined with the arrival of hundreds of Iroquois, convinced the Illinois that their qualms about the French had been well founded.

Tonty did little to ease their suspicions. When an Illinois chief explained, "our young men have gone to war and we have only bows and arrows," Tonty attempted to make peace with the Iroquois. As he approached their lines, an Onondaga warrior stabbed him in the chest, "severing a rib." Still, Tonty pleaded his case, warning the Iroquois that "they had come to make war upon a nation dependent on the Governor of New France." Meanwhile, Illinois women, children, and old men evacuated the Grand Village, traveling six hours down the Illinois River. The few remaining warriors burned part of the town and joined the rest downstream. After more than a week, the Iroquois insisted that they would "devour the Illinois" and told Tonty and the remaining French to flee, which they did. When Tonty was gone, Iroquois destroyed Kaskaskia, dug up graves, and mutilated the dead. Most Illinois had crossed to the west bank of the Mississippi, but some stayed east to hunt. The Iroquois army caught those who remained, killing a few and capturing "some seven hundred women and children." The invaders tortured and executed half of them on the spot and carried the rest back to Iroquoia.[18]

The attack at Kaskaskia and its gruesome aftermath announced the presence of a new threat to the Illinois Country. Illinois could no longer leave their villages lightly guarded as they journeyed into the west to hunt bison or raid for slaves. But, if the Iroquois sought to destroy the Illinois or discourage their alliance with the French, the attack failed. Unknown to French observers, the Grand Village of the Illinois was probably filled with slaves during the early fall of 1680, and they surely comprised the vast majority of those whom the Iroquois killed or captured. Most of the Illinois Nation survived, and when its forces returned from their slave raids in the winter of 1680–1681, they pursued the Iroquois. After seeing the "cruel marks" of the attack, one hundred Kaskaskias led by a chief named Paessa tracked the Iroquois to their makeshift winter quarters in Miami Country. Although outnumbered, Paessa and his warriors attacked and then, thwarted, "went to kill Iroquois hunters in the direction of Lake Erie."[19]

In the years that followed, Iroquois armies again invaded the midcontinent, but Illinois soon gained the upper hand through their own martial strength and through their vast network of allies. In 1682, Illinois defenders drove off 1,200 Iroquois warriors. La Salle and Tonty met the remnants of this party as they headed toward the Mississippi River and chose to steer clear, "for there is no pleasure in meeting warriors on one's road, especially when they have been unsuccessful." Again in March 1684, Illinois, aided by Tonty and a few French men, withstood an Iroquois siege for six days. Having blunted Iroquois attacks against their homes, Illinois went on the offensive. Along with Miamis, they ravaged Iroquois resources: "they cut down the

Trees of Peace that serv'd for Limits or Boundaries" to the "Frontiers" of Iroquoia. Then, they slaughtered the beaver on Iroquois hunting grounds, killing male and female alike, leaving none to reproduce. To Shawnees, they provided firearms. Illinois also drew their longtime allies the Kiskakon Ottawas into the conflict, after an Illinois man stabbed and killed a Seneca chief, a veteran of a recent Illinois Country raid, at the Kiskakon Feast of the Dead in 1681.[20]

By 1682, the war had ballooned to include most western nations. That year, a Jesuit among the Iroquois reported that "although the brunt of the war is to fall on The Ilinois," they would also target Miamis, Potawatomis, and others, as they included all of them "under the name of 'Ilinois.'" Jesuit predictions of the Iroquois "thunderbolt" poised to crash across the midcontinent failed to recognize that the sprawling Illinois alliance outmatched the Five Nations of the Iroquois Confederacy. By the middle of the 1680s, hundreds of Illinois warriors surged through Iroquoia, killing and capturing men, women, and children. In 1693, Tonty noted that Illinois "continually harass" the Iroquois. "Not a year passes," he wrote, "in which they do not take a number of prisoners and scalps." He reported in 1694 that, over the previous seven years, Illinois raiders had killed or captured 334 Iroquois men and 111 Iroquois women.[21]

Much to officials' chagrin, the ongoing war from Iroquoia to the Mississippi valley forced the French empire to pick a side. Into the early 1680s, Frontenac clung to the hope that New France could remain neutral and broker peace between the Iroquois and the western nations. In the summer of 1682, following the Illinois killing of the Seneca chief at Michilimackinac, Ottawas, Miamis, and Wendats journeyed to Montreal to seek France's backing in the war against the Iroquois. As Miami chief Alimahoué explained, he "wished not only to bite them . . . but also to eat them," and he asked that Frontenac "hinder him not." Frontenac demurred, insisting that he was "the common father" of his visitors and the Iroquois, and he asked the diplomats to offer presents to the Iroquois to cover the dead Seneca chief. Alimahoué and the Kiskakon leader, Nonteka, explained that "the Iroquois had made them suffer too long a time, and that they must avenge themselves." Frontenac recognized the precarious position he occupied. The "intimate bonds of relationship, alliance and friendship" that linked Illinois, Ottawas, Miamis, and Wendats ensured that the Iroquois war against the Illinois would soon engulf the entire region. France too would be caught up in the violence, as La Salle and other traders worked in those nations, making it "difficult" for Iroquois "to distinguish and separate them from those other nations."[22] Frontenac pled with Iroquois, just as he had the western nations, to end their war, but France held little authority to mediate between these powers.

Soon after Frontenac's conferences with the western nations and with the Iroquois, his fears came true. In February 1684, 200 Seneca and Cayuga warriors "strip'd, rob'd, and abus'd" fourteen *coureurs de bois* carrying weapons to the Illinois Country before attacking Fort St. Louis at Starved Rock. Later that year, Frontenac's successor, the inexperienced Joseph-Antoine Le Febvre de La Barre, led an ill-fated campaign into Iroquoia. He failed to achieve any military or diplomatic victory before returning to Montreal. King Louis condemned La Barre's fiasco and replaced him with Jacques-René Brisay de Denonville, whom he ordered to "humble the pride of the Iroquois" and "give assistance to the Illinois and the other Indian allies whom the Sieur de La Barre has abandoned." In 1687, Denonville led nearly 2,000 French and more than 1,000 Indians, including hundreds of Illinois warriors recruited by Tonty, into Iroquoia. The expedition's great achievement was destroying four Seneca towns before retreating. The Illinois contingent divided into smaller parties to continue the attack, returning having killed or captured sixty Iroquois men, women, and children. In the years that followed, Iroquois engaged in open war against New France. In August 1689, they brought the violence to within ten miles of Montreal, when 1,500 fighters raided Lachine, killed twenty-four colonists, and captured dozens more. A month later, in need of reinforcements, Denonville ordered Fort Frontenac's garrison to raze the outpost and return to Montreal.[23]

Abetted by Frontenac, La Salle had pursued a scheme that endangered New France. As a result, Louis XIV and Colbert's worries about the vulnerability of their "feeble colonies" had come to fruition. France could not defend its outposts, strewn across hundreds of miles of waterways from the St. Lawrence to the Mississippi, and Iroquois armies forced them to retreat. The war continued until the Iroquois Confederacy, France, and most of the nations of the Great Lakes signed an uneasy peace in 1701.[24]

While New France floundered, however, La Salle's endeavors in the Illinois Country flourished. During the 1680s, Tonty, La Forest, and the traders they employed transitioned from suspect outsiders to trusted allies. They had fought side by side with Illinois against the Iroquois. They engaged in a commerce that benefited both the *coureurs de bois* and Illinois traders. They also began to marry Illinois women on Illinois terms. Through military and economic alliances undergirded and reinforced by kinship ties, Tonty and La Forest secured their position in the Illinois Country, while the empire struggled with the consequences of La Salle's ambition and waffled on whether it should continue to allow French fur traders to operate in the West.

≈ In December 1680, upon returning to the abandoned ruins of Fort Crèvecoeur, La Salle discovered a declaration scrawled across one of the wrecked boards: "Nous sommes tous Sauvages." La Salle understood the gist of the brief message. Tonty and his dwindling garrison now lived among the Illinois. But the precise implication of Tonty's statement was more complicated. In saying "we are all *sauvages*," Tonty did not claim that he and his men had become "Indians." Instead, the four words announced that they had become "wild people," who had left French society. When they moved to Starved Rock, the 'six French men joined a community of thousands of Indians. Despite prejudices based on medieval European folk tales, Tonty and his men did not become "wild men of the woods," closer to the natural world than to human civilization. They relocated to an urban center. The Grand Village of the Illinois was more than five times larger than either Quebec or Montreal. Indeed, the Grand Village boasted a population nearly equal to that of the entire colony of New France. Once there, Tonty and his men, hoping to survive and to facilitate the fur trade, adapted to Illinois expectations of behavior, most notably by building kin ties in the community. They also maintained connections in Montreal and in France and would return to acquire more merchandise, hire employees, and visit relatives. Still, their conduct in the midcontinent alarmed imperial officials, who feared they were losing their grasp on their colonists as they became enmeshed in the world shaped and controlled by Native peoples.[25]

For more than a century, French officials struggled to make sense of intermarriage between colonists and Indians. On the one hand, empire was a family business. Private commercial endeavors as well as imperial politics relied on personal relationships. During the late 1670s and 1680s, La Salle depended on trusted friends, La Forest and Tonty, to manage his affairs. Similarly, Tonty called on relatives and friends—notably his brother Alphonse and his cousin Pierre Deliette—to manage his commercial and political interests as he traveled an estimated 35,000 miles back and forth between Canada, the Illinois Country, and Louisiana from 1678 to 1704.[26]

Interrelated families sprawled across France's colonies. Charlotte-Françoise Juchereau de St. Denis, who in 1702 married La Forest, was a cousin of the prominent Le Moyne family. At the end of the 1600s, Pierre Le Moyne d'Iberville founded the new colony of Louisiana on the Gulf Coast. Two of his brothers—Jean-Baptiste Le Moyne de Bienville and Antoine Le Moyne de Châteaugué—stood beside him. A fourth brother, Joseph Le Moyne de Sérigny, arrived in 1701. Several of Iberville's cousins, including Pierre Dugué de Boisbriand and Charles and Louis Juchereau de St. Denis, also joined the new colony in those early years.[27] For most of the next four decades, the Le Moyne brothers and their relatives controlled the colonial government as well as many of Louisiana's most important outposts. Colonial leaders, traders, and others all depended on networks of relatives and friends.

Kinship served such an important role in French North America in large part because other institutions were weak or absent. The empire held ten-uous authority beyond the towns of the St. Lawrence valley. In the Great Lakes and the Mississippi valley, imperial power ended not far out of sight of French forts. Other than the church, no civil organization commanded the devotion or obedience of the colonists, whose most important and lasting loyalty was to their families. More than the government and the church, rela-tives provided a network of support. In times of need, a colonist could turn to relatives for help because moral duty demanded that colonists aid their relations whenever possible. Thus, for the Tontys, Le Moynes, and other families, patronage to kin was both expected and necessary for success.[28]

As French claims extended beyond the St. Lawrence River valley, offi-cials relied on kin to build new colonies. Communication between these out-posts was difficult and sporadic, subject to the whims of environmental and political constraints. If a question needed a royal answer, officials had to wait months for ships to carry their letter to Versailles and then return with a response. As a Canadian governor explained, officers in France received their orders weekly. In New France, though, guidance arrived "only annually." As a result, "often a thing begins and ends before we have had time to notify you."[29] Commandants in the Great Lakes and Mississippi valley often adapted imperial policy to local concerns with little input from their supe-riors. Colonial administrators had no choice but to trust their discretion.

Examples abound of the dangers posed by unknown or unreliable com-panions and subordinates. In 1679, before La Salle set off for the Illinois Country, he sent a party of fifteen men ahead of him. When he reached Michilimackinac later that year, he discovered they had all stopped there, believing his expedition was doomed to failure. Six of the men deserted, stealing 4,000 livres of merchandise. La Salle's troubles continued after crossing the Chicago portage and entering the Illinois River. On the day they founded Fort Crèvecoeur, six more men attempted to kill him by poisoning the evening's meal and then fled. Then, when Tonty headed upstream to build a fort at Starved Rock, "all [his] men deserted" Fort Crèvecoeur, leaving it in ruins. Tonty's garrison shrank to two Recollect priests and three other men. Meanwhile, Tonty's compatriot Michel Accault abandoned Recollect Father Louis Hennepin on the upper Mississippi River, citing his daily prayers as a liability among his Dakota trading partners, who viewed the priest with suspicion.[30]

A lack of trust could have fatal consequences. In 1684, La Salle attempted to return to the Illinois Country from France via the Gulf of Mexico. Failing to locate the mouth of the Mississippi in the coastal swamps, La Salle's boats landed in preset-day Texas in 1685. Over two years of hardship, a party of 180 dwindled to fewer than fifty. In January 1687, La Salle took a portion of the survivors, including his brother and his cousin, to find Illinois by land. Two of his companions had grown disillusioned. One night in the spring of 1687, they killed La Salle's cousin and two other men, clubbing them with axes as they slept. The next morning, they ambushed La Salle and shot him in the head. He died an hour later. Taking command of the survivors, La Salle's murderers found the tables had turned. Other members of the party— driven by "jealousy and desire of command"—killed them.[31] Reliable partners could determine whether one lived or died, and French colonists trusted their bonds of kinship and reciprocity for safety and support in a dangerous world.

Still, for all of the significance that French officials placed on marriage as a source of wealth and power, they believed marriage between French men and Indian women required careful consideration. Their ideas about intermarriage stemmed from the notion of *mésalliance*, a concept devised to describe the marriage of aristocrats to socially inferior persons. In sixteenth- and seventeenth-century France, the educated and the elite held that virtues and physical characteristics passed through the blood from parents to children. When nonaristocrats introduced their inferior blood into noble lineages, this theory supposed, they damaged subsequent generations. However, the theory also held that women transmitted their husbands' traits rather than their own, so the aristocracy tolerated marriages between noblemen and women of lower status.[32]

In North America, French elites used the idea of *mésalliance* to explain cultural differences in addition to those rooted in class. At the founding of

New France, consequently, officials promoted the marriage of French men to Indian women as a way of introducing French virtues and civilization to Native communities and passing on those traits to a second generation of colonists. In the early seventeenth century, Samuel de Champlain, the founder of New France, proclaimed to a delegation of Indians in the St. Lawrence valley, "our young men will marry your daughters, and we shall be one people." Several decades later, Jean-Baptiste Colbert advocated a policy of *francisation* (Frenchification) in which French-Indian intermarriage would assimilate Native peoples into the French colony. The French government even established a fund to provide dowries for Indian brides.[33]

French men and Indian women fit their marital unions into their own cultural understandings about marriage, gender, and race. Many Native peoples, including Illinois, coveted the French as potential allies, just as French traders sought ties with Indian nations. Among Indians as well as the French, marriage was a common and trusted way to create ties between communities and nations. Yet, to fashion successful cross-cultural unions, Indians and French needed overlapping understandings of the roles of wives and husbands and the relationship between in-laws. Conditioned to expect the exotic and foreign, the French exaggerated the differences in gender roles in Illinois society and in their own. They highlighted divergences, often minor, and ignored the similarities in the two patriarchal cultures. In practice, however, French colonists found that similar understandings of courtship and expectations for spouses facilitated cross-cultural marriages in the Illinois Country.[34]

French and Illinois people alike emphasized the paternal line when figuring kinship. The French recognized bilateral kin—that is, relatives of both their mothers and fathers—but stressed the paternal line, as children took the surname of their father and lived in patriarchal households. Unlike Illinois couples, French newlyweds established new households separate from those of their parents, but they remained embedded in a web of kinship and reciprocity that linked them to their relatives and to the larger community. Illinois people organized their society around patrilineal households, a system that generally meshed well with French patriarchy.[35]

Still, the French found patrilineality confusing. In Illinois society, paternal uncles shared duties with biological fathers, and because of that, boys referred to both as *noohsa*. Children distinguished between *noohsa* and their maternal uncles *(nišihsa)*. Likewise, men differentiated between the daughters of their sisters *(nintaana)* and the daughters of their brothers *(nihšimihsa)*.[36] In short, men played an active role in the lives of their brother's children but took little responsibility for their sister's children, a distinction that made little sense to the French.

At times, Illinois kinship baffled French observers. Pierre Deliette noted, "It should be stated that they all call each other relatives, and such degrees of kinship . . . are often claimed by persons whom we should not even call cousins." Multigenerational ties became especially perplexing. Deliette noted, "I have seen men of eighty claim that young girls were their mothers." Although he did not know it, he described a practice called skewing, absent in bilateral societies, in which kin lump relatives of the same gender across generations. For example, a man's mother, mother's sister, and mother's sister's daughter would all be called "mother" (*ninkya* in Illinois).[37] These extensive family ties created networks of connection and reciprocity that permeated Illinois society, making marriage an institution that involved a far greater range of people than just the bride and groom.

In both France and the Illinois Country, families arranged or approved marriages. In France and its colonies, men under thirty and women under twenty-five required parental permission before marrying. Even after children reached the age when they could legally marry as they pleased, custom still led them to seek the approval of their parents. For most families, marriage was "too serious a matter to be left to the young couple." Likewise, Illinois people viewed marriage as an alliance between two families, and an Illinois family determined whether a union was beneficial before allowing a female relative to marry. Male relatives oversaw most of the courtship ritual, and families held the final decision on a marriage proposal.[38]

As in most societies that figure lineage partially or wholly through the father's line, both French and Illinois men ensured that they could establish a child's paternity with some degree of certainty by strictly regulating female sexuality. In doing so, they created a sexual double standard for men and women, reflected in punishment for adultery. In France and New France, social norms and the law treated female adultery as despicable, while accepting, if not encouraging, male promiscuity. In 1658, Louis XIV decreed that all women guilty of adultery, along with those convicted of prostitution and fornication, would be imprisoned until priests and nuns decided that they had reformed and repented. French courts granted husbands legal separations—although not divorces—from adulterous wives but refused to extend the same consideration to wives of profligate husbands. In Illinois society, men levied brutal punishments against adulteresses. Traders and missionaries noted that Illinois men scalped unfaithful wives or cut their noses. In other instances, husbands would gather gangs of "some thirty young men" to lay in wait on a road outside their town. When the wife passed, they ambushed and raped her. As in France, Illinois men involved with married women risked the wrath of the husband, who would sometimes attack or kill them, but there seems to have been no punishment for adulterous men on a societal level.[39]

Two significant differences distinguished Illinois marriage from that practiced in France: polygamy and divorce. Illinois people may have adopted polygamy in the seventeenth century to deal with new demographic realities created by warfare and slavery. During the 1600s, the Illinois carried war in all directions, leading to higher mortality rates among young men who carried out raids and campaigns. These wars may have decreased the young male population, but they also increased the nation's female population through the adoption and incorporation of female captives. By 1700, the Illinois may have had as many as four women for every man. Thus, when Jesuits and *voyageurs* arrived in the Illinois Country, they encountered sororal polygamy, in which Illinois men married a woman and her sisters. Although the French condemned polygamy as an abuse of Illinois women, plural marriage provided husbands in a society that was short of men as well as labor partners who could help perform household and agricultural work.[40] The demographic conditions that led to polygamy also sometimes prompted Illinois women to marry French men.

French and Illinois societies parted on the question of divorce as well. Linguistic evidence suggests that divorce was a strategy that allowed Illinois women to escape an abusive or unwanted husband. According to Jesuits, Illinois had words for a "woman who has had and left several husbands" *(pimit8a)* and a "woman separated from her husband who no longer wants to see him although in the same village" *(kissabamig8ta)*. French observers, especially Jesuits, found the practice shocking and a sign that disorder and lasciviousness defined Native cultures. They preferred their society, in which French women had no recourse to divorce. If a French wife could prove that her husband was irresponsible with the family's finances, she could seek a separation of property, in which she retained the rights to her own property to protect herself and her children from the husband's negligence. If a husband abused his wife, tried to murder her, committed aggravated adultery, or perpetrated some other form of "extreme wrongdoing," a court might grant her a separation, both of property and person, from her husband. These separations, however, did not grant the wife the right to remarry. Law and religion forever linked her to her husband.[41]

Despite these two differences, French *coureurs de bois* and Illinois women shared similar understandings of courtship and marriage, and they found common ground on which to build relationships. These marriages are by their nature difficult to track. No Jesuits recorded non-Catholic marriages, and Illinois left no documents like sacramental registers. Occasionally, specific marriages surface in travel accounts or official reports, but more often, they appear only as vague statements about *coureurs de bois* married to Indian women. But, from the scattered mentions, a composite image emerges. Instead of "Frenchifying" Native peoples, these marriages appear to have integrated French men into Indian society. They epitomized the crown's concerns that the fur trade would lure much-needed colonists away from the St. Lawrence valley.

Because the French empire desired wealth from the beaver trade but feared the growing number of *coureurs de bois* in the Great Lakes and Mississippi valley, it enacted complicated and contradictory policies throughout the late seventeenth and early eighteenth centuries. In 1678, Louis XIV banned the fur trade beyond the colonies of the St. Lawrence valley. The crown expected Indians to carry their furs to Montreal, thus removing French colonists from the distant countries in the West. At the same time, the company that monopolized fur exports from New France paid fixed prices set by the Minister of the Marine, and it bought all the furs that *voyageurs* and *coureurs de bois* brought to its offices. This system untethered the fur trade from the law of supply and demand, guaranteed profits to those who could return with large stocks of beaver pelts, and encouraged enterprising men to ignore the ban. Further emboldened by Frontenac's and La Salle's defiance of Louis XIV's trade restrictions, other French colonists disregarded the king's order as well. In 1681, Intendant Jacques Duchesneau reported that 800 or more *coureurs de bois* operated in the West, perhaps twice as many as a decade earlier.[42] Recognizing the limited reach of the law, Louis XIV and Colbert hoped to bring *coureurs de bois* back to New France by offering them amnesty and instituting a licensing system, through which traders could operate legally. Under the new plan, the governor of New France would issue twenty-five trade licenses each year. Each allowed one canoe of trade goods manned by three *voyageurs*, and no trader could receive a license in consecutive years.[43] At most, seventy-five *voyageurs* could operate legally, less than a tenth of the number of men Duchesneau estimated traded in the Great Lakes.

Meanwhile, Louis XIV allowed exceptions that compromised the licensing system. After La Salle's murder in Texas in 1687, his former subordinates Henri de Tonty and François Dauphin de La Forest applied for and received La Salle's old monopoly on the Illinois Country fur trade. In 1691, Tonty commissioned his cousin Pierre Deliette to erect a new trading post in the Illinois Country, replacing the original Fort St. Louis at Starved Rock. Kaskaskias and Peorias planned to relocate to a better source of firewood and water after a decade-long residence at Starved Rock. When Kaskaskias and Peorias chose a site on Lake Pimiteoui, near present-day Peoria, Deliette and Tonty began building the new trading post, bearing the old name Fort St. Louis, adjacent to the town. The next spring, La Forest arrived with "a considerable number of *engagés,* and of soldiers," who finished the construction. The large, wooden fort stood alongside an Illinois village numbering 6,000 or more inhabitants.[44]

Tonty and La Forest quickly expanded their operations, relying on relatives to manage distant trading posts and warehouses. From 1687 to 1691, they recruited no fewer than forty-two new employees from Montreal. In addition to Fort St. Louis, where they shared command, Tonty and La Forest ran a post at Michilimackinac—administered first by La Forest and then by Tonty's brother, Alphonse—and a warehouse at present-day Chicago, overseen by Deliette. In 1693, a party of *voyageurs* guided by Illinois Indians journeyed up the Missouri River to open trade with Osages and Missourias. Toward the end of the decade, Tonty trekked north of Lake Superior into Assiniboine Country, far beyond the limits of his grant.[45]

Although the Tonty brothers, La Forest, and Deliette were all commissioned officers in the French colonial army, and many of their men were enlisted soldiers, they acted little like representatives of the empire. In 1685, Governor Jacques-René de Brisay de Denonville complained, "Sieur de Tonty will not permit the French to trade in the direction of the Illinois." The Minister of the Marine decried this as a "ridiculous pretension" and reiterated the king's intent to "conserve to the French the liberty of trading among the Illinois." Denonville sent Captain Richard Pilette to command Fort St. Louis for the crown. When Pilette presented himself, Tonty declared that the fort was private property, not a possession of the empire. Pilette attempted to arrest the defiant commandant, but Tonty punched him in the mouth with his metal hand and knocked him down. Three of Tonty's employees picked up Pilette, carried him from the fort, and tossed him down the steep slope of Starved Rock. Despite his rough welcome, Pilette must have found the life of the *coureur de bois* appealing. He established his own trading post some distance from Fort St. Louis, married an Illinois woman, and carried on a bustling commerce, paying Tonty a percentage each year for the privilege of trading in his territory.[46]

The disposition of Tonty and his compatriots changed little in the next dozen years. In 1697, when Frontenac sent Alphonse Tonty to take command of the French post at Michilimackinac, Tonty sneaked out of Montreal with at least thirty fur traders and six canoe-loads worth of merchandise. Intendant Jean Bochart de Champigny complained of the Tonty–La Forest outfit, "All have the same spirit and a single interest, tending only to trading."[47]

In the Illinois Country, Tonty and La Forest relied on marriage to build connections with Peoria and Kaskaskia Indians who lived near Fort St. Louis. In 1687, a critic of their operations complained about the prevalence of intermarriage, "Every week, they marry, in the mode of the Indians of that country, Indian women who they buy from their parents at the expense of the merchants." Ignorant of the gift-giving customs surrounding marriage in the Illinois Country, this Frenchman believed that *coureurs de bois* engaged in something akin to prostitution. Jesuits contributed to this misapprehension, decrying the "libertinage" and "debauchery" that supposedly ran rampant among traders. They desired Catholic marriages that conformed to the expectations of the church, and the relationships of *coureurs de bois* and Illinois women did not meet those standards. French officials echoed these criticisms. Louis XIV complained that "libertines" of the midcontinent "live in extreme debauchery with the Indian women." Jesuits described Tonty as "a debauchée," while Deliette reportedly engaged in "scandalous conduct."[48]

The condemnations by Jesuits, colonial officials, and even the king failed to capture the realities of French-Illinois sexual and romantic relationships. Perhaps traders engaged in extramarital sex with Illinois women. But, given the harsh restrictions governing female sexuality in the Illinois Nation, it seems unlikely that Illinois fathers and brothers would have allowed such behavior. Almost certainly, traders sexually exploited the numerous enslaved Indian women in the Illinois Nation, but those encounters would have done little to further their trading endeavors. Enslaved women had no kin and offered little access to Illinois society. Many, perhaps even most, of the relationships that priests and others condemned as the products of "debauchery" or "libertinage" were in fact marriages conducted by the norms of Illinois society.[49]

Illinois women became essential to the fur trade, providing knowledge, access, and labor. Women worked as interpreters and mediators between their relatives and French outsiders. They understood the customs of exchange and the demands of reciprocity and could advise their husbands on appropriate behavior. Because they traditionally oversaw agricultural production, Illinois women fed their husbands. They handled household chores. And they cleaned and dressed pelts, preparing them for market or fashioning them into moccasins and clothing.[50] In short, they performed all of the duties expected of Illinois women and supplied the labor that drove the fur trade.

In the middle of the 1690s, imperial decrees disrupted Tonty and La Forest's business and pushed them toward illegal commerce. In 1696, Louis XIV again banned the fur trade, partially to curb "disorders" in the West and partially because of a saturated beaver market in France. The king ordered all western posts abandoned and destroyed. French colonists met the king's proclamation with outrage. Frontenac, given his continued personal stake in the fur trade, opposed the measure, as did traders and other officials worried about French prospects in the West. Some fretted about their own fortunes, but all worried about the growing presence of English traders in the midcontinent. In the end, the empire shuttered all of its western forts, except Tonty and La Forest's Fort St. Louis, which remained open as a bulwark against further English incursions on the condition that they not trade for beaver. Champigny had doubts about the arrangement. He believed that the order would result in a situation in which "they alone will trade with the Indians in the distant countries with *immense profits.*"[51]

After the traders had dedicated nearly two decades to their Illinois Country commerce, they had no intention of letting it wither. During the last years of the century, Tonty continued to expand operations into the regions north of Michilimackinac where he could acquire the most desirable beaver pelts. In 1700, when Tonty left the midcontinent to join the burgeoning French colony on the Gulf Coast, he did so to pursue new business schemes. He soon petitioned the crown "to confirm the gift" that La Salle had given him of "the river and country of the Akansas" and "to give him the Government of the post of the Ouabache, with a company to maintain with his family and the faculty of trading alone, to the exclusion of all others." Tonty also requested sanction to increase the number of canoes he could legally bring to the midcontinent from Montreal and to expand operations to "the Indians up to New Biscay," present-day northern Mexico. In the end, the crown ignored Tonty's requests and granted Iberville's cousin Charles Juchereau de St. Denis a concession to trade on the Wabash.[52]

Pierre Deliette, meanwhile, stayed in the Illinois Country, while La Forest went to France to push their case. With no governmental oversight, Deliette and La Forest expanded their operations, in the words of one official, "carrying on the trade with all sorts of tribes." In 1701, Governor Louis-Hector de Callières and Champigny complained that, much to their dismay, more illegal traders, including Tonty and La Forest, operated in the West than ever before. They noted, "We have learned that some of these bandits have been among the English of Carolina to link trade with them, where they have been very well received." The following year, Louis XIV ordered La Forest and Deliette to abandon their post. La Forest complied rather than lose his captain's commission, but Deliette and others defied orders and remained in the Illinois Country. Even so, La Forest seems to have maintained his interest in the fur trade. In late 1703, French officials caught an illegal shipment of furs belonging to La Forest and his wife, Charlotte-Françoise Juchereau de St. Denis, three-quarters of a league upriver from Quebec.[53]

Other illegal traders joined Tonty and La Forest in the Illinois Country, but *coureurs de bois* left little documentation of their shadowy world. Most *coureurs de bois* sneaked out of Montreal under the cover of night or conducted their journeys under false pretenses. At the end of the season, some slipped back into Montreal the same way they left, delivering their pelts to patrons who remained anonymous. Others sold their furs down the Tennessee River to Carolina, where English merchants welcomed the traders scorned by French officials.[54] In many cases, reports of their activities come shrouded in rumor and hearsay, revealing only bits and pieces of the commerce that continued in the face of imperial crackdowns.

Marriages between *coureurs de bois* and Indian women provided the foundation of the fur trade in the midcontinent, and they integrated the rogue traders into Indian nations, who supplied valuable pelts to their French relatives. The lawlessness of the fur trade, however, troubled French administrators. As they read reports from the Illinois Country and elsewhere in New France, the optimism of *francisation* gave way to fears about the *ensauvagement* (roughly meaning "becoming wild") of French men. Rather than assimilating Indians into New France, French men married Indian women in Indian Country, beyond the jurisdiction of the French colonial government or the Catholic Church. For nearly a century, officials from Quebec to Paris hoped that marriage would bring "order" to Indian Country, but by the first decade of the 1700s, they believed that it threatened to ruin New France.[55]

Intermarriage accompanied a whole host of other behaviors that officials viewed on a spectrum from frustrating to dangerous. As early as 1687, Tonty and La Forest's men, married to Illinois women, considered themselves "independent," and when Louis restricted the fur trade, they looked for new markets down the Tennessee River in English Carolina. King Louis XIV declared in his 1696 ban on the fur trade that the quest for beaver had lured men to the far reaches of North America, where they had "abandoned themselves to libertinage, to debauchery, to all sorts of disorder and crime." Having discarded French society and the agricultural life, they were no longer suitable to help build colonies. In 1709, New France's Governor Philippe de Rigaud de Vaudreuil and Intendant Jacques Raudot advocated a ban on intermarriage, warning, "one should never mix bad blood with good." In the middle of the next decade, the new king, Louis XIV's young grandson, and his regent agreed. They feared that "mixing by these marriages good blood with bad" would produce a colony of "mulattos, naturally lazy, libertines." Colonial officials should "prevent these sorts of marriages as much as possible."[56]

≈   The growing concerns of secular officials, however, met rising insistence on the part of Jesuits that intermarriage led to conversion, not only of Native peoples but also of *coureurs de bois* who had abandoned French society. For this plan to work, however, French men had to marry Indian women who had converted to Catholicism.[57] To see the benefits of this strategy, the Jesuits argued, one had only to look at the case of women such as Marie Rouensa, whose devotion to Catholicism brought her corrupted husband back to the faith and led to the conversion of thousands of members of her nation. Jacques Gravier's lengthy account of the struggle over Marie's marriage served as propaganda for the Jesuit missionaries and their projects in the midcontinent. But, at the same time, it captured a reality of intermarriage in the Illinois Country. France could not rely on French men to bring Indians into the empire, but it could use Indian women to convert their nations and to entice wayward male colonists to reaffirm their faith in the Christian God and their loyalty to the crown.

Marquette, Gravier, and other missionaries used familial and fictive kinship to build a multiethnic, Catholic community among the Kaskaskias. Just as the Illinois employed the calumet ceremony to transform strangers into friends and relatives, Jesuits used baptism to ritually adopt Native peoples into the Catholic family. Once baptized, Native peoples became "children of God."[58] Jesuits regularly employed kinship metaphors in their discussions of baptism, conversion, and their relationship to other Catholics and God, but they also facilitated and performed marriages between Indian women and French men. Jesuits and secular officials alike believed that Catholic families formed the building blocks of a stable, well-ordered society. Jesuits depended on Illinois, drawn by the relative opportunities for social status and spiritual power that Catholicism offered them, to convert their relatives and, through marriage, to bring nonbelieving or apathetic men, both French and Illinois, into the family of the church.

In the early years of the Jesuit mission, Kaskaskias and Peorias mistrusted the Jesuits. Before the 1680s, Illinois had no sustained contact with Europeans or their diseases. Jesuits and traders brought microbes with them. Soon, epidemics ravaged the Grand Village, and Illinois blamed Gravier for their sickness. They identified the right culprit for the wrong reasons, focusing on the priest's strange rituals. Gravier recognized the growing animosity toward him, noting that the Illinois, faced with a mounting death toll, believed he was the "bird of death." Following Catholic teachings that children who died unbaptized became "slaves of the devil," Gravier rushed to baptize Illinois children. When children died following their baptisms, parents of the deceased decried the priest and his rituals as killers. Other parents refused to allow baptism, but Gravier continued to perform them surreptitiously. For Gravier, eternal salvation justified any subterfuge to baptize sick children. "The little children who die," he wrote, "are grateful to me when they are before God." Illinois, though, saw a dangerous man who killed their children. Gravier survived through the intercession of Chief Rouensa, for, as the priest admitted, "without him the French would have been massacred here."[59]

As Kaskaskias and Peorias became increasingly wary of Gravier, young women continued to seek his tutelage and the comparative social and spiritual power that Catholicism promised them. Neither French nor Illinois society offered many opportunities for women to gain and exert power over their daily lives or their sexuality, whereas Catholicism—as practiced in the Illinois Country—offered more. In particular, the spiritual power of the Virgin Mary appealed to Illinois women. In the first days of the Mission de l'Immaculée Conception, Jacques Marquette demonstrated the importance of the Virgin Mary to Jesuits. He displayed four large pictures of her during his initial sermon to the Kaskaskias and named the mission to the Illinois in her honor. In translating Catholic concepts into Illinois, Jesuits raised Mary to a stature even higher than that she held among European

Catholics. In their worship, the Illinois and their Jesuit teachers promoted her from the position of the mother of God to the mother of all Catholics. In the Illinois translation of the Hail Mary, Catholic Illinois praised Mary not as "full of grace" but as "the master of all good hearts."[60] Jesuits in their instruction stressed the virtue of Mary's virginity and linked it to her power. Moreover, Mary's authority extended over men and women alike, and Illinois Country Catholics saw her as a positive and regenerative force.

Drawing on the power of Mary and other canonized women, Marie became a leader in the Catholic community of Kaskaskia. After orchestrating the conversions of her parents and her husband, which in turn led to the mass conversion of the town, Marie continued her efforts to strengthen the faith among Kaskaskia women and girls. She brought her newborn relatives to the chapel for baptism, and she led classes for Kaskaskia women and children in her home. Marie was a steady presence, reminding the baptized of the promises they had made to God and entreating them to maintain their faith and religious practice. She often acted as Gravier's agent. When he recommended ways to bolster Catholicism among Kaskaskias, she implemented them. In 1696, Gravier reported that he had converted more than 2,000 Kaskaskia Indians living at Mission de l'Immaculée Conception.[61] In many ways, the conversions of Kaskaskias were Marie Rouensa's success as much as Gravier's, and they provided a foundation for a Catholic Kaskaskia community separate and distinct from non-Catholic Illinois.

At Kaskaskia, Catholicism laid the groundwork for important changes in politics and economy. Jesuits linked Catholic practice to sedentary communities centered on wheat and livestock agriculture. At the turn of the eighteenth century, Kaskaskias altered their economy to more closely resemble the agrarian villages of France. Prior to their conversion, Kaskaskias spent part of the summer and most of the winter—sometimes more than five months total—hunting far away from their main town. When the Illinois dispersed in winter camps, the handful of Jesuits in the midcontinent struggled to provide regular services to the many bands. Jesuits tried to join Kaskaskias on their summer bison hunt and to travel between the camps during the winter, but they found the hardship unbearable.[62] Kaskaskias, who wanted to stay closer to their chapel and to the missionaries, adopted new forms of agriculture and husbandry that allowed them to remain in one location for more of the year.

The Jesuits introduced wheat to the Illinois Country around 1700. Within a decade, the Kaskaskias adopted the European plow and grew wheat "as fine as any in France." Before long, they expanded their field agriculture to include tobacco, flax, and hemp. Slaves and hired laborers worked these crops, replacing the labor of Kaskaskia women, who gave up the agricultural labor done by their ancestors. Some Catholic Kaskaskias had stopped so-journing for the winter hunt. They stayed behind to care for their cattle, horses, chickens, and pigs. Others continued to hunt, but their quarry changed. In earlier years, Kaskaskias had traded beaver, raccoon, deer, bear, and bison pelts to Canadian *voyageurs* at Fort St. Louis. By the 1710s, they hunted not for furs and skins but for meat and animal fat, which they con-sumed or sold to French colonists. In 1726, at the time of the first census of the Illinois Country, French-Illinois families maintained a way of life sim-ilar to that of their French neighbors.[63]

French and Illinois understandings of marriage and kinship further inte-grated Illinois women into the world of their French husbands. When an Illinois woman married a French man, she moved into his house, following Illinois and French customs regarding postmarriage habitation. Because Illinois Indians were patrilineal, the children of Illinois mothers and French fathers lacked kinship ties to their mother's community. An Illinois woman living with her French husband and French-Illinois children, consequently, drew closer to her in-laws. And Illinois women marked this evolution with changes in their material lives. In the years before Marie Rouensa died in 1725, she dressed as a Frenchwoman and lived in a French-style log house. The Rouensa home was decorated with a walnut table and chairs, a rope bed, and an array of European-manufactured cookware and dishes.[64]

Although Canadians believed that *francisation* was a fantasy, the experi-ence of the Jesuits among the Kaskaskias told a different story. Kaskaskias, especially women, became fervent Catholics, and their families exemplified piety and devotion. These female converts pushed their French husbands to accept and keep the faith. Father Julien Binneteau raved that they "would be a good example to the best regulated households in France."[65] Over time, as wheat and livestock agriculture took root in the Illinois Country, these Catholic French-Kaskaskia families moved ever closer to the ideal colony envisioned by French officials.

≈   Catholicism divided the Illinois Nation. The burgeoning French-Kaskaskia community bore little resemblance to the towns of most Illinois people, who resisted Catholicism and the wheat and livestock economy that flourished at Kaskaskia. In 1700, other Illinois lived in three towns on the

Illinois and Mississippi Rivers. Peorias and some Tamaroas remained at Pimiteoui, while the rest of the Tamaroas lived with Cahokias on the east bank of the Mississippi not far from the Kaskaskias. Michigameas lived farther south, about halfway between the mouths of the Illinois and Kaskaskia Rivers. While Kaskaskias developed a community centered on French-style agriculture, the other Illinois sustained their older economy of hunting combined with agriculture. French men married Illinois women at Pimiteoui and Cahokia, but in contrast with the Catholic marriages at Kaskaskia, those relationships incorporated French men into Illinois communities, much to the chagrin of colonial officials and missionaries.

Without prominent neophytes such as the Rouensas aiding missionary efforts in their communities, most Peorias, Cahokias, and Tamaroas remained hostile to the Jesuits. Peorias occupied a place of particular spiritual power in the Illinois Nation. Their name in the Illinois language, *peaareewa*, signified "dreamers," those who were in touch with the spirit world. Many Peorias also continued to hold Jacques Gravier responsible for the deaths of their children to epidemic disease. During the mid-1690s, Peorias watched the rapid conversion of the Kaskaskias and expressed grief for their friends and relatives "vexed" by the Jesuits. One Peoria chief proclaimed, "Let the *Kaskaskia* pray to God if they wish. . . . Are we *Kaskaskia?* And why shouldst thou obey him, thou who art a *Peouareoua?* . . . His Fables are good only in his own country; we have ours, which do not make us die as his do." A few years later, Cahokias and Tamaroas expelled Gravier when he tried to establish a mission at their town on the Mississippi River.[66]

At Pimiteoui and Cahokia, relations between the French and the Illinois Nation centered on the fur trade, and the crown's perplexing and everchanging regulations on that commerce confounded Illinois traders. After Tonty and La Forest left the Illinois Country at the turn of the eighteenth century, the fur trade in the region declined. Pierre Deliette remained at Pimiteoui, but he struggled to maintain the once-flourishing business. The decline in trade angered Peoria Indians. The reduction of the fort was not simply an economic matter for Peorias. Trade was also symbolic. Peorias interpreted the king's order as a sign of disrespect. In response, they rejected French pretentions to authority over them and missionary efforts to convert them to Catholicism. In 1705, Peoria chief Mantouchensa rallied his town against Father Gravier, whom they viewed as a spy for the crown. A Peoria man shot five arrows into the Jesuit. Gravier survived the attack, but one wound festered and killed him three years later.[67]

Likewise, Cahokia remained firmly rooted in the fur trade. Situated across from the confluence of the Mississippi and Missouri Rivers, the town served as a natural base of operations for traders headed up both rivers. The beaver pelts acquired at Cahokia paled in comparison to those from farther north or even those gathered by Tonty and La Forest at Fort St. Louis. In the warmer climate, beaver fur grew thinner and carried less value. Many *coureurs de bois* turned their attention instead to bear, bison, deer, raccoons, and other mammals.[68]

Traders flocked to Cahokia to exploit the advantageous location. In 1700, at least thirty traders lived there. By the early 1710s, that number had grown to fifty. In 1715, when France reopened its fort at Michilimackinac, one hundred *coureurs de bois* fled south to escape imperial governance. They cast their lot with the outlaws of the midcontinent. While the trader population grew, few farmers joined them. In 1724, one Frenchman counted only seven *habitants* at Cahokia. Eight years later, a census of the Illinois Country recorded three *habitants* along with two priests, one lay brother, and a hired worker at the Cahokia mission.[69] In both tallies, *coureurs de bois* and other itinerants went uncounted.

Most Cahokias and Tamaroas, like their relatives at Peoria, had little use for Catholic missionaries. In 1698, at the behest of the respected Henri de Tonty, they allowed fathers from the Séminaire des Missions Étrangères to establish a mission among them. Seven years later, Father Jean-Marc Bergier reported that he had converted sixty Cahokias and Tamaroas, probably attracted by the ample gifts he offered, but most of the 1,500 Illinois at Cahokia demonstrated apathy or hostility to his efforts. Jesuits made inroads at Kaskaskia and elsewhere in North America by adapting to the expectations of the Native peoples they encountered. Rival missionary orders, including the Missions Étrangères, considered Jesuit practice a departure from good Catholic teaching and from the behavior of respectable French men. As a result, Bergier made no effort to approach the Cahokias and Tamaroas on their own terms. By his own admission, Bergier spoke Illinois poorly, compounding the difficulty of his task. In November 1707, Bergier died, and Cahokia and Tamaroa Indians danced around a cross he had erected and praised their manitous (spiritual beings) for having killed him. At the end of their celebration, they "broke his cross into a thousand pieces."[70]

≈   In the fall of 1699, while at Michilimackinac, Henri de Tonty learned that Pierre Le Moyne d'Iberville had landed a small fleet on the Gulf Coast. Iberville had "long been a friend," and Tonty headed downstream to join the new colony. He hoped to parlay his friendship into a new officer's commission. When Tonty arrived in Lower Louisiana in February 1700, he brought with him about twenty traders married to Illinois women and living in their villages. They made the long journey to exchange beaver pelts for gunpowder and other items, unavailable and invaluable in the Illinois Country. Iberville knew that these *coureurs de bois* operated without license or sanction in the midcontinent. Yet he thought it better to accept their furs than force them to seek other markets, because he also knew that English traders had reached the Mississippi valley. After Tonty's arrival, he probably told Iberville that English traders threatened to become "masters of trade of [France's] allies, Miamis, Illinois, and Ottawas, without which the country cannot survive." In 1701, Iberville passed these concerns to his superiors in France. He had little ability to stop the trade. Instead, he suggested permitting the *coureurs de bois* to bring their furs to the ports of Louisiana.[71]

Tonty's meeting with Iberville at the beginning of 1700 marked the beginning of a long process of reincorporating *coureurs de bois* into the French empire. After many years of operating illegally, Tonty and other traders saw an opportunity to legitimize their enterprises. They presented themselves as valuable allies in these new endeavors. Tonty and La Forest promised Iberville that they could "facilitate" the success of his new colony "better than anyone else because of the authority they wield over the Indians."[72]

Like so many colonizers, Tonty and La Forest overstated their "authority" over the Indian nations of the midcontinent. But Tonty did know the geography of the Mississippi valley, he did speak the widely used Illinois language, and over two decades, he had built good relationships with Indian leaders. In early 1700, Iberville declared, "M. de Tonty will be of great help to me." Then, as the *coureurs de bois* attempted to gain legitimacy, two related developments aided them. First, the new Minister of the Marine, Louis Phélypeaux de Pontchartrain, and his son and successor, Jérôme, took a renewed interest in colonizing the Mississippi valley to secure a direct route between the Gulf of Mexico and New France. Second, increased English activity in the region threatened French interests.[73] Over time, as the empire moved away from the long-standing, antiexpansionist policy of Colbert, officials found that they could use the knowledge and experience of *coureurs de bois* to facilitate colonization.

By the time Iberville founded Louisiana, hundreds of *coureurs de bois* operated in the midcontinent. In 1700, the governor of Canada recalled 104 traders from Michilimackinac. Only twenty returned. Most of the rest sailed down the Mississippi. They loaded their furs on Iberville's ships and, like the traders from the Illinois Country, returned north with a new load of trade goods. In late February 1702, Iberville spoke with a cohort of Illinois Country *coureurs de bois,* who warned that if his market was closed to them, they would sell them to English merchants from Carolina, who had made them "grand promises." Two years later, Bienville, having taken over as governor following his brother's death, reported that over one hundred traders operated on the Mississippi and Missouri Rivers in small bands of seven or eight men. With little power to stop them, Bienville later downplayed the lawlessness of the Illinois Country, claiming that "only a few Frenchmen who married at the Illinois" remained in the midcontinent.[74]

Likewise, *coureurs de bois* began to rewrite their biographies to highlight their work for the crown and to minimize any morally or legally questionable behavior. As Tonty pushed for an official position in Louisiana, he presented himself as a loyal soldier in "the service of the king." He urged his brother to petition Pontchartrain, to detail his work with La Salle, and to "make the most" of his effort in 1687 to recruit and lead Illinois warriors to fight the Iroquois. To ensure that his brother captured the full value of his knowledge, Tonty included a long description of the Mississippi River valley and its inhabitants. "I have no doubt," he wrote, "that, by exposing all this properly, I shall get something from the Court." A few years later, when Pierre Deliette wrote a memoir on the Illinois Country, he obscured his outlaw years. He lied that he had left Pimiteoui in 1698 or 1699, well before the king had ordered the post shuttered and years before his actual departure.[75]

In the first two decades of the eighteenth century, France relied on *coureurs de bois* to help revitalize its imperial ambitions. The fledgling colony of Louisiana needed labor and local knowledge. *Coureurs de bois* provided both. Tonty never received another monopoly in the midcontinent, and his scheme to trade with the nations of the Southwest never materialized. But in Iberville, whom Tonty called "a great friend of mine," Tonty found a new patron. Not long after Tonty arrived on the coast, Iberville dispatched him to the Tunicas in what is now west-central Mississippi to "try to lure those Englishmen there under pretext of trading for beaver, and arrest them." A month later, Iberville sent him back to the Tunicas and also to the Chickasaws near present-day Tupelo to distribute gifts and inform them, "we have settled on the Mississippi—friends of all the nations nearby, with whom we are doing business in everything." Two years later, Tonty made another journey on Iberville's behalf, returning to the Chickasaw Nation to lay the groundwork for a peace conference between them and the French.[76] Then in 1704, Tonty died during a yellow fever epidemic that ravaged the region, cutting short his reintegration into the French empire.[77]

Over the next decade, officials in Canada and Louisiana struggled to bring the midcontinent under imperial control. Officials in Quebec complained to their superiors in France about disorder in the midcontinent, but they could do little to regulate the *coureurs de bois*. Illinois sat beyond the boundaries of Louisiana. Even as the ease of travel between the two regions brought them closer together economically, Bienville took only tentative steps to curb lawlessness. In 1708, he sent emissaries to Cahokia and Kaskaskia to plea for an end to the slave trade between the Illinois Country and Carolina.[78]

At the beginning of the 1710s, a series of events in Canada, Louisiana, and the Illinois Country forced the crown to pay increased attention to the midcontinent. At the end of the War of the Spanish Succession in 1713, French officials surveyed their claims in North America and found a dismaying picture. The previous year, a bloody battle outside the walls of Detroit marked the culmination of twelve years of blunders by colonial officials, who attempted to create a trading post open to all nations. Instead, Wendats, Illinois, Miamis, Ottawas, and others killed or captured 800 to 1,000 Fox Indians, their longtime enemies who had moved to Detroit in an attempt to build an alliance with France. To the southwest, illegal traders at Cahokia grew in number and in boldness. Canadian officials warned, "This settlement is a dangerous one, serving as a retreat for the lawless men both of this Colony and of Louisiana." In France, Canada, and Louisiana, officials decided that the time had come to rein in French subjects and prevent further English infiltration by paying closer attention to Middle America. In 1717, in an effort to spur Louisiana's economy, the crown granted Louisiana and the Illinois Country to a company of private investors.[79]

In the rush to bring order to the midcontinent, the empire turned to former *coureurs de bois*, men once condemned as outlaws, traitors, and degenerates. Over their decades in Indian Country, they had forged the close bonds that diplomacy required. In 1712, Governor Philippe de Rigaud de Vaudreuil demanded that Peoria chief Chachagouesse end war with the Foxes and make peace with the Miamis, who had flirted with moving east to trade with the English. Chachagouesse consented but only if Vaudreuil sent Pierre Deliette to the Illinois Country to reestablish his trading post. "Since Messieurs La

Forest, Tonty, and Deliettes were no longer among us," Chachagouesse insisted, "we have been unhappy." When Vaudreuil dispatched Deliette to the Illinois Country, he sent Jean-Baptiste Bissot de Vinsenne to the Miamis. Much like Deliette, Vinsenne had a long history with the Miami Nation. Also like Deliette, he had blurred the boundaries between official service and private enterprise, illegally trading with the Miamis in defiance of the king's prohibition on the beaver trade. The crown forgave his past sins in hopes of strengthening its empire. Even missionaries, longtime enemies of the *coureurs de bois*, admitted that Deliette was "the only Frenchman capable of putting these nations on the right path." In the decade that followed, *coureurs de bois* transformed into commandants at reopened forts, respected farmers and merchants, and pillars of their communities.[80]

≈   In 1718, Pierre Dugué de Boisbriand, Bienville's cousin, headed a contingent of about one hundred Louisiana troops who brought colonial rule to the Illinois Country. Boisbriand intended to extend the empire to the mid-continent by authorizing formerly illicit activities, including the trade of the *coureurs de bois*. Like officials in Canada, he turned a blind eye to the earlier defiance of men such as Deliette and others, only a few years earlier, condemned for leading "a life not only scandalous but even Criminal in many ways." By pardoning the illegal colonists, Boisbriand restored them as good subjects of the king. He also recorded French land claims at Kaskaskia and other towns, legitimating existing practice rather than implementing a new system.[81]

Boisbriand's actions had unintended cultural and political consequences. He brought with him metropolitan fears of intermarriage and *mésalliance*, and he upended the relationship between French *habitants* and Native peoples in the region by separating the multiethnic communities into racially distinct towns. Iberville, like Canada's founders before him, had advocated French-Indian intermarriage. But by the mid-1710s, Louisiana's political elites rejected that strategy, believing the success of the colony depended on French families under French authority. In 1716, the Council of the Marine banned French-Indian intermarriage. Boisbriand then pushed Kaskaskia Indians away from the joint French-Kaskaskia town to form a new, Indian Kaskaskia a few miles away. To the north, Boisbriand divided Michigamea and Cahokia Indians from other French villages.[82]

Although French officials initiated the segregation of the villages, many Illinois embraced the proposal because it allowed them to defend their sovereignty and their land from encroaching colonists. Indeed, Boisbriand lacked the power to force thousands of Illinois to relocate. His plan would not have come to fruition without Illinois supporting it. Michigamea chief Chikagou explained the situation to King Louis XV when he visited France in 1725. "The French are among us and we have ceded to them the lands we occupy in the Cascakias," he said. "We are content with this," Chikagou continued, "but it is not good that they come and mingle with us and install themselves in the midst of our villages and our wilderness." Illinois wanted "to remain masters of the lands where," he said, "we have placed our hearths." In the following decade, disputes over land at Cahokia created conflicts between missionaries and Peorias and Cahokias, whom the missionaries tried to convert to Catholicism. Tensions eased only when Peorias and Cahokias left the mission and returned to their former village at Pimiteoui.[83]

In order for Kaskaskia wives to keep their households united and to remain close to the church, they stayed with their French husbands in French Kaskaskia after the separation of the French and Illinois communities. From this moment, French-Kaskaskia families became more integrated into French colonial society, and they constituted a decreasing portion of the town's population. Some such as Marie Rouensa, Michel Accault, and Rouensa's second husband, Michel Philippe, died during these years. Other families may have found life in the French community increasingly isolating and relocated to Indian Kaskaskia. One of Marie Rouensa's sons chose that path in the early 1720s, and some Illinois widows rejoined their birth families after their French husbands died. Between 1720 and 1765, priests performed at least 272 weddings in the Illinois Country but married only thirteen French-Illinois couples—eight during the 1720s, another during the 1730s, and four during the 1740s. A number of these marriages occurred between French men and Illinois widows already living in French communities. When Marguerite Onaquamoquona married the French officer and minor noble Nicolas Pelletier de Franchomme, she was the recent widow of a wealthy trader, farmer, and militia captain. Befitting her status, she owned a French-style home in French Kaskaskia, which she decorated with walnut furniture, linen napkins and tablecloths, and pewter dishes. Meanwhile, between 1,000 and 1,300 Kaskaskias lived a few miles away and grew increasingly segregated from their French neighbors.[84]

Women such as Marie Rouensa and their children and grandchildren further integrated into French society as they married merchants, farmers, and soldiers. These relationships secured status within French Kaskaskia rather than building alliances between the French empire and the Illinois Nation. After all, according to the rules of patrilineal Illinois society, Rouensa's children were French, not Illinois. In 1727, when Marie Rouensa's daughter Marie-Joseph Philippe married Joseph Lorrain, their witnesses included Franchomme as well as two French officers, Jean-Baptiste Bissot de Vinsenne and a son of Robert Groston de St. Ange. In 1733, Vinsenne's son François Marie married Marie Philippe, the granddaughter of Marie Rouensa. By the end of the 1730s, through marriages to French officials and prominent merchants and farmers, Marie Rouensa's children and grandchildren occupied positions of wealth and influence in French Kaskaskia.[85] These marriages consolidated the status of the town's elites. However, their significance stemmed from the prestige that the spouses each held *within* French colonial society. They did not build connections across the borders between the French empire and the Illinois Nation.

As the eighteenth century progressed, most marriages that crossed those lines between French and Illinois society occurred in the context of the fur trade. In contrast to the marriages in Kaskaskia, these were *mariages à la façon du pays.* In the 1740s, the trader René de Couagne and Elisabeth Michel Rouensa married in an Illinois ceremony. One of their children may have been Jean-Baptiste Ducoigne, who became a prominent Kaskaskia chief. In the Miami Nation, a similar pattern occurred with Jean Baptiste Godfroy, who traded on the Wabash River and at Detroit no later than the end of the 1740s. By the turn of the nineteenth century, a likely descendant, Francis Godfroy or Pa-Lonz-Wa, had become chief of the Miami Nation, indicating an earlier alliance between Jean-Baptiste Godfroy and a Miami leader.[86]

When Boisbriand segregated the French and Illinois settlements in the Illinois Country, he enacted a specific vision for the future of the region. Boisbriand and his superiors expected the Illinois Country to become the breadbasket of the French empire. With the right guidance, they believed, French farmers in the midcontinent would feed Lower Louisiana and the Caribbean. Such a plan required a different society than the one that had developed independent of imperial oversight. Officials such as Bienville thought that marriage incorporated French men into Indian communities and sapped the agricultural labor force of Louisiana. Kaskaskia demonstrated the potential of the country with its fertile soil and temperate climate, but from the perspective of New Orleans and Versailles, only "the right people" would increase agricultural production in the midcontinent. Bienville and others depended on *habitants* dedicated to clearing and plowing fields, raising livestock, and living respectable lives. "All that is needed," wrote one Frenchman, "is some of these hard-working men and women accustomed to the cares of households."[87] Most officials carried prejudices that led them to see Kaskaskia as a promising but misguided settlement. In spite of all available evidence, they believed that French-Illinois families could not provide the foundation for stable colonies.

Despite an aversion to multiethnic families, French officials in Louisiana, Canada, and France recognized that the extension of the empire in the midcontinent required the assistance of Native peoples. Lacking the manpower to control or defend the region, France depended on alliances with Indian nations. During the ban on the fur trade, France had allowed its Indian alliances to go fallow. Now they required cultivation. The reopening of trade at Pimiteoui under Deliette probably pleased Peorias. But in separating Illinois and French settlements, Boisbriand undermined France's best chance at building a strong and stable alliance with Illinois Indians. In the future, when men like Pierre Deliette died or retired, no one with similar kinship ties would be available to replace them.

For Illinois, kinship, economics, politics, and religion converged as aspects of a single system, rather than operating as individual institutions. Although French imperialists relied on their Native allies, they refused to include them in the kinship networks that dominated the empire. As Boisbriand divided French and Illinois, he created a rift between French political interests in the region and the familial, religious, and economic bonds that linked Jesuits and *coureurs de bois* with the Illinois. In the following decades, France expanded its presence in the midcontinent, but without robust kinship ties, it struggled to maintain its alliances.[88]

CHAPTER THREE

Alliances and Fractures

In September 1737, Chickasaw chief Mingo Ouma joined the French officer Diron d'Artaguiette in council at Mobile. Chickasaws and the French had fought an intermittent war for decades, a conflict that culminated the previous year in two French-Indian campaigns into the Chickasaw homeland. Chickasaws had repelled both forces, and Mingo Ouma hoped to exploit French weakness to broker a peace favorable to his nation. As a diplomatic aid, Mingo Ouma presented a map of Chickasaw friends and enemies. Centered on the Chickasaw Nation, this map noted the relative importance of each nation to the Chickasaws and revealed how they were connected. Like other Native cartographers in the South, Mingo Ouma used circles to signify different nations, and the size of the circle represented the status of the nation. Large circles denoted dangerous allies or prominent friends, while smaller sizes indicated moderately or minimally significant nations. With three large circles, Mingo Ouma identified Choctaws, Illinois and Miamis, and Wendats and Iroquois as the Chickasaws' greatest enemies. Quapaws and Chakchiumas presented lesser threats. Along the Upper and Lower Trade Paths that connected Chickasaws to South Carolina, Cherokees and Creeks were the Chickasaws' most important allies. Tellingly, Mingo Ouma made no distinction between Indian nations and European empires. Without the key to the map, nothing would distinguish the British from another Chickasaw ally, nor the French from another enemy. Mingo Ouma did not grant Europeans any special prominence among the many polities vying for power. He marked the British and the French with medium-size circles approximately the same size as those used to indicate different divisions of the Creek Nation.[1]

Indian leaders such as Mingo Ouma carefully weighed the advantages and threats presented by Europeans and other Indians, and they negotiated their relations well aware of Middle America's complex politics. Indian nations pursued their own policies, shaped by concerns local and continental. As Mingo Ouma's map demonstrated, alliances and rivalries existed in a web of relations, sprawling across the waterways of the midcontinent. Through marriage, adoption, and fictive kinship, Miamis and Illinois had forged close ties with Ottawas and Quapaws, who in turn had built other alliances. Likewise, Mingo Ouma maintained alliances with his Cherokee and Creek neighbors. To be sure, Mingo Ouma worried about relationships between his nation and the French and the British, but he also acknowledged the power of Cherokees, Choctaws, Creeks, Illinois, Iroquois, Miamis, and Quapaws. As he guided his nation's foreign policy, Mingo Ouma had to balance friendly and hostile relations with all of those powers. He was but one of many Native leaders who recognized the intricate, kinship-based politics of the midcontinent. In this world, sometimes Native and European concerns converged, but just as often, Indians waged war and brokered peace without regard for European interests and demands.

Mingo Ouma's understanding of the midcontinent's political geography contrasted sharply with the self-perceptions of Europeans, who saw themselves as the protagonists in a global, imperial struggle. Studying their own maps of the Great Lakes, the Mississippi valley, and the unknown lands beyond, diplomats in Versailles and Quebec viewed their Indian allies as pawns in a much-larger game played by European empires. In their ethnocentric approach to Native peoples, imperialists exaggerated their own power and overlooked the complex factors that shaped events in Middle America. True, France, as well as Great Britain and Spain, influenced the course of events in the North American midcontinent. But as Mingo Ouma showed, Europeans stood in North American politics as middling players in a much-larger cast of actors.

During the mid-1710s, as France launched new efforts to bring Middle America under imperial control, officials struggled to reconcile their ambitions with their limited influence in North America. To strengthen their rule in the midcontinent, French imperialists focused their efforts on securing the Mississippi River and its tributaries from British incursion, safeguarding

NATIONS AMIES ET ENNEMIES DES TCHICACHAS.

Ces Figures ont êtées Tirées, D'aprés l'original qui etoient Sur une Peau, que Mingo-ouma Grand chef de Guerre de la Nation Tchikachas a donné au Capitaine de Pakama, pour apporter a Sa Nation, et aux François afin qu'ils Viſsent le Nombre de leurs amis et auſsy leurs Ennemis, les premiers Sont Marquéz en Noir et les Seconds en Rouge. ₽

Les Ronds marquez des Villages et Nations Entieres.

A. Les Anglois, B. Les Kaoüitas, C. Les Kachétas, D. Les Vtchiré, E. Les Toucoulou charakis, F. Les Charakis, Ceux cy parlent unelangue Differente des E. G. Les Aſſasquéz Abékas, H. Les Alybamonts, I. La Mobille ou les François, K. Les Tchakts,

L. Toute la Nation Tchikachas qui est Blanche en dedans mais d'on les Environs ne Sont que Sang: Elle est blanche par cequ'ils pretendent qu'il ne Sort que de bonnes paroles de leur Villages, mais que ceux des environs perdent l'Esprit en ne l'écourant point, Ce qui rend Ses Terres Teinte de Sang. M. Les Villages et Nations Heuronne Irquoise, et ceux qu'ils Appelent Nantouague. N. Les Villages et Nation des Tamarois Peanquichias &c. O. Les Arkansas, ou Okappa. P. Les Chakchouma Surlesquels ils doivent Aller Frapper inceſsament Q. Ce Sont des chemins de Guerre qui ne Se rendent pas, jusque au Villages, par ce qu'ils esperent qu'ils deviendront blancs, en faisant la paix avec ceux vers ou ils tendent R. Riviere des Alybamonts et chemin de cette Nation à la Mobille il n'arrive pas jus qua la Mobille, par ce qu'ils disent qu'ils ne seroient Y Aller, mais que Malgrez cela est blanc pour nous, S. chemin blancs qui vont chez leurs Amis, T. Chemins de Guerre, V. Chemins de chaſse des Alybamons. blancs: 7bre 1737.

travel between Louisiana and Canada, and protecting the Illinois Country, the crossroads of French North America. Yet the empire lacked the strength to accomplish much on its own. The French army in Louisiana usually numbered about 700 men scattered across hundreds of miles, and the *voyageurs* and *habitants* of the Illinois Country proved apathetic and unreliable imperialists.

The French depended on Indian nations to back their ambitions. However, because France and the Indian nations of the midcontinent employed different strategies to achieve diverse, sometimes competing, goals, France struggled throughout the first half of the eighteenth century to build a stable, lasting alliance in Middle America. In the centuries after the Seven Years' War, authors often employed a stereotype of the French as particularly adept at dealing with Indians with whom they lived in peace. But no French official in North America would have recognized that portrayal.[2] In Middle America, the French discovered that their alliance was an edifice built on ever-shifting ground, a structure with a fractured foundation always at risk of toppling.

In the midcontinent, kinship, whether real or fictive, had served as the basis of alliances since time immemorial, but France rejected French-Indian intermarriage as a political tool. During the 1710s, as the empire banned French-Indian intermarriage and Pierre Dugué de Boisbriand segregated the French and Illinois populations of Middle America, French officers refused to build familial relationships with Indian leaders. Instead, France sought to demonstrate its value as an economic and military ally, and imperial representatives had to build trust with Native leaders. In the absence of familial kinship, Indian nations used the calumet and other ceremonies to ritually adopt French officials. These alliances required constant reinforcing and reaffirming. Gift giving demonstrated France's value as an ally and its respect for Indian nations. But even as officials in the colonies recognized the need for generosity, they faced constant demands from Versailles to decrease expenditures.[3] To compensate, successful French officers relied on personal relationships with Indian leaders to soothe disagreements. In those instances, local officials established close relations with specific nations over years or decades of interaction. Unfortunately for the empire, short-tenured commandants too often found themselves in a confusing world, and they moved to

---

Fig. 3.1 Mingo Ouma, "Nations Amies et Ennemies des Tchicachas" (copy), 1737.

other assignments just as they began to understand their surroundings and their Indian allies and neighbors.

Beyond the difficulties created by limited resources and inexperienced representatives, France's strategy in North America, from its inception, contained a fatal flaw. France attempted to build its empire atop the existing political landscape, using good relations with powerful nations—notably Ottawas, Illinois, and Choctaws—to extend the influence of its empire. Far from serving as proxies for French imperial power, these nations demanded that their new allies aid them in wars against their enemies. France became entangled in conflicts that had long divided the midcontinent and that had little to do with imperial interests. At times, the empire and its allies joined together to fight a common enemy, as happened during the late seventeenth century when Great Lakes Indians and France united to defeat the Iroquois. More often, however, Native politics frustrated French imperialists, who struggled to stitch the nations of the Great Lakes and Mississippi valley into a grand tapestry of peace and cooperation only to discover that their would-be allies tore at the threads that held together the rival nations.[4]

The French could not impose their will on western nations because those powers ruled the waterways that connected New France and the Great Lakes to Louisiana and the Gulf Coast. In particular, three nations—the Illinois; their allies, the Miamis; and their mutual enemy, the Chickasaws—commanded the rivers of Middle America. Early in the eighteenth century, France believed that it could not afford to alienate any of these nations, because all of them could hamper travel, trade, and communication between the two centers of French North America. Because of Native diplomacy and demands in Middle America, the empire could not build and preserve an alliance that included Illinois and Miamis, on the one hand, and Chickasaws, on the other. By the end of the 1720s, the conflict between those nations consumed French interests in the midcontinent, and during the next decade, colonial officials in Louisiana joined the ongoing war against the Chickasaws to disastrous results.

In the first half of the eighteenth century, political and geographical realities thwarted French attempts to construct a mighty North American empire. The French were not powerless, but numerous limitations imposed by themselves, by Native peoples, and by geography hampered their efforts. With Versailles unwilling or unable to expend necessary resources, Canada and Louisiana depended on capricious local agents to cajole Indian nations into protecting French outposts and territorial claims. Reliant on their

Native allies, the French found themselves drawn into local conflicts that ballooned into expensive imperial wars. These wars curtailed French ambitions and, eventually, exposed French vulnerabilities and reduced the empire's influence among even its most trusted allies.

≈ During the early eighteenth century, France identified the Illinois Country as the keystone of its North American empire. French imperialists knew that the waterways of the Mississippi valley were crucial to commanding the midcontinent and to linking its holdings in Louisiana and Canada. With particular interest in the region as a connector, a strategic hub between Louisiana and Canada, France imposed a new understanding of space on the landscape of the midcontinent. Officials and cartographers emphasized the routes that connected the two halves of French North America and ignored waterways they considered marginal to their needs.

Three rivers—the Wabash, the Illinois, and the Mississippi—dominated French views of the region. Although the Ohio River gained importance later in the eighteenth century, French observers considered it a tributary to the Wabash, which in their understanding flowed into the Mississippi. Following the Ohio to its source, a French boatman would have found the western Iroquois Nation and British Pennsylvania, neither of which appealed as destinations. The Wabash, however, linked Montreal and the Illinois Country. Travelers from Canada exited Lake Erie at the mouth of the Maumee River, at present-day Toledo; journeyed upstream to the river's source at the current site of Fort Wayne, Indiana; and portaged a short distance to the headwaters of the Wabash. From there, the Wabash flowed past the mouth of the Ohio to the Mississippi River and the Illinois Country. (This understanding of the Wabash as the principal waterway and the Ohio as its tributary dated from the precolonial era and continued through the mid-eighteenth century.)[5]

Miami Indians controlled the route between Lake Erie and the Ohio-Wabash confluence. With regard to politics, language, and culture, Miamis shared much with the closely related Illinois. Like Illinois, Miamis recognized the power that came from controlling the region's waterways, and the three or four divisions of the nation each occupied a strategically significant village in the territory between the Great Lakes and the Ohio River. At the turn of the eighteenth century, some Miamis lived on the southwest shore of Lake Michigan, near the mouth of the St. Joseph River, which early French travelers called the "River of the Miamis." They controlled the entrance to the principal route from the western Great Lakes into the heart of Miami Country. By 1715, most of the nation lived in three groups that maintained villages at key spots along the Wabash-Maumee route that colonists used to travel from Canada to the midcontinent. The Miamis proper lived at the portage between the two rivers, while Weas occupied a location farther west at the confluence of the Wabash and Tippecanoe Rivers and Piankashaws resided on the Wabash a short distance above the Ohio.[6]

Since early in the seventeenth century, Illinois had ruled the Illinois River valley from the river's source to its mouth. Marquette took the advice of a slave given him by the Great Captain of the Illinois, and he and his party returned to Michilimackinac via the Illinois River with a short portage at present-day Chicago. Afterward, the way through Chicago became one of two main routes from the upper Great Lakes to the Illinois Country. The other, used by the French after 1679, followed the St. Joseph River through Miami Country to present-day South Bend, Indiana, where travelers portaged into the Illinois River system. Either route required negotiating Illinois control of their eponymous river.[7]

After the founding of Louisiana in 1699, one great benefit of the Illinois and Wabash River routes was that they ended at the Mississippi, which linked the French colonies in the Great Lakes to the burgeoning outposts on the Gulf of Mexico. Riding the rapid current of that mighty river, travelers could reach the Gulf, 800 miles downstream, in a month.[8] Making the voyage northward required more effort and more time, but throughout the eighteenth century, the river remained the most efficient way to journey from Lower Louisiana to the Illinois Country.

As France looked to strengthen its claims over Middle America, it recognized that the Chickasaws presented the greatest threat to French security in the lower Mississippi valley. From their homes in present-day northern Mississippi, Chickasaws lived on or near several key paths and rivers that linked them to Europeans and Indians across the South and throughout the Mississippi valley. Overland routes ran to Creeks, Cherokees, and English Carolina. The Tombigbee River flowed south to the Gulf, while the Tennessee River rolled north to the Illinois Country. The Yazoo and Wolf Rivers linked them to the Mississippi River. Using these waterways, Chickasaws could strike at river travelers making the journey between Illinois and the Gulf. Just as dangerous from the perspective of the French, they threatened to extend English influence from the Atlantic coast into the heart of the continent.[9]

By the end of the 1680s, French traders, officials, and cartographers realized that the Illinois, Wabash, and Mississippi were central to controlling the midcontinent, and during the next century, France employed two strategies to secure the long distances between Canada and Lower Louisiana. First, the empire erected a series of forts at key points along those waterways. Second, it built alliances with the nations that controlled the rivers.

Between 1715 and 1731, the French established outposts at choke points in the river valleys that linked the Great Lakes and the Gulf. On the Wabash during those years, France established Fort Miami (also called Fort St. Philippe) at the Miami towns at the Fort Wayne portage, Ouiatenon near the Weas and the Wabash-Tippecanoe confluence, and Vincennes among the Piankashaws above the junction of the Wabash and Ohio Rivers. On the Mississippi, the French built Fort de Chartres between the towns of Kaskaskia and Cahokia and not far from several Illinois Indian settlements.[10] They also established posts on the lower reaches of the river at New Orleans, Natchez, and Arkansas Post.

A crucial stretch of the Mississippi between Arkansas Post and Fort de Chartres remained unguarded, as did the lower Wabash—the section of the river later considered part of the Ohio. Even after the establishment of Vincennes in 1731, it sat too far north to protect the lower Wabash from British traders or southern Indians coming up the Cherokee (Tennessee) or Shawnee (Cumberland) Rivers. Due to the location of Fort de Chartres about one hundred miles north of the confluence of the Mississippi and Wabash (Ohio) Rivers, it offered little defense. In 1715, France began building a fort between the later site of Vincennes and the Mississippi River, but construction halted a year or two later because of limited supplies and manpower.[11] Beyond a handful of short-lived forts established and abandoned by French expeditions, no French fort ever filled the breach between Arkansas Post and the Illinois Country. The chain of French forts missed crucial links in the confluence region.

Small garrisons undermined the effectiveness of the forts. Between 1710 and 1740, Louisiana's army grew from two companies totaling forty-five men to sixteen companies, which were commissioned at fifty men a piece, although they regularly mustered only thirty-five to forty-five soldiers each. At the same time, Louisiana's claims expanded from a couple of small outposts on the Gulf of Mexico to ten forts stretching from the Illinois Country to New Orleans to Mobile. Illinois forts received three of the sixteen companies. The bulk remained at Fort de Chartres. Another twenty-five guarded Cahokia, and thirty manned Vincennes. During the 1720s, a small contingent defended a post on the Missouri River. Canada sent parties, ranging from ten to twenty-five men each, to Ouiatenon and Fort Miami.[12] In times of dire need, a few hundred ill-trained militiamen supplemented the regulars.

The protectors of New France also included some of the worst recruits in the French army. During the early years of Louisiana, few soldiers, much like the French population in general, wanted to immigrate to the colony. As with Canada, stories of hardship, deprivation, and Indian attacks painted the colony with a bleak brush, and most men with any options in France chose to stay in Europe. The empire enlisted orphans and vagrants to fill the ranks of Louisiana's army and shipped captured deserters to North America. In 1716, Jean-Baptiste Le Moyne de Bienville complained that not a single soldier in the colony knew the country or had ever fired a musket. Twenty years later, after a troop ship docked at New Orleans, Bienville reported that the new arrivals failed to match even the low standards set by their predecessors. Half of the "wretched blackguards" had already been punished as thieves since landing in New Orleans. Bienville found their physical stature disappointing as well, complaining that only two of the fifty-two soldiers stood taller than four feet, ten inches. Moreover, the new enlistees suffered from the diseases of the unfamiliar climate. Being stationed in Louisiana did not cure deserters of their urge to abscond, and many ran off soon after reaching the colony. At one point, Louisiana's companies faced a shortage of 142 men, not counting ten children who had been enlisted after their fathers died in combat, leaving the army about a fifth short of full capacity. Bienville predicted that his soldiers would "compromise the honor of the nation" and get their officers killed. With such a paltry, unreliable force, Louisiana's officials failed to extend French authority much beyond the walls of their forts.[13]

For want of troops, France relied on Indian allies to offset imperial weakness. To establish relationships with Indian nations, the French adopted Native diplomatic practices developed long before Samuel de Champlain set foot on the future site of Quebec. In the early 1700s, the French eschewed intermarriage as a route to alliance, but they routinely employed other customs borrowed from Native North America. The French offered gifts including weapons, beads, cloth, and kettles. In return, they accepted presents such as wampum belts, beaver furs, and slaves. Through the calumet and other ceremonies, intercultural alliances also employed ritual adoption and fictive kinship. Initially, like Marquette at Peouarea in 1673, French colonists found these ceremonies confusing and misunderstood their importance. Over time, officials learned the intricacies of Native diplomacy and alliance-building. These alliances required constant tending and bolstering, because Native peoples recognized them only as long as the French remained generous, respectful, and trustworthy.[14]

The strongest French-Indian pacts were those established by French officers over long periods of residence among individual Indian nations. Two families—the Vinsennes and the St. Anges—sustained French interests among the Illinois and the Miamis. In both instances, the fathers—Jean-Baptiste Bissot de Vinsenne and Robert Groston de St. Ange—moved to Middle America, bringing their children with them. Unlike many officers, who kept an eye open for opportunities to leave the Illinois Country or Wabash valley, both St. Ange and Vinsenne made their homes in the region. In this way, they signaled their commitment to strengthening the empire in the midcontinent.

Vinsenne served from 1704 until his death in 1719 as Canadian governor Philippe de Rigaud de Vaudreuil's primary informant on affairs among the Miamis, and for the last seven years of his life, he lived permanently in Miami Country. The most important duty of an ally was military support, and Vinsenne upheld his obligation in 1712 when he joined Miamis in their defeat of the Foxes at Detroit. At the end of the decade, Vinsenne died at Kekionga, a Miami village at the headwaters of the Maumee River. The governor of Canada believed that Miamis remained there rather than return to their old homes at Fort St. Joseph out of respect for the French officer who died there. Citing Vinsenne's influence among the Miamis, a decade after his death, the administrators of Louisiana believed that all they needed to get the Miamis to relocate was to move his bones from Kekionga to the desired spot.[15] These outsiders possessed poor understanding of dynamics that motivated Miamis to stay at or move from a particular spot, but the fact remained that Vinsenne had been a capable agent, trusted and admired by Miamis.

Like Vinsenne, Robert Groston de St. Ange dedicated decades to building relations between France and the Indian nations of Middle America. After moving to the Illinois Country with his wife and two of his sons in the early 1720s, St. Ange served among Miamis at St. Joseph, Missourias at Fort d'Orleans on the Missouri River, and finally, Illinois at Fort de Chartres. St. Ange helped Cahokia and Peoria Indians win a great victory against the Foxes in 1730. Around that time, he became commandant of Fort de

Chartres. In 1732, Bienville remarked that the "wise and prudent" St. Ange knew "perfectly the manner of conducting himself with the *sauvages*."[16]

The second generation of Vinsennes and St. Anges continued their fathers' work. François-Marie Bissot de Vinsenne and Pierre and Louis Groston de St. Ange all grew up in the midcontinent, and from their teenage or early adult years, they interacted with Native peoples. The young Vinsenne's superiors praised his early work among the Weas and the Piankashaws, noting those nations' high opinion of the young officer. We know little of the career of Pierre St. Ange other than that he served as an officer in the Illinois Country for fourteen years from 1722 until his death fighting alongside Illinois and Miami Indians in 1736. His brother Louis enjoyed a long career in the midcontinent, serving beyond the final days of the French empire. In 1736, not long after Louis's appointment as commandant at Vincennes, his superiors commented that he was "very well known and very well liked" by the Piankashaws who lived near the fort.[17] Thanks to the long histories of this generation of officers with Native communities, they guided French interests better than recently arrived appointees could.

In councils with Indian leaders, the French relied on the language of kinship to explain their relations with Indian nations as well as the relations that they expected Indians to have with each other. French officials posed as Onontio, the "father" of their Indian allies, whom they called their "children." In patriarchal French society, fathers commanded their children, and they expected to dominate their alliances. In the patrilineal Indian societies of the midcontinent, fathers gained authority and influence through generosity and by offering protection to relatives. Beyond the household, skill as a hunter or warrior added to a man's social capital. Most Indian leaders, whether at home or in politics, lacked coercive power. Native peoples welcomed Onontio as a wealthy and generous father, but they balked when his demands ran counter to their interests. For example, Onontio wanted peace among all of his "children," but in spite of French wishes, Illinois pursued war against Foxes, their longtime enemies, whom they took as slaves and used as commodities.[18]

Confusing the fictive kinship of the alliance, Indians did not recognize all French men, or even all French officers, as their father. By the early eighteenth century, the Illinois and other nations had interacted with French traders, missionaries, and explorers long enough to know that the king was also father to the impoverished, grubby French colonists of the midcontinent. Michigamea chief Jouachin made this distinction in council with the

French and Fox Indians in 1725. He acknowledged that the "Great Onon-thyo from the other side of the great lake"—the Atlantic Ocean—was his father. He referred similarly to Pierre Dugué de Boisbriand, the officer in command of posts in the Illinois Country. Other French men scattered through Middle America, however, were his "brothers." Like fathers, whose generosity and strength needed to be demonstrated frequently, brothers also had a role to fill. Native peoples expected them to fight together in battle against common enemies.[19]

The Indian expectation of military support complicated French ambitions to control the midcontinent. By the early decades of the eighteenth century, France maintained forts and trading posts among dozens of nations, and Onontio claimed countless clans, bands, and towns as his allies. In theory, with connections among many nations throughout Middle America, the French headed a vast alliance of Indian nations. Many French officials certainly be-lieved that to be the case.[20] French perceptions of their dominant place in North America, however, bore little resemblance to the complicated web of rivalries and alliances that stood between the French and their ambitions. For the French, the greatest challenge lay in negotiating the animosities that existed between the different nations that they considered their allies.

At least three precolonial alliances controlled the terrain from the western Great Lakes to the Illinois Country. Anishinaabeg, sometimes called the Three Fires Confederacy, comprised Ojibwes, Ottawas, and Potawatomis, who lived on Lake Huron, Lake Superior, and eastern Lake Michigan. Through Kiskakon Ottawas and later Potawatomis, the Anishinaabeg alli-ance maintained peaceful relations with the alliance that Illinois Indians had built during the seventeenth century. Consisting of Illinois, Missourias, Osages, and often Miamis, this coalition controlled the valleys of the Illinois, Mississippi, Missouri, and Wabash Rivers—the major waterways of Middle America. To the west of Lake Michigan and Green Bay, a third alliance—Foxes and Sauks, along with most Kickapoos and Mascoutens—opposed the Anishinaabeg and the Illinois. The rival alliances had been at war at least since the late seventeenth century.[21]

South of the Illinois Country, three large nations—Chickasaws, Choc-taws, and Quapaws—ruled the lower Mississippi. Chickasaws and Choctaws lived east of the Mississippi River in present-day Mississippi. Sometime in the distant past, the two nations had been united, but they parted ways long before the arrival of Europeans. Although Chickasaws were probably the smallest of the three nations in the late seventeenth century, they used

English guns to terrorize their neighbors and take slaves, whom they sold to Carolina traders. When Chickasaws opened trade with Carolina in the late 1600s, they exploited the weakness of Choctaws, a large nation but one lacking firearms. During the 1690s, Chickasaw slave raiders captured about fifty Choctaws a year and killed three times as many in the process. Quapaws lived west of the Mississippi on the lower Arkansas River. They became less attached to the Illinois alliance during the 1680s, not long after gaining direct access to the French trade. Like Choctaws, their primary antagonists were Chickasaws, who captured more than 1,000 Quapaws between 1670 and 1715.[22]

At the turn of the eighteenth century, the French, hoping to enhance the fortunes of their empire and to prevent their English and Spanish rivals from claiming the region, attempted to ally with all of these nations. French officials believed they could end conflicts between their desired allies using the same alliance-building strategies that Native peoples used to convert the French from strangers to fictive kin.[23] However, French mediation only worked if Indian nations desired peace. France lacked the power to compel Indian nations to do anything.

French mediation at its most successful reinforced preexisting bonds and smoothed tensions between nations that tended toward alliance anyway. Linguistically and culturally, Illinois and Miamis shared as much, if not more, than any other two nations in the midcontinent. They probably separated into different political groups during the early seventeenth century, as Illinois Indians moved into the Mississippi valley. Yet, in the late seventeenth and early eighteenth centuries, Illinois and Miamis occasionally fought each other, probably over disputed hunting territories or trade connections. By 1712, Pierre Deliette and Jean-Baptiste Bissot de Vinsenne had long histories of dealing with Illinois and Miamis, respectively. Exploiting that expertise, they settled one dispute between the two nations, allowing them to unite against their mutual enemy, the Foxes. In this instance, as in most successful French-brokered alliances, "those two nations," according to French officials, "seem[ed] to desire peace."[24]

Mediation could not repair deeper ruptures when only one, or neither, nation sought to end a war. During the eighteenth century, Illinois, Ottawas, and others wanted to keep the benefits of the French alliance for themselves and worked to exclude their enemies, notably the Foxes and their allies. In 1712, Illinois and Miamis along with their Anishinaabeg and Wendat allies surrounded a fortified Fox town near French Detroit. The besieged and beleaguered Foxes sent diplomats to meet with French commandant Jacques-Charles Renaud Dubuisson and enemy Indian leaders. Fox chief Pemoussa followed the protocols of alliance building by surrendering himself, along with seven slaves, to Dubuisson. He expected mercy in return. Dubuisson knew that the Canadian governor wanted peace, but he also recognized that his handful of soldiers could not enforce a peace settlement on the hundreds of Indian warriors who had come to fight the Foxes. He replied to Pemoussa that the decision was not his to make and deferred to the Indians at the council. The Illinois and the rest asked to kill the Foxes, and when Dubuisson refused the request, an Illinois spokesman warned the Foxes that they would soon be killed anyway. A few days later, an Illinois, Miami, Ottawa, and Wendat force killed or captured as many as 1,000 Foxes, while the French watched, unable to stop the fighting. Underscoring the limits of French influence, Miami Indians killed a group of Fox Indians, to whom the long-time Miami friend Jean-Baptiste Bissot de Vinsenne had "granted their lives and safety." The French negotiated a separate peace with the Foxes in 1716. Winning the war and profiting as the owners and sellers of Fox slaves, Illinois refused to honor the French-Fox accord. Instead, they continued to raid for captives among the Foxes and reignited a war that lasted for decades.[25]

The French alliance succeeded only within limited parameters. On a local level, officers such as the St. Anges and the Vinsennes formed ties with individual Indian nations or towns. Their presence helped France maintain good relations with those powers. France failed, however, to combine those individual relationships into a single alliance extending across Louisiana and Canada. In the midcontinent, French officials were caught between the demands of multiple nations with competing interests. As the eighteenth century progressed, war between Illinois and Chickasaws commanded French attention and resources. France wanted both nations as allies, but the empire could not mend the rift between the two polities. Instead, French officials found themselves drawn into a conflict they preferred to avoid.

≈ At the turn of the eighteenth century, Illinois and Chickasaws were expansionist powers, acquiring slaves and furs to trade for European goods, including guns. The slave trade was of particular importance in shaping inter-Indian relations in the early 1700s. At the turn of the century, the central Mississippi valley was the nexus of two slave trades. The Chickasaws, with their Carolina-based English trading partners, became "the scourge of the Mississippi." Illinois from their homelands captured slaves from the

Missouri and the lower Mississippi valleys, offering them to their French allies and trading partners, as well as to English traders operating on the Tennessee River. As Illinois ranged south for slaves and Chickasaws looked north, the two nations came into conflict. During one particularly devastating attack in 1698, Chickasaw slavers killed ten men at Cahokia and captured one hundred women and children, probably for sale to Carolina traders.[26] Illinois raiders retaliated. Warfare engulfed the region.

Soon after Governor Pierre Le Moyne d'Iberville established Louisiana in 1699, he recognized that he needed to forge an alliance with Chickasaws and to end the wars between the nations of the Mississippi valley. In early 1702, Iberville invited the *mingos,* or chiefs, of the Chickasaw Nation to join him in a council at Mobile, the capital of his fledgling colony. As the council began, Iberville made his case for peace. The English, he asserted, had no loyalty to Chickasaws. Once Chickasaws could no longer provide captives, the English, who liked "nothing but blood and slaves," would turn on them and sell them "in faraway countries" from which they could "never return." If Chickasaws were not convinced by Iberville's charges of English duplicity, the French governor had another strategy: threats. After promising to arm Choctaws, Natchez, and other Chickasaw neighbors, Iberville promised, "Far indeed from preventing the Illinois [Indians] from making war on you, I shall incite them to it. Certainly you see that you will be in no condition to hold out against so many nations; you will suffer the sorrow of seeing yourself killed at the gates of your villages, along with your women and children."[27]

Listening to Iberville's arguments, Chickasaws seemed amenable to peace, and after Iberville's offer of favorable trade relations, the two groups came close to an accord. One matter remained. Finally, Iberville promised to send three Canadians to the Illinois Country, where they would inform the Illinois of the peace and return with the Chickasaw prisoners held there. In exchange, the French would build a trading post on the edge of Chickasaw Country, providing an easy source of weapons, tools, and decorative items. When Chickasaws agreed to Iberville's terms, the governor distributed a plentiful assortment of guns, ammunition, metal tools and goods, and glass beads, a display of wealth and generosity that underscored his promises to his Chickasaws guests. With all parties satisfied, Chickasaws, traveling with Iberville's agents, headed north the following morning.[28]

Unfortunately for Iberville, the peace he negotiated with the Chickasaw *mingos* hinged on the acquiescence of absent Illinois. Iberville promised that he could restrain Illinois warriors from raiding southward, saying about the

Canadians he sent to Illinois, "[They will] notify [the Illinois] to make no further war on the Chicacha, as they are our allies, as well as to tell them I am holding back their tomahawk." In reality, Iberville could not force Illinois to do anything, and he had given them no reason to agree to his terms. He did not negotiate the release of Illinois captives among the Chickasaws, even though he knew about them. Those Illinois in bondage had relatives whose grief could only be satiated through vengeance or covering the dead, a ritual that compensated victims' families. In saying that he held back the Illinois' tomahawk, Iberville forbade revenge, but he made no arrangements to cover the dead. At the same time, he demanded the release of Chickasaw captives, who held immense material, cultural, and diplomatic value, and offered no compensation. In short, Illinois had no motivation to agree to Iberville's terms and every reason to refuse them. So they did. In 1708, an English trader in Chickasaw Country reported that Illinois—"the slyest and most patient men stealers of the World"—raided Chickasaws for slaves once or twice a year.[29]

In the next decade, the ongoing war between Chickasaws and Illinois endangered French efforts to strengthen their hold on the midcontinent. River travelers between Louisiana and the midcontinent had to journey through a war zone. The war began independent of the French, but Europeans became participants and often victims in the fighting. Chickasaw warriors targeted French traders who supplied the Illinois with weapons and ammunition. Even more troubling for Louisiana's administrators, the war expanded as allies of both Illinois and Chickasaws joined the fighting. In 1716, Jean-Baptiste Le Moyne de Bienville, Iberville's younger brother and successor as Louisiana governor, reported that the central Mississippi valley swarmed with "warriors of the Illinois, Miami, Chickasaw, and Cherokee nations who made war on each other and who ordinarily killed and plundered all those whom they found on the way." Five years later, as the Jesuit priest and historian Pierre de Charlevoix traveled down the Mississippi River, he spotted a decorated wooden post on the riverbank. As Charlevoix approached the post, he found representations of "two men without heads and a few in their entirety." The post told the story of a recent Illinois raid against the Chickasaws, in which Illinois had killed two men and taken others prisoner. In retaliation, Charlevoix reported, Chickasaws attacked two French travelers descending the Mississippi behind the Jesuit.[30]

By the 1720s, Chickasaws presided over a large section of the Mississippi River, and their power threatened both ends of French Louisiana. Chickasaw

Country was the true border between French claims in Upper and Lower Louisiana, and when Chickasaws restricted commerce and travel, they endangered the livelihood and lives of people hundreds of miles apart. By the 1720s, Illinois agriculture provided food for much of the colony, and in some years, Lower Louisiana received 100,000 pounds of flour from Illinois Country farmers. When flood, drought, or pestilence ruined crops around New Orleans and Mobile, French officials relied on Illinois produce to feed the soldiers and settlers of their posts. In exchange, the French in the midcontinent received goods and supplies from Lower Louisiana. Without passage on the Mississippi, French soldiers in Illinois faced shortages of guns, ammunition, and diplomatic presents, and Illinois and French *habitants* could not ship their produce—flour, salted meat, grease, and furs—to market.[31] Native peoples of the Illinois Country faced the same hardships as the French. Fort de Chartres and Vincennes served as primary distribution points for gifts and supplies for Illinois and Miamis.

Because the Illinois controlled the confluence of the Mississippi and Wabash (Ohio) Rivers, France identified them as their most important ally in the fight against English and Chickasaw expansion in the midcontinent. Illinois population declined in the late 1600s due to epidemic disease and chronic warfare. But, at the turn of the eighteenth century, they remained a formidable nation of at least 8,300 people and more than 1,600 warriors.[32] Moreover, the Illinois Nation controlled the most important real estate between the Great Lakes and the Gulf of Mexico. They offered France its best chance to stymie English and Chickasaw power on the Mississippi. Yet, while France sought peace with all the nations of the Mississippi valley, it could not ally with both the Illinois, its most important ally, and the Chickasaws, its most dangerous enemy and the rival of the Illinois. As the eighteenth century progressed, French dependence on the Illinois bound the two, even as Illinois policy toward the Chickasaws undermined the best interests of the empire.

Many Chickasaws, however, welcomed an alliance with the French. In the precolonial era, two Chickasaw officials—a peace chief and a war chief—shared power. With the rise of the slave trade, the war chief gained greater authority. Because slave raiding fell under his purview, he enjoyed access to trade goods denied to the peace chief. As a result, Chickasaw war chiefs valued and closely guarded their relations with the British. After the founding of Louisiana in 1699, peace chiefs sought to improve their own standing by dealing with the French, who, in turn, wanted to break the alliance between Chickasaws and France's imperial rivals. France's overtures produced results.

As late as 1720, the French believed that they and the British held equal influence among the Chickasaws.[33]

The façade came crashing down in 1729 when Natchez Indians destroyed the encroaching French settlement at present-day Natchez, Mississippi. In the preceding years, French colonists had demanded more and more Natchez land for their plantations. When the Natchez resisted, the French commandant threatened to burn their temple. The Natchez feigned acquiescence and then attacked the outpost. They killed more than 200 French men, women, and children and captured about 300 black slaves and fifty colonists. For the next two years, the French and their Choctaw allies retaliated against the Natchez with a war that crushed the nation and sent refugees fleeing throughout the South. Many Natchez found shelter among the Chickasaws, which the French interpreted as an act of war on the part of the host nation.[34]

Between 1731 and 1735, Chickasaws and the French fought an odd war, in which Chickasaws remained on the defensive and French refused to attack, instead encouraging their allies to invade Chickasaw Country. The French promised to continue the war unless the Chickasaws expelled the Natchez refugees. Most Chickasaws considered the condition unacceptable and a betrayal of their Natchez allies. By 1735, however, both Bienville and some Chickasaw leaders tired of war and sought a route to peace. Weighing the potential cost of an extended campaign in Chickasaw Country and the lack of French casualties thus far, Bienville believed that his superiors would not object to ending the conflict. At the same time, Chickasaw chief Ymahatabe, a leader among the towns closest to French Lower Louisiana and most vulnerable to Choctaw raids, approached the French to open peace negotiations.[35] But Ymahatabe represented only one faction of Chickasaws. In ensuing months, actions by other Chickasaws, the Illinois, and the French scuttled Ymahatabe and Bienville's efforts at peace.

In the spring of 1735, a Lieutenant Ducoder and ten soldiers journeyed from Fort de Chartres to Arkansas Post to retrieve 1,700 pounds of gunpowder abandoned the previous fall by three French officers. Although France was at war with Natchez and Chickasaws, those officers had left the gunpowder behind in order to make room in the semiannual French imperial convoy for the merchandise they would use to start their side business in the fur trade. As Ducoder made his way south, a party of Illinois Indians raided one of the northern Chickasaw towns clustered near present-day Tupelo, Mississippi. Like several parties the preceding winter, the Illinois

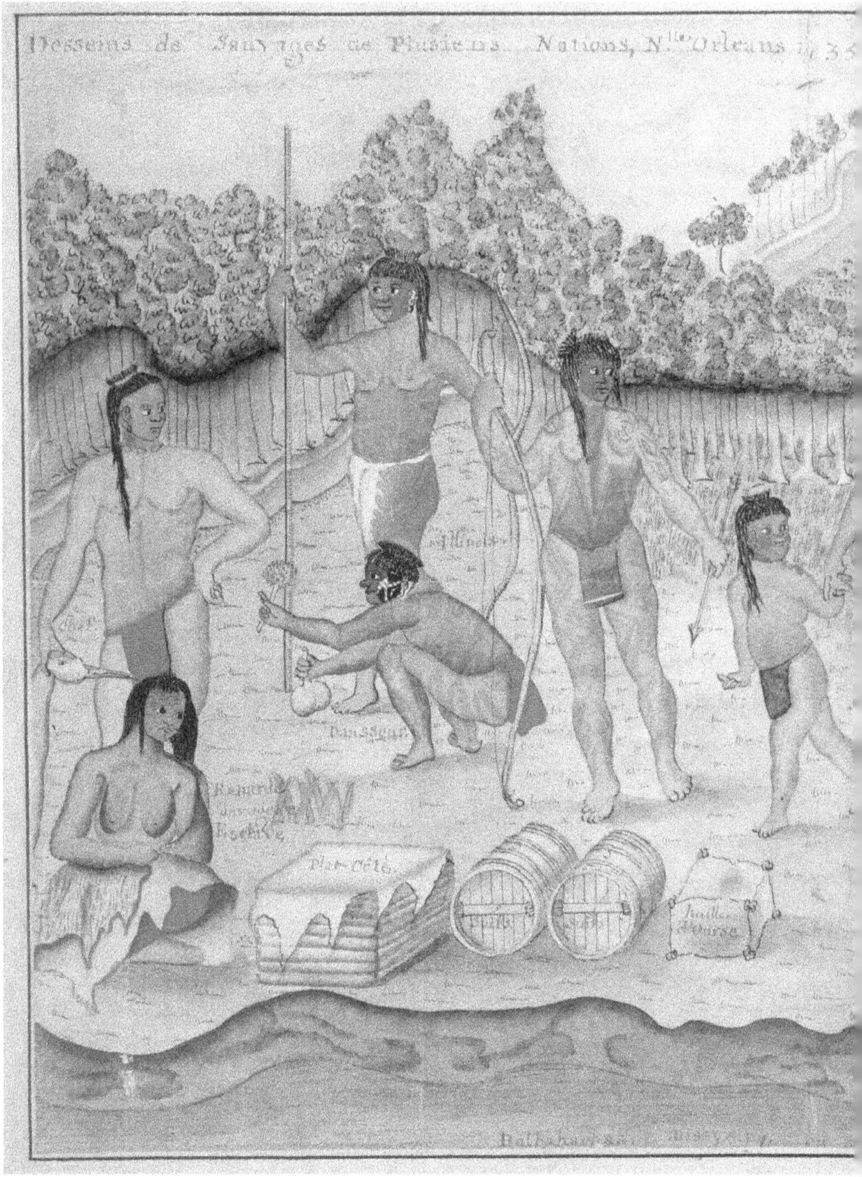

Fig. 3.2 Illinois Indians (center and left) with a Fox slave (sitting, left) and containers of tallow, bear oil, and meat at New Orleans.

sought captives. After abducting some Chickasaw women, the Illinois headed north to safety. Mingo Ouma, the Chickasaw chief and Ymahatabe's main rival, led 240 Chickasaw and Natchez men after their enemies, to rescue the women or exact revenge on the Illinois. Heading to the Mississippi River, the Illinois' usual return route, Mingo Ouma and his men discovered Ducoder's small force resting on the east bank of the river. As they approached, Chickasaws called out not to shoot, but the French, either too frightened to listen or unable to understand, fired at the Indians. Chickasaws and Natchez quickly counterattacked, killing nine soldiers and capturing Ducoder, one other man, and their valuable cargo. The next report from Ducoder came while he was a captive in the Chickasaw Nation.[36]

Each incident in that chain of events—the French officers' blunder, the Illinois raid, and the Chickasaw-Natchez capture of Ducoder's boat—might appear minor in the long history of fraught relations between Illinois, Chickasaws, and the French. But, together, they pushed Bienville to a course of action that wrecked French ambitions in the midcontinent. In capturing Ducoder and his men, Mingo Ouma ruined Ymahatabe's hope of making peace with the French. Bienville had used the absence of French casualties to justify ending the war. When he learned of the attack and the dead soldiers, he determined that war was "the only means that [he] had left to get out of this affair honorably."[37] Neither Bienville nor the empire could abide a direct attack on French troops. Bienville hoped that a campaign against the Chickasaws would restore his honor and that of the colony.

For a year after Ducoder's capture, Bienville planned his campaign against the Chickasaws and ignored the troubling omens that plagued him. First, Bienville knew that autumn, not spring, offered the best opportunity for a successful campaign against the Chickasaws. In the fall, the produce in Chickasaw fields would allow a longer campaign, and as an invading army consumed their food supplies, the Chickasaws would face starvation, weakening their resistance. A "slowness in preparations" delayed the campaign until spring 1736, an inauspicious season, but Bienville hoped a large-enough force could overpower the Chickasaws. The governor, however, mustered a limited number of able-bodied French soldiers. Drawing on the posts at New Orleans and Mobile as well as recruiting colonists from the Gulf Coast posts, Bienville gathered some 500 French men, still too few, he believed, to ensure success against the Chickasaws. To the north, Pierre d'Artaguiette, French commandant in the Illinois Country, led fewer than half the number that Bienville expected, marching with fewer than 150 officers, soldiers, and militia. Moreover, disease struck Illinois and Miamis, rendering them unable to raid the Chickasaws in the months leading up to the campaign.[38]

Crucially, Bienville's plan depended on close coordination with d'Artaguiette. Leaving from Mobile, Bienville and his army of French soldiers and militia would join Choctaw fighters before marching on the Chickasaws from the south. From the Illinois Country, d'Artaguiette's troops supplemented by a small force led by François-Marie Bissot de Vinsenne and aided by Illinois, Iroquois, Miami, and Quapaw warriors would attack the Chickasaws from the north. The French had difficulty communicating between Lower Louisiana and the Illinois Country in the best of conditions. With Chickasaws and their allies looking for French couriers, rapid communication was out of the question. By February 1736, with Bienville's legion running behind schedule, the governor had no way to alert d'Artaguiette of his new timeline. As a result, when d'Artaguiette arrived at the Prudhomme Bluffs—present-day Memphis—at the end of February, he did not know that he lacked support from the South.[39]

Early on the morning of March 25, 1736, Palm Sunday, d'Artaguiette stood just outside Chokkilissa—better known by its Choctaw name, Ogoula Tchetoka—which sat at the northwest corner of the clustered Chickasaw towns. Having left twenty-five French soldiers at Prudhomme Bluffs, d'Artaguiette had about 120 French troops, mostly militia, along with about 200 or 250 Piankashaws and Kaskaskias and another sixty to eighty Iroquois and Quapaws. With a small contingent ordered to guard the baggage train, d'Artaguiette's attack force numbered about 400 fighters. At six or seven o'clock, they assaulted the fortified town. Although Chickasaws retreated to their fortifications, the attacking Indians achieved some early successes. Kaskaskia and Piankashaw warriors attacked a small cluster of cabins, capturing several Chickasaws and killing a chief offering a calumet, while Iroquois and Quapaws captured those who were too slow to reach shelter.[40]

For fifteen minutes, all appeared well for the French and their allies, but the battle turned when 400 to 500 Chickasaw warriors roared over the crest of a hill on their flank. Indian military strategy centered on surprise and minimizing casualties. Seeing the Chickasaw force, Kaskaskias and Piankashaws fled the battlefield, living to fight again. The French troops and militia retreated to their baggage drop, where many of them died. As Chickasaws routed d'Artaguiette's army, they captured d'Artaguiette, Vinsenne, the Jesuit Antoine Senat, and as many as nineteen other officers, enlisted soldiers, and militiamen. Capture offered only a brief respite from death. Because the French had killed Chickasaws and invaded their homes, they had earned retribution.[41]

As Chickasaw warriors entered Chokkilissa with their captives, the towns-women built two large fires, where the French men would meet death. From the middle of the afternoon until midnight, the Chickasaws tormented the invaders, punishing them for their crimes and soothing the souls of the dead. Later accounts say that Chickasaws focused especially on two of the men, d'Artaguiette as the leader and Father Senat, whom they considered a "war prophet." Seventeen or eighteen French men burned in the fires, singing loudly to show their bravery in the face of death. Chickasaws spared only two captives, whom they would trade for a chief kept prisoner by the French. In all, Chickasaws killed at least a third and maybe close to half of the 145 French troops at Ogoula Tchetoka, along with an unknown, but probably lower, number of Indian fighters. Chickasaw defenders suffered only eight to twenty casualties.[42]

As late as May 1736, Bienville had little idea of what had transpired at Chokkilissa. Only at the end of that month, after watching his French-Choctaw army melt away before Chickasaw resistance at Ackia, one of the southern Chickasaw towns, did Bienville begin to piece together the total failure of his campaign. When he finally sent a report of d'Artaguiette's defeat, the governor admitted, "The circumstances . . . are reported so variously that I have difficulty in reconciling all the accounts that I have received on this subject and find myself somewhat embarrassed in preparing myself to inform your Lordship of it." In the pages that followed, Bienville reported what he had been able to gather. The governor knew that the Chickasaws had killed d'Artaguiette and many of his men. What he could not have known is that their deaths marked the high-water point of French power in Middle America.[43]

The Chickasaw victories over d'Artaguiette and Bienville reinforced their identity as great warriors, both at home and abroad. The battles of Ackia and Chokkilissa became central events in the military history of the Chick-asaw nation. Nearly a century later, Chickasaws still told stories of their tri-umphs and displayed trophies taken from their vanquished foes. In 2017, the Chickasaw Nation announced that it would produce a feature film about the battle at Ackia and Chickasaws' successful "defense of [their] homeland" against a "powerful French Army." In the immediate aftermath of Ackia and Chokkilissa, Chickasaws expanded their claims to the north. In July 1736, French officers learned that Chickasaws with their Cherokee allies had built

a fort on the Ohio River, eighty leagues north of its confluence with the Wabash River, probably near present-day Louisville, Kentucky. From this
stronghold, Chickasaws and Cherokees raided French *voyageurs* on the Ohio
and Wabash Rivers. Just as troubling for the French, they believed that English traders based at the fort worked to attract French-allied Miamis, Weas,
and Piankashaws on the Wabash River.[44]

Chickasaws also used their victories as diplomatic weapons. Speaking in
council with Diron d'Artaguiette, the brother of the defeated and executed
Pierre, the winter after the battle, Mingo Ouma identified a particularly
weak spot for the French as he mocked their military failures and the cow-
ardice of their Indian allies. "Are they [the French] not satisfied," he asked,
"with the two attacks that they have made and in which they have not succeeded, because of the great confidence that they have had in the Indians
who accompany them?" Mingo Ouma condemned Illinois and Miamis as
craven and claimed that they had intended to escort d'Artaguiette to the
Chickasaws and abandon him. He lampooned the lack of bravery among
Choctaws, whom Chickasaws could scare away only having "to beat drums
in [their] cabins."[45]

If Mingo Ouma was trying to divide his enemies, he could not have picked
a better line of argument. The French already believed that Illinois and Miamis were cowards after they fled the field of battle at Chokkilissa. When
Bienville's army melted away before Ackia, the French governor lost much
of his confidence in the Choctaws as well. In planning his next campaign
against the Chickasaws, Bienville believed that he "could avoid the misfor-
tunes" of 1736 by excluding Illinois and Miamis.[46]

Illinois and Miamis, for their part, retained little confidence in French
power. D'Artaguiette demonstrated in his battlefield decisions how different
French military goals were from those of their Native allies. For Illinois and
Miamis, the refusal to retreat in the face of overwhelming numbers revealed
a wanton disregard for the lives of one's troops. With the element of surprise removed, responsible leaders fell back and tried again another day.
D'Artaguiette and his army ignored this rule and paid with their lives. But
in Illinois and Miami military culture, retreat carried less disgrace than
death. Those warriors had no interest in sacrificing their lives for European
ideas of honor. Instead, they treated the French like disgraced warriors and
were wary of following them into battle again. Even as Illinois and Miamis
continued their war with the Chickasaws, they preferred small-scale raids
for captives, scalps, and plunder.[47]

The embarrassing defeats and heavy casualties rendered the failures at Chokkilissa and Ackia devastating for the French. The identities of the dead men made the losses catastrophic. The list of the deceased reads like a who's who of French colonial officers: Vinsenne, d'Artaguiette, St. Ange, Dutisné, Coulanges, Tonty. Many of these men were the sons or brothers of more famous officers, but they had all spent years and decades, often from childhood, living and working among Indian nations in the midcontinent. The greatest loss was François-Marie Bissot de Vinsenne. He, like Pierre Groston de St. Ange, Louis-Marie-Charles Dutisné, Pierre-Antoine Tonty, and many of the others, had worked in the midcontinent from a young age. Through nearly two decades of service among Miamis, Weas, and Piankashaws, Vinsenne built the sort of personal relationships on which the French empire depended. His reputation among the Indians of Middle America was such that, in late 1736 or early 1737, a party of Wendat Indians returning from a raid against the Chickasaws sought to replace Vinsenne by giving a captive to Detroit commandant Nicolas-Joseph de Noyelles de Fleurimont, formerly stationed at Fort Miami on the Wabash River. In turn, de Noyelles presented the captive to the Indians of Detroit, including some Miamis. Following custom, they burned the captured Chickasaw at the stake to assuage their grief over Vinsenne's death.[48]

Unable to admit defeat, Bienville mounted another campaign against the Chickasaws in the winter of 1739–1740. Illinois warriors joined the French army expecting to fight. Instead, Bienville put them to work "leveling a road" to transport artillery to the Chickasaw towns. After four months of digging in the dirt—time they felt would have been better spent killing Chickasaws—the Illinois returned home. At the end of March, after the Illinois left Fort Assumption, Chickasaw diplomats approached the French about making peace. Bienville and the Chickasaws came to terms, and the French agreed to "restrain the nations of the north and of the Mississippi" from attacking Chickasaws.[49] Once again, the French made peace with the Chickasaws without consulting their Illinois allies. As before, Illinois ignored the agreement.

French officials recognized the danger and futility of forging such agreements without the input of their allies, but Bienville hoped that a peace treaty, no matter how tentative or weak, gave the appearance of some return on the one million livres France had poured into its war with the Chickasaws. The treaty only enraged France's Indian allies. In early 1740, one French officer worried over how Choctaws would respond, noting that the nation "seems very much irritated and breathes nothing but vengeance." Iroquois warriors still in the region ignored the treaty and took five scalps and three captives before returning to Canada. A priest in the Illinois Country reporting on Cahokias and Tamaroas at his mission wrote, "The failure of M. de Bienville's army against the Chickasaws has strangely indisposed our domiciled savages against us, and I simply do not see why they do not rise up completely." Meanwhile, as early as the summer of 1740, Chickasaw and Cherokee raiders once again patrolled the Ohio and Mississippi Rivers, ambushing careless travelers.[50]

By the early 1740s, the French alliance in the central Mississippi valley was in tatters. Far from ending the Chickasaw threat, Bienville's failed campaigns devastated the French and alienated their Native allies. Distrust destroyed the once-close alliance between the French and Illinois and Miamis, as none of the parties thought the other dependable in battle or at the negotiating table. With the deaths of well-known and well-liked officers, the French lost the agents needed to repair relations. Meanwhile, newly arrived British traders on the upper Ohio River used their trade goods, which were superior in quality and less expensive than French-made items, to lure away Miamis and other nations of the Wabash River valley. For the next fifteen years, the French struggled to retain their Indian allies in the face of British incursions into Middle America.

≈   On June 1, 1752, 400 or 500 Fox, Sauk, Menonimee, and Sioux warriors, possibly joined by some Potawatomis and Ho-Chunks as well, attacked a combined Cahokia and Michigamea village about a mile north of Fort de Chartres. With only about one hundred fighting men from a total population around 400, the Cahokias and Michigameas were badly outnumbered. The raiders killed thirty Illinois, captured forty prisoners, and burned half the town, losing only four men in the process. Warfare between Illinois and Foxes was nothing new. They had been at odds for more than half a century. But this assault was different, because Jean-Jacques Macarty Mactigue, commandant of Fort de Chartres, had encouraged the Foxes and their allies to destroy the Illinois town.[51]

Less than three weeks later, about 250 Ottawa and Ojibwe warriors led by the French-Ottawa soldier Charles-Michel Mouet de Langlade surprised Pickawillany, a Miami town on the Great Miami River in what is now western Ohio. Anishinaabeg warriors captured several women and three British traders outside the walls of the palisaded town. The remaining

Miamis—a diminished population because most of the town's men were away hunting—took refuge inside the walls. Even with only fifteen to twenty men left in Pickawillany, Miamis held off the Ottawas and Ojibwes for several hours. Outside the town, Langlade and his men offered to withdraw if the Miamis would hand over the British traders still inside the walls. Miamis agreed on the condition that the traders would not be harmed. But when Miamis opened the gates to the town, an Anishinaabe warrior killed a wounded trader. Then Ottawas and Ojibwes seized the town's chief, Memeskia, also called La Demoiselle and Old Briton. Memeskia soon joined the trader in the afterlife at the hands of Langlade and the Anishinaabeg.[52]

A dozen years earlier, French-backed assaults on Miami and Illinois towns would have been unthinkable. But in the wake of the Chickasaw wars, the political landscape of Middle America shifted, creating a context in which French officials believed that violence against two of their most important allies served the empire's best interests. Bienville's failed campaigns against the Chickasaws demonstrated the attenuated military power of the French empire in North America. Continued Chickasaw aggression to the north following the 1740 peace agreement proved France's weakness as an ally. In 1745, Louisiana governor Pierre de Rigaud de Vaudreuil de Cavagnial complained that "the acts of brigandage" committed by Chickasaws on the Ohio River might "alienate all the nations of this continent" from the French. By posing his fear in the conditional tense, Vaudreuil failed to recognize the rifts that Chickasaws and their Cherokee allies had already created in French-Indian alliances in Middle America. Canadian governor Charles de Beauharnois de la Boische better understood the situation when he reported the increased difficulty in dealing with the Indians of the midcontinent following the French-Indian defeats of the 1730s. At the end of the 1730s, Pendalouan, an isolationist Sinago Ottawa leader, tried to end the alliance between the French and his nation by sneaking into the fort at Michilimackinac and blowing up its powder magazine. At Detroit, Wendats allied with southern Indians, angering their Ottawa, Ojibwe, and Mississauga neighbors. A number of Wendats then left for a new town about one hundred miles south of Lake Erie, where they forged new trade connections with the Iroquois and their British allies. Meanwhile, in what is now Mississippi, Choctaw chief Red Shoes plunged his nation into civil war after forging an alliance with Chickasaws and South Carolina traders.[53] These rifts originated in the context of politics between and within Indian nations. But in each instance, growing frustrations with the French proved to be a crucial factor in the shifting allegiances.

A lack of trade goods and gifts exacerbated the rifts in France's alliances and prevented the extension of French influence. The obligations of fictive kinship needed reinforcement through gift giving. Without periodic renewal of those bonds, onetime allies began to search for better opportunities. British traders courted midcontinent Indians by favorably contrasting the quality of their goods with those of France. In 1742, one Briton told a Kaskaskia man, "The Frenchman is a dog who devours you. He has only bad merchandise and sells it very dearly." At the start of King George's War in 1744, Great Britain blockaded French North America, drastically reducing the material support the colonies received from the empire. By 1747, French posts in the Illinois Country had not received supplies from New Orleans for more than a year. Chickasaw and Cherokee raiders waited on the Mississippi River hoping to stop the convoy before it reached its destination. That year and the next, rumors of anti-French conspiracies spread through Middle America. An official in Quebec worried that Claude de Bertet, the commandant at Fort de Chartres, could not quell the unrest without any gifts to offer. About Bertet and his situation, the Canadian noted, "his poverty has reached the point that there is not in the King's stores nor among the traders, an ell of cloth, nor a particle of ammunition." At different times, Vaudreuil pulled out of negotiations with potentially valuable allies, including the Chickasaws, citing French "indigence."[54] Even if he brokered accords, the governor lacked the goods necessary to seal the pacts. Alliances depended on generous and frequent gifts. By the late 1740s, the ongoing difficulty of supplying the Illinois Country had reached a critical level.

In this tumultuous political climate, France needed and lacked officers who could soothe tensions and reinforce weakening ties without the benefit of gifts. In particular, the empire needed men who could use their personal relationships with Native leaders to ease the strain caused by military defeats and missing goods. However, the French ban on intermarriage undercut the possibility of relying on family relationships to strengthen the empire's position. And many officers with fictive kin ties to Indian nations in the midcontinent had died on the battlefield or in Chickasaw fires at Chokkilissa. With the deaths of d'Artaguiette and the rest, France faced the challenge of replacing multiple post commandants and their key subordinates all at once. In better circumstances, they could have relied on military strength and generosity until new relationships and kin ties could be established. In the context of the 1740s, the French empire lacked both the resources and the time necessary to rebuild its fracturing alliance.

A few new officers met or exceeded the standards of their predecessors. At Fort de Chartres, the competent Bertet served well from 1742 until his untimely death in 1749. In 1748, despite a lack of material resources, Bertet had in fact foiled Memeskia's first attempts to gain Illinois support and prevented a rumored multinational attack on the French posts in Illinois. Upon his death, Canadian governor Roland Michel Barrin de La Galissonière remarked simply, "He was an excellent officer." On the Wabash River at Vincennes, Louis Groston de St. Ange et de Bellerive, the son of Robert Groston de St. Ange, replaced the post's namesake. At the time of St. Ange's appointment, Bienville reported that St. Ange's colleagues considered him "a brave lad of great merit." St. Ange spent the previous sixteen years as a junior officer at St. Joseph and then under Bourgmont on the Missouri River, before assuming command of a small fort on that river. He was well trained to replace the talented Vinsenne. The French soon benefited from the relationship he built with Piankashaws who lived at Chippekoke near Vincennes and at Vermillion just north of the French post. As couriers carrying wampum belts traversed the midcontinent urging action against the French, Chippekoke and Vermillion Piankashaws refused them, largely due to their relationship with St. Ange.[55]

Other new French commanders faltered, however, because they lacked the skill, knowledge, and connections necessary to smooth relations between the empire and Indian nations. In 1751, Jean-Jacques Macarty Mactigue assumed command of Fort de Chartres and soon found himself overwhelmed by his responsibilities. Writing of his many duties, Macarty complained that "one man only cannot suffice for it all." Macarty's taste for liquor compounded his woes. Within two years of his appointment, Macarty's superiors recommended his removal.[56]

Macarty even undermined the successes of other more competent officers such as St. Ange. In December 1751, not long after his arrival in Illinois, Macarty arrested Piankashaw chief Le Loup after he and a few warriors had skirmished in the woods with two French men. Le Loup's Piankashaws and the French hunters both knew that southern Indians roamed the woods of the Illinois Country, and they probably fired on each other due to mistaken identity and heightened anxiety. Macarty claimed, however, that Le Loup had joined the anti-French coalition and came to Illinois to attack its European residents. Fear and quick triggers created bad feelings where none had previously existed. Despite Le Loup's record of aiding the French and his protests that he and his men were traveling south to fight the Chickasaws, Macarty held the chief prisoner for six months. In that time, conditions on the Wabash deteriorated. St. Ange reported Piankashaw attacks on French traders and posts and warned his fellow commandants to prepare for "the storm which is ready to burst on the French." For half a decade, St. Ange had smoothed tensions between France and the Piankashaws, but Macarty through his incompetence and ignorance undid all that St. Ange accomplished. Perhaps Macarty grew into his position. He remained in the Illinois Country until 1760. But those first years in the midcontinent cast a troubling shadow over the rest of his tenure.[57]

The upheaval extended to the governor's chair. From 1703 to 1747, two men—Philippe de Rigaud de Vaudreuil and Charles de Beauharnois de la Boische—governed Canada. The long terms of Vaudreuil and Beauharnois provided much-needed stability to a colony, the rule of which depended on deep knowledge of local affairs and personal relationships that could only be formed over time and sustained effort. In the eight years between Beauharnois's retirement in 1747 and the appointment of Vaudreuil's son to the governorship in 1755, four different governors led Canada. Their tenures ran from as little as a few months to three years, and they all lacked enough time to learn how to administer the sprawling colony. Unfortunately for France, the revolving cast of governors presided over New France at a particularly tumultuous time. From Quebec, the inexperienced governors could only grasp at the loose threads of their unraveling alliances.[58]

At the end of the 1740s, despite a limited capability to provide military and economic support, a new guard of French officials determined to revitalize the fragmenting alliance. Due to a lack of experience, however, they pursued the worst possible strategy to accomplish their goals. In 1749, Antoine-Louis Rouillé replaced the long-tenured Jean-Frédéric Phélypeaux, Comte de Maurepas, as the French colonial minister. Possessing an exaggerated sense of French power in North America, Rouillé demanded subservience and obedience from France's Indian allies. France had strained to sustain its alliances even when seeking mediation and offering plentiful gifts. The empire only alienated its friends by demanding submission while providing little incentive to do so. Wendats who relocated from Detroit explained to an English trader that they had broken with their former allies because France demanded too many warriors and treated them as "Slaves," while offering trade goods that were too expensive for Wendats to purchase. In

1749, the new Canadian governor repeatedly offered few, if any, gifts to visiting Miami delegations, all the while condescending to his guests.[59] Throughout the midcontinent, longtime French allies began seeking new friends. They found a warm reception among British traders, who had been working to expand their influence in Middle America since the turn of the eighteenth century.

More than any other anti-French movement, Memeskia and his alliance reshaped the politics of the midcontinent and commanded the attention of French officials in both Louisiana and Canada. Memeskia's import stemmed from his place in the politics and geography of Middle America. In the 1740s, Memeskia's Miamis lived at Kekionga on the portage between the Maumee River and the Wabash River, near present-day Fort Wayne, Indiana, a crucial point in the travel route between Canada and the Illinois Country. But, in part due to the high price and low quality of French merchandise, he began pursuing new sources of European goods. Through Wendats, Memeskia sought an alliance with Iroquois, especially Senecas, and British traders from Pennsylvania. Encouraged by these new connections, Wendat chief Orontony, also called Nicolas, and Memeskia planned a large-scale attack on French posts in the lower Great Lakes. Memeskia would attack nearby Fort Miami, while Wendats pillaged Detroit and Ojibwes drove the French from Michilimackinac. Two of the three plans fizzled, but in the late summer of 1747, Memeskia attacked Fort Miami, capturing eight French men and their goods before burning part of the fort. Not waiting for French retaliation, Memeskia abandoned Kekionga, choosing a new site at Pickawillany on the Great Miami River. At the intersection of several trading paths, Pickawillany offered an advantageous location for the Miamis, much as Kekionga had in previous years.[60] From their new town, the dissident Miamis could easily travel east toward the Iroquois and British traders as well as contact Kickapoos, Illinois, Mascoutens, Potawatomis, and other potential allies in the west.

One British trader in particular—George Croghan—seized the opportunity to extend his trade network to the Miamis. Croghan had immigrated to Pennsylvania from Ireland in 1741 and almost immediately began to trade with Indian nations in the upper reaches of the Ohio valley. By the end of the decade, he probably commanded one hundred traders, drovers, servants, and slaves. Croghan had been active among Shawnees, Delawares, and Wendats to the north and the east of Pickawillany for several years. Using his connections with those nations, the Irishman wasted little time before approaching Memeskia and the Miamis. No later than the winter of 1749–1750, Croghan established a trading house at Pickawillany and began to broker new agreements between Miamis and the Pennsylvania government. Croghan's influence among the Miamis so frightened the French that the commandant at Detroit offered $1,000 for the Irishman's scalp.[61]

To the French empire, the potential loss of its Wabash River allies to the British made Memeskia's aggression a particularly dangerous challenge. Echoing earlier warnings about a Chickasaw-English alliance on the Mississippi River, French officials dreaded the risks posed by Memeskia and his English backers on the Wabash. French colonial minister Maurepas warned Louisiana governor Vaudreuil that Memeskia might break communication between Louisiana and Canada and "even occasion the loss of most of the posts of these two colonies." More than most French officials, Vaudreuil recognized the centrality of the Wabash River to the future of the French empire. He repeatedly wrote to France requesting authorization to build a new fort between Vincennes and the Mississippi River. Others likewise recognized the value of a new fort on the Wabash River and also understood the steps necessary to calm the unrest in the region. "By living among them [the Wabash River Indians]," one observer wrote, "we would further gain their confidence, which is very necessary to us; and as soon as they know that the French have strengthened themselves by a good settlement in that region . . . , they will lose the desire of trading with the English and will bring us their peltry."[62] By building relationships while demonstrating French power and wealth, the French hoped to resuscitate the alliances that had deteriorated in the previous decade.

Memeskia, though, not the French, possessed the kin ties necessary to construct far-reaching alliances. The three divisions of the Miami Nation formed the core of Memeskia's multinational coalition, and to them, he had recently added Wendats south of Lake Erie, Iroquois, and British traders from Pennsylvania. Memeskia sought to bind his new powerful friends in the east to the Miami alliance network in the west. The Miami chief used existing connections to enlist support from the three nations' western allies. For decades, a small band of Miamis had lived with the St. Joseph Potawatomis, and since the 1730s, Kickapoos and Mascoutens resided near the Weas at Ouiatenon. Memeskia gained support from all three of these nations, but only from those towns that lived near or with Miamis and not those located closer to Miami enemies such as the Foxes and the Sauks. Near the Illinois Country, Weas and Piankashaws maintained close ties with the

Kaskaskias. When Memeskia's ally La Mouche Noire, a Piankashaw chief, reached out to the Illinois, he contacted his two brothers, who were Kaskaskia chiefs. In turn, Kaskaskias contacted the other divisions of the Illinois, as well as their trans-Mississippi allies, the Osages and the Missourias, finding at least some success among all parties.[63] Kinship ties alone did not produce allies, but they opened the door for diplomats to forge new political associations.

Rarely did an entire nation join the Miami chief, and sometimes only fractions of towns allied with him; but those who stayed behind were hesitant to attack their kin at the behest of the French. Potawatomis remaining at St. Joseph promised Miamis that they would not attack them, and in 1751, they even refused to join Potawatomis of Chikagou and Ojibwes on a raid against the Miamis' close kin the Illinois. Late that winter, after a small French-Indian force killed two of Memeskia's followers, Kaskaskia chief Ousaouikintonga demanded answers from the governor of Canada, asking, "Why, my father, why do you not strike me myself? Why do you strike a tribe allied to me where all my relatives are?"[64] Ousaouikintonga may have preferred an alliance with the French to joining Memeskia, but the bonds of kinship preserved the peace between Ousaouikintonga's Kaskaskias and Memeskia's Miamis.

By the end of 1751, France had lost the nations of the Wabash valley, which, along with the Illinois Country, formed the base of its alliance network and of its empire in the midcontinent. Memeskia's followers and their neutral relatives stretched from Lake Erie to the Mississippi River. Weas stopped visiting Ouiatenon, while Miamis continued to attack Fort Miami. Near Vincennes, Piankashaws, disaffected after Macarty's arrest of their chief, killed nine French men and two slaves in the fall and early winter of 1751. At the same time, the French received word that Illinois, Weas, and Piankashaws were to join Delawares, Shawnees, and Iroquois in council at Pickawillany. Other Illinois and Piankashaws along with some Osages planned to build a fort between the Wabash and the Illinois Rivers from which they could attack French posts. Meanwhile, the French believed that neutrality was the best they could hope for from Kickapoos and Mascoutens near Ouiatenon.[65]

In this context, French officials determined to use their remaining allies to destroy Memeskia's alliance. Foxes and their allies welcomed the opportunity, because for decades, Illinois, Miamis, Anishinaabeg, and others had waged devastating wars against the Foxes rather than allow them to ally with the French. They needed little encouragement from Macarty to launch their raid against the Michigamea and Cahokia village. Unlike in the midcontinent, the Ottawas and Ojibwes of Michilimackinac who attacked Pickawillany remained staunch allies of the French, because they maintained kinship ties with French officials and built a truly multiethnic community. For example, Langlade, the French-Ottawa officer who led the Pickawillany raid, was a respected warrior among the Ottawas and an officer in the French *troupes de la marine*. He, along with other Anishinaabeg men and women, served as crucial links in the alliance with the French empire.[66]

The French-backed attacks on Pickawillany and the Cahokia-Michigamea town in June 1752 succeeded insofar as they stalled Memeskia's alliance and removed an influential man who was antagonistic to French interests. Additionally, British and Iroquois refusal to back retaliatory attacks proposed by Miamis, Shawnees, Delawares, and others demonstrated that they were feckless allies. But that summer's violence failed to resurrect the alliances between those nations and France. A veneer of reunion settled over the region, but it masked ongoing dissatisfaction with the French empire.[67] The issues that undermined the alliance—French military weakness, a dearth of gifts and trade goods, and a lack of kinship ties—prevented efforts at reconciliation between the empire and its longtime allies. By the early 1750s, France had lost most of its former influence in the midcontinent.

≈ After Memeskia's death, France sought to impose its own peace in Middle America. The French court wanted to avoid another war with Great Britain as well as with the Indian nations of the midcontinent, nations the French assumed acted as British proxies. The king and his ministers believed that the best way to keep peace between the two empires was to maintain clear borders between French and British claims in the Ohio valley. In 1749, near the height of Memeskia's influence, France sent Pierre-Joseph Céloron de Blainville to survey the Ohio valley and bury lead plates at the edge of French claims. Hidden plates did little to establish a boundary line, so in 1753, France began to build a line of border forts. With these forts guarding French claims, France hoped to remove the instability and uncertainty that might lead to war.[68]

Instead, the new fortifications exacerbated already-fraught relations with the British and with Native peoples in the region. In May 1754, an ambitious Virginia land speculator and militia officer, George Washington, marched with a small force of militiamen and Mingo Indians into present-day western Pennsylvania. There, he ambushed French troops led by Joseph Coulon de Villiers de Jumonville, charged with building a fort in the area. When the shooting ended, Jumonville lay wounded. Mingo chief Tanaghrisson walked over to the injured officer and stated, "Tu n'es pas encore mort, me père" (Thou are not yet dead, my father), and then buried his tomahawk in the Frenchman's skull.[69]

Like Jumonville, prostrate and bloody before the approaching Tanaghrisson, the French empire in North America was not yet dead, but it soon would be. The subsequent Seven Years' War shattered French ambitions in North America, but in the midcontinent, the war was something of a coup de grace, putting the French empire out of its misery. For decades, French officials had struggled and failed to construct a powerful empire out of a series of isolated posts stretched across half a continent. Years of warfare and poverty had eroded French authority in the midcontinent, relegating the empire's power to posts in the upper and eastern Great Lakes and in Lower Louisiana but not along the pivotal stretches of river that connected the two regions. Although French civilians built prosperous communities at Kaskaskia, Ste. Genevieve, and elsewhere in Middle America, the French empire struggled to link personal relationships to imperial goals. With French civilians focused on their own interests and Versailles unwilling to expend the necessary money or manpower, the French empire depended on Native allies both to maintain peace among the many nations in the midcontinent and to prevent British expansion into the Ohio and Mississippi River valleys. Although necessary, dependence on Indian allies drew France into costly local conflicts. The French government then poured millions of livres into unwanted wars that offered little benefit to the empire even had the French and their allies won. When they lost, France appeared a weak, unworthy ally to the Indian nations of Middle America.

During the 1740s, the French empire in its diminished stature watched as a parade of former allies spurned its soldiers or, worse still, joined English traders in new coalitions. With the outbreak of the Seven Years' War, the Indians of the midcontinent demonstrated their ambivalence about France even while they upheld the duties of allies when called on by other Indian nations. Illinois and Miamis were conspicuously absent at the defeat of British general Edward Braddock in July 1755. Then Illinois and Miamis' longtime Shawnee allies called for aid in addressing a growing list of grievances against the British. In 1753, South Carolinians had imprisoned some Shawnees as they returned from fighting Catawbas. A Shawnee chief died in captivity. The next year, British and Iroquois had conspired to steal Shawnee land in what is now central Pennsylvania. When a contingent of Shawnee and Delaware diplomats protested, British hanged them. Shawnees asked their western allies "to come and avenge the insult done them by the English." Illinois and Miamis traveled up the Ohio to meet their friends and pledged support. In the summer of 1756, thirty-two Shawnees, Delawares, and Illinois with a small party of French troops destroyed British Fort Granville, which was located on the stolen lands, and killed or captured its garrison. Meanwhile, Shawnees led 150 Miamis and Weas to South Carolina, where they attacked farms, towns, and a fort. Another group of Shawnees and Miamis destroyed Fort Vause in Virginia. Vengeance had been achieved. The dead had been soothed. Illinois and most Miamis returned home feeling satisfied at having performed the duties of good allies.[70]

Kinship ties continued to influence when and why people would or would not participate in war. French officers believed that Miamis and Illinois had entered the war on their side, but they soon learned the limits of their alliances with those nations. After the summer of 1756, France struggled to attract midcontinent Indians to its banner. In 1757 and again in 1759, Governor Vaudreuil gathered 1,800 Indians at Montreal for major campaigns. Allies came from as far away as present-day Iowa and Minnesota. No Illinois made the trip in either instance. In 1757, seventeen Miamis and Weas came from the Wabash River, and none came from that region two years later. The experiences of the previous two decades had loosed the bonds that might have influenced those nations to support France. Then, in 1758, the British agreed to return to Shawnees and Delawares the lands signed away by Iroquois diplomats a few years earlier. When British traders returned to the region soon after, Miamis declared that "they would remain stedfast Friends to the English as long as the Sun & Moon gave light."[71]

Afterward, France struggled to attract Native support from the upper Ohio to the Illinois Country. In 1759, the commandant at Fort de Chartres complained, "Most of our nations remained behind, having been spectators." After years of struggling to recruit allies in the Illinois Country, another French officer evinced his frustration by condemning Kaskaskia warriors as "Idle and very drunken." Too late, French officials realized that Native peoples "wish[ed] there were neither French nor English" in the Ohio valley. Well before the war ended—and, in some cases, before it started—nations that had once been France's staunchest allies abandoned the empire. These were the ramifications of Bienville's failures in Chickasaw Country, France's unreliability as a trading partner, and the lack of kinship ties between French officers and Native leaders in Middle America.[72]

However, the kinship networks that permeated Middle America could pull in a variety of directions. Because some Miamis and Weas at St. Joseph and elsewhere had married into Anishinaabe communities, they fought the British, making different choices than their Wabash River relatives. Connections between Anishinaabeg and the French remained strong, even while French relations with Illinois and Wabash River communities faltered. Those links made some Miamis and Weas more likely to join their Potawatomi, Ojibwe, and Ottawa relatives in Montreal. In 1757 and 1759, small numbers of Miamis from St. Joseph joined Potawatomis who made the trip to Montreal. As late as November 1760, interrelated Weas, Potawatomis, Wendats, and Ojibwes stood together and voiced support for the French. Kinship did not, however, guarantee that they would fight. In 1757, the eight St. Joseph Miamis who had traveled to Montreal left before the campaign began "without warning anyone," and their "contagious" example convinced "many others" to depart as well.[73] Getting Indian allies to the front lines remained complicated, but webs of kin ties opened doors that may have otherwise remained closed.

Despite decades of French colonialism, the political world of the midcontinent during the 1750s bore more resemblance to Chickasaw chief Mingo Ouma's 1737 map than to European conceptions of the region. When French imperialists thought of Middle America, they envisioned an ideal empire, in which they directed allied Indian nations against their Indian and European rivals. In reality, peoples such as the Illinois, Chickasaws, and Miamis pursued their own policies and employed diplomacy and warfare to achieve their own ambitions independent of European wishes. In the midcontinent, European colonies remained small circles surrounded by larger, more influential Indian nations. Far from French colonial power centers in Quebec and the Gulf Coast, officials in Middle America could achieve little without Indian support. But to gain that backing, the French tied themselves to the demands and expectations of their allies. The incompatibility of Native and European goals weakened and eventually fractured the French alliance in the midcontinent.

The work of empire and alliance was unremitting, exhausting, and aggravating, and at Paris in 1763, French diplomats happily washed their hands of their North American colonies. To Great Britain, they ceded all of their claims east of the Mississippi River. In a secret treaty the previous year,

France had granted to Spain everything west of the river. Without the troubles of North America draining its resources, France could focus on defending its more profitable colonies in the Caribbean.[74] However, the end of the Seven Years' War and the death of the France's North American empire brought more unrest to the midcontinent, as Indian nations, Great Britain, and Spain struggled for power in the absence of the French. In the years following France's departure from North America, new empires tried to navigate the region's politics and geography, while Native peoples envisioned a future with no empires at all.

CHAPTER FOUR

A New World?

In April 1764, Ottawa chief Pontiac arrived in the Illinois Country. Over the past year, Indian fighters allied with Pontiac had driven British forces out of nine forts in the Great Lakes and Ohio valley and laid siege to three others. Now Pontiac came to Illinois to expand his alliance and revitalize his war against the would-be conquerors. Standing before Fort de Chartres's French commandant, Pierre-Joseph Neyon de Villiers, Pontiac recounted the message of anticolonial, pan-Indian unity—nativism—that drove him to battle the British. He apologized to Neyon de Villiers for not listening to "the Words the Collers [wampum belts] and the Callumets of Peace" that he had sent to the region's Indian nations, but the French could no longer influence affairs in Indian Country. France had just concluded the Seven Years' War and surrendered its North American claims to Great Britain and Spain. Throughout Middle America, French officers urged their former Indian allies to make peace with the new British regime. Nativists rejected these overtures, fearing British land hunger and schemes to exterminate Native peoples. Pontiac told the French that, unless they would supply guns and ammunition, he and his allies had no use for them. Pontiac warned the French, "Thou goest against the orders of the Master of Life, & that all the red Men conform to his will, Thus I pray thee to talk no more of a Peace with the English, because I hate them." After more than a century of French demands, nativists envisioned a vast alliance of "all the nations of the Continent" that would rid North America of empires.[1]

A thousand miles away, merchants on the eastern seaboard also dreamed of the opportunities in postwar America. In designs incompatible with nativism, they lusted after the wealth to be extracted from the new British claims in the West. As Pontiac rallied support against Anglo colonialism, the Philadelphia businessmen John Baynton, Samuel Wharton, and George Morgan plotted to enter the region as traders and land speculators. In league with some of the most influential British officials in North America, they soon designed a much-larger endeavor in the West, one that would make them barons of an extensive colony on the Mississippi River. First, they needed to convince the British government of the colony's value to the crown. Their partner, New Jersey governor William Franklin, explained to a British minister, "The Country of the Illinois on the Mississippi, is generally allowed to be the most fertile & pleasant Part of all the Western Territory now in Possession of the English in North America." According to Franklin, lazy French farmers failed to take full advantage of the resources of the Illinois Country. Under British hands, the land would produce corn, cotton, hemp, flax, and silk. Illinois agriculture would feed Britain's North American empire, while also providing goods for export. Additionally, Franklin expected, "we might . . . carry on a more extensive & advantageous Furr-Trade, with the numerous Indian Nations . . . than was ever known since the first Settlement of America." All that was needed to acquire such riches was moderate support from the empire and the enterprise of "a Company of Gentlemen of Character & Fortune." In exchange for 1.2 million acres of land, Franklin along with Baynton, Wharton, Morgan, Superintendent of Northern Indian Affairs William Johnson, trader-turned-Indian-agent George Croghan, and four other men would exploit the potential of the Illinois Country for the profit of the empire.[2]

The upheaval of the Seven Years' War rarely reached the Illinois Country. But in the tumultuous years that followed, the region took center stage for Native peoples and Europeans who sought to impose a new order in the trans-Appalachian West. Following the 1763 Treaty of Paris, as France abandoned its Mississippi valley posts, Indians and Europeans alike observed a break with the past. It seemed as though a world of possibilities had opened up before them. In Great Britain and its Atlantic colonies, the acquisition of the Illinois Country sparked the imaginations of bureaucrats and colonists eager to expand their power and wealth. In London, the king's foreign affairs advisers saw an opportunity to shore up the defense of British North America. With France removed from the continent, the broad Mississippi would separate British holdings from Spanish rivals. With each empire on its own side of the river, they could avoid the territorial ambiguities that had sparked the Seven Years' War. Many Britons also expected to profit from trade and land speculation in the newly acquired region. The Philadelphia trading house Baynton, Wharton & Morgan and the related Illinois Company sought to rake in fortunes by becoming the region's first British traders and investors.[3] Native peoples saw other opportunities. Some called for a united front against all colonial powers, while others seized the chance to build alliances with the new regime.

All of these visions of the new, post-French world, however, overlooked that the Treaty of Paris changed little on the ground in Middle America. Great Britain may have pushed the French *empire* out of North America, but few French *colonists* left with it. Most of the French traders and farmers who lived and worked in the midcontinent remained in their homes and towns. Likewise, Indian nations, whose populations dwarfed the small French communities, welcomed or resisted newcomers in the context of the region's existing political relations. They continued to deal with one another and with Europeans on the basis of long-standing alliances and animosities.

In subsequent years, the interactions of Indians, colonists, and imperial officials in the midcontinent exposed a conflict between grand visions of possibility and the reality of the region's social landscape. Many Indians and "Interior French" (the British term for those francophone colonists who stayed) used their knowledge of local politics, customs, and geography to better their situations. Successful newcomers, whether individuals or empires, depended on the insights of local informants. Others, blinded by arrogance or prejudice, dismissed their potential allies and suffered the consequences. Nativists led by Ottawa chief Pontiac, British officials, and Anglo-American traders all came to Illinois with ideas about the possibilities of a North America without the French empire, and all three soon learned that the persistence of social networks created before and during the French regime limited their opportunities.

≈   Soon after the British completed their victory over French forces in Canada in 1760, the empire began to plan for the new realities of postwar North America. Not until 1763 would the final peace transfer all of France's holdings east of the Mississippi River to Great Britain. Well before the end of negotiations, imperial officials expected that Britain would add territory. Those new lands offered great opportunities to the empire and its subjects.

But Sir William Johnson recognized that Britain was not acquiring vacant acreage. The trans-Appalachian West was home to thousands of Indians belonging to dozens of nations. To gain a foothold beyond the mountains, the empire would have to extend its alliances into the interior of the continent. In August 1762, Johnson advised Sir Jeffery Amherst, commander in chief of Britain's forces in North America, that the "peace & security" of the country west of the Appalachians "must in a great measure depend on a due management of the Indians." The British Indian Department had to expand. It needed to hire new agents who would build alliances between western Indian nations and the empire. As these agents journeyed through Indian Country, they could not arrive empty-handed. Diplomacy depended on generosity, understood in the region as a sign of respect. British agents would have to present gifts of medals, clothing, gunpowder, and other items to the many nations west of the mountains.[4]

In the early 1760s, Shawnees, Delawares, and Cherokees consumed the alliance-building efforts of the Indian Department. At different times, these nations had allied with Great Britain, but during the 1750s, all had broken with the empire. After introducing Pennsylvania traders such as George Croghan to western nations during the late 1740s, Shawnees and Delawares spent the mid-1750s waging war against the land-hungry Anglos who invaded their homelands. When Cherokees entered the war allied with the Iroquois and the British, they shifted the balance of power in the Ohio valley. Their repeated attacks in the heart of Delaware and Shawnee country drove those nations to negotiate a peace with Britain. In the 1758 Treaty of Easton, British officials, including George Croghan, laid the groundwork for peace by promising to preserve the lands of western Indians. However, when the British stipulated that the Iroquois ruled over both western Indians and their lands, they weakened any chance of a lasting alliance.[5] Still, making peace with France's Native allies marked a major victory for British diplomacy in that moment.

However, as the Cherokees returned home from Pennsylvania, they suffered attacks at the hands of British colonists who could not or would not distinguish between Indian nations. When the leading Cherokee diplomat Attakullakulla left for home to soothe the growing tensions between his nation and Virginia, whose colonists had recently murdered thirty Cherokees, General John Forbes called him a deserter and ordered him captured and disarmed. Attakullakulla felt "like a child & no man." When British officials refused to make amends, Cherokees went to war against Virginia and

South Carolina. Hostilities largely came to an end by late 1761, but tensions remained for two years as British diplomats struggled to reassure Cherokees that they had no designs on western lands.[6] As British Indian agents navigated the diplomatic geography of the early 1760s, they discovered many fractures, but they hoped that a resurrection of earlier alliances would lay the groundwork for a peaceful transition to British rule in the West.

Stretched from New York to the Carolinas, British Indian agents relied on the knowledge and kinship ties they had established during their years and decades in Indian Country. In 1761, George Croghan advised hiring agents who would "Make themselves well acquainted with the Indians Custom, Maners & policys," in order to prevent the spread of anti-British sentiment. Neither William Johnson nor John Stuart, Johnson's counterpart in the South, needed to be convinced of the wisdom of such a strategy. By the winter of 1758–1759, Johnson had married Molly Brant (Konwatsitsiaienni), a member of a prestigious Mohawk clan and the stepdaughter of a Mohawk chief. Over the next fifteen years, Johnson and Brant had nine children, and Johnson became a mentor to Molly's brother Joseph (Thayendanegea), who was on his way to becoming the most prominent Mohawk leader of the era. Through Brant, Johnson gained greater knowledge about Mohawk and Iroquois affairs, but Molly also served as an influential ally. "One word from her," an observer later noted, "goes farther than a thous[an]d. from any white Man without Exception." An alliance with Brant was a powerful tie in matrilineal Iroquois society, in which women regularly participated in politics and decision-making. In the 1780s, Brant recalled that she often helped persuade Mohawk chiefs to accept Johnson's proposals.[7]

Meanwhile, Stuart married a Cherokee woman, Susannah Emory. Cherokees called Stuart "Bushyhead," in reference to his shock of red hair, and Stuart's Cherokee children took the sobriquet as their surname. Stuart also formed a close friendship with Cherokee chief Attakullakulla, who by some accounts adopted Stuart. In 1760, when Cherokee warriors attacked the British garrison at Fort Loudoun in present-day Tennessee, they brought Stuart to Attakullakulla, who helped him escape back to the colonies. Stuart and Attakullakulla saw mutual benefit in their friendship. In 1761, as Attakullakulla negotiated a peace with South Carolina, he requested that Stuart serve as Indian agent to the Cherokee Nation. According to Attakullakulla, "All the Indians love him, and there will never be any uneasiness if he is there."[8] With this vote of confidence, Stuart went to work in the Cherokee Nation, hoping his kinship ties and bond with Attakullakulla would smooth relations with the British.

Both Johnson and Stuart hired men who, as in Croghan's recommendation, were "well acquainted with the Indians Custom, Maners & policys."
In the regions north of the Ohio River, Johnson relied on Croghan with his
decades of experience and Alexander McKee, the son of an Irish trader and
an Anglo woman from North Carolina whom Shawnee Indians captured and
adopted when she was an infant. Beginning in 1755, McKee's father, Thomas,
worked for Croghan's trading enterprise, and when Croghan joined the Indian Department the following year, he employed Thomas McKee as an as-
sistant. Three years later, Croghan hired Alexander. Throughout the early
1760s, Alexander served as a translator and a trusted source of information
about activities and sentiments among Shawnee, Delaware, and Mingo Indians. By 1763, with Croghan absent dealing with private affairs in England,
the younger McKee took a lead role in diplomacy at Fort Pitt. As relations
with western Indian nations grew tense and then disintegrated, Johnson
advised McKee, "conciliate and fix to the British Interest, all the several
Nations and Tribes of Indians, who may fall within the Reach of your
Influence."[9]

In the South, Stuart likewise chose subordinates with intimate connections
to Indian nations. Stuart hired Alexander Cameron and John McDonald,
both of whom had also married Cherokee women. In the next decade, Henry
Stuart, John's brother and an officer in the Indian Department, stated that
Cameron "had lived so long among them [Cherokees] till he had almost
become one of themselves." Of course, Indian wives and mothers were much
more than helpmates to white relatives. They pursued their own interests,
worked to improve conditions for their families and nations, and used their
Anglo relatives' political and financial ties as sources of power and capital.[10]
From the perspective of Johnson, Stuart, and their subordinates, Indian
relatives were keys to repairing the empire's alliances in the West.

Regardless, Britain entered the new era impoverished by years of war, and
the empire intended to cut expenses wherever possible. In North America,
Amherst led the quest to reduce the costs of administering the growing empire. Compounding the general's fiscal concerns, Amherst approached Native
Americans with arrogance and ethnocentrism. He assumed that, in the absence of the defeated French, Indians depended on British largesse. Failing to
recognize the diplomatic significance of gift giving, Amherst believed that
robust trade would serve the same purpose while removing a financial burden
from the empire. This belief was compounded by his confidence that western
Indians would ally with Britain, gifts or not. Amherst ordered Johnson to
provide only those goods he considered "absolutely necessary." To the general,

unnecessary gifts amounted to little more than "Bribing the Indians, or Buying their good Behavior." Amherst stated bluntly, "it is not My Intention ever to Attempt to gain the Friendship of Indians by presents."[11] Amherst imagined that Indian nations would welcome Great Britain, and poverty would soon convince the reluctant to fall into line.

Agents within the Indian Department recognized the errors of the haughty Amherst. They had spent years or even decades living among Native peoples, and their experiences provided them with wisdom and perspective that Amherst, sequestered in New York City, lacked. Even before the end of the war with France, George Croghan foresaw that hubris and overconfidence would plague Britain as it attempted to take possession of the West after the Treaty of Paris. In the winter of 1759–1760, Croghan acknowledged that Great Britain had defeated France. But, he warned, "we have nothing to boast from the War with the Natives, yet it is thought every Penny, thrown away, that is given them." British officers, confident in their military victories against France, mistakenly believed they had also defeated western Indians, who could now be treated as subjugated peoples. Croghan wrote that western Indians remained unconquered, and they expected signs of friendship and generosity from the British. Failure to recognize those things, Croghan warned, portended trouble and played into the hands of Britain's enemies.[12]

As Native leaders learned of Amherst's miserly Indian policy, they grew increasingly distrustful of the British. Suspicion spread though Middle America. During the summer of 1762, Johnson sent Captain Thomas Hutchins on a diplomatic tour of the Great Lakes and Ohio valley. On the journey, Hutchins visited Ottawas, Ojibwes, Menominees, Potawatomis, Miamis, Weas, Piankashaws, Mascoutens, and Kickapoos. He discovered that these nations, crucial to the prospect of British control over the trans-Appalachian West, had already grown disillusioned with the empire. At Detroit, Ottawa and Ojibwe chiefs informed Hutchins's translator that they had expected the officer to bring them gifts. They "seemed much dissatisfy'd that they were disappointed." St. Joseph Potawatomis had a similar reaction. At Ouiatenon, Hutchins met with Wea and Kickapoo Indians, whose nations had been struck by "a Severe Sickness." A Wea chief lamented that the British commanded his people not to visit the French in the Illinois Country, yet they offered no replacement for the ammunition the French would provide. As Hutchins neared the end of his trip, he reached Fort Miami, where a British officer assured him "that it was almost impossible to keep friendship with the Indians here without allowing them some presents."[13]

Western Indians fretted especially over the scarcity of one item: gunpowder. France had struggled to supply its allies in the midcontinent in the decades before the fall of Canada. Years of war had consumed vast quantities of ammunition. As Indians watched France abandon outposts and cut ties with former allies, they expected Britain to fill the void. Jeffery Amherst did not intend to do so. Amherst believed that limiting access to ammunition would diminish western nations' ability to fight the British. He advised Johnson, "I Do not Doubt but all the Nations will Complain of not having powder sufficient; but I am for giving it to them with as sparing a hand as possible." By 1762, agents across Indian Country reported a "great demand" for gunpowder, which, even among traders, was scarce and expensive. Representatives of the Delawares, Shawnees, Weas, and western Senecas told George Croghan that the British, by stopping the sale of powder, had sent a "very Clear" signal that they were preparing for war.[14]

Across Middle America, Indians believed cutting off the supply of ammunition was the first step in a British scheme to exterminate them and seize their land. Since before the Seven Years' War, Indian leaders repeatedly voiced these fears. In 1758, Delaware leaders stated their belief that "the *French* and the *English* intend to kill all the *Indians*, and then divide the land among themselves." After the war, Amherst, Johnson, and the rest of the imperial administrators in North America insisted that Britain did not plan to snatch more land from the nations on its frontiers.[15] The actions of British colonists undermined these assertions.

As France and Great Britain prepared the final peace between the two empires, English colonists hovered on the edge of Indian Country, ready to seize new territory. Recognizing only European land claims, they believed that the defeat of France opened this country for Anglo settlement. At Fort Pitt, 400 men prepared to settle on the Ohio and Mississippi Rivers. Meanwhile, Delaware Indians accused Pennsylvania of a series of fraudulent dealings dating back decades, which had almost entirely dispossessed them of their homelands. All the while, 1,000 Connecticut families plotted to colonize Delaware lands to the west on the Susquehanna River. The scheme made the region's Indians "very uneasy," not least because Connecticut's claims rested on a sale made years earlier "in a very wrong manner" and disputed by Delaware and Iroquois chiefs. Amherst expressed confusion at the intended colonization along the Susquehanna. "I know nothing of the Motives," he wrote, "that can Induce the People of Connecticut to Act so Contrary to the Express Orders of their Government." If they were "Rash enough" to settle there, "they must Blame themselves if Consequences prove Fatal to them."[16]

The potential fallout from the ill-advised settlements extended far beyond the Susquehanna valley. William Johnson believed that New Englanders would irritate Iroquois and Delawares and draw in other Native nations, ultimately dragging "the American Colonies in[to] an Indian War." In December 1762, Croghan reported that Shawnees and Delawares "have No Intensions to Make Warr with ye. English Butt say itt is full Time for them to prepair to defend themselves."[17] Despite the best efforts of Indian agents across the frontier, imperial policies and the actions of unruly colonists undermined their ability to ensure peace.

≈   Not long after Great Britain and France signed the Treaty of Paris in early 1763, Indians across the midcontinent challenged the dreams of traders and speculators by launching a war against the would-be conquerors. In May and June, nativist forces seized nine British forts and threatened half a dozen others in the Great Lakes and upper Ohio valley. The coordinated attacks stretched from the Pennsylvania backcountry to southern Lake Michigan. By July 1763, British troops controlled only three forts west of the Appalachians: Niagra, Detroit, and Fort Pitt.[18] Over the next year, the nativist alliance expanded. By the spring of 1764, it controlled all of the waterways that connected the British colonies on the Atlantic coast to the empire's new claims on the Mississippi River. By commanding the Ohio, Wabash, Illinois, and Mississippi Rivers, Pontiac's allies prevented a British invasion of their homelands and thwarted British ambitions to extend their empire along the western waterways.

British imperialists claimed that French officials instigated the nativist movement, but nativists employed an Indian ideology to pursue ambitions that had little to do with the French. The nativist movement grew out of the teachings of Delaware and Shawnee prophets during the 1730s. Pushed west by British expansion in Pennsylvania, these holy men developed an anticolonial, pan-Indian ideology that rejected European goods, especially alcohol, and promoted a return to traditional lifeways. Perhaps most importantly, the prophets called for unity among Native peoples so they could better handle the challenges of colonialism. Around 1760, the Delaware Neolin was the first prophet to bundle the nativist message into a neat package. To the Indians of Pennsylvania and the eastern Great Lakes, Neolin narrated a journey in which he met the creator, the Master of Life. The Master of Life warned that he was displeased with his people. They drank too much, fought with one another, depended on European goods, ceded land to colonists, and worshiped the wrong spirits. Taking stock of Delawares' woes, the Master of Life offered a solution. By separating from Europeans, their customs, and their goods, Indians could return to the right path. Neolin returned to the Delaware towns. Using a map that depicted the physical world as well as Heaven and Hell, Neolin told his audience that "White people" and their "Sins & Vices" had diverted them onto the path to Hell.[19] Not all Delawares joined Neolin. For many, though, the prophet's message, combined with their lived experience of dispossession and diaspora from their homelands in Pennsylvania into the Ohio valley, sparked a fierce resistance against colonization. Two years later, Neolin joined forces with Ottawa war chief Pontiac. Together, they militarized nativist teachings and spread Neolin's message from the Appalachian Mountains to the Mississippi River.

As British forts fell, their leadership tried to understand the movement that had seemingly appeared out of nowhere to thwart their imperial ambitions. They identified Pontiac as the key leader of the alliance. They explained his authority by describing him as a great man and talented leader. British general Thomas Gage believed that Pontiac, "this turbulent and enterprising Savage," bullied the other nations to joining his cause and that Pontiac's death would effectively end the resistance to British rule. In early 1764, he advocated surprising Pontiac and "his Crew, and putting the whole to the Sword." The remaining western Indians, Gage hoped, would see the necessity of such an act and welcome the peace that followed. The British overstated Pontiac's role as a central leader. He was just one of many chiefs and warriors whose influence united the nativists. But Pontiac became particularly important in forming and extending the alliance because of his kinship ties in the Great Lakes and in the Illinois Country.[20]

Although Pontiac and the nativist prophets promised a new world free of Europeans, they had to negotiate an old world shaped by kinship-based politics of alliance and rivalry. The message of pan-Indian unity replaced tribal distinctions with a common, race-based identity, but Pontiac's alliance relied on the close relations developed between Delawares and Ottawas during the Seven Years' War. Adopting the nativist message from Delawares and Shawnees, who had been pushed west by British expansion, Pontiac returned to the Great Lakes, where he recruited Ojibwes and Potawatomis, his kin in the larger Anishinaabeg family. Pontiac's ties to Miami Indians brought an important ally along the Wabash River route that connected Anishinaabeg,

Delawares, and Shawnees to potential friends in the Illinois Country.[21] With this alliance of kin in place, Pontiac declared war on the British. For six months in the middle of 1763, nativists besieged and burned English forts in the Great Lakes and Ohio valley.

As the war stalemated in the winter of 1763–1764, Pontiac looked to expand his alliance. He believed that the Illinois Country held the key to future success. At first glance, Illinois Indians seemed an unlikely ally. Unlike Shawnees and Delawares, western nations had not yet lost most of their land to settler colonialism, and prior to 1763, they had limited contact with the British. Moreover, Kaskaskias had converted to Catholicism in large numbers. In general, Catholic Indians had little use for Neolin and nativist ideology.[22]

In other ways, however, the midcontinent's Indian nations were ideal recipients for the nativist message. Since the precolonial era, Illinois intermarried with neighboring nations to further their political and economic goals. Kinship ties linked the five divisions of the Illinois Nation—Kaskaskias, Peorias, Cahokias, Tamaroas, and Michigameas—with Piankashaws, Miamis, Weas, Kickapoos, Missourias, and Osages. During the seventeenth century, Illinois traded with all of those nations as they took control of the central Mississippi valley. Beginning late in the 1600s, the nations fought together against Foxes and Chickasaws. Many of them had joined Memeskia's anti-French alliance during the 1740s and early 1750s. Although local identities based on kinship and nation remained strong, Illinois and their allies recognized the power of multiethnic coalitions. But with the weather turning cold and British and Indian forces settling in for the winter, Pontiac waited for spring's thawed waterways and clear paths to continue his work.

While Pontiac wintered in a village on the Wabash River, the French commandant at Fort de Chartres, Neyon de Villiers, worked to keep the Illinois and their neighbors from backing Pontiac. As early as July 1763, British reports indicated that Illinois Indians sympathized with the nativists. The following winter, they served as messengers for the nativists, contacting their allies and spreading word of the opposition to the British. At the end of the year, Neyon de Villiers sent messages throughout the Illinois Country, urging Illinois, Potawatomis, Kickapoos, Mascoutens, Miamis, and others to stay at peace with the British. In response, chiefs demurred, stating that "they did not answer for their warriors, and that besides it was the Master of Life who was exciting them to war." The "prophetic spirit" of Neolin's message spread through the region, and Neyon de Villiers struggled to contain it. He hoped that his personal relationships with Indian leaders would enable him to influence their decisions, even if "necessity" broke "the bonds of respect they have always had for the French nation."[23]

In April 1764, Pontiac arrived in the Illinois Country, intending to draw on a history of multiethnic alliances and convince Illinois and their allies to join the war against the British. In his efforts, Pontiac was aided by the fact that he had married an Illinois woman. In later years, British reports documented Pontiac's regular travels along the Wabash River between his home in Detroit and his wife's family in the Illinois Country. By the time he arrived to bolster his alliance in the spring of 1764, he may have been a familiar face among the Illinois, and his familial ties may well have opened the ears of otherwise-reluctant allies.[24]

On that day in April 1764, Pontiac found a receptive audience among his wife's relatives, even as Neyon de Villiers spoke against him. Standing before the crowd, Pontiac presented a large wampum belt and explained the message of the Master of Life and the ongoing war against the British. The redcoats had dismissed the French as "little flies" and Indian warriors as "a lump of Earth which they break in their hands and give . . . to the winds to blow away like dust." Now, Pontiac's army had surrounded Detroit, and the British sought peace. The nativists refused. To continue the fight, they needed French gunpowder, but Neyon de Villiers, much less Louisiana's governor or the distant king, could not expect to control them or force them to seek a peace. Pontiac concluded, "We will not finish the War with the English whilst there remains one of us red men." In response, Neyon de Villiers repeated his exhortations to end the war and to befriend both the British and the French. Irritated, Pontiac interrupted that he could never make a peace with the British: "I hate them." Moreover, he said, "if this Peace is made it will not hold 40 moons, since it is true these are the sentiments of all thy Red Children." At some point during the proceedings, Neyon de Villiers returned Pontiac's wampum belt, a sign of refusal and disrespect. When Pontiac presented it again, the Frenchman kicked it from his hands. Leaving the council, Pontiac noted Neyon de Villiers's pleas: "Be quiet my Father I will not spill blood upon thy lands, what I will spill shall be on the water of thy River which the current will carry away." Despite Neyon de Villiers's counterarguments, the Illinois responded positively to Pontiac's message. A few days after the council, Neyon de Villiers reported that the Illinois had joined the nativists: "[Pontiac] destroyed in one night what I had accomplished in eight months."[25]

The addition of Illinois to the nativist alliance opened paths to nations throughout the central Mississippi River valley. To the west of the Illinois Country, Little Osage and Missouria Indians joined the Illinois and professed to follow "the Sentiments of all the redmen." Messengers from Illinois contacted Quapaws in present-day Arkansas, and they began to search French convoys on the Mississippi for British soldiers. Farther south in what is now Mississippi and Louisiana, Tunica, Ofogoula, and Avoyelle Indians joined Pontiac's alliance, probably through the influence of Quapaws. By the winter of 1764, Pontiac had utilized kinship ties to build a sprawling, anticolonial alliance throughout the waterways of Middle America. By controlling the Mississippi and Ohio Rivers, nativists ruled the routes to the Illinois Country and could stave off British incursions.[26]

In 1763, Amherst plotted a multipronged assault on the nativists. Key to the campaign was the Illinois Country, where French traders had surreptitiously supplied the nativist cause. That November, mounting failures led the British to replace Amherst as commander in chief of forces in North America. His replacement, General Thomas Gage, implemented Amherst's plan with few changes. In late 1763, Major Arthur Loftus relocated from Pensacola to New Orleans, where he would organize an expedition to ascend the Mississippi and take possession of Illinois. At the end of February 1764, Loftus set out at the head of a convoy of a dozen boats carrying more than 300 officers and soldiers and almost fifty women and children. Loftus knew that the nativists opposed his journey upriver, but he hoped to buy safe passage with a "few" gifts. From the beginning, soldiers feared Indian attack and grumbled about the "difficulties" of the trip. By the time the convoy passed Point Coupée in mid-March, eighty people had deserted or succumbed to disease. A few days later, thirty Tunica, Ofogoula, Choctaw, and Avoyelle Indians attacked the party just south of Natchez. Firing on the lead vessels, the attackers killed six British men and wounded as many more. The British disengaged and retreated to New Orleans and then to Pensacola.[27]

As Pontiac had promised, blood had been spilled on the river. Loftus blamed French duplicity and an overwhelming Native force for the British failure. Speaking at New Orleans, Tunica chief Perruquier echoed the rhetoric of the nativist prophets as he defended the assault. According to the chief, the British were liquor purveyors, smallpox carriers, and land thieves. "When I learned they were coming to our lands," Perruquier explained, "I said they would make us die, it is better to kill them." Perruquier warned, "if they [the British] wish to return, we shall have the glory of driving them away again."[28] As long as the nativist alliance held, the British could not reach the Illinois Country.

Despite the vast reach of the kinship networks that connected the diverse nations of the midcontinent, they were exclusive as well as inclusive. The pan-Indian teachings of nativism promoted a single identity and invited Indians of all nations to unite against European invasion. In practice, however, the nativist alliance excluded those nations that had long been enemies of Ottawas, Illinois, and its other members. Foxes and Sauks were notably absent and even hostile to the nativists. Since the late seventeenth century, they had tangled with Pontiac's Ottawas and their Ojibwe and Potawatomi relatives. But their deepest animosity was for the Illinois and their allies, with whom they had fought an ongoing, often devastating war dating back nearly a century. During the 1760s, a Sauk war chief declared that his nation's "perpetual war" with the Illinois would "Endure as long as the sun, moon and stars." He explained to a French officer why his nation could not make peace with its enemies: "was it possible our bones should meet after death, they would fight together 'till they would be broke to pieces." As Pontiac and his allies seized and besieged British forts, Sauks and Foxes allied with the British, promising Thomas Gage, "[We] are Resolved to remain always in your Interest, and Die with you." Similarly, south of the Ohio River, Chickasaws and Cherokees felt no common cause with their longtime adversaries to the north, and Cherokees, in particular, continued to wage their own war against the Indians of the Wabash River and the Illinois Country.[29] In these enemies of the nativists, British officers found an opportunity to defeat Pontiac and his allies.

By early 1764, Thomas Gage recognized that diplomacy was Britain's strongest weapon against the nativists. The Loftus expedition failed less than 200 miles north of New Orleans. At the same time, two British armies pushed into western Pennsylvania and present-day Ohio. They opened negotiations with Shawnees and Delawares but failed to provide the military victory that British leadership expected. Military power alone would not break the nativist alliance or allow the British to reach Illinois. Instead, Gage sought weaknesses in Pontiac's far-flung alliance. He hoped to dismantle it, piece by piece, nation by nation. Louisiana governor Jean-Jacques Blaise d'Abbadie had advised Loftus to take such an approach. But after Loftus's defeat, the Frenchman noted, "Commandant Loftus would have needed for that purpose more knowledge of their government than he had, and also a character more pliant than his."[30] To head diplomatic efforts, Gage relied on two men, both more knowledgeable and skillful than Loftus.

To Shawnees and Delawares on the upper Ohio, Gage deployed George Croghan. During the 1740s and 1750s, Croghan had built connections with Shawnees and Delawares and used those ties to attract trading partners among the Miamis, including Memeskia. Gage urged Croghan to revitalize those connections. Along with Lieutenant Alexander Fraser, Gage was to travel to the Shawnees and Delawares, broker a peace with them, and urge them to guide him to the Miamis and other nations on the Wabash River. After making peace with Miamis, they could lead Croghan and Fraser to the Illinois. "The Ilinois Indians if reconciled," Gage predicted, "will be easily brought to send Chiefs with Messages to the Akansas [Quapaws] to acquaint Them of Their Treaty with Us, And prevail on Them to do the same." If diplomacy faltered, Gage authorized Croghan to remind Miamis, Illinois, and others of "the satisfaction it would give the Chicasaws and Cherokees to enter their Country in Considerable Bodys so as to destroy and ravage all their Settlements." Sauks, Foxes, and Sioux had also offered to fight the nativists. Thus far, Gage noted, the British had discouraged these attacks, but if need be, they could call on these allies to devastate their enemies.[31]

In the South, Gage depended on John Stuart. Possibly more than any other Indian agent in the British service, Stuart understood the networks that linked Indian nations. By marrying a Cherokee woman, Stuart had created his own kinship ties among the southern Indians. At the end of the Seven Years' War, he employed those connections in negotiations with Cherokees, Chickasaws, and Choctaws. To forge an alliance with the Indian nations of the lower Mississippi valley, Stuart had to move beyond the limits of his own relations. He understood the necessary steps to take. He instructed his cousin and deputy, Charles, to gather as much information as he could from French officials in New Orleans about the nations along the river, their customs in negotiations, and the "proper Interpreters and Messengers" to bring to councils.[32] In taking stock of the politics of the lower Mississippi valley, Stuart relied on personal ties to gain Indian support for the next British convoy to ascend the Mississippi as well as to remove resistance from those nations between New Orleans and the Illinois Country.

The new strategy produced results. Shawnees and Delawares had grown discontented with the prolonged and stagnant war and quickly agreed to aid Croghan, serving, with some Senecas, as his guides. On June 8, three weeks into the journey, near the mouth of the Wabash River, eighty of the Shawnees' Kickapoo and Mascouten allies fired on the party, thinking they were Cherokees come to raid them. The volley killed three Indians and two British and wounded Croghan. Kickapoos and Mascoutens captured Croghan and the other wounded men, looted the goods he was carrying, and took him to Ouiatenon, a Wea, Kickapoo, and Mascouten village far upstream. When Croghan and his captors arrived at Ouiatenon two weeks later, Kickapoo and Mascouten chiefs recognized the potential fallout of the attack and feared retaliation from Shawnees and Delawares for the deaths of their relatives. They begged Croghan for forgiveness. By the end of July, Shawnees, Delawares, Mascoutens, Kickapoos, and some Miamis swore "they would become True and faithfull Allies to the King and his Subjects." They also promised to help the diplomat negotiate with the Illinois.[33]

Although relatively late to the alliance, Illinois remained steadfast supporters of Pontiac during the spring and summer of 1765. In April, in the presence of one British officer who had successfully sneaked north via Chickasaw country, Louis St. Ange de Bellerive, the last French commandant of the Illinois Country, held a council with the Illinois, hoping to convince them to make peace with the British. Referring to the Illinois' long-standing power in the region, he flattered his audience: "the Illinois Nations has always acted as they pleased without the Councel of other Nations. . . . You are your own Masters." Kaskaskia chief Tamaroa responded, "The Illinois Nations has always done formerly what they pleased . . . but in this afair we have followed the Sentiments of all the redmen." Tamaroa knew that his nation's power had dwindled in the preceding two decades as wars with Chickasaws and the Fox coalition, combined with disease, migration, intermarriage with the French, and a low rate of captive adoption, had reduced the Illinois population. More than ever, Illinois needed allies, and the nativists with their expansive coalition offered more support than the departing French. With that in mind, Tamaroa warned the British officer "to depart from hence as soon as possible." "Go away and never think of returning here," Tamaroa swore, "for if you presume to do it our Warriors . . . may perhaps make you fall in the Water."[34]

However, while Tamaroa insisted on the strength of the alliance, signs appeared that new imperial policies combined with Gage's diplomacy had weakened it. In October 1763, King George III issued the Royal Proclamation of 1763, which closed the trans-Appalachian West to British settlement and reserved those lands for Native peoples. After the Proclamation reached North America in December, William Johnson sent deputies throughout the

Northeast and Great Lakes, spreading the news and requesting that diplomats appear at a council the following summer at Niagara; 2,000 Indians from twenty-four nations joined the council and welcomed the king's overtures of peace.[35]

The Royal Proclamation proved an imperfect solution to a complicated range of imperial challenges—not least being the inability of the crown to enforce the prohibition on its colonists' westward movements—but in 1764, the document convinced many Indians that their homelands would be protected, a principal concern leading them to join the nativist war. None of the nativists attended the Niagara council, but their relatives and allies were present. Word of the Royal Proclamation soon spread through the eastern half of the continent. At the same time, Shawnee and Delaware leaders met with British diplomats, opening negotiations for an end to the conflict. When Pontiac and Illinois leaders traveled to Ouiatenon to meet Croghan at the end of the summer of 1765, the British agent brokered a peace with them. In no small part, Croghan succeeded because of the Wabash River Indians who pressured Pontiac and the Illinois chiefs to make peace. Ironically, Croghan noted, "my Success is entirely owing to my Misfortune in being taken and Plundered."[36]

Meanwhile, in the South, Tunica chief Perruquier saw political and economic opportunities better than those provided by his tenuous alliance with northern Indians. Four months after his attack on Loftus's convoy, Perruquier acquiesced to British passage on the Mississippi, under the following condition: "Let them not be ungrateful to us and . . . give us something." By the end of the year, Tunicas had allowed a British officer in their town and offered to invite the Quapaws to a council. Meanwhile, John Stuart completed two years of work drawing new boundary lines between Cherokee and British lands, a key stipulation of the peace established at the Treaty of Augusta in 1763. In negotiations in the spring of 1765, Stuart asked Chickasaws and Choctaws, who controlled the Mississippi River north of the Tunicas, to allow British safe passage. After promising that the British would respect the two nations' sovereignty, Stuart reached an accord with them. Satisfied with British promises, Choctaws, Chickasaws, and Cherokees agreed to allow British passage on their river and to escort them northward to the Illinois Country. These nations became key allies in the final phase of Gage's strategy against the nativists.[37]

In the summer of 1765, Gage sent British troops to Illinois from New Orleans and from Fort Pitt. Diplomacy had cleared the political obstacles that blocked British passage, but the expeditions still had to contend with the difficulties imposed by geography. Major Robert Farmar and the Thirty-Fourth Regiment of Foot left New Orleans in June—the worst time to journey upstream. In the late winter, the perilous ice of the upper Mississippi melted, and high water created a countercurrent along the banks, easing the burdens of travel upstream. In the summer, the waters receded, placing an added burden on the river men who powered the boats. French officials recommended leaving for Illinois no later than February. The few hundred Cherokee, Chickasaw, and Choctaw warriors accompanying Farmar's troops ensured they would meet no nativist resistance, but they could do nothing to improve travel conditions. Plagued by strong currents, scorching heat, boating accidents, and the desertion of experienced river men, Farmar's arduous journey lasted five months—two months longer than usual. In fact, the journey took so long to complete that Captain Thomas Sterling and another contingent of British troops arrived from Fort Pitt via the Ohio in October, two months before Farmar's men reached Fort de Chartres.[38]

In unraveling Pontiac's alliance, Thomas Gage demonstrated a keen understanding of the politics of the midcontinent. From his headquarters in New York City, Gage had little firsthand knowledge of Pontiac's network and what it would take to unravel it. But he recognized his shortcomings. Gage relied on his knowledgeable, experienced, and well-connected Indian agents to negotiate a political resolution to the war. From that foundation of alliances, the British then used ties linking Indian nations to one another to erode nativist power, at least temporarily. By the end of 1765, Great Britain had achieved diplomatic victory and avoided wasting the lives and money associated with a military campaign. Yet Farmar's difficult journey to the Illinois Country hinted at the burdens that distance would place on the empire's future in Middle America.

≈ With the Union Jack flying over Fort Chartres—the British dropped the "de"—the dawn of the British era in Middle America seemed auspicious. Resourceful British diplomats had ended the war in the midcontinent. Future wars between Britain and its French nemesis seemed unlikely. Not only had France ceded its claims in eastern North America to Great Britain, but as the British learned in 1763, it had also relinquished to Spain its rights west of the Mississippi River. When Thomas Gage heard of the cession, he rejoiced that Britain had lost "a most troublesome neighbor." From Fort Chartres, British troops could command the Mississippi River, which would serve as an unmistakable and easily defensible boundary with Spain. Built of stone, the fort's walls stood an impressive eighteen feet tall, two feet thick, and 490 feet long and enclosed nearly four acres of ground. In the communities along the Mississippi north and south of Fort Chartres, farmers tended herds of cattle, pigs, and other livestock and produced hundreds of thousands of bushels of wheat annually. Anglo observers expected these endeavors to boom as ambitious Brits replaced the supposedly slothful French.[39]

Yet changing one's perspective even slightly revealed a different future for Britain in the Illinois Country. The brokered peace to end the nativist war had depended on the assistance of Chickasaws and Cherokees, inveterate enemies of the Indians of the Illinois Country and the Wabash River. When France had claimed Middle America, war between those nations aided Great Britain. But as the British tried to maintain peace in their new colony, they viewed that animosity as a distraction. True, the Mississippi offered an unmistakable boundary, but with only a limited force stationed on the river, it was nearly impossible to guard against smugglers—often French traders tied to New Orleans markets—who slipped undetected into the Illinois and Ohio Rivers. Despite the impressive façade, Fort Chartres was crumbling, as the rapid current of the Mississippi washed away the bank supporting the fort's south wall. Its cannons had never been fired, because its walls were too weak to withstand the shock. Finally, with the cession of New Orleans to Spain, Illinois Country farmers lost the primary market for their produce, which was too bulky to ship the long distances overland or up the Ohio to the British colonies on the Atlantic coast. French traders and *habitants* continued shipping goods to New Orleans, but that market was closed to British produce.[40]

At the end of 1765, the British confronted the dark realization that they had inherited a troublesome colony from the French. They could do little to improve Fort Chartres' condition. British administrators found no better solution to the problem of distance, which slowed communication and made supplying the fort arduous and expensive, than had their French predecessors. More importantly, the British forgot the strategies that had succeeded so well during the nativist war. The diplomatic networks that agents such as Croghan and Stuart assembled did not extend to the Illinois Country, and after Britain took possession of the region, the two agents returned to their usual areas of operation—the upper Ohio valley and the South. The talented Gage could only administer the colony from afar, and for the day-to-day work of colony building, he relied on a series of officers who proved themselves unworthy of his confidence. To succeed in this isolated colony, the British needed to build new relations with the Indian and French inhabitants of the Illinois Country. Instead, after decades of warfare with the French and their Indian allies, British officers treated their potential allies as enemies and alienated the people who could determine the fate of the empire in Middle America. The war waged by Pontiac's alliance heightened Britain's deep mistrust of the French and Indians of the midcontinent. From the beginning of the conflict, British officers wrongly believed that the French had instigated the war and led nativist attacks. In reality, French officers in the Illinois Country and New Orleans had urged the nations of Pontiac's alliance to seek peace and accept the British as friends. In New Orleans, Governor d'Abbadie advised Loftus on how to safely proceed upstream. In the Illinois Country, Neyon de Villiers urged Illinois Indians to stay at peace with the British. His successor, Louis St. Ange, pleaded with Pontiac to make peace and protected British officials when they came to the Illinois Country. Nothing convinced the British that the French were sincere. British officers laid every failure at the feet of the French, although their own attitudes and short-sightedness were often to blame.[41]

More accurately, British officers accused French traders of supplying nativists with the guns and ammunition necessary to continue the war. The British exaggerated the extent of French power and also conflated the French empire and French traders. French officers worked tirelessly to end the nativist war and to ensure a smooth transition from French to British rule. On the other hand, French traders—the lawless *coureurs de bois*—pursued profit independent of the wishes of any empire. Louis St. Ange explained, "These same Frenchmen, since the capture of Canada, have always lived among the tribes, and are on that account beyond the control of the French government and that of England." St. Ange and his colleagues saw *coureurs de bois* as little more than criminals and "vagrants."[42] Far from encouraging them in any way, French administrators had struggled to control those scofflaws for nearly a century.

Once in the Illinois Country, British skepticism of French intentions led them to overlook the potential benefits of employing the soldiers and officers left without an empire in the midcontinent. When Britain took possession of the Illinois Country in late 1765, Gage directed his officers to "take care that every french Soldier is relieved, and that none of their troops remain in any part of the Illinois." Gage conceded that the French legal system would remain intact, in part to appease the remaining French colonists, but he ordered the removal of all French judges from the courts.[43] Sterling and Farmar encouraged the French military and civil officers to abandon their posts and head down the Mississippi as soon as possible.

Many of the French soldiers, including Louis St. Ange, had nowhere else to go, and they may well have joined the British service if asked. By the end of the Seven Years' War, St. Ange had lived in the midcontinent for more than forty years. He knew the region and its inhabitants, and that knowledge made him valuable to any empire trying to control Middle America. When the British urged him to leave the region, he crossed the Mississippi River and settled at the newly established St. Louis, soon to be the capital of Spanish Upper Louisiana. St. Ange served the Spanish government for another decade, both before and after Spain took formal possession of Upper Louisiana in 1769.[44] His defection represented a major lost opportunity for the British, who needed all the knowledgeable, capable officers they could find.

Despised and mistrusted by the new British government, many of the so-called Interior French had little interest in remaining under the British flag. In Kaskaskia, they worried that staying in the British settlements would put them in danger, as nativists "woud look upon them afterward as English and kill them all." Others feared that the new alliance between Britain and midcontinent Indians would lead to them "cutting the Throats of all the Frenchmen in the Colony." In October 1765, upon hearing of Sterling's arrival, hundreds of francophone colonists relocated to Ste. Genevieve and St. Louis on the Spanish side of the Mississippi. At Nouvelle Chartres, which had grown up around the walls of Fort Chartres, a few "poor families" stayed in the village. The rest left, packing up "the boards, the windows and door frames [of their homes] and everything else they could transport." Only a single inhabitant remained at St. Philippe, the smallest of the Illinois towns. Realizing the extent of the French exodus, British officials hoped that the colonists would eventually return after tiring of despotic Spanish rule.[45] This was wishful thinking. Most colonists who fled to St. Louis or Ste. Genevieve remained west of the Mississippi.

British officials emphasized building functional relationships with the region's Indian nations, but they had obstacles to overcome there as well. In counteracting Pontiac's alliance, the British had relied on George Croghan and John Stuart to gain support from their Indian friends and relatives. As their successes in 1764 and 1765 demonstrated, Croghan and Stuart were effective, but each man's influence was constrained to a finite region—

Croghan's in the upper Ohio valley and Stuart's in the South. Once in possession of the Illinois Country, Britain needed knowledgeable agents to strengthen ties with Illinois, Miamis, Kickapoos, Potawatomis, and other local Indians. By the end of 1765, most of the men and women who could fill that role had moved to Spanish Illinois. In particular, Louis St. Ange had maintained a close relationship with Piankashaws at Vincennes, even as defeat and dearth splintered the French alliance in Middle America during the 1740s and 1750s. Great Britain determined to make its own path with the French and Indians of the region. Like the French before them, the British made many missteps. To replace the veteran St. Ange, Britain sent Robert Farmar, whom a fellow officer described as "a good deal a Stranger seemingly to the Laws Customs & Dispositions of the French . . . and intirely so to dealing with Indians."[46] That initial error set the tone for much of what followed.

Moreover, Great Britain could not replace France and proceed as if little had changed. The British presence in the Illinois Country reshaped the political geography of the midcontinent. In particular, the new garrison at Fort Chartres attracted British-allied Indians, especially Chickasaws, hated by the Indian nations north of the Ohio. Since at least 1680, Illinois Indians had been hostile to Chickasaws, and that relationship showed no signs of improving in 1765, following decades of warfare. In contrast, Chickasaws were such important allies to the British that, in 1764, John Stuart could say, with only a bit of exaggeration, that they were King George's "most favoured children." With British possession of the Illinois Country, Chickasaws no longer had to trek hundreds of miles from Chickasaw Country to visit British officials in South Carolina or Georgia. Instead, they could make a short overland journey to the Tennessee River, which would carry them to within a few dozen miles of the British posts at Fort Chartres and Kaskaskia. With the British at Fort Chartres, Chickasaws enjoyed greater access to British gifts. Yet, to receive them, they had to travel into the homelands of their enemies. By bringing 125 Chickasaws to Fort Chartres in December 1765, the British demonstrated that, in the words of Thomas Gage, "we can introduce their enemies into the heart of their Country."[47] Gage wanted to display British power and encourage new alliances. Instead, he alienated many Illinois.

Native politics continued to shape the diplomatic opportunities open to empires. In 1765 and 1766, the British tried to force peace between Chickasaws and Illinois. Instead, many Illinois crossed the Mississippi

River, including Peorias who established a new town just south of St. Louis. More Peorias and some Kaskaskias considered moving in 1770 after Chickasaw attacks had increased and become, in one Spanish officer's view, a "continual war."[48] However, since the early 1750s, Illinois power had waned because of ongoing conflicts with multiple nations and a declining population. Those who remained east of the Mississippi needed an imperial patron for the first time. Soon they courted favor from the British.

In 1769, Peorias, Cahokias, Michigameas, and Kaskaskias remaining east of the Mississippi River united in one village under the protection of the British garrison at Fort Chartres. Afterward, Illinois scouts and informants paid regular visits to the commandant, trading knowledge for supplies. In 1771, enjoying closer ties with the British and facing persistent violence from Chickasaws, Illinois sought a lasting peace with their southern enemies. Chickasaws, having suffered their own population decline, accepted the overture as part of a larger effort to rebuild their nation as an economic rather than martial powerhouse. Peace with Chickasaws seems to have convinced about 400 Illinois to return from the Spanish side of the Mississippi in the four years following the Fort Chartres conference. The armistice between Illinois and Chickasaws ended only a fraction of the warfare directed at the Illinois Nation. In 1772, Peoria Indians reportedly sought refuge inside the walls of Fort Chartres because of persistent attacks by Sauk and Fox warriors.[49]

In the Wabash River valley, where French traders remained active and British officials had little influence, Indian nations ignored British demands for peace and waged war against their enemies. Finally free of the continuous demands of the French, those nations were reluctant to welcome another empire into the region. Even after Pontiac acquiesced to British rule in 1765, the Wabash River nations resisted the new regime. They attacked British traders and soldiers in the Illinois Country and waged war against Chickasaws, Britain's primary Indian ally in the region. Like Illinois and Miamis, Kickapoos had fought Chickasaws for decades. Even as the other nations raided less often into the South, Kickapoos continued their war against the southern Indians. Chickasaws recognized the threat, and even before their 1771 pact with the Illinois, they had increased their raids against Kickapoos. The British could do little stop the attacks, even as Kickapoos killed British soldiers and colonists around Fort Chartres and the neighboring towns.[50]

Farther north, St. Joseph Potawatomis thrived following the Seven Years' War, and they waged their own war on the British, who offered few incentives that were not provided by the Potawatomis' French relatives. In present-day southwestern Michigan, St. Joseph had been an important fur-trade center since the turn of the eighteenth century, and through decades of intermarriage between French men and Potawatomi women, St. Joseph Potawatomis built a strong community centered on a handful of French-Potawatomi families and the fur trade. As Illinois power declined during the final fifteen years of the French regime, Potawatomis advanced into strategically and economically valuable territory long held by their southern neighbors. During the late 1740s, St. Joseph Potawatomis established a new town on the Chicago River. After the Seven Years' War, many of them had moved to the Kankakee River. Thus, as the British took possession of the Illinois Country, St. Joseph Potawatomis controlled important lands between Illinois and Detroit. While the British needed safe passage through Potawatomi territory, Potawatomis saw little reason to ally with the British. In 1767, after killing a British trader, Potawatomis declared they "would not suffer an English Man to come near their Place." Over the next five years, they captured or killed numerous British soldiers and traders.[51] Unable to stop French trade with the Potawatomis and unwilling to pour money into a backcountry war, the British could do little to halt the violence.

Removed from the centers of British authority in the Illinois Country, Potawatomis, Kickapoos, Weas, and Piankashaws faced few repercussions from Great Britain. At Detroit, one British official complained, "The only method to Remove the French men from amongst the Indians, is first to order them to come in, which if they Refuse send a party of Indians and scalp them." British officers had few weapons beyond threats, and those lost their power once Native peoples realized they were empty. In August 1769, a chief, Hananaa, from one of the Wabash River nations mocked the threats of Fort Chartres commandant John Wilkins, "You talk to me of the stars, and say that you are as numerous as they are in the sky. The stars that fall hurt nothing." Hananaa continued, "As for me I am as the trees in the forests; and, when a tree falls, it does harm and kills a man."[52]

By 1772, violence and danger surrounded the British outposts in Illinois. That spring, Wilkins reported to Thomas Gage that enemy war parties constantly harassed his post. Following the 1768 Treaty of Fort Stanwix, by which Iroquois diplomats sold Shawnee and Cherokee hunting lands to the British, and the initial forays of British colonists into the upper Ohio valley, Shawnees and Delawares once again spread their message of Indian unity. Posing as messengers from William Johnson, two Shawnee chiefs traveled to the Illinois Country, where they asked for gifts from the British commandant before holding an anti-British council that attracted Illinois, Quapaws, and Great Osages. Already warring against the British, Kickapoos along with their Mascouten and Miami allies on the Wabash River needed little incentive to join the new alliance. Kickapoos even showed a willingness to set aside their differences with Chickasaws to further the cause of all Indian nations. Many Cherokee and Creek leaders, plagued by British incursions into their lands south of the Ohio, accepted the wampum belts of the northern nations and planned a conference together with Chickasaws. In sum, with Anglo colonists seizing Indian land all along the Appalachian Mountains, even nations that had worked against Pontiac recognized the benefits of a pan-Indian resistance to British encroachment.[53]

Less than a decade earlier, British agents had used personal relationships and knowledge of the political landscape to end the nativist war and gain access to the midcontinent. In many ways, the achievements of 1764 and 1765 marked the apex of British diplomacy. From Gage to local agents, British officials worked to understand local politics and used existing alliance networks to their advantage. However, after removing the immediate threat of Pontiac and his nativist alliance, the British seemed to forget the value of working with rather than against people on the ground. Instead, they entered the Illinois Country full of suspicion of the region's French and Indian inhabitants. At the same time, Great Britain and its colonists made increased demands for Indian land, and the empire failed to halt the outlaws who illegally crossed the Proclamation Line of 1763 into the trans-Appalachian West. As long as British officials tacitly supported those colonists, they provoked more animosity from the revitalized nativists and their new allies, and they could call on few Indian nations to defend the interests of the empire.

≈   During the French era, many traders thrived even as the empire struggled. *Voyageurs* and *coureurs de bois* intermarried with Indian nations and forged the kinship ties necessary to maintain economic relations. The experience of British traders during the 1760s and 1770s differed from that earlier era. Unlike the British empire, which met with early success in part because of French imperial failures, Anglo merchants found few openings in a market saturated by francophone entrepreneurs. Those well-established traders retained much of their earlier commerce. Arriving without local connections and with an arrogance that prevented building relations with either Indians or French, British traders found Illinois' markets closed to them.

After King George III issued the Proclamation of 1763, prohibiting British settlement west of the Appalachian Mountains, traders and land speculators focused their attentions on the Illinois Country, which had been excluded from the ban because it was already a European colony rather than Indian Country. In late 1764, while Britain still struggled to gain more than a fragile foothold in the West, George Croghan encouraged the Philadelphia traders John Baynton, Samuel Wharton, and George Morgan to expand their trade and land interests to the Illinois Country. Croghan advised that the traders who arrived in the region first stood to gain the most.[54] Baynton, Wharton, and Morgan believed that by entering the trade early they could exploit a wide-open market. At the same time, in the one western region open to British commerce, the firm could buy land from French *habitants* and sell it to newly arrived Anglo colonists. Calling on their powerful friends in London and in colonial governments, the speculators hoped to gain official sanction.

In early 1765, Baynton, Wharton, and Morgan seemed, like the British empire as a whole, on the cusp of achieving their ambitions. The three Philadelphians enjoyed the support of powerful friends positioned throughout the mid-Atlantic colonies. George Croghan and Sir William Johnson backed their trading interests from their positions in the British Indian Department. On the advice of Croghan and Johnson, Baynton, Wharton, and Morgan dispatched a wagon train carrying their goods to Fort Pitt in advance of word that the British government had reopened the western trade. The firm had a head start on any potential competitors on the East Coast. Over the next year, the three merchants continued working their connections in the British imperial government. In March 1766, Croghan, Johnson, and New Jersey governor William Franklin joined them to form the Illinois Company. The company conspired to buy French land titles on the Mississippi River, but Franklin recognized that the deeds held little value unless the British government established a colony there. Croghan, Franklin, and Johnson tried to cast themselves as impartial, all keeping their membership in the outfit a secret while they lobbied for the company's schemes. In London, Franklin's well-respected and highly connected father, Benjamin, advised British officials of the need for a colony in the West.[55] Baynton, Wharton, and Morgan, with their powerful friends backing them, anticipated good fortune.

Nevertheless, the endeavor began to go poorly almost immediately. In April 1765, the Paxton Boys, an anti-Indian mob, attacked Baynton, Wharton & Morgan's shipment before it reached Fort Pitt, believing it contained presents for Indians allied with Pontiac. The destruction of that cargo, which included some goods belonging to the Indian Department, led Thomas Gage to conclude that Croghan was illegally involved in trade. Croghan maintained his secrecy about his role within the firm, withdrew from the enterprise, and with help from William Johnson, saved his job as an Indian agent. Still, Croghan continued to aid the firm in an unofficial capacity. Also, in the spring of 1765, the defections of junior partners Robert Field and Robert Callender posed more serious challenges, as they had agreed to oversee the firm's interests in the West. When both men quit the firm, much to Morgan's chagrin, the duties fell to him.[56]

The partners chose Morgan to go west because he had both a financial and familial stake in the enterprise. In addition to his partnership in the firm, Morgan had married John Baynton's daughter Polly. Like many European trading houses, Baynton, Wharton & Morgan relied on kinship to reinforce business agreements. In addition to the Baynton-Morgan marriage, the firm's suppliers included the Chevalier family, another group of Philadelphia merchants married to the Baynton family.[57] The partners of Baynton, Wharton, and Morgan understood the security and power that came from combining business and kinship, but once in Illinois, prejudice or ignorance prevented them from recognizing that similar patterns regulated trade there as well.

Morgan found limited access to the social networks that controlled trade in the midcontinent. For decades, Indians of the Illinois Country had dealt with French traders, who had integrated into the region's kinship-based trade networks. Through George Croghan, Morgan had contacts with upper Ohio valley Indians such as his Seneca guide, Silver Heels, and the Ottawa Indians who carried messages for him. In Illinois, those connections held little value. Additionally, Morgan failed to develop lasting relations with the French merchants engaged in the Indian trade. These Interior French businessmen controlled an extensive, kin-based trade network that stretched from Montreal to the Mississippi valley to New Orleans. Morgan struggled to enter the existing power structure that governed the fur trade. As a result, the fur trade never constituted more than 5 percent of the firm's business.[58]

More troubling, tense and tenuous relations with British officials and colonial regulations further limited Morgan's trade. When he arrived in the Illinois Country in the spring of 1766, Morgan discovered to his dismay that a few local traders had contracted with Fort Chartres's commandant, John Reed, to supply the post's garrison.[59] As a result, Morgan had no market with the British army. At the same time, in an effort to prevent smuggling and to limit French influence on Native peoples, Great Britain prohibited traders from traveling to Indian villages. They were supposed to operate at posts, where British officers could supervise their commerce. The policy carried little weight among French traders, who flouted English rule, or with smugglers from Spanish Illinois.[60] Even British merchants sneaked off into the backcountry, hoping to profit beyond the purview of the empire. But the policy tethered lawful British traders to forts and towns, where they waited, often in vain, for Indians to come to them. Morgan established four stores in Illinois, but for months at a time, few Indians visited.

Although few Indians traveled to Baynton, Wharton & Morgan's stores, Morgan's ample supply of goods—approximately £30,000 worth—attracted a stream of customers during the Philadelphian's early days in the Illinois Country. However, most of the transactions were small, usually amounting to less than one hundred livres (or about nine pounds sterling). Between May 1766 and February 1767, British soldiers and officers made nearly 60 percent of the purchases at Morgan's Kaskaskia store. French *habitants* made up the rest. Morgan's shoppers took advantage of his diverse stock of cloth, hats, knives, handkerchiefs, rum, and metal goods. The purchasing habits of British soldiers and officers varied little from those of French *habitants*, although they spent an inordinate amount on rum and other alcoholic beverages. The British Indian Department and its employees purchased more from Morgan than did any other customers. This commerce kept the firm afloat but fell far short of the partners' expectations.[61]

During Morgan's travels from Philadelphia to the Illinois Country and back, he learned what Anglo-Americans discovered repeatedly in the late eighteenth century. The region's rivers made a westward journey relatively easy. Getting back was a different matter. In ideal conditions, the trip from Philadelphia to Illinois took about two months, while the return voyage via New Orleans took twice as long. Morgan noted that, due to river conditions and the possibility of Indian attacks, only two months—January and February—were recommended for shipping goods down the Ohio. The return route posed greater challenges. From the Illinois Country, Morgan was "at a Loss" for how to get even the few furs received back to Philadelphia. Shipment required a series of transfers from canoes to bateaux to ships, and adverse winds and currents made delays inevitable. Without proper care, furs and skins could rot in the southern heat. The circuit from Philadelphia to Kaskaskia and back remained too long, too impractical, and too expensive to be profitable. At the end of 1766, Baynton, Wharton, and Morgan found themselves, because of travel delays, unable to transport the furs they had collected in the Illinois Country in time to pay their outstanding debts. Owing £3,000 to a company in London, the firm asked the Franklins to cover the loan for six months, until the firm could transport its furs to market.[62]

Local conditions and imperial policies converged to undercut Morgan's modest successes in the West. First, in March 1767, under pressure from London to reduce expenses, Gage ordered officers in the Illinois Country "to deal out Presents with a sparing hand." Early the following year, Morgan complained that his accounts with the Indian Department had become "contemptible."[63] Business with the Indian Department would not fund Baynton, Wharton & Morgan's western venture. Second, limited to a small share of the Illinois Country fur trade, Morgan acquired more grain, livestock, and meat than beaver pelts, bison robes, or deerskins. Unlike furs, agricultural produce and game meat were not valuable enough to ship back to Pennsylvania or to Europe. However, Morgan and his partners recognized that a ready market for such products sat nearby in the Fort Chartres garrison.

At the end of 1766, Morgan returned to Philadelphia, and he and his partners redoubled their efforts to gain the contract to supply Fort Chartres. Multiple roadblocks stood in their path. Beyond John Reed's refusal to deal with them, the trio learned sometime that winter that the British government had granted another Philadelphia firm an exclusive contract at the fort. Baynton, Wharton, and Morgan hoped that they could convince the British administration to choose them instead. Writing to Gage, British administrators, and the Board of Trade, the three men explained that they could provision the British garrison more reliably and less expensively. Worried that their pitch would not convince officials, Baynton, Wharton, and Morgan offered Lauchlin Macleane, an undersecretary in Secretary of State Lord Shelburne's office, one-seventh of the profits from the venture, if he could convince the government to choose their firm. Macleane rejected the overture and reported it to Shelburne.[64] In the end, the letter-writing campaign came to naught.

Thwarted in London, Baynton, Wharton, and Morgan turned their attention in 1768 to currying favor with Colonel John Wilkins, the incoming commandant of Fort Chartres. The previous year, Morgan worked with French *habitants* disgruntled over John Reed's excessive taxing and fining of colonists to force the recall of the corrupt and heavy-handed commandant. As the administration changed in the spring of 1768, Baynton, Wharton, and Morgan seized the opportunity to win an ally. When Wilkins stopped in Philadelphia on his way to the Illinois Country, Baynton and Wharton agreed to pay him 5 percent commission on their business as well as a biannual stipend of £500, in exchange for preferred status as suppliers and a promise to reduce illicit trade. Soon after Wilkins arrived in Illinois that fall, Morgan reported that business had "greatly & agreeably increased." Morgan and Wilkins also purchased title to 100,000 acres for the Illinois Company, adding to the firm's holdings.[65]

The agreement between Wilkins and Baynton, Wharton & Morgan began auspiciously. But as it crumbled in 1769 and 1770, it wrecked the career of the commandant and destroyed the firm. The French traders who had supplied Fort Chartres during John Reed's tenure resented being pushed aside. They appealed to Thomas Gage, condemning Wilkins as corrupt. According to one British soldier in Illinois, by 1769, George Morgan was "universally hated" by the Interior French and possessed "but few friends of any other Nation here." Once agents of the rightful owners of the Fort Chartres contract arrived in early 1770, Morgan lost his best and largest market. Having sunk most of his available cash into unsellable land, Morgan could not pay Wilkins's fee when it came due, and his poverty angered the colonel.[66]

Because of the firm's troubled relations with the Interior French, Indians, and British officials, Morgan could do little to improve its "unfortunate Situation." Baynton, Wharton, and Morgan had invested £75,000 in trade goods but had sold little of the merchandise they had purchased. Morgan focused on other enterprises, especially agriculture and distilling, but in each endeavor, his conflicts with the local population and his distance from Philadelphia greatly reduced the possibility of success. Meanwhile, hostility between Wilkins and Morgan led to a protracted legal battle, which sullied the reputations of both men.[67]

Land speculation and trade brought disappointment for the Philadelphia merchants. In 1767, unbeknownst to George Morgan, who continued buying land in the Illinois Country, the partners of the Illinois Company abandoned their ambitions in the Mississippi valley. Instead, they turned their attention to lands in western Virginia and present-day Ohio, more appealing because of their proximity to the British colonies. Samuel Wharton asked William Franklin to stop lobbying for the Mississippi River colony in favor of their new scheme, which they called "Vandalia." Two years later,

Wharton's interests converged with those of other land speculators, whom Benjamin Franklin united to promote Vandalia and the twenty million acres it would encompass. Yet British colonists did not wait for recognition of the colony. They poured into the upper Ohio valley and further antagonized the nativist alliance. Official sanction for Vandalia never came, because the conflict between Native peoples and Anglo invaders became a full-fledged war in 1774.[68]

Meanwhile, for the five years that Baynton, Wharton and Morgan traded in Illinois, business never matched expectations because of their ignorance of the social landscape of Illinois, an inability to maintain good relations with British officials and the Interior French, and a business model constructed on a poor understanding of the geography of Middle America. By 1770, George Morgan regretted the exuberance that had driven his entrance into the Illinois trade. The visions of wealth—"the Golden Dreams of Tagus," in Morgan's words—had been replaced by the reality of what Morgan took to calling "this more than accursed Country."[69] In 1771, Morgan returned to Philadelphia, where he spent the next four years extricating himself from the rubble of his firm's failure.

The conflict between George Morgan, John Wilkins, and the Interior French exacerbated the growing British problems in the Illinois Country and the West. When Thomas Gage sent Wilkins to the Illinois Country in 1768, he had told the new commandant that the post needed "some sensible and discreet Officer." Four years later, complaints of abuse and corruption against Wilkins swamped Gage. No one defended the once-promising administrator. Gage soon recognized that Wilkins deserved the fault for the unrest. "That you have many Enemies is certain," the general wrote, "but how they became so, you may devise better than me."[70] Gage refused to accept any further responsibility for Wilkins and his many errors.

In 1772, Gage washed his hands of Wilkins, the Illinois Country, and the West. Tired of the expense of distant, decaying outposts, he ordered the evacuation and destruction of Fort Chartres and Fort Pitt. At Fort Chartres, the troops turned their cannons on the fort's walls and opened its floodgates to let the Mississippi do the rest of the work. Most of the garrison removed to other posts in North America. Only a minimal force at Kaskaskia remained in the Illinois Country. Four years later, as Britain faced challenges from a revolutionary movement in its Atlantic colonies, Gage recalled the remaining troops from Illinois. Ironically, given British attitudes toward French officials a decade earlier, Philippe-François de Rastel de Rocheblave, a Frenchman and former officer in Spanish Illinois, took charge of the colony, becoming its last "British" commandant.[71]

≈ Before Pontiac's rapt audience in April 1764, he professed to represent the interests of a vast alliance determined to prevent Britain from extending its empire west of the Appalachian Mountains. Indeed, Pontiac claimed that "all the nations of the Continent" shared his ideology and that they stood united against their British foes.[72] To be sure, Pontiac exaggerated the extent of the alliance. But between 1763 and 1765, he had built an extensive network of allies that halted the ambitions of a powerful empire. The dreams of pan-Indian unity shared by Pontiac, Neolin, and their many compatriots proved fragile. British used their own ties to western nations to dismantle the alliance.

After 1765, Pontiac lost much of his influence, but the highest-ranking British officials believed that he remained the leading authority in the West. In 1767, even while noting the growing faction of Ottawas opposed to Pontiac, the British commandant at Detroit expressed his wish that Pontiac would attend an upcoming council: "I am Sensible his presence will always have a good effect." British intentions of using Pontiac as their agent weakened his position among the Ottawas. One British official reported that Ottawas sought to replace Pontiac as chief, believing him too close to the British. In 1768, another stated that he had suffered "severall Beatings" at the hands of "his own tribe."[73]

Pontiac's interactions with Illinois Indians shaped the trajectory of his life at the end of the 1760s. As he worked to regain influence, he regularly traveled back and forth between the Ottawas of Detroit and his relatives on the Wabash River and in the Illinois Country. Despite his familial connections with the Illinois, their encounters could turn violent. At Detroit in the spring of 1766, for unknown reasons, an altercation broke out between Pontiac and three Illinois diplomats on their way to meet with William Johnson. In the fight, Pontiac stabbed the Peoria chief, Black Dog. Yet, two years later, Pontiac returned to the Illinois Country to visit "the brothers of [his] wife." Illinois were unsure of what Pontiac intended. In the spring of 1769, reports circulated that Pontiac was headed to the Illinois Country with 150 canoes of warriors, who intended to "Cutt off the nations of the Illinois." Pontiac insisted that he came only to trade. On April 20, almost five years to the day since he convinced the Illinois to go to war, Pontiac walked out of the Cahokia store operated by Baynton, Wharton, and Morgan. The world went black. A nephew of Black Dog clubbed Pontiac in the head and then stabbed and killed him. Pontiac's death came in retribution for the stabbing at Detroit three years earlier.[74] The kinship ties that Pontiac had utilized so successfully in his war against the British led to his demise in the streets of Cahokia.

The decade following the Seven Years' War was an era of great hopes and great frustrations, in which Great Britain, British colonists, and Native peoples put forth new visions for the North American midcontinent only to have their ambitions dashed by political and geographical realities. The persistence of alliances, kinship ties, and other relationships, some of which predated the French colonial era, restricted the possibilities for remaking the midcontinent. Pontiac's nativism advocated pan-Indian unity, but his alliance only connected those nations already linked by kinship. British agents used their own alliance networks to chip away at the nativist coalition, achieving victory through diplomacy.

Once in control of the Illinois Country, however, British operatives dismissed the lessons of their triumph. Great Britain was a financially destitute empire struggling to fund its colonies, and it had taken on an impossible task in the Illinois Country. The attitudes of its officers toward Native peoples and the Interior French exacerbated British woes. Stationed far beyond the usual reach of British traders and agents and unwilling to work with either French or Indian locals, Anglo imperialists lacked the influence necessary to form alliances and to stop violence. Meanwhile, lack of knowledge about Illinois geography and the people who lived there wrecked Baynton, Wharton, and Morgan's Illinois venture. All the while, traders and officials struggled to contain animosities that predated or originated independently from British concerns in the region. Baynton, Wharton, and Morgan discovered those perils in the aftermath of Pontiac's death, when five warriors led by his Ojibwe relative Minweweh (also called Le Grand Sauteux) murdered three of their storekeepers in Cahokia.[75]

Britain expected that the Illinois Country would be a boon to the empire. Within a few years, the colony had lost much of its sheen. In 1768, less than three years after imperial troops arrived at Fort Chartres, Thomas Gage lamented, "The Ilinois has been a gulph that has swallowed up every thing, and returned nothing back."[76] Matters hardly improved in the years that followed. The British repeated many of the mistakes and suffered many of the failures of the French empire. A thousand miles from Fort Pitt, the last post on the route from the Atlantic coast to the Illinois Country, Fort Chartres stood well beyond the reach of British diplomatic networks. But the geography of the empire alone did not produce failure. Across the Mississippi River, a new settlement at St. Louis overcame many of the same geographical obstacles that hindered British Illinois. Its merchant founders prospered where Baynton, Wharton, and Morgan failed. In contrast to Britain's antagonistic relationship with Indians and francophone colonists, French traders, Spanish imperialists, and Native peoples merged personal, kinship-based ties and the resources of the empire to pursue complementary goals.

CHAPTER FIVE

An Empire of Kin

The beginning of 1804 found Auguste Chouteau in a contemplative mood. The new century, only four years old, had brought much upheaval to the fur magnate and his home city of St. Louis. In 1800, Spain returned Louisiana, including St. Louis, to France, which sold its claim to the fledging American empire less than three years later. Now, on the eve of the colony's official transfer to the United States, Chouteau looked back forty years to another moment of transition in the region's imperial history. Following the Seven Years' War, much as in early 1804, Louisiana's colonists knew they would soon be subjects of a new empire, but the handover had not yet occurred. In 1763, six months after France ceded its North American holdings to Great Britain and Spain, the teenage Chouteau left his birth city of New Orleans, probably for the first time. He made the thousand-mile trek up the Mississippi River to the Illinois Country, a place unfamiliar to both Chouteau and his stepfather, the merchant Pierre Laclède Liguest. Across the intervening four decades, the Chouteau family, with Auguste at its head, had risen from its initial status as ill-informed newcomers to command much of the Missouri River fur trade. The Chouteaus' ascent to the top of the region's most lucrative industry stemmed from two factors: their accurate reading of the geography of Middle America and their ability to build personal, kinship-based ties with Indian leaders, rival traders, and colonial officials.

Awaiting the Americans' arrival, Chouteau penned an account of those early years of St. Louis in a lengthy "journal," combining myth and fact to

Fig. 5.1 Auguste Chouteau.

stress his and his stepfather's role in founding the city. According to Chou-teau, Laclède sought an ideal place to base his fur-trading operations. Dis-satisfied with the poor selection of buildings for sale in the "small village" at Ste. Genevieve, he determined to establish an outpost of his own. At the end of 1763, Laclède headed north toward the mouth of the Missouri. Upon spotting the bluff that would soon house his new city, the "beauty" of the site attracted the Frenchman. Even more, "he found there all the advantages that one could desire to found a settlement which might become very con-siderable hereafter." Particularly notable was the bluff's close proximity to both the Missouri and Mississippi Rivers. As soon as the ice thawed and river traffic opened in February 1764, the thirteen- or fourteen-year-old Chouteau led thirty men to the site to begin erecting the city.[1] Chouteau's "journal" is equal part eyewitness account and mythical origin story. Not without some justification, he cast himself and his family as the founders and leaders of the fledgling settlement, but he probably omitted the contributions of longtime Illinois residents, who might have directed Laclède to the bluff or perhaps even lived there already.[2] Yet Chouteau's account, for all of its mythmaking, documents how the Laclède-Chouteau family emerged as economic and political leaders in St. Louis, the most important city in the midcontinent.

In many respects, Laclède and the Chouteaus used strategies familiar to other successful polities and families in Middle America. Chouteau reported that Laclède chose the bluff overlooking the Mississippi River because "so many advantages were embraced in this site by its locality and its central position."[3] From St. Louis's "central position" at the confluence of the Missouri and Mississippi Rivers, the family connected fur production in the West to markets in New Orleans. At the same time, Laclède and the Chouteaus built an extensive social network of traders, colonial officials, and Native peoples that placed them at the core of economic and political life in the midcontinent. They valued close relationships with people such as Louis St. Ange de Bellerive, a French officer later employed by Spain. Chouteau's "journal" includes an account of St. Ange's early career in the Illinois Country, underlining the significance of the relationship between the family and the man, who while serving as an adviser for Spain, lodged in the family's home.

The existence of Chouteau's account reveals a third strategy for success in the midcontinent: the control of information and the crafting of narratives favorable to the family. Throughout the late eighteenth century, Laclède and especially Auguste Chouteau told stories to fellow colonists and Native leaders that highlighted their importance in the region. These stories attracted new allies and helped the Chouteaus gain even greater power and influence.

By the end of the eighteenth century, the Chouteaus occupied key positions in the economy and politics of the midcontinent. They built close relationships with a series of Spanish officials and married into elite Osage families. Kinship served as a kind of passport. It opened gateways and created bridges between culturally and politically distinct communities. The Chouteaus controlled the passages between the Spanish empire and the Osage Nation, making them important partners for both polities. Their trade network

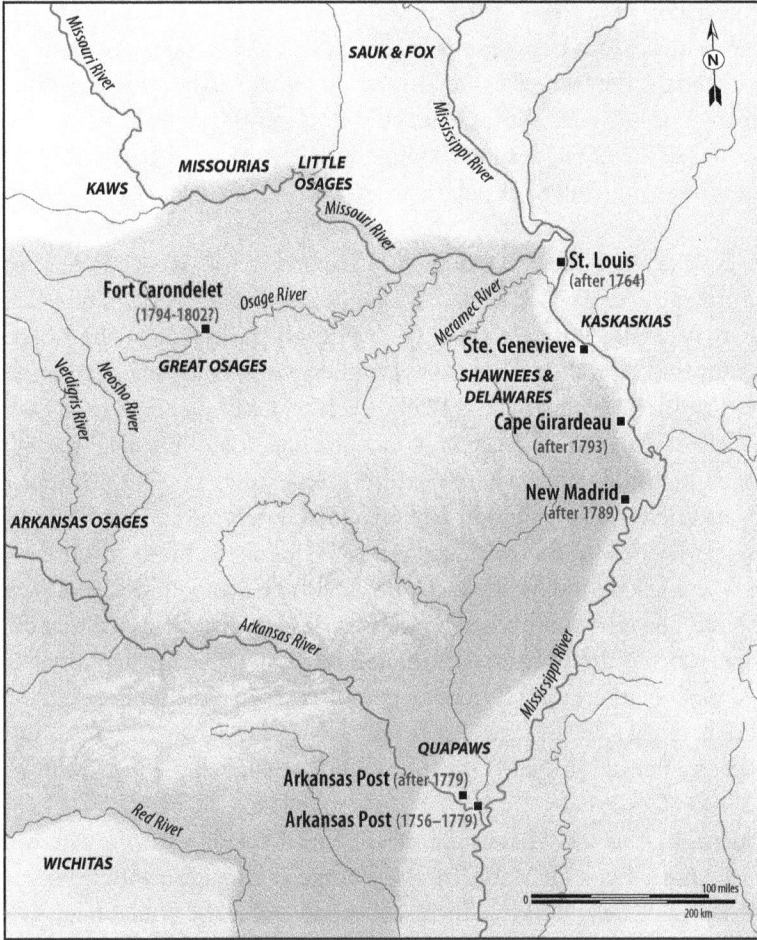

The North American Midcontinent, 1763–1804

░░░ Osage Nation, ca. 1790

ILLINOIS Indian Nation

■ Indian and French Towns

Map 4 The North American midcontinent, 1763–1804.

stretched along the rivers of the midcontinent, eventually reaching from the Osage Nation to St. Louis to colonial hubs and European ports. By the end of the century, they served as trusted advisers to the highest-ranking officials in Spanish Louisiana. Throughout, they pursued their own interests, using the power of the Osage Nation and the Spanish empire to buttress their position in the region and to enrich themselves and their relatives.

≈   By the time Pierre Laclède and his stepson arrived in the Illinois Country at the end of 1763, he had already cultivated the types of relationships that would lead to his family's eventual dominance of the Missouri River fur trade and its influence on both the Spanish and American empires. Sometime in the last half of the 1750s, Laclède, a recent émigré from France, met Gilbert Antoine de Maxent, a local merchant and his neighbor in the city's multiethnic, multiracial fourth militia district. In 1749, Maxent had married a rich widow and soon after bought a warehouse, where he supplied *voyageurs* headed up the Mississippi to the Illinois Country. Both men on the make, Laclède and Maxent schemed to escape their working-class neighborhood of taverns and tradespeople. Together, they determined that direct participation in the Indian trade offered more lucrative opportunities than did supplying others with European manufactures. In the twilight of French Louisiana, they received a monopoly on the Missouri River fur trade. Maxent would stay behind in New Orleans, while Laclède handled their affairs in the Illinois Country.[4]

Journeying up the Mississippi meant that Laclède and Auguste would leave behind a pregnant Marie Thérèse Bourgeois Chouteau with three young children. Laclède and Marie Thérèse met soon after the Frenchman arrived in New Orleans in 1755. At that point, she was the mother of a young son, Auguste, and the recently abandoned wife of the baker and tavern keeper René Auguste Chouteau. Catholic doctrine prevented Marie Thérèse from divorcing her wayward husband, but she and Laclède pursued a relationship without the sanction of the church. They set up housekeeping near the Maxent family. In 1758, they welcomed a new son, Pierre. The boy was baptized with the last name Chouteau, as were his three sisters, born over the following six years. Meanwhile, Laclède pretended to be a lodger in the Chouteau home.[5]

Neither Maxent's and Laclède's humble circumstances nor Laclède's curious living situation hampered their ambitions. As they planned their trading venture, the two men cultivated close connections with the French leadership in New Orleans, including Governor Louis Billouart, Chevalier de

Kerlerec. Once in the Illinois Country, Laclède and Chouteau further drew on Kerlerec's familial ties. The governor's brother-in-law, Pierre-Joseph Neyon de Villiers, commanded Fort de Chartres. When the merchants arrived with their goods in November 1763, Neyon de Villiers offered them storage space in the fort until they could establish their own warehouse. The following year, Jean-Jacques Blaise d'Abbadie, Kerlerec's replacement and another friend of Maxent and Laclède, ordered the closure of all French forts in the Illinois Country in preparation for the arrival of British troops. In executing d'Abbadie's order, Neyon de Villiers also closed Fort de Cavagnial, a French outpost on the Missouri River near present-day Leavenworth, Kansas. As far as d'Abbadie and Neyon de Villiers knew, the Missouri River and Fort de Cavagnial were to remain French possessions, but they aided their friends by shuttering the post.[6] As Laclède and Maxent commenced their endeavor, their allies in the government did all they could to ensure their success.

Not long after Laclède and Chouteau arrived in Illinois in November 1763, locals learned that the west bank of the Mississippi River belonged to Spain, the result of a secret 1762 treaty. Spain viewed its new Mississippi River border as a way to improve colonial defenses. The unmarked boundaries between Spanish and French holdings in Texas had provoked conflict between the two empires. The new boundary with Great Britain was clear and undisputed. In accepting western Louisiana, including the Illinois Country, Spain sought a buffer zone between the expansionist British empire and the rest of Spain's North American colonies. In particular, Spain wanted to protect the silver mines and Indian trade of northern New Spain and prevent British incursions to the Pacific Ocean. Louisiana would serve as a valuable first line of defense.[7] Yet, for years after the news arrived, Spain delayed taking possession of the colony and gave little indication of how it would govern once it did. In St. Louis, Laclède and the other residents continued building their lives and their community, in spite of the uncertainty that loomed over all preparations for the future.

In 1765, after surrendering Fort de Chartres to Britain, St. Ange moved his garrison across the Mississippi to St. Louis, which he selected as the new seat of government. The nearby Missouri River gave St. Louis strategic value, especially in preventing incursions from the British side of the river. Additionally, it sat on a limestone bluff, which protected it from floodwaters. And, even before St. Ange's arrival, St. Louis had become the beneficiary of the French exodus from British Illinois. St. Ange's choice benefited Laclède and Chouteau and their young town, guaranteeing that it would become the political, as well as the economic, heart of Spanish Illinois. At the end of 1765,

British officials reported that St. Louis, "only founded last year," was "flour-ishing" and rivaled what had been the "best settlement" east of the river.[8]

For two years, St. Ange commanded alone, anticipating the arrival of the Spanish. He met with visiting Indian diplomats. He oversaw the civil gov-ernment and signed deeds formalizing land grants given by Laclède. And he waited. In March 1766, Governor Antonio de Ulloa landed in New Orleans and soon sent word to St. Louis that Spain had taken possession of the colony. St. Ange responded with a warm letter, informing Ulloa of all of the work he had done to smooth the transition from French to Spanish governance. Most significantly, he had met with diplomats from "the different nations," whom he informed that "the Spanish and the French were the same nation." He predicted that Spain "will take possession of this district with as much ease as if nothing had changed between the two crowns."[9]

St. Ange had laid the groundwork for an easy transfer in the Illinois Country, but his efforts did not speed the arrival of Spanish government. A year after St. Ange's initial correspondence with Ulloa, the aging officer re-ceived word that Ulloa had dispatched Captain Francisco Ríu y Morales upstream with a contingent of Spanish troops. Surprisingly, he also learned that he and Ríu would share command: "You will each have your depart-ment." St. Ange would oversee Indian affairs, while Ríu headed the Spanish troops and erected a fort at the mouth of the Missouri River. Ulloa retained the experienced St. Ange in recognition of his "merit" and his "power in all regards." St. Ange wrote directly to Ríu, welcoming his troops as much-needed reinforcements and promising to provide advice and knowledge about "the state of this country and of the character of those who inhabit it as well as the dispositions of the various Nations and even of the maneuvers of our neighbors the English."[10]

The situation in St. Louis reflected a broader trend in the early years of Spanish Louisiana. The Spanish empire employed French officers to augment its small garrisons and to advise on local conditions. When Ulloa arrived in New Orleans in 1766, he brought too few troops, he believed, to command the colony. He sensed hostility from the thousands of francophone colonists who remained in New Orleans. For much of his tenure, he governed from La Balize, a small outpost near the mouth of the Mississippi. In early 1767, he signed an agreement with Louisiana's French governor, Charles-Philippe Aubry, to share command of Louisiana. Ulloa raised the Spanish flag at La Balize, while the French standard waved over New Orleans. Aubry continued at his post, through the uprising that drove Ulloa out of the colony in 1768 and the arrival of a new Spanish government the following year. Less extreme examples occurred throughout the Mississippi valley. From St. Louis to Arkansas Post to Natchitoches to New Orleans, men who once served France Hispanicized their names and took jobs under the new regime.[11]

Although St. Ange's position in the new empire originated from need as much as design, he served a crucial role in Spain's strategy toward Louisiana. Because Louisiana offered little economic benefit compared to the wealthier mining colonies to the southwest, Spain sought to maintain the colony as inexpensively as possible, in part by implementing an Indian policy that it believed mirrored French practices. French officials laid the groundwork for this practice by telling Native audiences that the transfer of Louisiana from France to Spain meant that "the two nations have become one." Spanish officials played up the kinship ties of the ruling Bourbon families, noting "the close bonds of blood and alliance between the kings of Spain and France." They promised to continue the diplomatic practices of the prior regime, emphasizing trade-based alliances over military domination.[12]

Spanish officials had little of the knowledge required to implement this plan. When the French empire handed over Louisiana and its officials vacated their posts, they left behind few descriptions or maps of the region. Instead, the Spanish relied on individuals such as St. Ange, whose personal experience could fill in the gaps in colonial records. As Ríu headed to St. Louis, Ulloa advised him that St. Ange, "being a man experienced in treating with savages will give instruction as to how they must be treated."[13]

In this context, the close relationship between St. Ange and Laclède became crucial to the latter's success in the Missouri River fur trade. Although Spain hoped to replicate French rule, it issued new regulations on commerce with Indian nations, including instituting a licensing system and limiting or prohibiting the trade in brandy, firearms, and slaves. St. Ange helped Laclède navigate the new government and presented him as an ally to the Spanish government. Through the bond with St. Ange, Laclède merged his personal interests with those of the empire. By 1770, Laclède provided the Spanish government with supplies to offer Indian visitors and served as a landlord to the empire, renting buildings to house the lieutenant governor and his garrison. Until St. Ange's death in 1774, he remained a key adviser for Spanish officials at St. Louis and a valuable friend to the Laclède-Chouteau family, with whom he lived in his final years.[14]

≈   Connections to the French and Spanish officials of Louisiana eased the path to success, but the Chouteaus' prospects depended on safe passage and abundant commerce on the Missouri River, the key to the St. Louis fur trade.

The Missouri and its tributaries offered access to the interior of the continent. In 1766, Aubry anticipated, "One will take from there very beautiful and rare peltries." Sitting at the confluence of the Missouri and Mississippi Rivers, St. Louis provided a natural stopping point for Missouri furs on their way to the markets of New Orleans—a fact exploited by the town's founders.[15] Laclède and Chouteau realized that any future success depended on carefully navigating the geography and political world of the lower Missouri valley.

However, Aubry noted the river's perils as well. The governor wrote that the valley had been "little frequented up to this time . . . on account of the ferocity of the tribes and of the difficulty of navigating the Missouri." The Missouri has a swift current that carves channels and ridges into the river's sandy bottom. During the eighteenth century, its course was notoriously turbulent. Navigation changed from one year to the next, as late-winter and early-spring floods washed away sandbars, opening new paths and blocking old ones. Navigation information became outdated almost as soon as it was recorded. Travelers needed to know and understand the river if they were to avoid all the obstacles that could sink or snag their canoes and pirogues.[16]

In contrast to the volatile river, diplomacy hewed to predictable channels, even if colonists struggled to identify them. From St. Louis's earliest days, Native nations hoped to render Laclède and Chouteau's outpost a dependency. After all, these wealthy colonists squatted on their land. In July 1764, hundreds of Missouria Indians arrived at Laclède's trading post. The older man was absent, so they spoke first with Chouteau. They announced that "they wished to form a village around the house [Laclède and Chouteau] were building." Chouteau recalled that he sent for Laclède, absent at Fort de Chartres, who convinced the Missouria visitors that settling at St. Louis would expose them to attack from the powerful nations east of the Mississippi.[17] The Missourias dropped their request to surround the outpost with their own village, but this moment signaled that the nations of the lower Missouri, most notably Missourias and Osages, would attempt to use the new outpost as a source of wealth and influence to support their regional ambitions.

Native polities had their own criteria for who could or could not trade on the Missouri River. Because the fur trade brought guns and ammunition to Native communities, it presented both advantages and disadvantages to Missouri River nations. To better regulate commerce between St. Louis and groups upriver, Indian nations controlled the flow of river traffic, stopping travelers to determine their motives, trade with them, and request gifts. Traveling upstream from St. Louis, traders encountered, in order, Missourias, Osages, Kaws, and Otoes. When Laclède and Chouteau founded St. Louis, French and Spaniards knew little about the nations farther up the river and its tributaries: Poncas, Omahas, Pawnees, Arikaras, and Mandans.[18] Before the end of the eighteenth century, traders reached those nations and others 1,000 or more miles up the Missouri, but such journeys depended on negotiations with the many nations that lived along the river. Each nation sought trade and to exclude its enemies from that trade, particularly in arms and ammunition.

The Osage Nation exerted unmatched authority over the lower Missouri valley, dominating the river from St. Louis to the future site of Kansas City. In 1758, Governor Kerlerec advised that Europeans working in the region had to "show consideration" to the Osages, in particular. Osages often detained traders or otherwise discouraged them from engaging in commerce with the nations farther upriver, because they held an advantage over their rivals as long as they could prevent them from trading for weapons. In 1772, Pedro Piernas, the lieutenant governor at St. Louis, complained to his superior about Little Osages, who had "always shown themselves daring and insolent." Recently, they had been "forcing of contributions from traders" traveling to nations farther up the Missouri River. In effect, Osages ran a tollbooth. They demanded tribute in exchange for passage. When their security trumped other concerns, Osages halted river traffic, forcing traders to turn back. A 1775 report totaling trade among the tribes of the Missouri River noted that traders who were sent beyond the Osages to Kaws and the Republic band of Pawnee Indians were "not able to enter."[19] St. Louis traders dealing with Osage enemies posed a threat to Osages, and the nation used its location to improve its position in the Missouri River fur trade. To overcome these obstacles, French traders needed to build good relations with Osages. Without their support, the traders could not operate on the Missouri.

Since at least 1700, Osages ruled the prairies along the Missouri and Osage Rivers. A flood early in the nation's history divided Osages into five towns. Although dispersed geographically, Osages remained united by culture, politics, and kinship. One town, the Down-Below-People, or *U-Dse-Ta*, moved north to the Missouri River, where its residents became the first Osages to meet Europeans. During an early encounter, French travelers asked the Down-Below-People for their name. Communication problems led the

French to call them the "Little Osages." That misunderstanding among out-siders rendered Little Osages more visible in European documents than the other Osage towns were. Colonists referred to the other four towns simply as the "Great Osages." By the mid-eighteenth century, the separation be-tween Little Osages and Great Osages became firmly implanted in the minds of colonists, although it held little significance among Osages.[20]

As early as the turn of the 1700s, French traders braved the Missouri River to seek out new sources of wealth. Having witnessed the rise of the Illinois, Missourias and Osages were reluctant to let Europeans ally with their rivals farther west. In 1718, Charles Claude du Tisné made his first attempt at as-cending the Missouri, only to be waylaid by Missourias who refused to let him pass when they learned he was headed to the Wichitas. They were, ac-cording to du Tisné, "jealous of the French going among the other nations." He returned to the Illinois Country. The following year, du Tisné reached the Osages, who offered him gifts—horses stolen from the Pawnees and furs—and welcomed his plans to forge an alliance and open regular trade. Their mood turned hostile when du Tisné announced that he intended to continue westward to the "Panis," a reference to either the Pawnees or Wich-itas. They allowed him passage only after he promised to carry firearms with him for personal use only, not trade. Still, Osages worried about du Tisné's mission. They sent messengers to the "Panis," warning that the French intended to capture them and "render them all slaves." Their plan backfired when du Tisné convinced "Panis" that Osages had lied and then sealed an alliance through trade, including the firearms he carried. However, "Panis" then refused to let du Tisné continue westward to meet Padoucas, "their mortal enemies." When du Tisné passed through Osage towns on his re-turn, he learned that his actions among the "Panis" had soured relations with Osages. They refused to provide guides, and du Tisné had to find his own way back to Kaskaskia.[21] This early encounter between the French empire and the Missouri River nations established the pattern for decades of inter-action, as nations guarded access to trade and blockaded their enemies.

Still, a small but valuable trade thrived on the lower river in the decades following du Tisné's journey. Each year, *voyageurs* set out from Cahokia and Kaskaskia to buy the pelts of bears, deer, beavers, and other creatures har-vested by Missouri River nations. When conflict broke out on the Missouri, officials accused the traders of stoking rivalries and encouraging violence. More likely, these clashes were but a new chapter in long-standing hostili-ties. Once again, France believed it could bring peace and tranquility by exerting control over its subjects.[22]

From 1724 to 1736, France maintained Fort d'Orleans next to a Missouria town in what is now central Missouri. For all but the first several months of the fort's existence, the St. Ange family commanded the post and profited from its trade. In October 1726, commandant Robert Groston de St. Ange paid a debt in Kaskaskia with 800 livres worth of pelts, indicating more than a little interest in the fur trade. Although the governor reassigned St. Ange in 1727, his elder son, Louis, supervised the fort for another nine years, until he replaced the deceased François-Marie Bissot de Vinsenne on the Wabash, following the disastrous 1736 Chickasaw campaign. In the next decade, officials began to worry once again about the "vexations" of the voyageurs who "cause disturbances and dissension" among the Missouri valley nations.[23]

In 1744, Governor Pierre de Rigaud de Vaudreuil de Cavagnial ordered a new fort built on the Missouri in the Kaw Nation, probably near either present-day Kansas City or Leavenworth. The commandant of Fort de Cavagnial enjoyed a commercial monopoly in the region, although illicit independent traders continued to work on the river. For the rest of the French colonial period, a small but valuable trade in beaver, deer, and bear skins flourished on the lower Missouri River. Each year, Fort de Cavagnial sent one hundred bundles of beaver pelts downstream to the Illinois Country, while Osages and Missourias produced an additional eighty packages of deer- and bearskins each year. (In comparison, most of the posts in the Illinois Country and Wabash valley produced between 200 and 400 bundles of pelts annually.)[24]

At the founding of St. Louis, the Osage Nation was a rising political and economic power in the midcontinent, enjoying control of the lower Missouri River and having recently driven rival nations out of prime hunting lands in the Arkansas valley. Little Osages lived on the Missouri, about 250 river miles west of St. Louis, while Great Osages resided on the Osage River in what is now southwestern Missouri and were expanding farther south and west at the expense of Caddoan speakers in the upper Arkansas River valley. Osages pushed their Taovaya and Kadohadacho enemies across the Red River, which runs along the present-day boundary between Texas and Oklahoma before flowing through Arkansas and into the Mississippi River. Rich in bison, these new hunting lands added to the Osages' power. By the early 1760s, their territory stretched from the Missouri River south to the Arkansas River and beyond. Continuing a tradition in the midcontinent, they used their location on those waterways to isolate their rivals and prevent them from trading with Europeans. Their control over these rivers made the Osages the most powerful polity in the lower Missouri valley.[25]

Whether or not Laclède and Chouteau knew it, Osage politics shaped their entry into the Missouri valley fur trade. Maxent, Laclède & Co.'s monopoly—aided by Neyon de Villiers closing Fort de Cavagnial and ordering the return of all traders from the Missouri—reduced Osage access to European goods at a crucial moment. Osages needed weapons and ammunition to continue their expansionist wars in the Red River valley, and they wanted to trade furs and slaves acquired in the Southwest for European goods. In this context, the Osages welcomed Laclède and Chouteau and their stores of merchandise into their towns.

Domestic Osage politics also shaped Laclède and Chouteau's experience. Two chiefs and a council of priests *(non'-hon-zhin-ga)* headed the Osage Nation. The chiefs each came from one of the nation's two moieties, and each handled distinct duties. The chief from the *Tsi-zhu* moiety handled peace and diplomacy. His counterpart from the *Hon-ga* moiety oversaw war. Because traders came to the Osages as friendly visitors, they dealt with the *Tsi-zhu Ga-hi-ge*, or peace chief. The *Tsi-zhu Ga-hi-ge* came from the Great Crane clan, which performed the duties of peacemaker for the nation. Although the *non'-hon-zhin-ga* wielded more power than the chiefs did, they mostly remained unremarked on by Europeans, who seem to have dealt more with the *Tsi-zhu Ga-hi-ge*. By the middle of the eighteenth century, the *Tsi-zhu Ga-hi-ge* was a man named Clermont, and he and his clan became the primary beneficiaries of foreign trade. As in most other Indian nations, neither chief possessed absolute power. They could not command Osages to take any course of action, but they could cajole and sway people to follow them. Displays of generosity, including feasts and gift giving, helped convince skeptics. Although Clermont and his *Hon-ga Ga-hi-ge* counterpart, Jean Lafond, held equal but distinct authority, Spain identified Clermont as the nation's principal chief, probably because of his ties to European traders.[26]

Like the *Tsi-zhu Ga-hi-ge* and *Hon-ga Ga-hi-ge*, whose power balanced each other, Osage men and women held complementary roles that together preserved the nation and its status. Women represented the creation of life, and in their roles as farmers and mothers, they tended the crops necessary to feed their communities and birthed and raised the children that ensured the survival of their nation. They were "the channel through whom all human life must proceed and continue." In contrast, men represented the destruction of life. They provided food through hunting and protected and expanded the nation through warfare. Both male duties required killing.[27] This balance created mutual obligations between male and female relatives, with each having expectations they were required to fulfill.

This gendered balance of power extended to political and spiritual life as well. A man had to be married before he could join the *non'-hon-zhin-ga*, and his wife acquired her own responsibilities. She became the keeper of the *wa-xo'-be*, the sacred war bundle. If a warrior wished to carry the bundle with him for protection, he had to ask the keeper's permission. If she agreed, she then performed a series of ceremonies for four days following the men's departure to guarantee their safe return. After a priest's death, his wife could join the *non'-hon-zhin-ga*. The other priests performed the same ceremony they had used to induct her husband, except "all references to the destruction of life are carefully avoided."[28]

Yet, despite the balance between *Tsi-zhu* and *Hon-ga* and between men and women, Osage society could be quite hierarchical. In some instances, individual and clan status were fixed by Osage tradition. Age and birth order mattered. Children and teenagers had little say over their lives, up to and including their choice of spouses. Children were ranked by birth order, with the eldest son and daughter occupying positions of privilege. Likewise, according to custom, chiefs could only come from certain clans. Other clans possessed esoteric knowledge that gave them status within the nation. However, through personal deeds and wealth, individuals could gain prestige. A man who wished to join the *non'-hon-zhin-ga* first had to acquire one skin from each of seven exotic animals. With that quest complete, he held a four-day feast, where he fed and provided gifts to priests from all twenty-four Osage clans. If his widow wished to take his place, she had to pay "a suitable fee." These requirements set a high bar of entry for would-be priests. Still, men of any clan or class could rise to prominence as hunters and warriors. Society rewarded the individual acts of bravery or skill through which men provided meat for their families, defended their communities from raiders, and participated in successful attacks against enemy nations.[29]

Pierre Laclède and Auguste Chouteau had to navigate this unfamiliar world when they opened trade relations with Osages. As a *négociant*, or merchant, Laclède helmed trading operations but rarely dealt with the day-to-day work of the fur trade. Like most men of his stature, he managed his firm's business in St. Louis, but he delegated the trips up the Missouri and negotiations with Indian trading partners to his sons. Both Auguste Chouteau and his half brother, Pierre, worked extensively in the Osage Nation. They built relationships with Osage leaders and forged the kinship ties that allowed them to trade on the Missouri River. In the 1760s and 1770s, Auguste and Pierre became adopted members of the Osage Nation and married Osage women. The elder of the two brothers, Auguste Chouteau probably made his first foray into Osage Country shortly after he and Laclède established St. Louis in 1764. Eight years younger than Auguste, Pierre Chouteau began his relationship with the Osages when he joined the family business as a teenager in the mid-1770s.[30] Auguste arrived in Osage Country a stranger, a man with no reputation or honors. But he carried a cargo of trade goods that drew the attention of leading Osages. They sought to incorporate him and, by extension, to increase the prestige of their families, clans, and nation.

For Osages, as well as the French, marriage was a common and trusted way to forge political, military, and economic alliances and to create ties between families, communities, and nations. A set of rules dictated who could and could not marry in Osage society. Osages had to choose spouses from the opposite moiety. For example, a *Tsi-zhu* man had to marry a *Hon-ga* woman. This symbolized the unification of sky and land in the universe and of the Osage people as one nation. Men reached marriage age when they had established themselves as hunters or warriors. If a man attempted to marry before that, "he would be sure to suffer the painful mortification of a rejection; he would become the derision of the warriors, and the contempt of the [women]." Women married soon after reaching puberty. Within those guidelines, parents arranged marriages, whether between *Tsi-zhu* and *Hon-ga* or between Osages and outsiders.[31]

Osage hierarchies shaped these marriages. About the Osages, one French observer stated, "Marriages are concluded for material interests." Usually, a man's family identified a prospective wife for him. Mothers may have conducted an initial round of negotiations to test the waters. Then the man's family recruited four *ni'-ka don-he* (good men) to establish that the man and woman met the clan and moiety requirements and, then, to negotiate an appropriate exchange of gifts—horses, bison robes, blankets, and the like. Once a man became a husband, he had to provide for his family and negotiate marriages for his children and grandchildren. Only after fulfilling those duties as a husband and father could he become a *ni'-ka don-he* and a respected elder in the community. Each obligation required skill or wealth. As a result, economic and social position affected whom a man could marry and whether a woman's family would accept an offer of matrimony.[32]

Sometime during the eighteenth century, even though lineage passed through the father's line, Osages began practicing matrilocal residence, meaning that the family lived with the wife's kin. The combination of patrilineality and matrilocality was unusual, but it probably emerged from the particular context of the mid-1700s, when Osages increased their wars in the South. In a society in which war parties often originated from a single clan, patrilocal residence posed a risk in that all the men from a single household might be killed if a raid went badly. The new arrangement spread male relatives across many households. Matrilocality also probably increased the economic power of Osage women. Indeed, one Frenchman noted that after a father's death, "the eldest son keeps his father's horses, the eldest daughter becomes the owner of the lodge." As matrilocality became more deeply rooted in Osage society, a woman obtained divorce by throwing her husband's personal belongings out of their home. She retained control of the lodge and all household goods.[33]

As aspirants to a strong and productive relationship with Osage leaders, the Chouteau brothers followed these practices as they married into Osage families. An illegitimate marriage might have brought food, shelter, and labor from an individual Osage woman, but it did not come with the family ties necessary for good relations over the long term. Instead, Auguste and Pierre conformed to Osage expectations. They demonstrated their value as husbands and allies by providing suitable gifts, and soon, they became relatives of both Osage chiefs and the French-Osage Mongraines, another important trading family. By fulfilling their obligations as husbands and relatives, they secured their position in the nation. The adoption of these French traders guaranteed that their children would belong to Osage clans.[34]

Cross-cultural marriages brought prosperity and influence to Osage women and their families. These unions created bonds of reciprocity that required French men to support their Osage kin. Among Osages, as elsewhere in Indian Country, prestige stemmed in part from generosity. Prominent men, including chiefs and head warriors, demonstrated their skill as hunters and diplomats by distributing gifts to the people of their towns. These presents could be trade items, such as metal goods or cloth, or proceeds from a hunt, such as meat or animal skins. Although often misconstrued as a disdain for personal wealth, these rituals were in fact displays of affluence and brought respect in return.[35] Through intermarriage with wealthy newcomers, Indian women ensured that their families maintained or increased their standing in the nation.

With various ties in New Orleans, St. Louis, and the Osage Nation, Maxent, Laclède & Co. sat at the center of a network of economically and politically powerful people and promised to turn those advantages into profits. In November 1765, British Superintendent of Indian Affairs Sir

William Johnson reported that "a Frenchman" at the mouth of the Missouri "carries on a vast Extensive Trade, and is acquiring a great influence over all the Indian nations." The following year, a British officer visited St. Louis and claimed that Laclède controlled the fur trade of not just the Missouri River but also the upper Mississippi and large parts of British Illinois. In the six years between Laclède's arrival in Illinois and the dissolution of the firm, the wealth of Maxent, Laclède & Co. grew at a rapid rate. In 1763, Maxent had imported 9,000 livres of trade goods to launch the endeavor. During Laclède's years in St. Louis, the firm had amassed over 100,000 livres worth of furs, slaves, livestock, property, and implements and held promissory notes worth tens of thousands of livres.[36]

However, the last half of the decade also brought setbacks. In 1765, the firm lost its monopoly. Following complaints from other traders in New Orleans, the Minister of the Marine ordered Governor Aubry to revoke all such contracts. Granting monopolies had been a wartime measure designed to produce a steady stream of supplies and gifts to Indian allies. With the signing of the Treaties of Paris and Fontainebleau, they were no longer necessary for an empire whose days were numbered. Instead, as Aubry informed the monopoly holders in New Orleans, "all honest people can enjoy the liberty of commerce." In April, two months after the minister's order but three months before Aubry relayed the message to Upper Louisiana, Pierre Laclède insisted that "employees of the government" seize the goods of the traders Louis Viviat and Jean-Baptiste Datchurut for attempting to trade on the Missouri and "violating the laws of the Indian trade." Viviat and Datchurut filed a lawsuit, demanding reimbursement for their losses. In 1767, the Superior Council of Louisiana ruled against Laclède and Maxent. Maxent later fumed that he had been "extremely wronged" by the council, which "did not judge it appropriate to respect" his privileges granted by the governor and backed by the power of the king. Laclède and Maxent had to pay nearly 6,500 livres to their two rivals.[37]

The removal of Maxent, Laclède & Co.'s monopoly initiated competition and uncertainty in the Missouri River trade. Initially, Ulloa issued strict regulations. Traders had to apply in New Orleans for licenses to conduct business on the river. As St. Ange explained, St. Louis traders were generally too poor to make the trip to New Orleans, and the plan would produce discontent among the Missouri River nations, which were "accustomed to the same needs" that the Spanish "deprived all of a sudden." Soon after, when Osage, Kaw, Oto, and Pawnee diplomats visited St. Louis, Ríu learned how troublesome his orders would be. The Kaw chief complained to Ríu and St. Ange that, for four years, French officers had assured them that Spain would continue the practices of its predecessors. "We were all happy awaiting your arrival," he said. But now Spanish officials offered only paltry gifts. Great Osage chief Clermont informed Ríu that the lack of traders made him "very disgusted." Acting on the advice of St. Ange, Ríu reopened the trade.[38]

Afterward, Laclède faced increased competition on the Missouri. Laclède was not one of the traders licensed to work among the Pawnees, Otos, or Kaws. In 1769, Maxent requested permission to trade with the Osages and Otos, but on the same day, he and Laclède dissolved their firm. That year, Laclède, hoping to reenter the fur trade, led a group of "merchants and habitants" who petitioned Ríu to expand the commerce for the safety of St. Louis. The limited trade amounted to "depriving those tribes of the aid which it has been customary to take them." The nations grew dissatisfied and began to threaten European outposts, forcing the colonists "to shut [them]selves up in our villages, destitute of all fortification and with no hope of relief, and in danger of seeing [their] wives and children murdered." The only way to prevent violence, the petition warned, was commerce. The traders licensed in 1768 were eager to guard their privileged position, and none of them signed the document.[39]

Laclède continued to play a substantial role in the St. Louis fur trade. He supplied merchandise to other traders in return for payment in furs at the end of the hunting season. Either through these deals or his own trading operations, he acquired a large portion of the pelts that moved through the city. In the summer of 1770, one of his boats carried 300 packages of skins and furs to New Orleans. When the boat stopped in Ste. Genevieve, Auguste Chouteau, briefly in town as agent for his stepfather, purchased another sixty-nine bundles of furs to add to the load. At the same time, Laclède diversified his interests in St. Louis. After he built a new, larger home for his wife and children, he rented their old house to the Spanish government to use as a barracks. He deployed his boats to ship merchandise from New Orleans to St. Louis for both private and public interests. And he bought a grist mill and produced flour from local wheat. Such an enterprise was probably profitable in a city once nicknamed "Pain Court," or "short of bread."[40]

Whatever financial struggles Laclède faced during the late 1760s, he appears to have mounted something of a comeback as a *négociant* by the start of the new decade. In addition to shipping hundreds of bales of furs to New Orleans, he formed a new partnership with Auguste Chouteau and Sylvestre

Labbadie, another Missouri River fur trader who reportedly married into the Osage Nation. Labbadie had also been granted, in 1768, a trade license to operate in the Kaw Nation. These new partnerships placed the Laclède-Chouteau family at the center of the St. Louis fur trade. By 1777, they controlled the bulk of commerce with the Osage Nation. In that year, Spain authorized Auguste Chouteau to trade 10,000 livres worth of merchandise to the Great Osages, while it granted Labbadie another 6,000 livres of the total Great Osage trade worth 24,100 livres. A rival trader later complained that Chouteau, Labbadie, and their partner, Gabriel Cerré, commanded "all the posts of the Missouri."[41]

Kinship undergirded these new enterprises. Labbadie married Pelagie Chouteau, Auguste's half sister and Laclède's daughter. Labbadie's business partner, Joseph-Marie Papin, also married into the Chouteau family, wedding Laclède's middle daughter, Marie Louise. In doing so, Labbadie, Papin, and the Chouteaus merged their financial and familial obligations to one another. Behind the scenes, Pelagie and Marie Louise were probably active participants in their family's commercial interests. Thanks to the legacy of the French legal regime, women in colonial St. Louis wielded substantial influence over their families' finances. In the contracts signed at weddings, men and women each identified the property they were bringing into the union, and women retained a right to that property for the life of the marriage and in divorce. A widow acquired all of her husband's property after he died, unless they had children, in which case she inherited half of the estate, with the rest divided among their offspring. As a result of the shared stake in community property, women and men often conferred about family finances. An Anglo-American visitor marveled at the power women had in their marriages, over both the household and financial affairs. "Even in most instances of purchase and sales, the women are consulted," he wrote, "and they not unfrequently assume the management of property." Pelagie and Marie Louise, with their husbands frequently away on business, could oversee affairs in St. Louis. And the sisters had a strong example from which to draw inspiration. Their mother, Marie Thérèse, had fended for herself and young Auguste when her husband abandoned them. Years later, he reappeared, and at his request, the governor of Louisiana ordered her to return to New Orleans. She refused and continued to live with Laclède. And Madame Chouteau was quick to protect her property. She once filed a lawsuit against her son-in-law Papin in which she charged him as responsible for the death of an enslaved man whom she owned and demanded compensation.[42]

While the Laclède-Chouteau family extended its connections in the St. Louis merchant community, Laclède's former partner Maxent and his children nurtured alliances with colonial leaders. During the 1770s, two of Maxent's daughters, Marie Elizabeth and Marie Félicité, married Spanish governors, Luis de Unzaga y Amezaga and Bernardo de Gálvez, respectively. Both individual and family interests shaped these unions. Maxent probably arranged the marriage of the teenage Marie Elizabeth to the fifty-five-year-old Unzaga. Marie Félicité was already a widow when she married Gálvez in 1777 at the age of twenty-one and possessed more autonomy than her older sister did. She controlled a considerable fortune, and although widows frequently remarried, she was under no obligation to do so. Yet she and Gálvez seem to have felt a strong attraction. They married about ten months after Gálvez's arrival in New Orleans, a speedy courtship. Gálvez risked losing his governorship by not obtaining the royal license required for him to marry within his jurisdiction. (Spain rightly feared that its officials would become ensnared in the local interests of their in-laws at the expense of the needs of the empire and seems to have wanted to keep track of those men who posed such a risk.) Perhaps Gálvez knew that his uncle and the minister of the Indies, José de Gálvez, would grant him an exception. Marie Félicité, for her part, may have found the cosmopolitan Gálvez intellectually stimulating. In later years, she ran a political and literary salon in her Madrid home. Of course, romance and material interests were not necessarily at odds. By marrying Gálvez, Marie Félicité became a countess and a member of the highest levels of Spanish colonial society. Those connections empowered her father as well. Together, Unzaga and Gálvez governed Louisiana from 1769 to 1785 and appointed Maxent to key roles in the colonial government, including head of Indian affairs. At some moments during that period, Maxent was reportedly the only New Orleans merchant who could sell supplies for the Indian trade. During these years, Laclède continued to draw on his increasingly well-connected friend for support. With the connection to Maxent, Laclède and Chouteau enjoyed a supply of trade merchandise. Their competitors risked shortages.[43]

Great changes came to Middle America and to the Chouteau family in 1778. In May, Pierre Laclède died near Arkansas Post. Laclède's death was a blow to the family's business, but like many other family enterprises in early America, the Chouteaus divided and dispersed skills and responsibilities so their commercial affairs could persist. Auguste Chouteau stepped into the role of patriarch of the growing family, and he maintained commercial ties with Maxent, sending him furs and accepting the merchant's power of attorney for transactions in St. Louis.[44] Auguste lost his surrogate father, but Laclède's mentorship served him well in the years to come. Although Laclède's endeavors had often been unsuccessful, he offered an important model of how to navigate changing imperial regimes and how to combine personal and business interests to build and expand economic power. Two months after Laclède's death, American troops arrived in the Illinois Country and provided Chouteau with an opportunity to put those lessons into practice.

≈   On July 4, 1778, the American Revolution reached the midcontinent. On that day, Virginia troops led by George Rogers Clark captured Kaskaskia. Within two weeks, the patriot army seized Cahokia and Vincennes—all French towns masquerading as British posts. Never particularly fond of the British empire or its traders, French merchants on both banks of the Mississippi welcomed Clark's army, which shared their antagonism toward Britain and gave the traders a new clientele. The recent alliance between France and the fledgling United States drew support to the Americans as well. Auguste Chouteau crossed over from St. Louis and, along with Cahokia and Kaskaskia traders such as Charles Gratiot and Gabriel Cerré, offered goods to the beleaguered Americans.[45] Clark had no money, but the merchants accepted his notes for tens of thousands of dollars worth of supplies. Since Clark represented the state of Virginia, they trusted that the government backed the officer's promises.

After an initial period of optimism, the merchants of Illinois grew increasingly skeptical about the Americans, their wealth, and the future of trade under the new regime. With Clark's victories, the fledgling United States claimed what had been British Illinois. Traders in that area, however, depended on their connections to markets in British Canada. Without access to Montreal, Gratiot and Cerré had no buyers for their furs and no suppliers of trade goods. During the late 1770s, the Americans offered no markets for the western traders, making the newcomers a poor replacement for the merchants of Montreal. Meanwhile, the Virginia government, due to economic hardship, could not pay Clark's promissory notes, infuriating Illinois traders and impoverishing Clark. As Virginia disregarded its obligations, the Americans became less attractive customers and allies. Even when American buyers offered to pay in cash, merchants soon learned that American paper money held little or no value. Gratiot noted that, at St. Louis, American currency would not even "buy a cat [pelt]."[46]

Cerré and Gratiot continued to conduct business with their partners in Montreal. Cerré later professed to Clark that "he never conserned himself about State affairs further than the Interest of his trade required." But, in wartime, such a position was untenable, and the two French merchants drew the ire of Americans and British alike. Upon Clark's arrival in Kaskaskia in 1778, he learned that Cerré was transporting a load of furs to Michilimackinac and Quebec. Cerré's business rivals—Clark believed they were probably in debt to him—characterized the absent merchant as "one of the most inveterate Enemies of the Americans." Although the Virginian questioned the motives of Cerré's accusers, he wanted to determine Cerré's loyalties for himself. Until Cerré returned to Kaskaskia, Clark's troops detained the Frenchman's family and seized his stores. Clark reported that he eventually earned the goodwill of Cerré, but the antagonism of their initial encounter must have remained prominent in the merchant's mind. In June 1779, Cerré purchased a lot in St. Louis. By the spring of the next year, he had moved his family to their new home.[47]

Charles Gratiot faced other challenges in the wake of the American takeover. In 1777, Gratiot immigrated to Cahokia as a partner in a Montreal-based trading house. His financial well-being depended on shipping furs to his partners in Prairie du Chien, Michilimackinac, and Montreal and receiving merchandise in return. In early 1780, Gratiot obtained the necessary passports from American and Spanish officials to send a boat of goods to Prairie du Chien. British troops and Menominee Indians seized Gratiot's cargo just south of its destination. In the Illinois towns, rumors circulated that Gratiot intended the boat to be captured and was secretly aiding the British.[48] Unable to conduct his business in British Canada and mistrusted by his American neighbors, Gratiot grew dissatisfied with his life at Cahokia.

The Americans further aggravated Gratiot as they demonstrated themselves undependable and, in Gratiot's mind, apathetic about the war. In late 1779, Richard McCarty, the American commandant at Cahokia, granted Charles Sanguinet, a resident of St. Louis, the right to trade on the Illinois River. Excluded from trading in Spanish Illinois, Gratiot could not conceive of why McCarty allowed Spanish traders to operate in American territory. Feeling betrayed, Gratiot informed one American officer that he would be "obliged . . . to become a Spaniard." Additionally, Gratiot believed that he had contributed more to the American cause than the Americans had. Gratiot provided more than $8,000 worth of goods to Clark's army.

Yet, at Kaskaskia, in May 1780, Gratiot watched American soldiers vote to campaign against the British and their Indian allies on the Wabash River and then refuse to help supply the expedition. Not long after, he wrote to Clark, "I cannot help regreting the Time and trouble I have lost in trying to serve a People so Destitute of Patriotic Sentiments, who are totally guided by a vile Particular Interest never doing any thing or even caring about the General Benefit of a Country."[49] Within the year, Gratiot joined Cerré in St. Louis.

The relocations of Gratiot and Cerré proved a boon for Auguste Chouteau. For more than a decade, Chouteau had depended on the markets of New Orleans and especially his stepfather's old partner, Maxent. Auguste and his kin had dealt with Gratiot and probably Cerré when they lived on the east bank of the Mississippi. Their moves to St. Louis offered a host of new opportunities for Chouteau. In 1778, most St. Louis fur traders shipped their furs to New Orleans. As Laclède and Chouteau learned, this commerce could be very profitable for men with the right connections. At the same time, however, dealing only in New Orleans offered limited profits. Laclède and Chouteau could buy European goods cheaply in New Orleans, but the merchants of Lower Louisiana likewise offered low prices for Missouri River furs. Traders such as Gratiot and Cerré faced a similar challenge in Montreal, where firms paid well for furs but charged high rates for trade goods. The arduous journey from Montreal to the Illinois Country added exorbitant transportation costs. Great profits would come from combining the two markets. If a merchant could buy goods in New Orleans but sell furs in Montreal, he would profit more than was possible by dealing with firms in either city alone.[50]

At the turn of the 1780s, the Chouteau family joined their commercial network with the connections Gratiot and Cerré had in Montreal. In 1781, Auguste Chouteau's sister Victoire married Gratiot, and five years later, Auguste married Cerré's daughter Marie Thérèse. Other Chouteau relatives, particularly Joseph-Marie Papin, had dealt with Montreal trading houses in the past, but not until Gratiot and Cerré joined the family did the Chouteaus open a regular commerce with Canada.[51] The Chouteau sisters and their counterparts in the Cerré family extended the family's economic connections and solidified their position as the leading families of St. Louis. Their marriages reveal a conscious strategy to protect and expand the family's position in the fur trade. By 1786, Auguste Chouteau and his siblings sat at the center of a kinship-based trade network that linked Indian nations of the Missouri

River to markets in New Orleans and Montreal and eventually to European ports such as La Rochelle in France and London in Great Britain.

≈   While the Chouteau family's commercial network grew, Spain lost face owing to repeated challenges from the Osage Nation, which resented European encroachments on its territory. Poachers in the Missouri and Arkansas River valleys stole food and pelts from Osage land, presenting a direct threat to Osage subsistence and commerce. By 1786, 200 white hunters operated on the Arkansas River alone. When Osages discovered intruders, they relieved them of their supplies and their furs, usually expelled them, sometimes took them captive, and, in rare instances, killed them. In contrast, Osages recognized that St. Louis sent traders to their towns. While they considered trespassing hunters enemies, Osages saw the people of St. Louis as their friends, relatives, and allies. Even when the Osages stopped traders from traveling farther up the Missouri River, they infrequently caused them harm, choosing instead to turn them away or take payment for the right to continue upstream. Ste. Genevieve and the fledgling colonies on the Meramec River south of St. Louis fell in a gray area between friend and foe, which made them a mark for Osage warriors and traders seeking horses.[52]

Although these attacks resulted in few deaths, Osage raids scared off much-needed inhabitants in the fledgling towns of Upper Louisiana. During the 1780s, Spain had recruited American colonists to cross the Mississippi, swear allegiance to the crown, and set up farms south of St. Louis. But Osage attacks undermined efforts to attract settlers, since most colonists valued their lives more than they valued wages or homesteads. In Ste. Genevieve, if colonists learned that Osages had killed one person, his or her neighbors would cease farming, even when they had little to fear. A once-thriving settlement on the Meramec River showed "only traces of habitations, abandoned, and left to desertion." At New Madrid, employers faced such a shortage of workers that they offered double the wages paid at New Orleans. Spanish officials worried that, if the attacks continued, residents throughout the region would flee their homes and maybe even seek refuge in the American settlements on the east bank of the river.[53]

Throughout the empire, Spanish officials believed they could use trade to build peaceful relations with Indian nations, and they hoped they could use that strategy against the Osages. In theory, trade rendered Native peoples dependent on European manufactures and compelled them to obey Spanish commands in order to enjoy the benefits of commerce. Spanish policy forced the empire, however, to rely on local traders whose primary loyalties were to themselves, their partners, and their families. When those interests aligned with those of the empire, both groups benefited. When money could be made and influence acquired in defiance of the empire, traders followed their own course. Spanish strategy may have worked in isolated areas, but the many factions of Native peoples and Europeans in Middle America precluded the empire from sequestering the Osages and severing their supply routes. Additionally, as one observer noted, so long as the Missouri River trade continued, Little and Great Osages would find ways to acquire goods: "Traders will go to the other nations, and before they return they will be stopped or pillaged by these two nations."[54]

Rampant illicit trade, especially by the Chouteaus, scuttled Spanish bans on commerce with the Osages during the 1770s and early 1780s. Still, Spanish officials persisted in this strategy, in part because it was the only tool at hand. In 1790, Governor Esteban Miró again forbade commerce with the Osages. In 1792, Miró's successor, Francisco Luis Héctor de Carondelet, reiterated the ban. The Chouteau brothers, meanwhile, continued their operations in Osage Country. At Arkansas Post, hunters testified that Pierre Chouteau and Sylvestre Labbadie regularly traded among the Osages, bringing them gunpowder and other goods. On the Mississippi in 1793, an Osage woman who was held captive by a party of Chickasaws and Quapaws told a Spanish officer that Pierre Chouteau had brought ten pirogues of supplies to her town the previous summer.[55]

Lieutenant Governor Zenon Trudeau, a friend of the Chouteaus, tried to justify their actions to his superiors. First, he claimed that the traders had left St. Louis before word of the trade ban arrived. Then, when that line of defense became untenable, he acknowledged that, like many others, they traded with Osages but "avoided as much as possible that they not be given arms and munitions." Carondelet found little satisfaction in those excuses. He noted that, thanks to Chouteau and Labbadie's trade, the Osages had plenty of weapons to continue their attacks. He promised that if the two men continued to flout Spanish rule, he would "make an example of them capable of giving warning to those who look with so little conscience and honor on the public good." They would be treated as "true enemies" of Spain.[56]

By late 1792, the continuing Chouteau-Osage commerce induced Carondelet to supplement the ban on the Osage trade by secretly supplying munitions to the Osages' enemies. According to Carondelet's plan, after two years of cutting off trade to the Osages and supplying their enemies, Spain would join forces with those Indian nations to defeat the Osages. Carondelet believed, "It is extremely important to humble or destroy those barbarians . . . by force." Earlier governors had also wished to dominate the Osages, but Carondelet was the first to set a plan of war into motion. Previously, the challenges of reaching Osage Country and the expense of a Spanish-led campaign had prevented Spain from going to war with the powerful nation. When Carondelet took office in January 1792, though, he lacked the experience of Miró, who had governed for a decade. He came to New Orleans from Guatemala, where Spain had subjugated Native peoples with force. Applying that strategy to Louisiana, Carondelet overestimated the reach of the empire and underestimated the power of the Osages. Rejecting the advice of his subordinates to the contrary, Carondelet marched toward war.[57]

Louisianans greeted Carondelet's plan with a mix of enthusiasm and ambivalence, depending on whether they had antagonistic or fruitful relations with the Osages. Hunters from Arkansas Post and farmers at Ste. Genevieve and on the Meramec River had suffered the brunt of Osage attacks, and they welcomed official sanction to attack the Osages. On the Arkansas River, 120 hunters offered to lead a campaign against the Osages, "for the good of humanity" and their "private interests." Unlike those hunters, the merchants and *habitants* of St. Louis had no interest in going to war with the Osages. Even when Spanish officials stopped the Missouri River trade, Osages left St. Louis unscathed, instead targeting Ste. Genevieve and the burgeoning settlements on the Meramec River. The relationship between St. Louis and the Osage Nation was mutually beneficial, and despite the demands of Carondelet, few St. Louisans would fight the Osages. Trudeau anticipated that he could coerce 200 men to join a campaign into Osage Country, but he warned that "not a single one would volunteer."[58]

Demographics skewed against Spain as well. In 1791, about 2,500 residents, including enslaved people of Native and African descent, lived in St. Louis, Ste. Genevieve, and the scattered surrounding towns. Nearly twice as many people lived in the Osage towns on the Arkansas and Missouri Rivers and their tributaries. Carondelet hoped to even the numbers by recruiting Indians hostile to the Osages, but only 100 Shawnees and Delawares, frequent victims of Osage raids on Cape Girardeau, joined the force gathering at St. Louis. Across the Mississippi, other nations including Kickapoos, who lived beyond the reach of Osages, faced a greater challenge from the U.S. empire, which in 1790 and 1791 sent armies to destroy the nations north of the Ohio River. Rather than join the Spanish war, those peoples stayed home to defend against anticipated attacks by the U.S. Army and by other Indians.[59]

The distance from St. Louis to the Osage settlements, combined with the seasonal rhythms of colonial warfare, posed an additional difficulty. Any Spanish army would have to journey more than 400 miles via river between St. Louis and the Osage heartland. The route from Arkansas Post was longer. Such a trip would provide the Osages many opportunities to spot the army. Zenon Trudeau noted, they "might withdraw at the least signal of attack only to reappear later and render my expenditures without effect." Only in August, when Osage crops ripened, could a Spanish army destroy enough of the nation's provisions to justify an expensive campaign. War preparations in St. Louis began too late in 1793 to be carried out that autumn.[60] Carondelet would have to wait another year.

A growing number of threats to Upper Louisiana further diminished the possibility of a successful war against the Osages. In particular, Carondelet worried about the loyalty of the francophone colonists of Spanish Louisiana, suspecting that they sympathized with the French revolutionaries who had toppled the monarchy in 1789. Then, in 1793, Spain declared war on Revolutionary France. Edmond-Charles Genêt, the French ambassador to the United States, recruited George Rogers Clark, retired from military service and living in Louisville, Kentucky, to lead a French army against Spanish Louisiana. Many inhabitants of Middle America remembered Clark's daring campaign against British Illinois in 1778–1779, and his reputation loomed large, although his military career had faltered during the 1780s. By the spring of 1794, Clark reportedly had recruited 2,000 Kentuckians ready to declare themselves citizens of France and attack Louisiana. The specter of Clark at the head of a revolutionary army spooked Spanish officials in St. Louis and New Orleans. Faced with the prospect of defeat, Trudeau reported from St. Louis that he had "already taken steps to facilitate [his] retreat." Although that threat passed, Carondelet still worried about Louisiana's francophone colonists. In New Orleans, Jacobin sympathizers marched and sang in the streets. Reports from St. Louis, likely overblown, informed Carondelet that a *sans-culottes* club had formed in the city and had the "audacity" to sing revolutionary songs and celebrate New Year's Day in September, following the new republican calendar.[61]

At the same time, British traders from Michilimackinac and Prairie du Chien expanded their commerce in Spanish territories. Since the 1760s, these smugglers followed a centuries-old route and crossed the Mississippi at the

Des Moines River in present-day Iowa. They traveled up that river and, with only a short portage, entered the middle Missouri valley. In doing so, they avoided the risk of being detected by the Spanish settlements near the mouth of the Missouri, while still enjoying the benefits of working on the river. By the early 1790s, British traders operated among the Pawnees and the Otoes, while Sauk Indians, supplied by British firms, reached out to Osages, farther downstream. Carondelet began to worry about the future of St. Louis and the neighboring towns, caught between British-armed Missouri valley Indians and French-backed Americans.[62]

Sensing an opportunity and suffering from the Spanish ban on the Missouri River trade, the Chouteau brothers offered to facilitate peace between Spain and the Osages. The Chouteaus knew that the governor could do little to placate scheming Americans or dreaming French diplomats, but he could reconcile with the Osages—with Auguste and Pierre Chouteau's help. On behalf of the empire, Auguste offered to erect a fort in the Osage Nation, where Pierre would serve as commandant. The Chouteaus promised that, using their influence among prominent Osages, they could expand Spanish presence on the river and quell the conflict between Spain and the Osages. In Auguste's words, the Osages would be "subjected and reduced to reason." As reward, Auguste and Pierre would receive a six-year monopoly on the Osage trade, valued at over half of Spain's total commerce on the Missouri River.[63]

Other traders had proposed building posts among the Osages and elsewhere, but the Chouteaus possessed the necessary connections in the Spanish administration and in the Osage Nation to make their plan a reality. Spain closely monitored kinship ties between its officials and colonists, fearing the influence of local interests on administrators. Marriage between imperial officers and locals was forbidden without permission from the crown. Likewise, officers could not serve as godparents or witnesses at weddings. Nor could they engage in business or buy real estate. Such rules closed off many of the avenues the Chouteau family used to build affective ties. Still, the Chouteaus found another way to court potential allies. During the late 1780s, as frequent travelers between New Orleans and St. Louis, the Chouteaus began to accompany incoming lieutenant governors on their journey north. In 1787, Pierre Chouteau and Manuel Perez shared a boat as the latter traveled to his new post. Using the long voyage to shape Perez's perception of the region and the Chouteaus' place in it, Pierre turned Perez into an ally before the officer ever reached St. Louis. This initial trip may have been an accident, but in subsequent years, the Chouteaus made a point to arrive in town with Upper Louisiana's chief official.[64] Trudeau soon became an important friend. The Chouteau brothers' relationship with Lieutenant Governor Zenon Trudeau became especially significant in gaining approval for their proposal.

In return for Trudeau's backing, Chouteau vouched for his performance with the Osages, telling Carondelet that his lieutenant governor had "reduced" the Osages to a "state of distress"—a bold exaggeration. Trudeau, for his part, advocated the building of a fort among the Osages, anticipating it would have a great effect on the Osages, "particularly if an official capable of making himself loved and respected by them and knowing how to govern them could be found." Trudeau had already found the man for the job. A few days later, he praised Chouteau's influence over the Osages and his friendship to Spain.[65]

Little did Trudeau know that Carondelet had already decided to make peace with the Osage Nation. The threats to Upper Louisiana had become too great. As Trudeau scribbled his praises of Auguste Chouteau, Carondelet authorized the lieutenant governor to allow "only one commercial house of [his] selection" to reopen commercial relations with the Osages. Meanwhile, with Trudeau's blessing, Auguste traveled south to New Orleans with six Osage diplomats. He would make his case to the governor that he and his brother should be the sole firm trading with Osages and to present his plan to build a fort in their nation. Standing before Carondelet alongside the Osage chiefs, Chouteau could demonstrate his close relations with the nation. He used the occasion to persuade Carondelet that Spanish security depended on a fort among the Osages and that only he and his brother could oversee such an endeavor. Carondelet agreed. Soon the governor praised the St. Louis merchant as "a rich man, very friendly to the name of Spaniard, and held in the highest esteem" by the Osages. He later told a subordinate headed to St. Louis that the Chouteau brothers "deserve all confidence."[66] Neither Carondelet nor anyone else mentioned that the Chouteaus had run afoul of the governor the previous year for illegally trading with Osages.

Osages allowed the Chouteaus to build the fort because it reinforced their command over the Missouri valley. In Osages' view, Fort Carondelet did not extend Spanish authority into the Osage Nation. Instead, they regarded it as a tribute to their power, recognition of their dominant role in the region. Moreover, as the fort sat on Osage land, it was an Osage possession. One Spanish official noted, "They regard it all as their own property." Also, the fort provided a regular source of European goods, especially much-needed guns and ammunition, increasing Osage military strength. Noting the advantages brought by "our friends the whites," one Osage proclaimed, "When they keep themselves distant, we have no nerves in our arms and we can scarcely move our bows." He continued, "Now that they will not abandon us any more, we have them so strong that we can break trees."[67]

As commandant of Fort Carondelet, Pierre Chouteau used the power of the Osages and the resources of Spain to increase his family's influence in the region. Despite the Spanish fort's palisade and handful of cannons, it was little more than a Chouteau trading post. In the contract with Auguste Chouteau, Carondelet agreed that the Spanish crown would pay the salaries of twenty militiamen to garrison the fort. Chouteau hired a bevy of St. Louis traders, including Noel Mongraine and Paul Loise, a French-Osage man reported to be the son of either Auguste or Pierre. Trusting the Chouteau brothers, Spanish officials never visited the fort, and the Chouteaus may have intentionally withheld its location to prevent oversight. Thus, Pierre Chouteau controlled the flow of information between the Osage Nation and St. Louis. He, along with Auguste, reinforced the Spanish image of the brothers as expert diplomats, and officials filled their correspondence with praise for the wonders the Chouteaus worked on the Osages.[68]

≈ Just as the Chouteau brothers recognized the significance of kinship in their commercial affairs, they used those connections to shape regional politics and further enhance their standing in Missouri River commerce. Once in place at Fort Carondelet, Auguste and Pierre drew on the authority of the Spanish empire to buttress their influence in the region. They also drew on imperial resources to support their Osage friends and relatives as they sought new positions of power within the nation. The shift in Osage political authority began in the spring of 1794, when Auguste Chouteau and six Osage leaders—four from the Great Osages and two from the Little Osages— traveled to New Orleans to make peace with Carondelet. Each of the five major Osage towns had its own chief, but two hereditary chiefs, drawn from the preeminent town, handled those duties on a national level. In 1794, Jean Lafond was the "Grand Chief" of the Earth moiety, *Hon-ga*, while Clermont headed the Sky moiety, *Tsi-zhu*. Probably only a boy in the mid-1790s, Clermont was the son of a recently deceased chief of the same name, and his father's brother, Pawhuska, acted as regent until the younger Clermont came of age.[69]

When the six Osage chiefs, council members, and warriors traveled to New Orleans, Pawhuska joined Jean Lafond as the leading representatives

Fig. 5.2 Osage Chief Pawhuska.

of the Great Osages. Clermont stayed behind in Osage Country. Pierre Chouteau reported that Clermont worried that he would be killed if he made the journey to New Orleans.[70] He may have thought it safer to allow Pawhuska to make the voyage and assume the risk while also representing Clermont's interests. If that was the case, he placed too much faith in the older man's loyalty. Pawhuska wanted to be chief, not regent.

Pawhuska and the Chouteaus joined forces because their ambitions were mutually beneficial, and family ties shaped their interests and their strategies. Pawhuska had to cultivate support from powerful men and women in his nation and moiety if he was to supplant Clermont. When a chief died or grew too old to serve, his son replaced him. Yet a council of ten warriors called *a'-ki-da* could choose another successor if they considered the heir unfit to serve. Pawhuska needed their backing and received it. Zenon Trudeau reported that Pawhuska "is related by marriage to a very large number of warriors and *considerados* who support him." Pawhuska probably sought the approval of the priests of the *non'-hon-zhin-ga*, the most powerful political body in the nation, as well as their wives. All major decisions and many minor ones required their approval. In some ceremonies, women sat behind the *non'-hon-zhin-ga* and "symbolically represent the voice of the people." Their support would bolster Pawhuska's claim. Outside the nation, the Chouteaus were all too happy to aid Pawhuska, because it benefited them. Pierre Chouteau's marriage into the Mongraine family linked the Chouteaus and Jean Lafond, and when Noel Mongraine married Pawhushan, the daughter of Pawhuska, they added a direct link to the regent.[71] If the Chouteaus could help Pawhuska ascend to the chieftainship, they would enjoy close ties with both of the chiefs of the Great Osages.

In Clermont's absence from the New Orleans council, the Chouteau brothers worked to undercut the young chief's authority and move Pawhuska, their friend and ally, into a position of greater authority. No doubt relying on information provided by the Chouteaus, Zenon Trudeau described Clermont as "stupid and incapable," while noting that Pawhuska was "already considered as the chief since he governed his nephew." Carondelet received Trudeau's account on the eve of his council with the Osages where he awarded peace medals to the chiefs. Jean Lafond received the large medal of a head chief, while Pawhuska accepted the small medal of a second chief.[72] Clermont received no medal at all, removing him from the hierarchy of Spanish-recognized headmen.

Carondelet's medal ceremony was part of a deliberate effort by the Chouteau brothers and Pawhuska to wrest authority from young Clermont. Spain could not make or unmake Osage chiefs. However, when Spain honored a chief, it indicated to observers inside and outside the nation that he was a man to be respected.[73] As in many venues of diplomacy, image could become reality. Such recognition offered tangible benefits as well. The higher a chief's rank, the greater number of gifts he received. Moreover, good relations with the empire could bring access to trade goods, as medal chiefs became the people with whom traders and others needed to negotiate when crossing political boundaries. Wealth bought power, as the chief demonstrated his prestige by distributing gifts to his people. Pawhuska arrived in New Orleans as the representative of Clermont. When he left, he had become a chief in the eyes of Spain.

A tragedy on the return voyage accelerated Pawhuska's rise to power. Two days north of New Orleans, Chickasaw Indians, fighting another in a long history of wars against the Osages, attacked the diplomatic party. When the shooting ended, Jean Lafond and the two Little Osage chiefs lay dead. Pawhuska, the two other Great Osages, and Auguste Chouteau escaped harm. Upon returning to their homes, Pawhuska and the Chouteau brothers both used the attack to further their own ambitions. Pawhuska's brother became regent for Jean Lafond's young son, even though they belonged to different moieties and Pawhuska's family had no claim on the office of *Honga Ga-hi-ge*. At the same time, Auguste Chouteau depicted himself once again as enjoying unmatched access to and respect among the Osages. Writing to Carondelet, the merchant reported, "The deaths of the three Osage chiefs frightened everybody, and there was only my brother or myself who could go to these nations without risk. All others would have experienced unpleasantness."[74] In this way, Auguste set the stage for himself and Pierre to serve as mediators between Spain and the Osage Nation.

In the winter and spring of 1794–1795, Pawhuska via Pierre Chouteau drew on the Spanish empire to complete his ascent to chief. During those months, Pierre Chouteau requested a series of medals to distribute among Osage chiefs. In the wake of Jean Lafond's death, Spain needed to promote someone to the rank of large medal chief. In a clever bit of deception, Chouteau asked for a large medal for "Gredomanse," noting that he was also called Cheveux Blancs (White Hair). However, Gredomanse, or more accurately *Gra-to-moh-se*, was another name for Clermont, while White Hair referred to Pawhuska. Spanish officials knew the names Gra-to-moh-se and White Hair, and Carondelet had even met "White Hair" the previous spring. By combining the two men into a single person, Chouteau further undercut Pawhuska's rival. Either the Spanish officials did not realize White Hair and Gra-to-moh-se were two different people, or they did not care. Regardless, Pawhuska received the big medal, and Clermont disappeared from imperial correspondence. Afterward, Spanish officials considered Pawhuska the "great chief" of the Osages.[75] With this quiet coup, the Chouteau brothers completed their network of Spanish officials, British and French merchants, and Osage leaders.

As the eighteenth century ended, the ties between Pawhuska and the Chouteaus brought wealth and power to both. Supplanted and isolated, Clermont eventually left the Missouri valley to Pawhuska, taking his remaining followers to join another Osage town in the Arkansas valley. Clermont informed onlookers about the betrayal of Pawhuska, declaring his uncle and the Chouteaus his "mortal enemies." But few imperialists cared as long as Upper Louisiana enjoyed peace and prosperity.[76] In the years that followed, all parties learned that relations between Osages, Spain, and the Chouteaus required careful and frequent tending.

Initially, Spain desired an impossible balance in its dealings with the Osages. Carondelet sought to end Osage attacks on European squatters and poachers and relied on the Chouteau brothers to broker peace. In the years immediately following the construction of Fort Carondelet, the threat of violence declined in the Spanish towns south of St. Louis. That fact emboldened colonists, who moved farther into the interior. One such colonist, Henry Payet, explained that he established a homestead on the Grand River about fifteen miles west of Ste. Genevieve because Auguste Chouteau had promised to end Osage violence. Only with that assurance did Payet move into Osage territory. By 1797, Osages once again reasserted their territorial boundaries. From Ste. Genevieve, François Vallé complained that Osages "pillaged an American family," stealing six of their horses. At the same time, they took horses from the Spanish mines and from Peoria Indians encamped on a creek west of town. Vallé wrote, "Already all the new families established of the interior are abandoning their establishments." Mining and logging operations came to a halt. In Ste. Genevieve, Vallé reported, "we are working, sowing our seeds, while trembling."[77] When Osages extended peace to the Spanish towns, colonists saw it as an opportunity to expand west, forcing Osages to reassert their dominance in the region.

Yet the reports of Osage activity reveal that they were reluctant to kill or even injure colonists, partially because their motivation was to drive them away and partially because they knew colonists' deaths would spark retaliation by the Spanish government. Spanish officials complained of Osage "evildoers" who committed "depredations," "disorders," and "brigandages." But warriors usually limited their activity to stealing horses and household goods and destroying what they could not carry. In the winter of 1797 and spring of 1798, small parties of Osage warriors harassed outlying farms west of Ste. Genevieve and New Bourbon, but only one resident suffered personal injury: a gunshot to the leg. During the same months, when Osages appeared on the Meramec River, three inhabitants faced off against raiders, who retreated.[78] By turning back in the face of even minimal resistance, Osages showed that their goal was driving off, not killing, colonists, even if officials failed to understand the message.

Still, the attacks provoked a Spanish response, because they threatened the agricultural communities of Upper Louisiana. As Zenon Trudeau admitted, those farmers were "more important than the few hunters of the

Arkansas river." In 1797, shortly before the end of Carondelet's term as governor, he ordered the Chouteaus to stop the violence and threatened "to annul [their] contract and to forbid all commerce with the Osage nation." Not even an Osage chief, much less the Chouteau brothers, could command young men to stop their raids on the Spanish towns. Adding another complication, most of the warriors responsible for the attacks lived on the Arkansas River, where Pawhuska had little influence. Auguste and Pierre would have to negotiate a settlement that would satisfy Pawhuska while also convincing Spain of Pawhuska's continuing power. At that moment, Pierre Chouteau was laid low by "a complete hernia" and had returned from Fort Carondelet to St. Louis to recover. Nevertheless, he made his way to the Osage Nation with the full confidence of the new governor, Manuel Gayoso de Lemos, who wrote, "I do not doubt that Cadet Chouteau will bring the Little Osages to reason and even have them return the stolen property and give satisfaction." By late 1798, Auguste reported that his brother was "doing everything possible to keep [the Osages] in subordination and comply in that way with the views of the government."[79]

Meanwhile, ever eager to cut costs, Spain wanted to end the annual 2,000-peso subsidy that funded Chouteau's militia at Fort Carondelet. Gayoso de Lemos received orders to find a solution "most useful and advantageous for the security of these territories [and] economy of the royal interests." This change in policy put the Chouteaus in a perilous position, for they had enjoyed Spain paying the salaries of their employees. A contingent of regular troops would not serve their interests as well. Gayoso de Lemos identified another potential problem. Spain required that regular troops be commanded by a regular officer. Pierre Chouteau would lose his authority over the fort's garrison. Fortunately for the Chouteau brothers, Auguste was a trusted friend of the new governor and the previous year had stood in for Gayoso de Lemos as godfather at the baptism of Zenon Trudeau's son. Rather than force the Chouteaus to accept a new garrison of Spanish troops, he offered a more favorable proposal: Pierre would "continue to command this fort and to form a garrison of [his] hunters without cost [to Spain]." Perhaps knowing that Spanish Louisiana perpetually lacked a full complement of soldiers and could not spare twenty men for Fort Carondelet, Auguste insisted that the fort needed troops, not simply hunters. His plea convinced the governor to continue paying the garrison from the king's coffers, until more troops arrived in the colony.[80]

Spain and the Osage Nation made peace again in 1800. That year, Pierre Chouteau led a contingent of Osage leaders, headed by Pawhuska, to

St. Louis, where they met with the new lieutenant governor, Charles Dehault Delassus. Having emigrated from France following the overthrow of
the monarchy, Delassus and his father both served as Spanish officers in
Upper Louisiana, where they became enmeshed in the network of Chouteau social ties. Delassus's father enjoyed a particularly close relationship with
Auguste's brother-in-law Antoine Soulard, another aristocratic refugee from
France whom the elder Delassus considered something of an adopted son.[81]

Delassus, like Trudeau before him, relied on the Chouteau brothers to ed-
ucate him about the region's politics and to ease tensions with the Osages.
Pierre played that role in St. Louis in the summer of 1800. Accompanied by
some 200 Osages, Pawhuska arrived in St. Louis to surrender a man responsible for killing two colonists on the Meramec River. Pawhuska and the
other speakers asked for mercy, which Delassus was inclined to offer if the
Arkansas Osages would return to the Osage River and live under Pawhuska's leadership. Pawhuska informed Delassus that he needed resources to reinforce his authority: "Although I am chief of my nation, as thou [are] of
thine, I lack the means." Another trade ban would only weaken his position. Pawhuska's message convinced Delassus, who agreed to release the prisoner once the Osages reunited under Pawhuska. He also distributed gifts
provided by Auguste Chouteau. When Pawhuska and the Osages left
St. Louis, they carried with them one hundred new muskets and hundreds
of pounds of ammunition, as well as cloth, tobacco, and metal goods and
tools, courtesy of the Spanish empire.[82]

The new Spain-Osage peace came at a convenient time for the Chouteau
brothers. Six years had passed since Auguste's meeting with Carondelet in
New Orleans, and their monopoly would soon expire. Perhaps that fact ex-
plains, at least in part, the smooth negotiations of that summer's council.
The Osages arrived, knowing they could surrender a prisoner, possibly not
even the actual culprit, to Spain with near certainty that he would not be
executed. Pierre Chouteau would convince the relevant officials to release the
man, as he had before in 1797. The Arkansas Osage chief present, La Chenière,
could promise to rejoin Pawhuska to appease Delassus, and the Chouteaus
would confirm that they had followed through on the vow, whether or not
they had.[83]

Regardless of the legitimacy of the conference, it reinforced the image of
the Chouteau brothers as invaluable advisers and skilled negotiators. In the
fall of 1800, Delassus urged the empire to extend the Chouteaus' monopoly
for at least another six years. Delassus reported, "From the time they took

over the trade, it is agreed that the nation has greatly lessened its raids against the rest of us." He continued, "Now, when anything happens, the Osage nation gives satisfaction for it in every way that can be expected." All thanks went to the Chouteau brothers. "I know of no one who deserves this great favor more," Delassus wrote, "than Don Augusto Chouteau both for his loyalty toward the government and for his ability, and likewise his brother Don Pedro Chouteau, who alone carried with him to that nation the greatest daring that was possible." Spain renewed the license for four years, and the governor noted that Chouteau was "truly worthy of it."[84]

Less than a year into the new contract between the Chouteaus and Spain, rival traders in St. Louis began to attack the brothers and their monopoly. Manuel Lisa, the leader of the faction, protested to yet another new governor, Juan Manuel de Salcedo, that the monopolies on the Missouri River had divided the trade into the hands of a few, favored merchants. The rest of the commercial community in St. Louis suffered and struggled in poverty. Lisa suggested that a new contract, granted to him and a few other traders, would better serve St. Louis and its residents. The Chouteau family, he argued, had controlled the best part of the Missouri River trade for too long. If his group received a monopoly, he argued, more traders would enjoy the benefits of commerce with the Osages. Learning of Lisa's petition, Delassus spoke in favor of the status quo. He presented Lisa as a jealous schemer. Lisa cried hardship, which he laid at the feet of the monopolies, but Delassus offered another theory for Lisa's alleged business troubles: "Few inhabitants like to trade with him because many times it ends in disputes on his part."[85]

Although Lisa sought to undermine the Chouteaus' place in the Missouri River trade, he employed the strategies that they had perfected over the previous four decades. At the helm of a group of intermarried families, he curried favor with a new governor and argued that his cohort would better serve the needs of St. Louis and the empire. Salcedo knew that Lisa argued his case with what Delassus termed "inconsistency." If he was awarded the Osage monopoly, Lisa would not expand access to the trade. One close-knit group of intermarried traders would replace another. Salcedo also knew that Lisa's colleagues had all held their own monopolies among the Pawnee, Kaw, and Ponca Nations. Indeed, two of his partners had received two-year monopolies less than a year earlier. Still, in June 1802, Salcedo granted the Osage monopoly to Lisa and his partners, over the objections of Delassus, who accused Lisa of "imprudent and seditious conduct." With no sense of irony,

Salcedo explained, "it is just that all the honorable and powerful residents profit from trade with the Indians."[86]

Stripped of their monopoly, the Chouteaus, like Laclède before them, suffered a serious blow. But the ever-crafty brothers found ways to usurp Lisa's commerce. Auguste retained the contract to provision Fort Carondelet's garrison, which offered a pretense for shipping goods up the Missouri into the Osage Nation. He and Pierre also argued that the monopoly only extended to Osages on the Missouri River, not those on the Arkansas, and worked to curry favor with Arkansas River Osages. Meanwhile, they sponsored illicit traders to trade with Pawhuska's towns. In St. Louis, Auguste bought up $1,500 of his rivals' debt and demanded full payment when it came due in April 1803. When Lisa would not pay his share of the note, Delassus ordered his partners to withhold "from the funds of the association the amount due by Lisa."[87] Soon after, the Chouteaus set their sights on bigger quarry. In the summer of 1803, word arrived that Spain returned Louisiana to France and that France had sold Louisiana to the United States. Auguste likely recalled the early days of his forty-year-long career, when Maxent and Laclède had lost their monopoly in a similar period of upheaval. Lisa's monopoly would matter little if the Chouteaus played the transfers to their advantage.

≈   In early 1804, as Auguste Chouteau crafted his account of the founding of St. Louis, he perhaps found solace in the fact that moments of transition provided as many opportunities as risks to those who were poised to grab them. He knew that the transfer of power was not simply a time for reflection. Chouteau wrote the story of early St. Louis for U.S. officials, subtly shaping their understanding of the region and highlighting the importance of his family. Such a practice was old hat to Chouteau after his years of massaging details and crafting narratives to earn the favor of Spanish officials. Looking back to 1764, Chouteau recorded what had made the town and his business so successful: St. Louis's "central position" and close relations with the region's inhabitants.[88] From Osage towns to St. Louis to New Orleans and Montreal, the Chouteaus stood tall as the central node in a network of relatives and friends. They merged diverse economic and political interests to elevate themselves in Middle America. Chouteau and his family had turned a bluff overlooking the Mississippi River into the center of a fur-trading empire that stretched across much of the North American interior. In the process, Chouteau had transformed his position in the region from that of a newcomer who needed to create connections to that of a power broker whom new arrivals needed to court as an ally.

When Chouteau and Laclède arrived in the midcontinent in November 1763, they entered a social world shaped by nearly a century of interaction between French colonists and Native peoples. In the intervening decades, neither they nor Spain nor Great Britain had dislodged the region's French and Indian communities. Instead, those who built fortunes and power worked with those peoples. During the Chouteau brothers' first four decades in the Illinois Country, they constructed a web of allies that crossed borders drawn by Europeans and Indians alike. In many ways, the influence of the Chouteaus was an image carefully constructed by the brothers as they worked in the space between the Spanish empire and the Osage Nation. Yet Spanish officials and certain Osage leaders used that image to their advantage, rendering it real. In 1804, as Auguste Chouteau looked into the future, decades of knowledge and experience convinced him that, once again, the region's social networks would shape the new empire. The brothers hoped to use their decades of experience to build relationships with Americans and to harness the resources of the empire for personal gain.

CHAPTER SIX

Conquest

On a bright, clear morning in November 1804, Charles Dehault Delassus shivered aboard the *Esperanza*. Eight months earlier, he had transferred claim of Upper Louisiana from Spain to the United States, but due to a lack of boats at the time, he had been unable to depart the colony. The new American officials grew frustrated with Delassus, asking "why the troops of Spain remain here so long after the term proscribed by treaty for their departure." Delassus sought boat builders to construct the needed vessels, but only Auguste Chouteau accepted the job and only after he surveyed nearby woods to guarantee he could acquire enough timber for the project. Not until October did Delassus acquire the craft necessary to remove the garrison and the accompanying artillery, ammunition, and miscellaneous goods, the few remnants of the Spanish colony in the midcontinent. Now, plagued by icy nights and frigid mornings, the crew of the *Esperanza* and the rest of the small flotilla followed the Mississippi's current south. Early on the second day of the voyage, nine miles south of St. Louis, Delassus spied another boat, heading in the opposite direction. The boat, Delassus noted, "knew the current." Scanning the deck of the northbound vessel, Delassus recognized a friend, Pierre Chouteau. Chouteau had gone to Ste. Genevieve to intercept William Henry Harrison, who was visiting St. Louis for the first time since learning that Upper Louisiana would fall under his purview as governor of Indiana Territory. Delassus would not have been too surprised at the sight of Chouteau and Harrison conversing aboard their

195

boat. He had probably introduced them, after Harrison informed Delassus of the impending transfer of Louisiana to the United States, noting, "it may give me an opportunity of serving some of your friends."[1]

These encounters and negotiations, along with more formal ceremonies and celebrations, eased the incorporation of Upper Louisiana into the United States. In March 1804, Captain Amos Stoddard announced the arrival of the new regime by marching his troops through town, before raising the American flag and firing "a federal salute." When the rituals were complete, Stoddard, his soldiers, and a crowd of St. Louisans retired to a lavish ball hosted by the Chouteaus. Stoddard's displays were the public face of a more complicated process that occurred along unofficial channels of power. The written exchanges between officials of rival empires, the conversation between Chouteau and Harrison, and countless other moments at dances and dinners, in the streets and homes of St. Louis and on the decks of riverboats, all built and strengthened ties between francophone colonists and U.S. officers and diplomats. During the years following the Louisiana Purchase, the U.S. depended on the advice, support, and service of the colony's longtime residents.[2]

U.S. officials both in Washington and in the West, like French and Spanish imperialists before them, needed allies in St. Louis and Upper Louisiana to overcome the limits of distance and demography. U.S. officials and the St. Louis elite understood the political practices of the other, as both relied on kinship, real and fictive, to rule their dominions. The Chouteau family had risen to power by building reciprocal ties with Osage and Spanish elites, and Auguste and Pierre Chouteau pursued a similar strategy with the new regime. In turn, American officials hoped that patronage and friendship would build affective ties between Louisianans and the United States. Over time, American colonists married into old St. Louis families. They gained entry to local society while also furthering the interests of their francophone relatives as lawyers and politicians. From the late summer of 1803, when word of the purchase arrived in the West, to the end of 1804, the Chouteau brothers and U.S. agents laid the foundation for the political networks that ruled the midcontinent for decades to come.

At the same time, the United States brought a new form of imperialism to the midcontinent. The United States planned to transform Indian Country into Anglo-American homesteads. For centuries, colonists had sought two commodities: furs and souls. Now they fixated on land. Thomas Jefferson believed that independent farmers were the ideal citizens of a republic, and he understood the vast trans-Mississippi West to be crucial in creating his ideal society. The Louisiana Purchase removed French and Spanish claims to 828,000 square miles of the trans-Mississippi West, but it did not make that region part of the United States. For more than half a century after signing the treaty with France, the United States convinced and coerced Indian nations to sign over ownership of their territory.[3] In 1804, the United States stood in the footsteps of the empires it had replaced—a pretender to a vast western domain. Unlike its predecessors, however, the United States expended the resources required to integrate the region into its empire. U.S. military presence west of the Appalachians reassured western colonists. The Louisiana Purchase guaranteed that westerners would be able to transport their produce downstream to market in New Orleans. As a result, colonists flocked over the Appalachians and across the Mississippi. They propelled the empire ever further west.

Kin ties continued to shape colonialism, but Americans enforced far more restrictive ideas about who could and could not join their families. Drawing on Enlightenment-era notions of race and "civilization," U.S. officials thought that with proper education and training Indians could join "civilized" society. At times, some Americans, notably Thomas Jefferson, avowed that they and Native peoples would eventually form "one family." Echoing the rhetoric of Samuel de Champlain from 200 years earlier, Jefferson proposed "to let our settlements and theirs meet and blend together, to intermix, and become one people." He believed that "this is what the natural progress of things will of course bring on, and it will be better to promote than to retard it."[4] Yet the "natural progress of things" did not bring intermarriage in substantial numbers. Instead, the American colonists who flocked into the West generally rejected Indians as marriage partners. Their brand of colonialism centered on the acquisition of land, and as a result, they sought the dispossession and displacement of Native peoples. Anglo-Americans still built alliances with knowledgeable and influential midcontinent families, but they extended kin ties to francophone colonists, not Native peoples. Americans increasingly relied on race as the marker for who could or could not join their families. As the United States expanded its geographic boundaries, Americans contracted the borders of kinship.

The United States also governed its empire differently than France or Spain had administered theirs. Rather than holding Louisiana as a dependent colony, the United States incorporated the new territory into the nation, urging the formation of territorial and then state governments, equal in standing to those east of the Mississippi. Such a policy encouraged westward migration, but it also generated loyalty from francophone Louisianans. When Amos Stoddard addressed the crowd gathered to watch the transfer ceremony in March 1804, he swore to the St. Louisans that planning had begun to form a territorial government, which would lead to statehood. "Thus you will perceive," he continued, "that you are divested of the character of Subjects, and clothed with that of citizens—You now form an integral part of a great community."[5] The Chouteaus and others in the audience demanded and received the power and authority promised by Stoddard.

In the wake of the Louisiana Purchase, the Chouteaus and other Louisianans adapted to new roles in the changing political landscape. They proved essential to the expansion of the United States as they brokered land cessions from Indian nations to the United States. During the Spanish era, the Chouteaus rose to prominence as traders and mediators. In tandem with their commercial endeavors, they forged alliances and settled conflicts, both for themselves and for Spanish officials. After the Louisiana Purchase, the Chouteaus discovered that fortunes could be made by dispossessing Indian nations of their lands. Auguste and Pierre Chouteau, along with their sons, nephews, and cousins, learned how to make money at every step of the treaty process. They served as interpreters in councils, supplied goods given as gifts at the end of negotiations, inserted clauses into treaties guaranteeing personal land holdings or debts would be honored, and furnished Indian nations with the annual allotments of goods. By the 1830s, this new style of colonialism had transformed the region, as American colonists flooded into the trans-Mississippi West and dispossessed Native peoples. By adapting to the demands of the new regime, the Chouteaus facilitated the remaking of Middle America and amassed vast fortunes.

≈   Few Americans or francophone Louisianans expected theirs would be a natural union. Americans worried that, as longtime imperial subjects, Louisianans lacked the proper mind-set and training for self-governance. They were too used to monarchy to make good republicans. In this judgment, Americans ignored that they had been subjects of the British crown but two decades earlier. They also questioned whether Catholics could be loyal both to the United States and to the pope. Francophone Louisianans, for their part, held most Americans in low regard. Many shared the view of one Spanish lieutenant governor, who described Americans as "a people without law or discipline."[6] Yet Anglo-Americans and Louisianans in their political

practices found much common ground. St. Louis elites such as the Chouteaus recognized the power of an alliance with U.S. officials, just as those
administrators understood that working with local power brokers would
accelerate Louisiana's incorporation into the empire.

In the years following the Louisiana Purchase, the United States faced
the same challenges as earlier outsiders—nations, empires, and private enterprises—in extending authority and exerting control over the North Amer-
ican midcontinent. Although the newly acquired lands adjoined existing
U.S. claims, those acquisitions far outstripped the immigration of Anglo-
American colonists to the territories on the east bank of the Mississippi River.
Only about 2,500 non-Indians lived in Indiana Territory in 1800, and about
10,000 lived in Upper Louisiana at the time of the Louisiana Purchase.[7] In
Indiana, they gathered at Vincennes, Kaskaskia, and other towns along the
Mississippi, Ohio, and Wabash Rivers. Similarly, colonists in Louisiana
Territory lived in St. Louis and a handful of other towns stretching south
along the Mississippi. A few newer outposts dotted the lower Missouri River
above St. Louis. More colonists populated these settlements than had under
earlier regimes, but these colonies remained distant from the imperial capital and difficult to command.

The United States depended on kinship ties to link colonial—or territorial, to use American nomenclature—officials to the central government and
to collapse the distance between the empire's frontier and its capital. As a
result, the U.S. government in 1803 was particularly well suited to the Chouteaus' style of political dealing. Since the inauguration of Thomas Jefferson
in 1801, Virginians led the government in Washington and in the hinterlands of the trans-Appalachian West. Jefferson hesitated to appoint family
members to office. Instead, he relied on a new form of fictive kinship based
on a common birthplace and shared political allegiances. In the decade following the Louisiana Purchase, young Virginians controlled western territorial governments. The president trusted William Henry Harrison, Meriwether
Lewis, William Clark, Frederick L. Bates, and others, as Jeffersonians and
Virginians, to administer the far reaches of the growing U.S. empire. Three of
the four governors of Louisiana Territory—Missouri Territory after 1812—
came from Virginia. Lewis and Clark spent their formative years in Albemarle
County, the home of Jefferson. Benjamin Howard grew up in an adjacent
county and was a close friend and relative of the extended Clark family.[8]

The Chouteaus initially identified William Henry Harrison, the governor
of Indiana Territory, as the key leader among the western American officials.

By 1803, Harrison, still only thirty years old, had enjoyed considerable success as a politician and military officer and had demonstrated himself to be
both able and ambitious. His birth into a prominent Virginia political family
also ensured that Harrison received many political opportunities. In 1791,
friends of the Harrison family called on George Washington to commission the eighteen-year-old Harrison as a junior officer in the U.S. Army. Nine
years later, while Harrison served as a U.S. congressman from Virginia, his
political patrons obtained for him the post of governor of Indiana Territory.
His appointment came from the Federalist John Adams, but Harrison made
sure to get guarantees from the Democratic-Republican Thomas Jefferson
that he would not be replaced should Jefferson defeat Adams in that year's
presidential election. Jefferson kept his promise and reappointed Harrison
to the governorship twice during his presidency.[9]

Harrison also drew on relationships with fellow army officers. In the trans-
Appalachian West, American men often shared a fictive kinship based on
military service, and Harrison had served with three men who became
important friends to the Chouteau brothers. When Harrison introduced
General James Wilkinson to Auguste Chouteau, he noted that his friendship with Wilkinson had begun when Harrison was "yet a youth," referencing
his years with Wilkinson in General Anthony Wayne's Legion of the United
States in the Northwest Territory. Harrison had served Wayne as aide-de-
camp, while Wilkinson had been Wayne's second in command. During those
years, Harrison had met William Clark, then a young lieutenant, and the
two men began a decades-long friendship. One of the men then under Clark's
command was Meriwether Lewis, a fellow Virginian with whom Clark
would soon be forever linked. A decade later, Lewis noted their "long and
uninterupted friendship," when he asked Clark to colead an expedition to
the Pacific. Clark replied "that no man lives whith whome I would perfur to
undertake Such a Trip &c. as your self."[10] Harrison, Wilkinson, Clark, and
Lewis constituted the first set of U.S. officials in Louisiana Territory. Through
Harrison, the Chouteaus tapped into a powerful network of political allies.

In Indiana Territory, Harrison used his position and isolation from federal oversight to build his own fiefdom. In 1803, Harrison dominated the
U.S. government north of the Ohio River and west of Ohio Territory. Ostensibly, his command encompassed the present-day states of Illinois, Indiana, Michigan, and Wisconsin, along with part of Minnesota. In reality,
American control over the region was largely an illusion, much as it had been
with earlier empires. Only in the rapidly expanding American settlements

on the Ohio and Wabash Rivers did the United States exert authority. There, Harrison amassed growing power and influence. He appointed cronies to office and used dubious election practices to ensure his followers gained control of the territorial legislature.[11]

With the Louisiana Purchase, Harrison saw an opportunity to expand his authority westward across the Mississippi. He recognized that Louisiana was too large to be governed as a single territory. Harrison hoped that Upper Louisiana would be added to Indiana Territory, greatly increasing his power and importance in the West. The governor began to build relations with the power brokers of St. Louis. In the three years that his territory bordered that of Charles Dehault Delassus, Harrison developed a surprisingly close relationship with the Spanish-appointed lieutenant governor. In August 1803, upon learning that the United States had purchased Louisiana, Harrison informed Delassus of the news and extended an offer: "Should this be the case it may give me an opportunity of serving some of your friends—if this opportunity *does* offer be assured my dear Sir that it Shall not be neglected." Taking Harrison up on his proposal, Delassus probably introduced the Chouteau brothers to the governor shortly thereafter.[12] The Chouteaus and Harrison both sought to profit during the transition by helping one another.

Harrison served as the perfect ally for the Chouteaus because of his own power and because of his many connections in Virginia and in Washington. Writing to his friends and allies in the East, Harrison described Pierre Chouteau as a great asset to empire: a "man of the Strictest Honour" and more knowledgeable about Upper Louisiana "than any other man in the world." Harrison considered Auguste Chouteau "the Most respectable Citizen of Upper Louisiana whether it respects Character fortune or information." The young governor advised Thomas Jefferson that Auguste was "the first Citizen of Upper Louisiana" and that "every thing that Comes from him may be relied upon with the utmost Confidence."[13] Such praise facilitated the Chouteaus' integration into the western leadership of the United States.

Soon after making Harrison's acquaintance, the Chouteau brothers began to reap the benefits of their new friendship. In December 1803, Meriwether Lewis and William Clark arrived in St. Louis, heading the Corps of Discovery on its mission to explore the Missouri River valley and map a route to the Pacific. The Americans, however, lacked the necessary passports to travel through Spanish territory. Louisiana had not technically been a Spanish colony since October 1800, when Spain returned it to France, but Lieutenant Governor Delassus still waited for someone to take possession of the colony.

Fig. 6.1 William Clark by Charles Willson Peale, ca. 1807.

Lewis expected to encounter a French governor when he arrived and acquired the necessary documents from the French minister to the United States. Lewis was unprepared to meet Delassus.[14] Lacking the paperwork to enter Spanish territory, Lewis and Clark spent the winter and spring waiting for the colony's transfer to U.S. rule.

During the winter of 1803–1804, the two Virginians built close ties with the St. Louis elite. Clark had visited St. Louis once before. During a 1797 journey through present-day Illinois and Missouri, Clark stopped in St. Louis. After dining with Delassus, Clark attended a ball at Pierre Chouteau's home, where he mingled with the friends and relatives of the Chouteau brothers. Clark spoke no French, and most of his fellow party-goers were unfamiliar with English. The bilingual Charles Gratiot, a brother-in-law of the Chouteaus and a former ally of Clark's older brother George Rogers Clark, served as Clark's host and translator through the evening and into the night.[15] Half a dozen years later, Clark and Lewis called on those men and laid the foundation for the alliances that were to rule the city and the newly formed Louisiana Territory for the next generation. The Virginians established their base of operations across from St. Louis on U.S. land, but they frequently visited St. Louis and lodged in the home of Pierre and Brigitte Saucier Chouteau. Auguste and Pierre represented themselves—not incorrectly—as experts on the midcontinent and its Native peoples. The Chouteaus supplied the expedition with the goods Lewis and Clark needed to offer as gifts to Indian diplomats along their route. Pierre Chouteau also hired seven *engagés* to lead Lewis and Clark up the Missouri River to the Mandan towns in present-day North Dakota. For Jefferson, an avid natural scientist, the Chouteau brothers and Charles Gratiot provided samples of minerals as well as western flora and fauna. Auguste offered the Americans a map of the lower Mississippi River, while they all contributed their knowledge of the Missouri valley to a chart drafted by the explorers. On the eve of departure, Lewis appointed Gratiot as one of his representatives in St. Louis to greet Indian delegations, pay his bills, and receive and forward his mail.[16] By the time Lewis and Clark set forth in late May 1804, the extended Chouteau family had become partners of the American adventurers.

Even before Pierre Chouteau and William Henry Harrison landed in St. Louis together, the Chouteau brothers stood at the governor's right hand. They advised him on conditions in the colony, particularly Indian affairs. The brothers attended Harrison's negotiations with Sauk and Fox Indians that November and surely influenced the addition of a clause protecting the owners of Spanish land grants, principally Auguste Chouteau, in the territory ceded by the Sauks and Foxes. They also received appointments in local, territorial, and federal government. While Pierre received a position as a federal Indian agent, Auguste accepted multiple positions in the civil government of St. Louis and Upper Louisiana, including justice of the peace and justice of the Court of Common Pleas. Chouteau brother-in-law Charles Gratiot also received an appointment to the Court of Common Pleas.[17]

When General James Wilkinson took over the governorship of Louisiana Territory in July 1805, Harrison informed his old friend of his "sentiments" about the Chouteaus, advising him to seek their friendship. In contrast, Harrison warned his friend about fraught relations between the U.S. military commander Major James Bruff and the St. Louis elite, "the bare Idea, of his being in your confidence would frighten some of them out of their senses." In particular, Bruff had alienated the Chouteaus during a dispute about

Indian affairs. Leaving nothing to chance, Pierre Chouteau sailed down the Mississippi to greet Wilkinson as he approached St. Louis. On Wilkinson's first night in St. Louis, he snubbed Bruff and dined instead with Auguste.[18] Wilkinson recognized the power of the Chouteau family and sought the favor of its patriarch.

In Wilkinson's fifteen months in office, he aided the Chouteaus and other wealthy St. Louisans, most notably in their efforts to secure title to lands granted by the Spanish crown. The question of Spanish land grants became one of the most contentious and one of the longest-running conflicts in the territory's history. Beginning in 1804, American colonists arrived in Louisiana Territory only to discover that most of the desirable land had already been claimed for 300 miles along the Mississippi and as far as 120 miles west of the river.[19] The question for the new regime was how that had happened. According to the new arrivals, St. Louis elites spent the final years of Spanish Louisiana colluding with Delassus and Antoine Soulard, the royal surveyor and Chouteau in-law, and acquiring as much land as they could before the colony changed hands. They backdated claims to before the retrocession of Louisiana to France and edited surveys and plats to increase land holdings.

The francophone residents told a different story. Many of these deeds confirmed ownership for colonists, who had lived in homes and worked on farms without acquiring formal deed. The relatively small European population of Upper Louisiana generated little competition for property and lax enforcement of Spanish law removed much of the motivation to register and survey claims. The reality most likely existed somewhere between these two extremes. Amos Stoddard believed at first that the residents of Upper Louisiana had defrauded the United States. But during his months in St. Louis, he decided "that many of these suspicions arose from other causes not difficult to explain." Fraud existed, he admitted, but it failed to account for most of the grants awarded by Spain. Yet, without question, Delassus and Soulard dealt generously with claimants, and the city's wealthiest residents amassed vast holdings. The Chouteau brothers alone obtained several hundred thousand acres of land, most of it from grants signed by their friend Delassus and recorded by their relative Soulard.[20]

Jefferson's enthusiasm for the Louisiana Purchase grew out his belief that the United States needed more land to create the small farms that he believed served as the bedrock of a republican society. Initially, Jefferson thought that Indians east of the Mississippi could be convinced to exchange their territory for land west of the river, while French and Spanish colonists could be enticed to move east. Jefferson's western advisers warned against the scheme, as it would further alienate Louisianans, many of whom expected mistreatment from the United States. Jefferson turned his attention to the potential of the region for his beloved yeoman farmers. To open the newly acquired land for white colonization, the United States would have to settle the issue of Spanish land grants. Jefferson created a three-man commission to inspect grants, surveys, and deeds. It would affirm legitimate claims and overturn any found to be fraudulent.[21]

Through the newly appointed Governor James Wilkinson, the Chouteaus gained advocates on the land commission. Of the three commissioners, one was Wilkinson's nephew and another a longtime political ally. The Chouteaus' brother-in-law Charles Gratiot served as the commission's clerk, while Soulard acted as territorial surveyor. The commission's majority rubber-stamped the titles of the St. Louis gentry. American colonists, including the third commissioner, wanted the land for themselves. They alleged corruption and accused Wilkinson and his appointees of engaging in "the most abominable practices to the injury of the U.S." Taking stock of the reports from St. Louis, Secretary of the Treasury Albert Gallatin claimed that Wilkinson had "united with every man in Louisiana who had received or claims large grants under the Spanish Govt. (Gratiot, the Chouteaus, Soulard &c)." In March 1806, Jefferson determined, working in consultation with his cabinet, that "no improper motive" had influenced the commission's actions, but nevertheless, they had committed "an error . . . wandering entirely out of the views of the law." The commission was urged to reconsider its initial rulings in favor of the claimants. Meanwhile, despite the efforts of Harrison and Wilkinson, the U.S. surveyor general replaced Soulard with an American.[22]

The land controversy consumed the Wilkinson administration. Jefferson transferred the embattled governor to the border between Louisiana and Spanish Texas. In early 1807, Gallatin ordered the commission to suspend rulings until Congress could revisit the issue. The issue was far from solved, but Wilkinson and his friends had advocated for the francophone elites whom American colonists condemned as the "land junto" or "the Junto of speculators." On Wilkinson's departure from the midcontinent, Auguste Chouteau, writing on behalf of "the citizens of St. Louis," thanked the general for "the benefits they have derived" from Wilkinson's administration and expressed his hope that he would "long remain the guardian of the rights of this people."[23]

The Chouteaus, with the help of their western allies, gained a direct line to the highest echelons of the U.S. government. In February 1804, Lewis appointed Pierre Chouteau to lead a delegation of Osage leaders, including Chouteau friend Pawhuska, to Washington, DC, to meet President Jefferson. Such an assignment was a boon to the Chouteaus. The brothers handled all the expenses of the Osage delegation, and the U.S. government reimbursed them, including for $3,500 worth of gifts given to the Osage diplomats before they left St. Louis. The Chouteaus sold the items at retail prices, offering no discount to the United States. Additionally, Pierre Chouteau joined the Osages in their audience with the president. Over the years, the Chouteaus had counted many prominent and powerful men as their friends but had never enjoyed direct access to a head of state. In the ensuing years, both Pierre and Auguste kept up a regular correspondence with the president, informing him of activities in St. Louis, the disposition of Osage leaders, and the progress of the Lewis and Clark expedition. A decade after these initial encounters, Jefferson wrote that he "always considered" Auguste Chouteau "the most respectable man of the territory."[24]

U.S. officials recognized the opportunities and risks that Chouteau presented. During Pierre's visit to Washington, he twice met with Secretary of the Treasury Albert Gallatin. Writing to Jefferson, Gallatin reported, "He seems well disposed, but what he wants is power and money." In their conferences, Chouteau pushed the secretary to craft Indian trade policies that would benefit the Chouteau family, requesting a renewal of their Osage trade monopoly. The United States did not agree. Federal officials considered monopolies incongruous with republican ideals. Still, Gallatin dealt carefully with the Chouteaus, because he recognized that they could be "either useful or dangerous" to the new regime. In the end, Jefferson and his subordinates seized on the brothers' utility. The president chose the younger Chouteau brother to serve as U.S. Indian agent for Louisiana Territory.[25] The Chouteaus carried influence in St. Louis and in the Osage Nation. As the United States extended its empire into the West, it needed allies like Pierre and Auguste.

≈ For all of the success of the Chouteaus' relationships with Harrison, Wilkinson, Lewis, and Clark, Auguste and Pierre also realized that the American regime could be inconsistent in practice and policy. The brothers had always relied on personal ties to gain standing. Americans often engaged in similar behaviors. In other instances, they condemned such arrangements as nepotism and corruption. In the decade that followed the Louisiana Purchase, the Chouteaus deployed many of the strategies they had honed under Spain. They developed close ties with imperial officials and merged public and private interests to their advantage. Still, in politics and in the fur trade, they faced setbacks as they dealt with the fickle U.S. empire.

James Wilkinson, with his penchant for controversy and scandal, proved an unreliable ally. Shortly before his departure from St. Louis, Wilkinson became embroiled in former vice president Aaron Burr's supposed conspiracy to secede from the United States and build a new empire in the West. The Chouteaus needed to sever ties with their onetime collaborator and remove any taint of treason. Fortunately for them, Lewis and Clark had been absent during the Wilkinson administration. They had not been sullied by associating with Wilkinson, nor had Wilkinson's actions soured them on the Chouteaus. On the night Lewis and Clark landed in St. Louis on their return from the Pacific, the explorers took up residence in the home of Pierre Chouteau and dined with the two brothers and some of their "old friends."[26] In October 1806, a month after the return of the Corps of Discovery, Pierre Chouteau joined Lewis and Clark on their journey to the East, accompanying a delegation of Osages and other Missouri River Indians. Pierre and Auguste used their friendships with Lewis and Clark to circumvent potential charges of conspiracy or disloyalty.

During these early years, the Chouteaus also lost their near monopoly on knowledge about the Osage Nation and Missouri valley politics. In 1804, on Pierre's first visit to the U.S. capital, he repeated many of the stories that he, Auguste, and Pawhuska had told Spanish officials in the previous decade. Pawhuska, after a decade of conflict with his adversary Clermont and the growing number of Osages living on the Arkansas River, needed the backing of the United States, especially gifts, trade, and other material support, to maintain his advantage over his rivals. Standing before the U.S. president, Pawhuska depicted himself as the legitimate chief of the Great Osages and discredited his rivals on the Arkansas River. He blamed Clermont's Osages for violence in the West and asked the United States to aid him in bringing Arkansas Osages back under his authority. Jefferson welcomed Pawhuska and accepted his version of the Osage schism. The president promised support, particularly distributing goods to Pawhuska and not Clermont, in reuniting the Osage Nation under Pawhuska's leadership.[27]

Yet, by the time Pierre returned to Washington in 1806, the United States had begun to build its own library of information about the West, thanks to the reports of the Corps of Discovery and three other expeditions into the Louisiana Purchase. During the 1806 trip, Pierre Chouteau used familiar diplomatic strategies but achieved diminished returns. Little Osage chief Tuttasuggy (The Wind) refused to make the trip to the U.S. capital. Chouteau invited the chief's younger brother Nezuma (Traveling Rain) to take his place. Challenged by the intransigent Tuttasuggy, Chouteau attempted to maneuver around him as he and Auguste had done with Clermont and Pawhuska a decade earlier. However, Chouteau failed to promote Nezuma, in part because U.S. officials possessed greater knowledge of Osage politics than did their Spanish predecessors. Within a few months of Chouteau's visit to the Little Osages, a U.S. officer traveled to Tuttasuggy's town, where the chief informed him of Chouteau's duplicity. By 1808, Nezuma seems to have become the head chief of the Little Osages but only after the death of his elder brother.[28]

Meanwhile, the Chouteaus' new enterprises faced increasing scrutiny as they drew on imperial resources for personal gain. In 1807, Lewis and Clark returned to St. Louis from the East. Lewis replaced Wilkinson as governor. Clark became the new Indian agent for Upper Louisiana, unseating Pierre Chouteau, who took a new, diminished role specializing in Osage affairs. The restructuring may have resulted from Secretary of War Henry Dearborn's mistrust of Chouteau, whom he had criticized the previous year for trading while serving as Indian agent. However, as Dearborn also explained, "the extent of our Indian relations in the Territory of Louisiana" made the job too great for one man, and the United States needed Chouteau for his "particular acquaintance with the great and little Osages."[29]

Chouteau squashed any frustration he felt over his demotion and maintained good relations with Clark. In 1809, the two men helped cofound the St. Louis Missouri Fur Company (later shortened to the Missouri Fur Company), a joint venture of the commercial and political elite of St. Louis, Kaskaskia, and Louisville. The impetus came from Manuel Lisa's profitable return from the upper Missouri River in 1808. After a short but successful season of trapping and trading, he turned to his longtime rivals, the Chouteau brothers, for additional financial support. The Chouteaus did not particularly like or trust Lisa, but they loved money. Since the arrival of the U.S. government, federal trading posts, or factories, had cut into their business. The factories used trade to aid diplomatic goals. As a result, they were not bound by the need to turn a profit, and they could undersell private traders. After 1808, when the United States opened Fort Osage, some 330 miles west of St. Louis, the Chouteaus faced a rival that was not limited by the usual rules of competition. The wealth to be made in upper Missouri and Rocky Mountain furs convinced Pierre Chouteau to gather his allies and relatives and join Lisa. The partners of the Missouri Fur Company included Pierre Chouteau; William Clark; Auguste Chouteau, Jr. (probably backed by his father); Reuben Lewis, brother of the governor; Chouteau nephew Sylvestre Labbadie, Jr.; Lisa's partners and sometime Chouteau business associates Pierre Menard and William Morrison of Kaskaskia; Benjamin Wilkinson, nephew of former governor James Wilkinson; and Dennis Fitzhugh, a Clark brother-in-law who had conducted business with Lisa. Meriwether Lewis was probably a silent partner in the outfit.[30] The web of connections linking all of the partners would have struck the Chouteaus as a perfect mixture of interests and power.

With the backing of Governor Lewis and Indian agent Clark, the Missouri Fur Company drew on governmental connections to jump-start its business. In 1806, Clark, Lewis, and Pierre Chouteau escorted Mandan chief Shahaka and his family to Washington, DC, as part of the Indian delegation that met Jefferson following the return of the Corps of Discovery. The United States promised to return the Mandans to their town. But in 1807, Arikara Indians turned back the convoy escorting them. Shahaka spent the winter of 1808–1809 in St. Louis with his wife and children. Through the influence of Clark and Lewis, Congress appropriated $7,000 to pay the Missouri Fur Company to take Shahaka home. Lewis also promised that he would license no other traders to operate on the upper Missouri until after the Missouri Fur Company's convoy left St. Louis.[31] Given a head start on any competitors, the Missouri Fur Company possessed a similar advantage to that previously enjoyed by the Chouteau brothers among the Osages.

William Clark brought economic as well as political connections to the Missouri Fur Company. Clark's brother, nephew, and brother-in-law ran mercantile establishments in Louisville, and the river route between Louisville and St. Louis offered advantages over the Montreal–St. Louis–New Orleans network that the Chouteaus had built. The difficult journey from Canada to St. Louis and the seasonal vagaries of the Mississippi River created a cycle of feast and famine for Upper Louisiana's merchants. At certain times of year, stores in St. Louis and traders on the Missouri River offered a wealth of goods, but those supplies sometimes waned before the arrival of the next shipments. The voyage down the Ohio could be made any time of year except the dead of winter, when the region's rivers could freeze. Thus, Louisville became an important market for St. Louis merchants.[32] Adding Clark's contacts to those of the Chouteaus, Lisa, Menard, and Morrison, the company maintained a dependable network of suppliers and enjoyed a choice of where to buy goods and where to sell furs.

Trade on the upper Missouri proved more difficult and dangerous than operations lower on the river. The Indian nations of the Missouri posed the greatest challenge. The farther traders and trappers journeyed upriver, the more nations they had to negotiate with. Native peoples determined right of way much as the Osages had on the lower Missouri in the late eighteenth century. And like Osages, each faced a decision of whether the traders offered more advantages or disadvantages. On the upper Missouri, Blackfoots, Gros Ventres, Arikaras, and Lakotas determined that traders posed a threat as they traversed their nations, heading north and west. They raided vessels loaded with merchandise and pelts. Omaha chief Blackbird became famous for his demands on traders voyaging through his nation. To reach the upper Missouri, traders called on government power to back their endeavors. The Missouri Fur Company traveled with 140 militia volunteers to defend against Arikaras, who turned back the first effort to take Shahaka home. Along the way, Pierre Chouteau and his partners distributed gifts to ensure, as he put it, "the free passage of the Mandan chief."[33]

Departing in groups in May and June 1809, the Missouri Fur Company's partners, nearly 200 traders, and the militia contingent reached Mandan Country in late September. Hardship filled the first season of trapping and trading. Some excursions produced few furs, and one trading post filled with pelts burned to the ground. Near the headwaters of the Missouri, Blackfoot Indians killed company trappers, who poached on their land. The company also faced the misfortune of undertaking a large trading venture just as the United States enacted the Embargo Act of 1807, which depleted the supply of British trade goods to the midcontinent. In early 1810, Manuel Lisa journeyed to Canada in defiance of the law. Writing Pierre Chouteau from Detroit, he complained of the many U.S. guards on the border and the harsh penalties for smuggling: a 500-piastre fine and twenty-five days in prison. Lisa remarked, "I think that this time I will go to prison, for I cannot suffer it that they will not let me pass with merchandise." The firm's partners began looking for an exit.[34]

Meanwhile, in Washington, DC, U.S. officials became apprehensive about the Missouri Fur Company and its ambitions. Coming on the heels of the

Burr-Wilkinson conspiracy, the Missouri Fur Company's initial expedition drew suspicion that its partners planned something larger and more nefarious. Meriwether Lewis insisted that returning Shahaka and trading furs constituted the whole of the mission's interests. He promised that the company had no plan "to enter the Dominions, or do injury to any Foreign Power." Despite the insinuations about him, Lewis swore, they could "never make 'A Burr'" of him.[35]

Government officials also worried about the company's mix of political and commercial, public and personal, interests. Learning that Pierre Chouteau helmed Shahaka's escort, new secretary of war William Eustis dismissed Chouteau as agent to the Osages. The move shocked Chouteau, and Clark and Lewis came to his defense. Noting the delicate state of Osage relations with the United States, Lewis warned of war as he waited for all of the Osage leadership to sign a treaty between the two nations. Lewis insisted that Pierre would return from the Mandan towns quickly and that while he was away, Auguste could take his place. Pierre Chouteau, Jr., in his father's absence, explained to the secretary of war that Pierre Sr. "did not think it [joining the company] any dereliction of his duty since he was authorized to do it by the example of General Clark." Following the deluge of letters from St. Louis, Eustis relented and restored Chouteau, for the United States still needed the Chouteaus to mediate between the empire and the Osage Nation.[36]

In January 1814, despite reorganization and an influx of capital from new investors, the Missouri Fur Company dissolved. Most of its members, including the Chouteaus, lost interest after the company's initial struggles. The demise of the Missouri Fur Company marked a turning point for the Chouteaus. For years, the fur trade had proved an increasingly uncertain way to make a fortune. The Rocky Mountains and the upper Missouri offered a wealth of furs, but retrieving them required more effort and risk than the deerskin and bison robe trade of the lower Missouri. Deteriorating relations between the United States and Great Britain and the War of 1812 added more insecurity, as St. Louis merchants still depended on Montreal fur houses to obtain British manufactures. Meanwhile, government trading posts undersold private traders, benefiting Indians while hurting the Chouteau brothers and their competitors. Finally, the Chouteaus were growing too old for the day-to-day hardships of fur expeditions. In 1814, Auguste turned sixty-five; Pierre was fifty-six. Younger members of the family sustained the fur business, usually with Auguste and Pierre's backing, but the elder Chouteaus sought a steadier and more secure source of revenue.[37]

During the decade following the Louisiana Purchase, the Chouteau brothers employed strategies honed during the Spanish era to gain influence and wealth under the U.S. regime. But a number of setbacks forced Auguste and Pierre to adapt to the new government's expectations. The fallout from their friendship with James Wilkinson and the disappointment of the Missouri Fur Company convinced them that they needed to be subtler in their merger of public and private business so as to avoid suspicion from the United States. At the same time, the growing number of U.S. officials in the West ended the Chouteaus' monopoly on information about Indian nations in the Missouri valley. The Chouteaus recognized that they had to serve the objectives of an empire that wanted to transform Middle America into a world of Anglo-American farmers. Still, despite their mounting frustrations and failures during the early 1800s, Auguste and Pierre Chouteau retained important connections in Indian Country, the U.S. government, and the fur trade. They used those relations to transition into a new business built on dispossessing Indian nations and feeding the land hunger of the United States and its colonists.

≈   In July 1804, Pawhuska and Pierre Chouteau presented Thomas Jefferson with a carefully constructed narrative of the past and a vision for the future of Louisiana and relations between the United States and the Osages. Jefferson, in turn, seized the opportunity to shape the expectations of his western guests. The president welcomed Pawhuska and the other Osage leaders, proclaiming, "we are all now one family, born in the same land, & bound to live as brothers." Jefferson highlighted U.S. interest in the fur trade and promised it would continue. He assured Pawhuska that the empire would work to reunite the divided Osages under Pawhuska's leadership. To facilitate good relations and communication, he appointed Pierre Chouteau as U.S. agent to the Osages. Both Pawhuska and Jefferson concealed much about the past and their intentions, but their speeches in those initial meetings shaped the future of U.S.-Osage relations. Jefferson did not broach one of his two intended topics of discussion, "the plan of inducing the Indians on this [side of the Mississippi], to remove to the other side of that river."[38] In this omission, Jefferson hid his desire to acquire Indian land, the central piece of his plan for the Louisiana Purchase.

In the United States' administration of Louisiana Territory, it introduced a brand of colonialism born out of three decades of warfare and violence in the Ohio valley. Rather than alliance and trade, which had been the corner-

stones of previous empires, the United States sought land. In the years following the Revolutionary War, relations between the United States and the
Indian nations north of the Ohio River deteriorated. The United States
claimed Indian lands by right of conquest, having defeated Great Britain,
but Indian nations rightly asserted that they had not been conquered, nor
had they ever acknowledged British authority over them. Drawing on the
kinship ties and alliances that Memeskia used in the 1740s and 1750s and
that Pontiac employed following the Seven Years' War, Miami, Delaware,
and Shawnee leaders forged the powerful Northwest Confederacy to preserve their territory and stave off invasion by Americans. In 1790 and 1791,
Josiah Harmar and Arthur St. Clair led armies against the confederacy. The
Northwest Confederacy defeated both forces on the battlefield. St. Clair's
army suffered near annihilation. It was far from certain that the United States
could defeat the Northwest Indians militarily. Plus, war was too costly for a
fledgling nation that was short on cash and credit. Anthony Wayne's Legion
of the United States, which finally defeated the Northwest Confederacy at
Fallen Timbers in 1794, cost the federal government more than $1 million
each year. Such an expenditure would consume about half of the federal
operating budget.[39] Wayne proved that the United States could achieve
military victory but only at a high cost.

Faced with choosing between embarrassing defeats and crippling costs,
Secretary of War Henry Knox and key subordinates devised a third path:
"civilization" policy. Knox advocated recognizing Indian rights to their land,
purchasing that land rather than taking it, training Indians in Euro-American
agriculture and animal husbandry, and thereby imparting to them "a love
for exclusive property." At the same time, missionaries would convert Indians
to Protestant Christianity and establish schools in their nations. Having
changed into educated, Christian yeoman farmers, Indians would become
U.S. citizens. Knox admitted that his program "would be an operation of complicated difficulty" and that it required "a steady perseverance in a wise system
for a series of years." Despite hardships entailed in implementing "civilization"
policy, Knox expected to reap great benefits, particularly avoiding the costs of
war and gaining the affections of Native peoples.[40] He believed that Indians
and Americans alike would enjoy peace and prosperity under his program.

In formulating the plan, Knox tapped into Enlightenment theories, well
intended but ethnocentric, that were dominant among U.S. elites. Environ-
mentalist theories of race posited that climate, diet, and local conditions
influenced human character and behavior. This theory considered Indians

"noble savages," uneducated, childlike primitives, living in nature and un-
touched by civilization. Many Americans believed that the United States
held a moral obligation to prevent the extermination of Native peoples, whose
"savagery" stemmed not from innate qualities but from their surroundings.
In this view, "civilization" had begun its inevitable advance across North
America, destroying barbaric societies. With the aid of American philanthropy, Indians could join the ranks of the civilized world. They would be
transformed through education and training, just as nature, inherently wild,
could be made into cultivable land by the axe and plow.[41]

Knox advocated his new program as "the obligations of policy, humanity,
and justice." But he and other officials also recognized the material benefits
to the United States of reducing Indian land holdings. U.S. officials believed
that, by restructuring Native economies around farming and transforming
the landscape from game-filled woods and prairies to homesteads, they would
open territory for American colonists. In Knox's initial formulation, he noted
that expanded agriculture and the accompanying decline in game would
allow the United States to purchase land for "small considerations." Soon the
emphasis on land cessions dwarfed the other tenets of "civilization" policy.
In 1803, Thomas Jefferson concisely enumerated the duties of Indian agents:
"1. the preservation of peace. 2. the obtaining [of] lands."[42]

Knox built "civilization" policy on theories formulated by thinkers who
had mostly never encountered Indians, and Native peoples defied the expectations of imperialists who anticipated malleable and pliant students. Many
eastern Indian nations, or at least factions within them, adopted aspects of
the program. But they did so on their own terms. In the government's plan,
they saw avenues to rebuild their economies after years of war. They welcomed new agricultural methods and tools. They adapted some industries
to suit their needs and interests. For example, encouraged to replace hunting
with animal husbandry, Indian men often let their cattle and pigs roam wild,
and at time for slaughter, they tracked them down like game. But they rejected those parts of "civilization" policy that defied Native cultural norms.
They had little interest in religious education. Despite U.S. pressure to take
up agriculture, most men refused to expand their involvement, and women
retained much of their control of field agriculture. And Indian nations
would not surrender their land or their sovereignty in exchange for farming
implements, religious schools, or possible U.S. citizenship. "Civilization"
policy failed to produce the sweeping changes that Knox and his backers
envisioned.[43]

From the beginning, "civilization" policy contained two impulses running counter to each other. On the one hand, the program intended to "civilize" Indians and convert them as citizens of the republic, which, as Knox noted in his original statement, required time. On the other, behind the benevolent talk that buttressed "civilization" policy, the United States worked to destroy Indian nations and acquire Indian lands. At the turn of the nineteenth century, the two goals of "civilization" policy perplexed U.S. officials. Should they allow Indian nations to determine for themselves that they no longer needed certain tracts of land? Or should they force cessions? Would they protect Indian land rights from American squatters? Or should they compel Native peoples to surrender territory and move westward away from the frontiers of the United States? In the contest with patience, greed prevailed.

The tensions between "civilization" and dispossession in U.S. Indian policy extended to the highest levels of the empire. After Thomas Jefferson became president in 1801, he demonstrated that U.S. officials could speak eloquently about transforming Native peoples while working also to seize their land. In early 1803, writing to William Henry Harrison, Jefferson reiterated his belief that eastern Indians would "in time either incorporate . . . as citizens of the United States or remove beyond the Missisipi." Jefferson affirmed Knox as he advocated western training and education and predicted changes in Indian societies that would reduce their territorial needs. Yet the tenets of Jeffersonian Indian policy made removal more probable than incorporation. By 1803, Jefferson encouraged underhanded means to ensure land cessions. He insisted that officials should "be glad to see the good and influential individuals among them run in debt," as the leverage to coerce land sales. If any nations resisted, the United States would seize their lands and deport them to the trans-Mississippi West. Before closing, Jefferson noted the retrocession of Louisiana to France and implored Harrison to acquire as much land as possible before the changing political landscape made Indians reluctant to cede territory.[44]

The Louisiana Purchase served an integral role in Jeffersonian Indian policy. It provided a region where "uncivilized" Indians could be deported to live away from Americans and "civilized" Indians. James Wilkinson advised, "Depopulation must precede the transfer of the Indians."[45] Jefferson and his subordinates focused on the territory of the Osages. If the United States could force them west, it would open a large region for removed eastern Indians. With the United States dedicated to acquiring Osage land, Jefferson's language of kinship and brotherhood between the United States and the Osages had already outlived its usefulness.

In the fall of 1808, Pawhuska welcomed U.S. negotiators, because he needed American backing to galvanize his position within the Osage Nation. His power in the 1790s stemmed in no small part from the wealth provided by his Spanish and Chouteau allies. Fort Carondelet, a trading post and an indicator of Osage prestige, buttressed Pawhuska's claims to authority. But all the while, Clermont denounced Pawhuska's reign as illegitimate. A series of factors weakened Pawhuska's authority. In 1804, Manuel Lisa, who assumed the Chouteaus' monopoly two years earlier, abandoned Fort Carondelet after the end of Spanish rule had canceled his exclusive trade privileges. Although Pawhuska's Great Osages and Little Osages maintained permanent residences on the Osage and Missouri Rivers, respectively, they traveled to the Arkansas valley for their winter bison hunt. The Arkansas valley and the lands to the south and southwest had long been prime Osage hunting territory and the nation's primary source for food and furs. From the Arkansas valley, Osages ranged south and raided Wichita and Caddo villages for horses, which they used in warfare or traded. In Osage society, young men rose to prominence by demonstrating their prowess as hunters and warriors, and the Arkansas valley offered more opportunities for both.[46]

The Missouri and Osage valleys lost much of their appeal for Osages as commerce dwindled and violence increased, and the center of Osage power shifted to Clermont and the Arkansas valley. After Fort Carondelet closed, Pawhuska's territory held little advantage in trade over that of Clermont. The Chouteaus had turned their focus to the Arkansas Osages after Lisa took over their monopoly among the Osages in the Missouri valley. At the same time, the influx of American colonists and campaigns by the U.S. military north of the Ohio River convinced some Delawares, Potawatomis, Sauks, and Shawnees to relocate west of Mississippi. Along with Ioways and Otoes already living west of the river, they moved into Osage territory along the Missouri River, where border conflicts grew into ongoing wars. Reports of those attacks fill the correspondence and journals of early U.S. observers. In 1804, Sauk warriors attacked the Osage delegation traveling to Washington, DC, and killed a chief. The following year, Kaskaskia chief Jean Baptiste Ducoigne held a council of Delawares, Miamis, Ojibwes, Ottawas, Piankashaws, Potawatomis, and Shawnees and advocated uniting to war against the Osages, because the United States seemed to offer them special favor and consideration. In an 1805 attack, Potawatomis killed more than thirty Osage women and children and took sixty more as captives. Two years later, Potawatomis killed two Osage chiefs while raiding their village. Thomas Jefferson feared that the endemic warfare between the Osages and the refugee nations was turning the Mississippi into "a river of blood."[47] Without Fort Carondelet to anchor Osages, warfare with emigrant Indian nations pushed more and more Osages away from the Missouri River.

Between 1800 and 1810, when the non-Indian population of Upper Louisiana increased from about 7,000 people to nearly 20,000, thousands of American colonists joined eastern Indians as interlopers in Osage Country. Towns and farms sprung up along the Meramec and Missouri Rivers, impinging on the Osage Nation, which used violence to intimidate the intruders. Osages raided Indian and American settlements, stealing horses, destroying farms, and occasionally killing a squatter. Unable to stem the incursion, many Osages relocated southward to the Arkansas valley, where they joined Clermont. Pawhuska, with his followers evacuating the Missouri valley, felt his power slipping away.[48]

The actions of Louisiana territorial officials, especially Governor Meriwether Lewis and Indian agent William Clark, exacerbated Pawhuska's woes. Because of their success in negotiating with Indian nations as leaders of the Corps of Discovery, Lewis and Clark overestimated their own knowledge and skill in such situations. In their new roles in the U.S. empire, Clark and Lewis often mishandled the customs and formalities of Indigenous diplomacy. Pawhuska employed common tropes in his speeches to the Americans. He blamed uncontrollable young men for violence, praised U.S. power, and requested protection. More experienced diplomats would have recognized Pawhuska's speech as flattery rather than reality, but the two Americans took the chief's statements at face value. In 1808, Lewis declared war on all but Pawhuska's Great Osages and some Little Osages. Lewis, like the Spanish governor Carondelet before him, banned trade with the Osage Nation and encouraged their longtime enemies to attack them. Pawhuska knew that the United States could not control Missouri River trade, but he feared that U.S.-backed attacks would drive more Osages from the Missouri valley and further weaken his position.[49]

In the fall of 1808, when William Clark led a contingent of U.S. troops to Fire Prairie on the Missouri River northeast of present-day Independence, Missouri, Pawhuska welcomed the opportunity to negotiate. For a moment, the interests of Pawhuska's Osages and the United States converged. Clark journeyed to Fire Prairie to build a trading post for the Osages, not to negotiate a treaty, but he returned to St. Louis with a pact in hand. By Clark's account, Pawhuska and Little Osage chief Nezuma ceded to the United States 50,000 square miles of land east of a line running from Fire Prairie south to the Arkansas River. They would relocate their towns to the site of the new outpost, Fort Osage. In exchange, the United States would reopen trade with the nation except those living on the Arkansas River, provide Osages an annual annuity of gifts and supplies, pay any claims held by U.S. colonists for property destroyed or stolen by Osages, and end the war between the Osages and their enemies to the north and east. Osages also retained hunting rights on the lands east of the boundary line.[50]

Osages, for their part, believed that they had only given the United States the right to hunt in the eastern part of the Osage Nation. Although they fiercely defended their hunting territory from poachers, Osages often shared those lands with friendly nations as a gesture of alliance. Granting hunting rights to the United States, especially on areas that Americans and eastern Indians had invaded, in exchange for peace and a dedicated Osage trading post seemed like a reasonable trade. In late 1808, when Osage chiefs learned of the more sweeping U.S. interpretation of the treaty, they condemned the proceedings at Fire Prairie. Pawhuska and Nezuma insisted they had been tricked, while other leaders complained that those chiefs had lacked the authority to cede land without permission of the nation. Clark insisted that he used "no unfair means" to induce the Osages to cede their land, but the Osages believed they had been swindled.[51]

In December 1808, Meriwether Lewis dispatched Pierre Chouteau to renegotiate the treaty. Pawhuska and Nezuma may have lacked the authority to agree to Clark's demands, but the United States used the disputed agreement as the starting point in Chouteau's negotiations. Meriwether Lewis warned that those who refused to sign the treaty "can have no future hopes, that their pretensions to those lands now claimed by them, will ever be respected by the United States."[52] The large numbers of American colonists moving up the Missouri gave weight to Lewis's words. The remainder of the Osage leadership had two options: they could agree to the terms and negotiate for remuneration or refuse and probably lose their territory anyway. The attitude of the United States rendered the second round of negotiations a farce.

As Pierre Chouteau negotiated the second treaty, he found that the ambitions of the United States limited his opportunities for profit. In the only substantial change between the two treaties, Pierre Chouteau inserted a clause preserving his Osage land grants and those of his French-Osage kinsman Noel Mongraine. Osages had given those lands—about 25,000 acres on the Lamine River—to Pierre Chouteau in 1792 in gratitude for his years of advice and assistance. In 1799, Spanish governor Delassus upheld the grant in part, because, as he noted, "the tract of land which he solicits is situated at too great a distance from these settlements to be prejudicial to any person." By 1808, Chouteau's claims sat in the middle of a large swath of territory that U.S. officials, including Lewis, wanted to open to American colonists. To that end, Lewis struck Chouteau's additions from the treaty before sending it to Congress for ratification.[53]

Despite the loss of land that accompanied the construction of Fort Osage (also called Fort Clark), Pawhuska believed that the outpost would serve the Osages much as Fort Carondelet had during the 1790s. U.S. treatment of the Osages, however, paled in comparison to the favoritism the Chouteau brothers showed Pawhuska and his town. The greatest blow came from the revelation that Fort Osage would not serve the Osages alone. In the summer of 1808, Meriwether Lewis commended Fire Prairie for its central location, not just to Great and Little Osages but also to Kaws, Ioways, and Sauks. While the fort was still under construction, George C. Sibley, soon to take charge of the post's commerce, anticipated that Fort Osage would "become a great place of rendezvous for the Indians of a great many Tribes to come and trade."[54] Had Pawhuska been privy to that correspondence, he would have been more reluctant to treat with the United States, which soon invited enemy nations to journey through and trade in the Osage Nation.

U.S. officials seemed either unaware or indifferent to the fact that their plan for the fort insulted Osages and would spark violence between Osages and their enemies. Further demonstrating Lewis's inexperience in Indian diplomacy, he believed that "by compelling several nations to trade at the same establishment they will find it necessary to live in peace with each other." Lewis could scarcely have made a worse prediction. By the spring of 1809, before the Treaty of 1808 was even ratified, William Clark learned that Sauk warriors marauded against the Osages. In the fall and winter of 1809–1810, large numbers of Great Osages left Fort Osage and returned to their old homes on the Osage River. The next spring, most of the remaining Great Osages joined them, as did some Little Osage families. When the time came to plant the year's corn crop, only about half of the Little Osages still lived around the fort. The death of Pawhuska in 1809 and the reopening of U.S. trade with the Arkansas Osages accelerated Osage abandonment of Fort

Osage. In 1810, about 3,000 Osages, more than half of the nation, lived on the Arkansas River, an increase of 1,000 or so people from the beginning of the decade.[55]

The shrinking Osage population at Fort Osage became more vulnerable to attacks by the nation's enemies. In May 1811, as Little Osages prepared to leave Fort Osage for the summer bison hunt, they suffered nighttime raids waged by Ioway and Oto Indians stealing horses. Late on May 6, Osage sentries discovered three Ioway raiders lurking just beyond the town. In a brief skirmish, the Osages killed one man, an Ioway war chief, and drove the others away.[56] Despite the success in repelling the attack, Little Osages failed to recover their stolen horses, a loss rendered particularly devastating on the eve of their annual hunt.

The violence around Fort Osage limited its effectiveness as a trade hub and a site of diplomacy. In 1809, Fort Osage's first year of operation, Sibley shipped 28,000 deerskins, 4,000 beaver pelts, and 2,500 bearskins, among others, to New Orleans. In the years that followed, those totals fell dramatically. The fort was dangerous, and the U.S. garrison offered little protection. In the spring of 1811, a party of Great Osages from the Osage and Arkansas Rivers journeyed to the fort to trade and collect their annuities. Sauk, Ioway, and Ho-Chunk warriors waited on the prairies to the south. As the Osages returned home, the warriors attacked. In the defeat, Osages suffered "the slaughter of many of their people and the loss of a great part of their goods & horses." Only when the garrison escorted the survivors a dozen or so miles beyond the fort did they attempt the journey again. Under the protection of the U.S. Army, they escaped without further violence on that trip.[57]

Danger persisted. The next summer, a U.S. officer reported that northern Indians were "continually hovering arround the neighbourhood of the Fort . . . looking out for Osages." Osage leaders complained, "the bones of several of my Nation lie *unburied* and bleaching on the Prairie between my Village & Fort Clark." Witnessing the violence, the officers stationed at Fort Osage took a dark view of the post and its failures, because the Osages increasingly stayed away. In 1812, one American officer concluded, "the Object of this establishment is distroyed." The next year, some Great Osage leaders requested that the fort be moved south to the Osage River. Others favored a location near Arrow Rock, a sizeable American town, which they believed would offer more security from enemy attacks. Even those Little Osages who continued to live near Fort Osage and liked the location condemned the feeble U.S. Army. The Big Soldier told Sibley, "I have seen [the president] and his Country and Millions of his People, and am very certain that he is able to protect a Trading House wherever he is bound by contract to keep one." That the fort had failed, he believed, rested squarely at the feet of the U.S. government. The president had promised to "plant an Iron Post there that could not be pulled up," but instead, he "intends to let the old *wooden* one rot."[58]

The Treaty of 1808 and its aftermath revealed the extent of American demands for land—the facet of U.S. Indian policy hidden by Jefferson during his 1804 meeting with Pawhuska—and set the tone for future U.S. treaties in the midcontinent. U.S. officials, from Indian agents to the president, professed desire for friendship and peace between the empire and Indian nations. But as Clark and Lewis showed, those overtures were merely way stations on the path to dispossession. The Treaty of 1808 and the violence at Fort Osage compelled Osages to abandon the Missouri River, the key to much of their power during the eighteenth century.

In the early nineteenth century, the United States pursued a deliberate strategy of driving Native peoples away from rivers. The Missouri River would be the future great commercial avenue of the trans-Mississippi West. For the United States to thrive, Osages had to move. By 1815, most Osages had moved to the Arkansas valley, where they reunited under the leadership of Clermont. Meanwhile, the Chouteau brothers learned that they would need to change their strategy if they wanted to retain power and influence in the new regime. Spain had largely been content to let the brothers shape policy toward the Osages, because their interest was in preserving peace and promoting trade. In contrast, the United States wanted land and to encourage American colonists to erect homesteads. After the Treaty of 1808, the Chouteaus continued to serve the United States as negotiators, advisers, and mediators by facilitating land cessions.[59]

≈   As the Chouteaus brokered land sales from Indian nations to the United States, they discovered that they could profit by serving as employees of the empire and by providing the merchandise promised to Indians in treaties. They continued to draw on their many connections in Indian country, the U.S. administration, and the trading world, but they depended on them to deal in land rather than furs. In short, the Chouteau family profited from the misfortune of their Indian relatives and trading partners. At the conclusion of the War of 1812, Secretary of War James Monroe picked Auguste

Chouteau to serve as one of three commissioners to negotiate treaties with Indian nations in the Mississippi valley. Joining Chouteau were William Clark, now governor of Missouri Territory, and Ninian Edwards, governor of Illinois Territory. Although the aging Chouteau was on the verge of retiring from public life, he accepted this appointment. He surely saw the opportunity to funnel government contracts to his relatives. In 1815, he participated in negotiations with twenty-one nations at Portage des Sioux, where the U.S. government dispersed $20,000 in merchandise as gifts. It must have pained him that those items had been purchased in Washington, DC, rather than from him. Over the next five years, Auguste Chouteau represented the United States at the negotiations of fifteen treaties between Indian nations and the U.S. empire. In 1818 and 1825, Pierre Chouteau took part in two other treaty councils between Osages and the United States. Other relatives served as translators and subagents. In addition to receiving pay for services rendered, the Chouteau family became one of the largest suppliers of goods to Indian agents in St. Louis. The Chouteaus dealt in the same merchandise that they used in the fur trade. But when the Chouteaus worked as government contractors, the United States guaranteed and underwrote their business.[60]

Auguste Chouteau's appointment as an Indian commissioner in 1815 coincided with a growing drive in the United States to deport Native peoples. Americans believed that "civilization" policy had failed, although they disagreed about why. Some insisted that the program remained workable but that poor westerners—"bad white men"—had negated the positive influence of missionaries, government agents, and others. The geographer and author Jedidiah Morse argued, "It is very difficult to prevent these evils while Indians and white people live in the near neighborhood of each other." To give Native peoples more time to "civilize," people such as Morse advocated removing Indians beyond the borders of the United States, where they would live free from corrupting influences and could adapt at their own speed. Others adopted increasingly popular theories that proposed that intrinsic qualities, not environmental factors, produced a hierarchy of races. By the 1830s, American scientists and philosophers posited that the Christian God had created four distinct races of humans: Africans, Caucasians, Indians, and Mongolians. These authors asserted that Caucasians, due to their natural abilities, thrived while the other races faltered. U.S. officials in Washington and in the West argued that the extinction of Native peoples was imminent and inevitable. Many Americans, such as the Kentucky politician Henry

Clay, "did not think them, as a race, worth preserving."[61] Regardless of the logic, American thinkers and politicians came to believe that Indian removal was the next step in U.S. Indian policy.

As the vanguard of colonization, westerners drove American demands for Indian land, and they had never shared the dream of "civilization" policy with U.S. officials. Western Americans moved to the trans-Mississippi to acquire land, and in their pursuit of property, they disregarded the borders of the United States and the laws that regulated land use in the territories. The influx of colonists after the War of 1812 only aggravated matters. In 1810, about 20,000 colonists lived in Louisiana Territory. Ten years later, the American population had jumped to more than 66,000. The itinerant preacher John Mason Peck recalled, "the 'new-comers,' like a mountain torrent poured in the country faster than it was possible to provide corn for breadstuff." Some came in 1815. Then, in 1816, "they came like an avalanche." The demand for land skyrocketed. The U.S. government repeatedly banned squatting on Indian land—a policy pursued for peace, not in recognition of Indian sovereignty—but such prohibitions did little to curb the incursions. The militia, made up primarily of recently arrived Americans looking for their own land, refused to enforce unpopular land laws. The U.S. Army was scarcely more reliable. In 1808, Captain George Armistead, U.S. captain on the St. Francis River, informed a civil official that "white people are at liberty to settle where they please." He swore to support the squatters and "let them see who prevent it."[62]

Capricious U.S. officials promised to uphold treaties, but they lacked the ability and, in many instances, the desire to stop American intrusions into Indian Country. In 1816, William Clark learned that American squatters had moved to Osage land in the Arkansas valley. Rather than request support to arrest the intruders, he noted the difficulty of removing them and commented on the significance of the country, which connected Missouri to Louisiana and on "which the Indians set but little value." Rather than force Americans out at gunpoint, Clark suggested purchasing those lands and extending the Osage boundary line. In the Northwest Territory and then in Louisiana, the United States repeatedly backed squatters. Instead of enforcing existing treaties, the empire pushed Indians for more land cessions. One U.S. official in St. Louis noted, "there is so many precedents of Pre-emption rights, Donations &c. that these folks . . . will become very numerous & Clamorous for the same favors from Government that others have received under similar Circumstances." A colonist noted, "American settlements *never recede.*

Whoever heard of two hundred farms, cultivated by wealthy and respectable American citizens, being abandoned by their cultivators and turned into Indian hunting grounds?" Americans knew that eventually the government would back them, whether they had broken the law or not, "however wrongfully" they acquired land, so they pushed into Indian Country.[63]

"Civilization" policy died a slow death in those years, as officials and colonists conspired to seize Indian land to push the boundaries of the United States westward. The United States still offered farming implements and livestock to Indians, but Jefferson's dream of incorporation had evaporated. Osages showed little interest in changing their economy, but many Indians, such as a number of Shawnees and Delawares in southeastern Missouri, welcomed Euro-American-style agriculture. In particular, Shawnees built log cabins and enclosed their fields with split-rail fences. Their farms looked much like American homesteads. Some men adopted animal husbandry as an alternative to hunting. These émigrés from the Ohio valley did well for themselves. In the 1810s, some individual Shawnees in that region owned more than 200 cattle, horses, and pigs. Missourians coveted Shawnee and Delaware lands at Cape Girardeau, and in 1817, the territorial legislature passed a resolution authorizing the exchange of those lands for "other lands in some more remote part of the Territory which is better adapted in indian persuits."[64]

Because Americans considered Indians migrant hunters, roaming across rather than owning land, they refused to acknowledge that the "persuits" of Delawares and Shawnees in Missouri were virtually indistinguishable from those of their American neighbors. One Shawnee chief protested, "our behavior has been such that no honest white man can have any cause to find fault with us." That mattered little to land-hungry colonists. In fact, wealthy Indians made more attractive targets for American violence. Between 1811 and 1814, Americans stole more than 150 pigs, horses, and cattle from Shawnees living on Apple Creek in southeastern Missouri. Around 1821, the squatter William Fulbright drove the Shawnee Indian Petatwa off his homestead on the Meramec River, seizing "a good Cabin." Petatwa returned, only to be beaten and chased off by a different American. Petatwa's brother Little Captain suffered similar depredations. Indian agent Pierre Menard worked to bring redress to the Shawnees, but the new state of Missouri blocked prosecution until the statute of limitations expired.[65] Such actions sent a clear message to Shawnees that they were not welcome in American Missouri.

U.S. officials believed that the best way to halt the violence was to deport Indians, and as a bonus, land cessions opened more territory for the thousands of Americans arriving annually. Auguste and Pierre Chouteau and their legion of kin took full advantage of the new emphasis on removal. In 1819, Auguste Chouteau and Benjamin Stephenson negotiated the removal of the Kickapoos from their remaining land on the Wabash River. In exchange, the Kickapoos received new territory on the Osage River, and by the stipulations of the treaty, "some judicious citizen shall be selected to accompany them, in their passage through the white settlements, to their intended residence." The United States tapped Pascal Cerré, brother-in-law of Auguste Chouteau, to escort the Kickapoos to their new homes. The United States paid Cerré $6 a day, a higher daily salary than even Clark received. In 1825, Pierre Chouteau, Pascal Cerré, and Pierre's son Paul Liguest Chouteau aided in the negotiation of a new treaty with the Osages, which completed their removal from Missouri and ceded the lands that would become Indian Territory. The final treaty included provisions to repay debts that the Osages owed St. Louis traders, including $1,000 due Pierre's son A. P.[66]

The Chouteaus also made money by providing the goods offered as gifts at treaty councils and those given as part of the annuities guaranteed in the treaties. These goods included all of the items the Chouteaus had traded for furs in earlier decades. They added a new customer, selling to the United States as well as trading with Indian nations on the Missouri. In 1820, Berthold & Chouteau, the mercantile house run by Pierre Chouteau, Jr., and his brother-in-law Bartholomew Berthold, supplied nearly 60 percent of the $11,600 in Indian gifts that Clark distributed that year. During the mid-1820s, William Clark acquired tens of thousands of dollars worth of Indian Department supplies from a new firm owned by Pierre Chouteau, Jr., and his brothers- and cousins-in-law Berthold, Jean Pierre Cabanné, and Bernard Pratte.[67]

While the children and in-laws of Pierre and Auguste Chouteau served as guides and suppliers for the empire, the brothers sought U.S. confirmation of their Spanish land grants, as the titles to tens of thousands of acres remained in dispute. During the transfer from Spanish to French to U.S. governance, the Chouteaus had claimed prime land around St. Louis, St. Charles, and the other towns near the junction of the Missouri and Mississippi Rivers and stretching up the Missouri River into the central part of the state. During the 1810s, thousands of Americans followed the Missouri River to Boone's Lick, which was fast becoming the agricultural heart of the state. As John Mason Peck wrote, "Caravan after caravan passed over the prairies of Illinois, crossed the 'great river' at St. Louis, all bound to the Boone's Lick." Kentucky and Tennessee, it seemed, were "breaking up and moving to the 'Far West.'" Others came from throughout the Upper South, "while a sprinkling found their way to the extreme west from Yankeedom and Yorkdom."[68]

As Americans moved into those growing towns and pushed up the Missouri, the Chouteaus' claims became particularly valuable because of their location. The brothers pursued title to every acre to which they had any claim. Among the unsettled claims, the 1792 Osage grant of about 25,000 acres dominated Pierre Chouteau's land interests. Situated near the confluence of the Lamine and Missouri Rivers in central Missouri, Chouteau's Osage grant occupied one of the fastest growing regions of Missouri Territory during the 1810s. When the United States sold the first public lands in the area in 1819, demand drove up prices from the federal rate of $2 per acre upward of $26 per acre. Determined to gain title, Pierre offered shares of the tract to powerful allies in exchange for their support, because without confirmation of his title, Pierre would lose all potential profits. For three decades, Pierre petitioned to have his grant upheld, but only in 1833, after the intercession of William H. Ashley—a former fur trader turned U.S. congressman and the owner of a quarter stake in the tract—did the land commission confer title to Chouteau. Pierre promptly sold his share of the land for $43,000. Auguste preferred to rent rather than sell his holdings. At his death in 1829, he still owned about 50,000 acres of land and held unconfirmed claims to more than 8,000 acres.[69]

As Pierre and Auguste Chouteau profited from American imperialism, they also used their position to shield their Osage relatives from displacement and dispossession. The 1825 Osage treaty, negotiated partly by Pierre, included an article creating "reservations, for the use of the half-breeds." At the Marais des Cygnes in western Missouri and at the Three Forks of the Arkansas River, both near Chouteau trading posts, thirty-nine French-Osage men, women, and children received allotments under the treaty. Many of Pierre Chouteau's grandchildren, Chouteau employees and interpreters, and assorted Chouteau relatives dominate the list of recipients, indicating that the plots were given to a select group of friends and kin. Notably, the Chouteau relative and longtime ally Noel Mongraine, ten of his children, and four of his grandchildren received half of the total land. The treaty also recognized the daughter of Paul Loise, sometimes called Paul Chouteau, and the

Fig. 6.2 Mi-Ho'n-Ga and her daughter Maria-Elizabeth, 1830. Along with thirty-eight other French-Osage people, most of them relatives of the Chouteau family and other French traders, Mi-Ho'n-Ga's older daughter, Amelia, received a plot of land in the 1825 treaty between the United States and the Osage Nation.

daughter of Mi-Ho'n-Ga, an Osage woman possibly married to a Chouteau. William Clark justified these grants to his superiors, explaining that they "have a good effect in promoting civilization, as there attachment is created for a fixed residence & an idea of separate property is imparted, without which it is vain to think of improving the minds and morals of Indians."[70] Despite Clark's talk of "civilization," the exclusion of other Osage people, including those with francophone fathers or grandfathers and those who had been baptized by Christian missionaries, reveal the limited reach of this program. Those who received land did so because of their personal connections to the treaty's negotiators, not because of American largesse.

The deportation of the midcontinent's Indians was a joint enterprise between the U.S. government, American colonists, and francophone entrepreneurs. The empire and its colonists desired land, and the Chouteaus brokered the deals that dispossessed Native peoples. The Chouteau family thrived in the business of Indian removal, and it used those profits to offset the risk of trading on the upper Missouri River and other regions west of Missouri. Once the United States reached those areas, the Chouteaus transitioned again to brokering land cessions. Years before the passage of the Indian Removal Act of 1830, the U.S. empire had expended immense energy and resources dispossessing Indian nations in the midcontinent.

Indeed, acquiring Osage lands was a prerequisite for Indian removal of the 1830s and 1840s. Immediately after the Louisiana Purchase, Thomas Jefferson envisioned the new territory as a home for "uncivilized" Indians from the East. The Virginians he sent into the West set to work acquiring land, and the 1825 treaty between the United States and the Osage Nation was the final step to obtaining the land necessary to enact Jefferson's dream. Over the next fifteen years, the trails of tears and death that took Indians from their eastern homelands ended in Osage Country. Some 75,000 Indians from nations from the Great Lakes to the Gulf Coast recovered from the trauma of Indian removal on lands that had recently been the heart of the Osage Nation. William Clark in his later years described the Osage Treaty of 1825 as "the hardest treaty on the Indians he ever made." He predicted "that if he was to be damned hereafter it would be for making that treaty."[71]

≈   As Pierre Chouteau floated up the Mississippi with William Henry Harrison in November 1804, he could hardly have expected that the new regime, propelled by land-hungry colonists, would completely remake Middle America by seizing Indian land and deporting Native peoples. In the wake of the Louisiana Purchase, a flood of Americans moved into the region. In 1800, 7,000 colonists populated a handful of towns on the Mississippi and Missouri Rivers. By 1830, more than 140,000 Americans spread across the state.[72] As Americans drove Indians from the region, the United States integrated Louisiana rather than holding it as a buffer between the heart of the empire and its enemies. This policy spurred westward migration and secured the loyalty of the fringes of the empire.

In the early years of U.S. rule, the Chouteaus built alliances with officials, acted as mediators between the empire and the Osage Nation, and demonstrated their skill and knowledge of a region largely unfamiliar to American empire builders. The Chouteaus, like other powerful individuals, depended on kinship and other personal relationships to acquire influence, and in turn, they used their ties to the empire to support private enterprises. These strategies had served them well during the Spanish regime, but Americans' disdain for nepotism—in theory, more than practice—forced them to act covertly. The Chouteaus relied on William Henry Harrison, James Wilkinson, William Clark, Meriwether Lewis, and others to open doors for them. Through trial and error, the brothers learned to disguise the power of their personal relations. Although they became more circumspect, the Chouteaus continued to draw on a host of allies in public office. Even after Missouri statehood, when electoral politics replaced the appointment system of the territories, the Chouteaus built a coalition of friends and relatives, Louisianans and Americans, to represent their interests in the state and in Washington. One of their most valuable allies, Thomas Hart Benton, had gotten his start in St. Louis as Charles Gratiot's attorney before editing the *St. Louis Enquirer*, a mouthpiece for the city's fur-trading community. In 1821, Benton became one of Missouri's first U.S. senators, and in office, he waged war against the factory system, leading to its abolition the following year.[73]

At the same time, Americans' desire for land opened a position for the Chouteaus within the empire as facilitators of land sales. The United States arrived in the midcontinent intent on incorporating the populace of Upper Louisiana as citizens. Francophone colonists would become Americans, bound to the new government by rights, friendship, and patronage. Through the "civilization" policy, the United States planned to convert Indians into republicans—small freeholders and citizens. Henry Knox's Indian policy, ethnocentric and based on a fundamental misunderstanding of Native peoples, failed to produce idealized "civilized" Indians. By the mid-1810s, Americans decided that the empire had a place for francophone Louisianans but not for Indians. Into the 1820s, officials referenced future incorporation of Indians, but their actions along with those of American colonists revealed that the acquisition of land was the most important goal of U.S. imperialism.[74] Over the course of two decades, the empire began defining potential citizens in narrower and narrower terms.

The convergence of Anglo-American and francophone Louisianan kinship networks formed the foundation for the American empire in the transMississippi West. The Chouteaus accumulated influence and wealth by insinuating themselves into the new regime, but the United States used Auguste, Pierre, and their relatives to negotiate treaties, broker land cessions, and push Indian removal. Their ambitions were distinct but complementary. The Chouteaus amassed power. U.S. officials strengthened the empire's tenuous claims in the Louisiana Purchase. Francophone Louisianans and

Anglo-Americans merged their families and their political interests to their mutual benefit.

During the first decade of U.S. rule, Indian nations worked to build alliances with the new regime, but Americans made unprecedented demands on Indian territory and resources. During the 1790s, Spain authorized Fort Carondelet, an exclusive trading post, in the Osage Nation in exchange for peace. At the end of the next decade, the United States offered Fort Osage but wanted thirty million acres of land. The treaty process became a vicious cycle for Native peoples. The Treaty of 1808 established a clear boundary line between the United States and the Osage Nation, but Americans and eastern Indians refused to recognize that border. When Osages used violence to defend their nation from invaders, the United States demanded reparations in the form of land cessions. The sequence repeated until Indian nations surrendered all but a few small parcels of land in the midcontinent.

By the early 1830s, the United States had become master of the middle waters. For the first time in centuries, a single polity controlled the entirety of Middle America. Although the United States created an empire that differed radically from its predecessors, its rise to power had stemmed from familiar sources. U.S. officials had built close relationships with local elites. Anglo-Americans and Louisianans had intermarried, cementing ties between the new empire and longtime residents of the midcontinent. Meanwhile, the United States had also gained control of the region's many waterways and the trade, travel, and communication that occurred along them. The United States supplanted the longtime rulers of the midcontinent, not because it brought new imperial strategies to the region but because it perfected old ones.

Conclusion

The Deep History of the Midcontinent

A s Edmund Flagg roamed the midcontinent during the 1830s, he witnessed the transformation of Middle America. American colonists were erasing the Native past from the landscape. Indian removal constituted one part of the process, and with the deportation nearly complete, Americans inscribed the landscape with new meanings. In western St. Louis, Americans leveled mounds to make way for streets, homes, and shops. Believing that the city could have easily incorporated the structures into the urban landscape, Flagg lamented the destruction: "they are passing rapidly away; man and beast, as well as the elements, are busy with them, and in a few years they will quite have disappeared." Across the river in Illinois, Flagg found an American farmer living and laboring on top of Monk's Mound, the largest of ancient Cahokia's earthworks. The homesteader had built a house and planted a cornfield, orchard, and garden. When Flagg visited, the owner was considering an offer to sell his homestead to an entrepreneur from St. Louis, who intended to open "a house of entertainment" on the site.[1] With plows and carts, axes and hoes, Americans obscured evidence of a Native presence or co-opted it into the new American imperial landscape of cities and farms.

With the stories Americans told about the mounds, they further removed Indian ties to Middle America, for they disassociated the monumental architecture of the earthworks from their builders, the ancestors of the Indians recently deported from the midcontinent. Eager to discredit Indian land

231

Fig. C.1 Thomas M. Easterly, "Big Mound, Fifth and Mound Streets," ca. 1854.

claims, nineteenth-century Americans attributed the mounds to some long-deceased race, unrelated to and probably destroyed by the ancestors of Native Americans. Because Flagg met no Indians during his walks through ancient Cahokia, he incorrectly insisted, "The present race of aborigines can tell nothing of these tumuli. To them, as to us, they are veiled in mystery."[2]

Such opinions were widespread in the United States. A dabbler in natural history, the American lexicographer Noah Webster posited an array of possible mound builders: Goths, Vandals, Carthaginians, "Siberian Tartars," and even the Spanish conquistador Hernando de Soto. Early in the nineteenth century, John Evans and John Mackey, two Missouri River explorers, professed, "the present race of Indians were not its [North America's] first Inhabitants & if they were their Descendants has degenerated much both in numbers & Knowledge." Of the mounds, Evans and Mackey wrote, "The monuments of industry found in Different parts of America Cannot with any degree of probability be supposed to be the work of a race of Beings so excessive indolent & lazy as the present Indians of America." Instead, to explain the mounds, the authors invoked fantastical tales of Prince Madoc, a

Fig. C.2 Thomas M. Easterly, "Big Mound during Destruction. The Last of the Big Mound," 1869.

twelfth-century Welshman who allegedly traveled to North America.[3] To legitimize Anglo-American imperialism, Flagg, Webster, Evans, Mackey, and other Americans clung to myths that disputed Indian ownership of the continent.

Although fascinated by, even obsessed with the ruins of ancient Native societies, Flagg and his contemporaries refused to view nineteenth-century Indians as peoples with either history or a future. They considered the 600 years between the collapse of Cahokia and the rise of the United States as little more than a footnote, an era of paltry significance wedged between the stories of two great powers, neither of them associated with the recently dispossessed Native peoples of the midcontinent. Yet entangled Native and imperial histories from those six centuries offer a new history of colonialism in North America and the processes that culminated in the American conquest of the midcontinent. Rooting Indian and imperial histories in the social geography of North America yields a long history of the borderlands of the midcontinent.

From the fall of Cahokia to rise of the United States, political and economic power originated in kinship-based social and alliance networks that
controlled river-based trade and diplomacy. In contested Middle America,
influence stemmed from the control of space, especially key river crossings
and confluences. Along those waterways, Indian nations adapted to the pressures of colonialism, but a Native political world continued to operate by its
own cultural logic, even as European imperialists attempted to reshape and
control it. Despite the many changes of the seventeenth and eighteenth centuries, power still flowed through the kinship networks that ruled the landscape and, thus, commanded trade and diplomacy. Native nations lost their
authority over Middle America only in the first decades of the nineteenth
century, when the United States dismantled Native-centered social networks
and subjugated and deported Indians. In its conquest, the United States
fractured and reconstituted the kinship networks of the midcontinent. Even
as Anglo-Americans expelled Native peoples, they still relied on personal
relations and drew francophone Louisianans into the empire.

Despite the violence and upheaval of Indian removal, deported Indians
retained the ties that connected them to one another. As they rebuilt their
nations in Indian Territory, Indians relied on longtime allies for assistance.
They moved to lands adjacent to those of former neighbors to facilitate mutual aid. In 1839, as the U.S. surveyor Washington Hood accompanied
Wendat chiefs to investigate potential sites, he noted that they preferred to
live next to Shawnees and Delawares, their allies and former neighbors. In
present-day Kansas, south of the Santa Fe Trail, Peorias and Kaskaskias
shared property that bordered the new home of Weas and Piankashaws,
whose southern neighbors were the Miamis. The Three Fires of the Anishinaabeg lived next to each other as well, with Ottawa lands bordering that of
their longtime Peoria and Kaskaskia allies. In the context of Indian removal,
groups that had grown separate reunited. In 1832, Peorias and Kaskaskias
agreed to live together, possibly for the first time since the end of the 1600s.
Two decades later, they joined Weas and Piankashaws to form the Peoria
Tribe of Indians, which brought together nations that had split at a time recorded only in oral histories.[4] Looking to the past and to the future, the
Native peoples of the midcontinent found power in old associations to rebuild and to adapt to the new political landscape of North America.

Meanwhile, the links between francophone St. Louisans and the American empire multiplied. In 1825, the New York fur magnate John Jacob
Astor's right-hand man, Ramsay Crooks, married the daughter of Bernard

Pratte, the relative and partner of Pierre Chouteau, Jr. Crooks began addressing Chouteau as "*cher* cousin." The next year, Pratte, Chouteau, & Co. signed an agreement with Astor's American Fur Company, which resulted in them partnering in the Missouri River fur trade. In 1834, Astor retired, and Pratte and Chouteau bought out the New Yorker's interests in the endeavor. Eight years later, after the failure of the American Fur Company under Crooks, Chouteau opened his own office in New York, in effect absorbing the firm into the new Pierre Chouteau, Jr., & Co. Chouteau funneled his fur trade profits into other industries, investing in railroads, iron, real estate, and agriculture and accumulating a fortune estimated to amount to "several millions."[5]

Both independently and in alliance with other firms, Pierre Chouteau, Jr., and his partners expanded their interests in the Far West. In the final years of the 1820s and early 1830s, the Western Department of the American Fur Company—the joint venture of Astor and the Chouteaus—established new trading posts on the upper Missouri River and its tributaries. This new generation of Chouteaus, like their ancestors, placed their outposts at confluences, recognizing them as convenient meeting places and entrepôts for the import of manufactured goods and the export of pelts. In 1832, a company steamboat, the shallow-draft *Yellowstone*, inaugurated a new era in the history of the fur trade when it reached Fort Union, some 1,800 river miles above St. Louis. Ramsay Crooks congratulated Chouteau on the feat, declaring, "You have brought the Falls of the Missouri as near, comparatively, as was the River Platte in my younger days." In the following years, Chouteau's steamboats plied the Missouri from its mouth to the Yellowstone River, drawing closer the posts of the upper Missouri and the markets of New York and Europe.[6]

In the Far West, the Chouteaus, their relatives, and their friends continued to use kinship ties to support their commercial interests. In 1833, Charles and William Bent and Ceran St. Vrain, the foster son of Pierre Chouteau, Jr.'s partner Bernard Pratte, began construction on the Arkansas River trading post that would soon be known far and wide as Bent's Fort. Five years later, Chouteau struck a bargain with Bent, St. Vrain & Co. to market its furs and provide it with trade goods in exchange for one-third of the company's profits. At the Arkansas River trading post, William Bent married Owl Woman, a Southern Cheyenne woman from a prestigious clan. When Charles Bent and St. Vrain expanded the firm's operations into New Mexico, they soon established common-law marriages with New Mexican women, smoothing their entry into a new lucrative market.[7]

With Chouteau's outsized control over the infrastructure of the western fur trade, he became a key ally for the U.S. empire. Officials depended on him to supply and transport goods and officials up the Missouri. During the 1840s, the United States purchased Chouteau trading posts, most notably Fort Laramie, and converted them into military forts.[8] The Chouteau family and its allies helped build the foundation of the U.S. empire in the Far West.

When Edmund Flagg entered the midcontinent in 1836, he resisted linking the ruins of Cahokia and the burgeoning U.S. empire because Americans justified colonization by erasing and reinterpreting the Native past. They understood the mounds and Indian history as alien and separate from the future of the continent. Yet the past proved difficult to escape because Cahokia's mounds provided an ever-present reminder of the region's deep history and because the region's waterways continued to shape its politics and commerce.

Many Americans believed that, because of the power of the Mississippi and Missouri Rivers, St. Louis would soon serve as the center of their transcontinental empire. In that regard, too, they followed in the footsteps of Cahokians, the Illinois, the Chouteaus, and others who, for centuries, relied on those waterways. As Flagg stood atop the "Big Mound" at St. Louis, he scanned the Mississippi. His eyes fell on the floating dry docks, "an ingenious contrivance" recently invented by a St. Louisan. There "an indefinite number of floats" could service the growing number of steamboats that trafficked humans and goods up and down the Mississippi and its tributaries. Steam power drove these vessels upstream in the face of the swift current, revolutionizing river travel. Yet, even with smokestacks belching fire and paddle wheels churning water, pilots navigated old roads. They remained subject to shifting channels and hidden snags. They docked where dugouts and birchbark canoes had once landed. They disembarked passengers on banks trod by centuries of chiefs, traders, diplomats, slaves, missionaries, hunters, and farmers.[9] Like the Mississippi rushing to the Gulf, the history of the midcontinent ran wide and deep.

ABBREVIATIONS

NOTES

ACKNOWLEDGMENTS

CREDITS

INDEX

ABBREVIATIONS

ANOM   Archives Nationales d'Outre-Mer, Aix-en-Provence, France

APNDC   Abraham P. Nasatir Document Collection, Bancroft Library, University of California, Berkeley

ASPIA   *American State Papers: Indian Affairs,* 2 vols. (Washington, DC: Gales and Seaton, 1832–1834)

ASPPL   *American State Papers: Public Lands,* 8 vols. (Washington, DC: Gales and Seaton, 1833–1861)

B   Série B, Correspondance au départ avec les colonies, Fonds Ministériels, Premiere Empire Colonial (XVIIe–début XIXe siècle), ANOM

BLC   A. P. Nasatir, ed., *Before Lewis and Clark: Documents Illustrating the History of the Missouri, 1785–1804,* 2 vols. (St. Louis: St. Louis Historical Documents Foundation, 1952)

BWM   Sequestered Baynton, Wharton & Morgan Papers, Manuscript Group 19, Pennsylvania State Archives, Harrisburg, PA

C11a   Série C11a, Correspondance à l'arrivée, Canada et colonies du nord de l'Amérique, Fonds Ministériels, Premiere Empire Colonial (XVIIe–début XIXe siècle), ANOM

C13a   Série C13a, Correspondance à l'arrivée, Louisiane, Fonds Ministériels, Premiere Empire Colonial (XVIIe–début XIXe siècle), ANOM

C13b   Série C13b, Correspondance à l'arrivée, Louisiane, Fonds Ministériels, Premiere Empire Colonial (XVIIe–début XIXe siècle), ANOM

CRP   *Colonial Records of Pennsylvania*, 16 vols. (Harrisburg, PA: Theo. Fenn, 1838–1853)

DCB   *Dictionary of Canadian Biography/Dictionnaire biographique du Canada*, 22 vols. (Toronto and Quebec: University of Toronto and Université Laval, 1966–present), available at http://www.biographi.ca/en/index.php

FHS   The Filson Historical Society, Louisville, KY

HNAI   William C. Sturevant, ed., *Handbook of North American Indians*, 17 vols. (Washington, DC: Government Printing Office, 1978–2008)

IHC   Clarence A. Alvord et al., eds., *Collections of the Illinois State Historical Library*, 38 vols. (Springfield: Illinois State Historical Library, 1903–1973)

JCB   John Carter Brown Library, Brown University, Providence, RI

JR   Reuben G. Thwaites, ed. and trans., *The Jesuit Relations and Allied Documents*, 73 vols. (Cleveland: Burrow Bros., 1896–1901)

KM   Kaskaskia Manuscripts, Randolph County Courthouse, Chester, IL, available at www.familysearch.org/search/catalog/show?uri=http%3A%2F%2Fcatalog-search-api%3A8080%2Fwww-catalogapi-webservice%2Fitem%2F58291, numbering system refers to year:month:day:document

LC   Library of Congress, Washington, DC

MHS   Missouri Historical Society Library and Research Center, St. Louis, MO

MPA:ED   Dunbar Rowland, ed., *Mississippi Provincial Archives: English Dominion* (Nashville, TN: Brandon, 1911)

MPA:FD   Dunbar Rowland, Albert G. Sanders, and Patricia Galloway, ed. and trans., *Mississippi Provincial Archives: French Dominion*, 5 vols. (Jackson: Mississippi Department of Archives and History, 1927–1932; Baton Rouge: Louisiana State University Press, 1984)

MPHC   *Michigan Pioneer and Historical Collections*, 40 vols. (Lansing: Michigan Pioneer and Historical Society, 1874–1929)

NARA   National Archives and Records Administration, Washington, DC

NYCD   E. B. O'Callaghan, ed., *Documents Relative to the Colonial History of the State of New York*, 11 vols. (Albany: Weed, Parsons, 1853–1861)

OV-GLEA   Ohio Valley–Great Lakes Ethnohistory Archive, Glenn A. Black Laboratory of Archaeology, Indiana University, Bloomington, IN

PC   Papeles Procedentes de Cuba, Archivo General de Indias, Sevilla, Spain. Microfilm at Historic New Orleans Collection, New Orleans, LA.

PFFA   Marthe Faribault-Beauregard, *La population des forts français Amérique (XVIIIE siècle): Répertoire des baptêmes, mariages et sépultures célébrés dans les forts et les établissements français en Amérique du Nord au XVIII siècle,* 2 vols. (Montreal: Éditions Bergeron, 1982–1984)

PSWJ   James Sullivan et al., eds., *The Papers of Sir William Johnson,* 14 vols. (Albany: University of the State of New York, 1921–1965)

RAPQ   *Rapport de l'Archiviste de la province de Québec,* 40 vols. (Quebec: Imprimeur de Sa Majesté le Roi/la Reine, 1921–1960)

SLML   St. Louis Mercantile Library, St. Louis, MO

SRM   Louis Houck, ed., *Spanish Regime in Missouri,* 2 vols. (Chicago: R. R. Donnelly, 1909)

SMV   Lawrence Kinnaird, ed. and trans., *Spain in the Mississippi Valley, 1765–1794,* 3 vols. (Washington, DC: Government Printing Office, 1949)

TGP   American Series, Thomas Gage Papers, William L. Clements Library, University of Michigan, Ann Arbor, MI

TPUS   Clarence Edwin Carter and John Porter Bloom, eds., *The Territorial Papers of the United States,* 28 vols. (Washington, DC: Government Printing Office, 1934–1975)

VP   The Vaudreuil Papers (French Colonial Manuscripts), The Huntington Library, San Marino, CA

WHC   Lyman C. Draper and Reuben G. Thwaites, eds., *Wisconsin Historical Collections,* 21 vols. (Madison: State Historical Society of Wisconsin, 1855–1915)

WMQ   *The William & Mary Quarterly,* 3rd series

NOTES

Introduction

1. Edmund Flagg, *The Far West; or, A Tour beyond the Mountains*, 2 vols. (New York: Harper and Brothers, 1838), 1:134–135, 2:76, 216–217.

2. Flagg, *Far West*, 124–133, 156–174 (quote on 127).

3. Flagg, *Far West*, 1:160; 2:22, 76.

4. The question of power relations between Indian nations and European empires has been one of the key issues in early American history, and over the past dozen or so years, scholars have demonstrated the strength of Native peoples and the precarious positions of Europeans and Euro-Americans well into the nineteenth century. For example, see Kathleen DuVal, *The Native Ground: Indians and Colonists in the Heart of the Continent* (Philadelphia: University of Pennsylvania Press, 2006); Juliana Barr, *Peace Came in the Form of a Woman: Indians and Spaniards in the Texas Borderlands* (Chapel Hill: University of North Carolina Press, 2007); Brian DeLay, *War of a Thousand Deserts: Indian Raids and the U.S.-Mexican War* (New Haven, CT: Yale University Press, 2008); Pekka Hämäläinen, *The Comanche Empire* (New Haven, CT: Yale University Press, 2008); Christina Snyder, *Slavery in Indian Country: The Changing Face of Captivity in Early America* (Cambridge, MA: Harvard University Press, 2010); Barr, "Geographies of Power: Mapping Indian Borders in the 'Borderlands' of the Early Southwest," *WMQ* 68 (January 2011): 5–46; Brett Rushforth, *Bonds of Alliance: Indigenous and Atlantic Slaveries in New France* (Chapel Hill: University of North Carolina Press for the Omohundro Institute of Early American History and Culture, 2012); Michael Witgen, *An Infinity of Nations: How the Native New World*

Shaped Early North America (Philadelphia: University of Pennsylvania Press, 2012); Michael A. McDonnell, *Masters of Empire: Great Lakes Indians and the Making of America* (New York: Hill and Wang, 2015). For a competing view that centers Indian power in nations' ability to "play off rival rulers" against one another, see Jeremy Adelman and Stephen Aron, "From Borderlands to Borders: Empires, Nation-States, and the Peoples In Between in North American History," *American Historical Review* 104 (June 1999): 814–841 (quote on 840); Aron, *American Confluence: The Missouri Frontier from Borderland to Border State* (Bloomington: Indiana University Press, 2006).

5. On entangled histories, see Eliga H. Gould, "Entangled Histories, Entangled Worlds: The English-Speaking Atlantic as a Spanish Periphery," *American Historical Review* 112 (June 2007): 764–786. Kathleen DuVal urges considering "interdependence" in early America; DuVal, *Independence Lost: Lives on the Edge of the American Revolution* (New York: Random House, 2015), xx–xxiii.

6. For layered pasts, see Daniel K. Richter, *Before the Revolution: America's Ancient Pasts* (Cambridge, MA: Harvard University Press, 2011), 3–8.

7. I borrow the tripartite model from the anthropologist Julian Pitt-Rivers's study of ancient Mediterranean society; Pitt-Rivers, "Women and Sanctuary in the Mediterranean," in *The Fate of Shechem, or, The Politics of Sex: Essays in the Anthropology of the Mediterranean* (Cambridge: Cambridge University Press, 1977), 113–125, especially 116–117. See also Andrew Shryock, Thomas R. Trautmann, and Clive Gamble, "Imagining the Human in Deep Time," in *Deep History: The Architecture of Past and Present,* ed. Andrew Shryock and Daniel Lord Smail (Berkeley: University of California Press, 2011), 52–54.

8. An excellent introduction to kinship among Native peoples is Raymond J. DeMallie, "Kinship: The Foundation for Native American Society," in *Studying Native America: Problems and Prospects,* ed. Russell Thornton (Madison: University of Wisconsin Press, 1998), 306–356. For the importance of kinship among Europeans and Euro-Americans in early modern Europe and the Atlantic world, see Toby L. Ditz, *Property and Kinship: Inheritance in Early Connecticut, 1750–1820* (Princeton, NJ: Princeton University Press, 1986); Sharon Kettering, "Patronage and Kinship in Early Modern France," *French Historical Studies* 16 (Autumn 1989): 408–435; Julie Hardwick, *The Practice of Patriarchy: Gender and the Politics of Household Authority in Early Modern France* (University Park: Penn State University Press, 1998), 159–193; Lorri Glover, *All Our Relations: Blood Ties and Emotional Bonds among the Early South Carolina Gentry* (Baltimore: Johns Hopkins University Press, 2000); Peter N. Moogk, *La Nouvelle France: The Making of French Canada—A Cultural History* (East Lansing: Michigan State University Press, 2000), 177–233; Naomi Tadmor, *Family and Friends in Eighteenth-Century England: Household, Kinship and Patronage* (Cambridge: Cambridge University Press, 2001); Julia Adams, *The Familial State: Ruling*

Families and Merchant Capitalism in Early Modern Europe (Ithaca, NY: Cornell University Press, 2005); David Warren Sabean, Simon Teuscher, and Jon Mathieu, eds., *Kinship in Europe: Approaches to Long-Term Development (1300–1900)* (New York: Berghahn Books, 2007); Sarah M. S. Pearsall, *Atlantic Families: Lives and Letters in the Later Eighteenth Century* (New York: Oxford University Press, 2008); "Centering Women in Atlantic Histories," special issue, *WMQ* 70 (April 2013): 205–424; Susanah Shaw Romney, *New Netherland Connections: Intimate Networks and Atlantic Ties in Seventeenth-Century America* (Chapel Hill: University of North Carolina Press for the Omohundro Institute of Early American History and Culture, 2014).

9. For the calumet ceremony, see Nicolas Perrot, *Memoir on the Manners, Customs, and Religion of the Savages of North America*, in *The Indian Tribes of the Upper Mississippi Valley and Region of the Great Lakes*, ed. and trans. Emma Helen Blair, 2 vols. (Cleveland: Arthur H. Clark, 1911), 1:182–186; Donald J. Blakeslee, "The Origin and Spread of the Calumet Ceremony," *American Antiquity* 46 (October 1981): 759–768; Ian W. Brown, "The Calumet Ceremony in the Southeast and Its Archaeological Manifestations," *American Antiquity* 54 (April 1989): 311–331; James Novotny Gundersen, "'Catlinite' and the Spread of the Calumet Ceremony," *American Antiquity* 85 (July 1993): 560–562; Robert L. Hall, *The Archaeology of the Soul: North American Indian Belief and Ritual* (Urbana: University of Illinois Press, 1997), 1–4, 48–58. For European rituals, see Patricia Seed, *Ceremonies of Possession in Europe's Conquest of the New World, 1492–1640* (Cambridge: Cambridge University Press, 1995); Lauren Benton, *A Search for Sovereignty: Law and Geography in European Empires, 1400–1900* (Cambridge: Cambridge University Press, 2010), 55n40. See also Tracy Neal Leavelle, *The Catholic Calumet: Colonial Conversions in French and Indian North America* (Philadelphia: University of Pennsylvania Press, 2012), 47–71.

10. The literature on intermarriage between colonists and Native peoples in early America is extensive, especially in the context of the fur trade. See Sylvia Van Kirk, *Many Tender Ties: Women in Fur-Trade Society, 1670–1870* (1980; paperback ed., Winnipeg: Watson and Dwyer, 1999); Jennifer S. H. Brown, *Strangers in Blood: Fur Trade Companies in Indian Country* (Vancouver: University of British Columbia Press, 1980), especially 51–110; Jacqueline Peterson, "The People In Between: Indian-White Marriage and the Genesis of a Métis Society and Culture in the Great Lakes Region, 1680–1830" (Ph.D. diss., University of Illinois at Chicago Circle, 1981); Tanis C. Thorne, *The Many Hands of My Relations: French and Indians on the Lower Missouri* (Columbia: University of Missouri Press, 1996); Albert L. Hurtado, *Intimate Frontiers: Sex, Gender, and Culture in Old California* (Albuquerque: University of New Mexico Press, 1999); Susan Sleeper-Smith, *Indian Women and French Men: Rethinking Cultural Encounter in the Western Great Lakes* (Amherst: University of Massachusetts Press, 2001); Theda Perdue, *"Mixed-Blood" Indians: Racial Construction in the Early South* (Athens: University of Georgia

Press, 2003); Andrew K. Frank, *Creeks and Southerners: Biculturalism on the Early American Frontier* (Lincoln: University of Nebraska Press, 2005); Kathleen DuVal, "Indian Intermarriage and Métissage in Colonial Louisiana," *WMQ* 65 (April 2008): 267–304; Jennifer M. Spear, *Race, Sex, and Social Order in Early New Orleans* (Baltimore: Johns Hopkins University Press, 2009), especially 17–51; Anne F. Hyde, *Empires, Nations, and Families: A History of the North American West, 1800–1860* (Lincoln: University of Nebraska Press, 2011); David Wallace Adams and Crista DeLuzio, eds., *On the Borders of Love and Power: Families and Kinship in the Intercultural American Southwest* (Berkeley: University of California Press, 2012); Robert Michael Morrissey, "Kaskaskia Social Network: Kinship and Assimilation in the French-Illinois Borderlands, 1673–1735," *WMQ* 70 (January 2013): 103–146; Ann McGrath, *Illicit Love: Interracial Sex and Marriage in the United States and Australia* (Lincoln: University of Nebraska Press, 2015); Natalie R. Inman, *Brothers and Friends: Kinship in Early America* (Athens: University of Georgia Press, 2017); Erika Pérez, *Colonial Intimacies: Interethnic Kinship, Sexuality, and Marriage in Southern California, 1765–1885* (Norman: University of Oklahoma Press, 2018). For an overview of alliances in Native North America and Europe, see Nancy Shoemaker, *A Strange Likeness: Becoming Red and White in Eighteenth-Century North America* (New York: Oxford University Press, 2004), 83–103. For other works that have demonstrated power and centrality of Native women, see Patricia Albers and Beatrice Medicine, eds., *The Hidden Half: Studies of Plains Indian Women* (Washington, DC: University Press of America, 1983); Laura F. Klein and Lillian A. Ackerman, eds., *Women and Power in Native North America* (Norman: University of Oklahoma Press, 1995); Nancy Shoemaker, ed., *Negotiators of Change: Historical Perspectives on Native American Women* (New York: Routledge, 1995); Theda Perdue, *Cherokee Women: Gender and Culture Change, 1700–1835* (Lincoln: University of Nebraska Press, 1998); Perdue, ed., *Sifters: Native American Women's Lives* (New York: Oxford University Press, 2001); Lucy Eldersveld Murphy, *A Gathering of Rivers: Indians, Métis, and Mining in the Western Great Lakes, 1737–1832* (Lincoln: University of Nebraska Press, 2000); Rebecca Kugel and Lucy Eldersveld Murphy, eds., *Native Women's History in Eastern North America before 1900: A Guide to Research and Writing* (Lincoln: University of Nebraska Press, 2007); Barr, *Peace Came in the Form of a Woman.*

11. Ives Goddard, "Delaware," in *HNAI*, vol. 15, *Northeast*, 235; James A. Clifton, "Potawatomi," in *HNAI*, vol. 15, *Northeast*, 741; John H. Moore, Margot P. Liberty, and A. Terry Strauss, "Cheyenne," in *HNAI*, vol. 13, *Plains*, 2:881; Thomas W. Kavanagh, "Comanche," in *HNAI*, vol. 13, *Plains*, 2:902; David J. Costa, "On the Origins of the Name 'Illinois,'" *Le Journal* 24 (Fall 2008): 6–10; Snyder, *Slavery in Indian Country*, 8–9, 17–19, 36–37, 56–58.

12. Sebastien Rale to "Monsieur and Very Dear Brother," 12 October 1723, in *JR*, 67:173–175; Pierre Deliette, "Memoir," in *IHC*, 23:387; Daniel K.

Richter, "War and Culture: The Iroquois Experience," *WMQ* 40 (October 1983): 528–559; Snyder, *Slavery in Indian Country*, 65–67, 101–126; Francis La Flesche, *A Dictionary of the Osage Language* (Washington, DC: Government Printing Office, 1932), 35, 110, 111; Willard H. Rollings, *The Osage: An Ethnohistorical Study of Hegemony on the Prairie-Plains* (Columbia: University of Missouri Press, 1995), 34. For an older but still useful account, see James Axtell, "The White Indians of Colonial America," *WMQ* 32 (January 1975): 55–88.

13. Alden T. Vaughan, "From White Man to Redskin: Changing Anglo-American Perceptions of the American Indian," *American Historical Review* 87 (October 1982): 917–953; Karen Ordahl Kupperman, *Indians and English: Facing Off in Early America* (Ithaca, NY: Cornell University Press, 2000); Roxann Wheeler, *The Complexion of Race: Categories of Difference in Eighteenth-Century British Culture* (Philadelphia: University of Pennsylvania Press, 2000); Joyce Chaplin, *Subject Matter: Technology, the Body, and Science on the Anglo-American Frontier, 1500–1676* (Cambridge, MA: Harvard University Press, 2001); Shoemaker, *Strange Likeness*, 125–140; Snyder, *Slavery in Indian Country*, especially 101–126; Benjamin Braude, "The Sons of Noah and the Construction of Ethnic and Geographical Identities in the Medieval and Early Modern Periods," *WMQ* 54 (January 1997): 103–142; Guillaume Aubert, "'The Blood of France': Race and Purity of Blood in the French Atlantic World," *WMQ* 61 (July 2004): 439–478; Saliha Belmessous, "Assimilation and Racialism in Seventeenth- and Eighteenth-Century French Colonial Policy," *American Historical Review* 110 (April 2005): 322–349; Bernard W. Sheehan, *The Seeds of Extinction: Jeffersonian Philanthropy and the American Indian* (Chapel Hill: University of North Carolina Press for the Institute of Early American History and Culture, 1973); Robert F. Berkhofer, Jr., *The White Man's Indian: Images of the American Indian from Columbus to the Present* (New York: Vintage, 1979); Reginald Horsman, *Race and Manifest Destiny: The Origins of American Racial Anglo-Saxonism* (Cambridge, MA: Harvard University Press, 1981); Anthony F. C. Wallace, *Jefferson and the Indians: The Tragic Fate of the First Americans* (Cambridge, MA: Harvard University Press, 1999).

14. Horsman, *Race and Manifest Destiny*, especially 98–157. On the development of scientific racism, see also William Stanton, *The Leopard's Spots: Scientific Attitudes toward Race in America, 1815–59* (Chicago: University of Chicago Press, 1960); Winthrop Jordan, *White over Black: American Attitudes toward the Negro, 1550–1812* (Chapel Hill: University of North Carolina Press for the Institute of Early American History and Culture, 1968), especially 486–541; George M. Fredrickson, *The Black Image in the White Mind: The Debate on Afro-American Character and Destiny, 1817–1914* (1971; repr., Middletown, CT: Wesleyan University Press, 1987), especially 71–96; Bruce R. Bain, *A Hideous Monster of the Mind: American Race Theory in the Early Republic* (Cambridge, MA: Harvard University Press, 2003); Ann

Fabian, *The Skull Collectors: Race, Science, and America's Unburied Dead* (Chicago: University of Chicago Press, 2010); Audrey Smedley and Brian Smedley, *Race in North America: The Origin and Evolution of a Worldview*, 4th ed. (Boulder, CO: Westview, 2011), especially 213–226; Ibram X. Kendi, *Stamped from the Beginning: The Definitive History of Racist Ideas in America* (New York: Nation Books, 2016). On resistance to those ideas among Anglo-Americans, see Nicholas Guyatt, *Bind Us Apart: How Enlightened Americans Invented Racial Segregation* (New York: Basic Books, 2016). Native peoples also formulated theories about polygenesis, and beginning in the mid-eighteenth century, Nativists called for disentangling from Europeans; Gregory Evans Dowd, *A Spirited Resistance: The North American Indian Struggle for Unity, 1745–1815* (Baltimore: Johns Hopkins University Press, 1992), 21; Snyder, *Slavery in Indian Country*, 160–161.

15. Instead of focusing principally on ecology, I am interested in how command and knowledge of geography and natural resources led to political and economic power. For example, see Cynthia Radding, *Wandering Peoples: Colonialism, Ethnic Spaces, and Ecological Frontiers in Northwestern Mexico, 1700–1850* (Durham, NC: Duke University Press, 1997); Elliott West, *The Contested Plains: Indians, Goldseekers, and the Rush to Colorado* (Lawrence: University Press of Kansas, 1998); James C. Scott, *The Art of Not Being Governed: An Anarchist History of Upland Southeast Asia* (New Haven, CT: Yale University Press, 2009); Pekka Hämäläinen, "The Politics of Grass: European Expansion, Ecological Change, and Indigenous Power in the Southwest Borderlands," *WMQ* 67 (April 2010): 173–208; Elizabeth A. Fenn, *Encounters at the Heart of the World: A History of the Mandan People* (New York: Hill and Wang, 2014); Robert Michael Morrissey, "The Power of the Ecotone: Bison, Slavery, and the Rise and Fall of the Grand Village of the Kaskaskia," *Journal of American History* 102 (December 2015): 667–692.

16. Stephen Aron has also noted that rivers brought diverse peoples together in this region; Aron, *American Confluence*.

17. For landscape and Native American studies, see Keith H. Basso, *Wisdom Sits in Places: Landscape and Language among the Western Apache* (Albuquerque: University of New Mexico Press, 1996); James Taylor Carson, "Ethnogeography and the Native American Past," *Ethnohistory* 49 (Fall 2002): 769–788; Lisa Brooks, *The Common Pot: The Recovery of Native Space in the Northeast* (Minneapolis: University of Minnesota Press, 2008); Jon Parmenter, *The Edge of the Woods: Iroquoia, 1534–1701* (East Lansing: Michigan State University Press, 2010); Ari Kelman, *A Misplaced Massacre: Struggling over the Memory of Sand Creek* (Cambridge, MA: Harvard University Press, 2013); Joshua L. Reid, *The Sea Is My Country: The Maritime World of the Makahs* (New Haven, CT: Yale University Press, 2015).

18. John Joseph Mathews, *The Osages: Children of the Middle Waters* (Norman: University of Oklahoma Press, 1961), 15, 106–108; La Flesche, *Dictionary of the Osage Language*, 110, 209–210; Garrick A. Bailey, "Osage," in *HNAI*, vol.

13, *Plains*, 1:493; Alice C. Fletcher and Francis La Flesche, "The Omaha Tribe," in *The Twenty-Seventh Annual Report of the Bureau of American Ethnology* (Washington, DC: Government Printing Office, 1911), 36; Margo P. Liberty, W. Raymond Wood, and Lee Irwin, "Omaha," in *HNAI*, vol. 13, *Plains*, 1:413; Gloria A. Young and Michael P. Hoffman, "Quapaw," in *HNAI*, vol. 13, *Plains*, 1:510–511.

19. Wallace, *Jefferson and the Indians*, 239.
20. Hattie M. Anderson, "Missouri, 1804–1828: Peopling a Frontier State," *Missouri Historical Review* 31 (January 1937): 150–51, 180; Perry McCandless, *1820–1860*, vol. 2 of *A History of Missouri*, ed. William E. Parrish (Columbia: University of Missouri Press, 1972), 35–37.
21. Flagg, *Far West*, 1:131.

1. In Cahokia's Wake

1. Pierre Deliette, "Memoir," in *IHC*, 23:318, 339–340; Le Boullenger Dictionary, s.v. "Lune," JCB; Largillier Dictionary, "Anacapi Kiris.," p. 32, Miami-Illinois Digital Archive, available at http://ilaatawaakani.org; E. R. Cook and P. J. Krusic, *The North American Drought Atlas* ([New York]: Lamont-Doherty Earth Observatory and the National Science Foundation, 2004), available at http://iridl.ldeo.columbia.edu/SOURCES/.LDEO/.TRL /.NADA2004/.pdsi-atlas.html; Sebastien Rale to "Monsieur and Very Dear Brother," 12 October 1723, in *JR*, 67:169; *Relation of 1666–1667*, in *JR*, 51:49–51; *Relation of 1669–1670*, in *JR*, 54:161, 191; Jacques Marquette, "Of the first Voyage made by Father Marquette toward new Mexico . . . ," [1674], in *JR*, 59:127.
2. Marquette, "Of the first Voyage," in *JR*, 59:113–115.
3. Marquette, "Of the first Voyage," in *JR*, 59:113, 115.
4. Marquette, "Of the first Voyage," in *JR*, 59:87–89; Jean Delanglez, *Life and Voyages of Louis Jolliet (1645–1700)* (Chicago: Institute of Jesuit History, 1948); Joseph P. Donnelly, *Jacques Marquette, S.J., 1637–1675* (Chicago: Loyola University Press, 1968); Raphael N. Hamilton, *Marquette's Explorations: The Narratives Reexamined* (Madison: University of Wisconsin Press, 1970), 158–165.
5. Marquette, "Of the first Voyage," in *JR*, 59:91; *Relation of 1640*, in *JR*, 18:231–233, 237; *Relation of 1642–1643*, in *JR*, 23:235, 277–279; *Relation of 1655–1656*, in *JR*, 42:221; *Relation of 1657–1658*, in *JR*, 44:247; *Relation of 1666–1667*, in *JR*, 51:47 ("continual"); *Relation of 1669–1670*, in *JR*, 54:167 ("five large"), 187; *Relation of 1670–1671*, in *JR*, 55:207.
6. *Relation of 1669–1670*, in *JR*, 54:185–191; Marquette, "Of the first Voyage," in *JR*, 59:117 (quote).
7. Thomas E. Emerson, *Cahokia and the Archaeology of Power* (Tuscaloosa: University of Alabama Press, 1997); Timothy R. Pauketat and Thomas E.

Emerson, eds., *Cahokia: Domination and Ideology in the Mississippian World* (Lincoln: University of Nebraska Press, 1997); George R. Milner, *The Cahokia Chiefdom: The Archaeology of a Mississippian Society* (Washington, DC: Smithsonian Institution Press, 1998); Thomas E. Emerson and R. Barry Lewis, eds., *Cahokia and the Hinterlands: Middle Mississippian Cultures of the Midwest* (Urbana: University of Illinois Press, 2000); Timothy R. Pauketat, *Ancient Cahokia and the Mississippians* (Cambridge: Cambridge University Press, 2004); Pauketat, *Cahokia: Ancient America's Great City on the Mississippi* (New York: Penguin, 2009); Larry V. Benson, Timothy R. Pauketat, and Edward R. Cook, "Cahokia's Boom and Bust in the Context of Climate Change," *American Antiquity* 74 (July 2009): 467–483; Christina Snyder, *Slavery in Indian Country: The Changing Face of Captivity on the Early American Frontier* (Cambridge, MA: Harvard University Press, 2010), 29; Thomas E. Emerson and Eve Hargrave, "Strangers in Paradise? Recognizing Ethnic Mortuary Diversity on the Fringes of Cahokia," *Southeastern Archaeology* 19 (Summer 2000): 1–23; Emerson, *Cahokia and the Archaeology of Power*, 151–192; Susan M. Alt, "Cahokian Change and the Authority of Tradition," in *The Archaeology of Traditions: Agency and History before and after Columbus*, ed. Timothy R. Pauketat (Gainesville: University Press of Florida, 2001), 141–156; Timothy R. Pauketat, "Resettled Farmers and the Making of a Mississippian Polity," *American Antiquity* 68 (January 2003): 39–66; Thomas E. Emerson and Randall E. Hughes, "Figurines, Flint Clay Sourcing, the Ozark Highlands, and Cahokian Acquisition," *American Antiquity* 65 (January 2000): 79–101; Thomas E. Emerson and Randall E. Hughes, "De-mything the Cahokia Catlinite Trade," *Plains Anthropologist* 46 (May 2001): 149–161; Robert A. Birmingham and Lynne G. Goldstein, *Aztalan: Mysteries of an Ancient Indian Town* (Madison: Wisconsin Historical Society Press, 2005); Danielle Benden, "The Fisher Mounds Site Complex: Early Middle Mississippian Exploration in the Upper Mississippi Valley," *Minnesota Archaeologist* 63 (2004): 7–24; Robert F. Boszhardt, "The Late Woodland and Middle Mississippian Component at the Iva Site, La Crosse County, Wisconsin, in the Driftless Area of the Upper Mississippi River Valley," *Minnesota Archaeologist* 63 (2004): 60–85; William Green and Roland L. Rodell, "The Mississippian Presence and Cahokia Interaction at Trempealeau, Wisconsin," *American Antiquity* 59 (April 1994); 334–359. For historians' views, see Neal Salisbury, "The Indians' Old World: Native Americans and the Coming of Europeans," *WMQ* 53 (July 1996): 435–458; Alan G. Shackelford, "The Frontier in Pre-Columbian Illinois," *Journal of the Illinois State Historical Society* 100 (Fall 2007): 183–194; Daniel K. Richter, *Before the Revolution: America's Ancient Pasts* (Cambridge, MA: Harvard University Press, 2011), 21–33.

8. Lawrence A. Conrad, "The Middle Mississippian Cultures of the Central Illinois Valley," in Emerson and Lewis, *Cahokia and the Hinterlands*, 124–132; Duane Esarey, "The Late Woodland Maples Mills and Mossville Phase

Sequence in the Central Illinois River Valley," in *Late Woodland Societies: Tradition and Transformation across the Midcontinent,* ed. Thomas E. Emerson, Dale L. McElrath, and Andrew C. Fortier (Lincoln: University of Nebraska Press, 2000), 387–410; Ellen Wohl, *Wide Rivers Crossed: The South Platte and the Illinois of the American Prairie* (Boulder: University of Colorado Press, 2013), 165–184.

9. Thomas E. Emerson, "The Langford Tradition and the Process of Tribalization on the Middle Mississippian Borders," *Midcontinental Journal of Archaeology* 24 (Spring 1999): 3–56; Michael C. Stambaugh, Richard P. Guyette, Erin R. McMurry, Edward R. Cook, David M. Meko, and Anthony R. Lupo, "Drought Duration and Frequency in the U.S. Corn Belt during the Last Millennium (AD 992–2004)," *Agricultural and Forest Meteorology* 151 (February 2011): 159.

10. Dawnie Wolfe Steadman, "Warfare Related Trauma at Orendorf, a Middle Mississippian Site in West-Central Illinois," *American Journal of Physical Anthropology* 136 (January 2008): 51–64; Conrad, "Middle Mississippian Cultures," 133; George R. Milner, "Nineteenth-Century Arrow Wounds and Perceptions of Prehistoric Warfare," *American Antiquity* 70 (January 2005): 144–156.

11. Jane E. Buikstra and George R. Milner, "Isotopic and Archaeological Interpretations of Diet in the Central Mississippi Valley," *Journal of Archaeological Science* 18 (May 1991): 319–329; Jeremy John Wilson, "Modeling Life through Death in Late Prehistoric West-Central Illinois: An Assessment of Paliodemographic and Paleoepidemiological Variability" (Ph.D. diss., State University of New York, Binghamton, 2010), 68–69, 290–295, 527–529. For an insightful look at precolonial disease ecology, see Paul Kelton, *Epidemics and Enslavement: Biological Catastrophe in the Native Southeast, 1492–1715* (Lincoln: University of Nebraska Press, 2007), especially 1–46.

12. Steadman, "Warfare Related Trauma at Orendorf," 51–64; Wilson, "Modeling Life through Death," 65–70, 316–317, 528; Gregory D. Wilson, "Living with War: The Impact of Chronic Violence in the Mississippian-Period Central Illinois River Valley," in *The Oxford Handbook of North American Archaeology,* ed. Timothy D. Pauketat (New York: Oxford University Press, 2012), 528; Conrad, "Middle Mississippian Cultures," 141–144.

13. Emerson, "Langford Tradition," 21–33; Michael Strezewski, "Patterns of Interpersonal Violence at the Fisher Site," *Midcontinental Journal of Archaeology* 31 (Fall 2006): 249–279.

14. Conrad, "Middle Mississippian Cultures," 141–144; Alan D. Harn, *Variation in Mississippian Settlement Patterns: The Larson Settlement System in the Central Illinois River Valley,* Reports of Investigations 50 (Springfield: Illinois State Museum, 1994), 43.

15. Emerson, "Langford Tradition," 34; Duane Esarey and Lawrence A. Conrad, "The Bold Counselor Phase of the Central Illinois River Valley: Oneota's Middle Mississippian Margin," *Wisconsin Archeologist* 79 (1998): 38–61;

R. Eric Hollinger, "Conflict and Culture Change in the Late Prehistoric and Early Historic American Midcontinent" (Ph.D. diss., University of Illinois at Urbana-Champaign, 2005), 151–163.

16. Paul Radin, "The Winnebago Tribe," in *Thirty-Seventh Annual Report of the Bureau of American Ethnology* (Washington, DC: Government Printing Office, 1923), 50; Douglas R. Parks and Robert L. Rankin, "Siouan Languages," in *Handbook of North American Indians*, vol. 13, *Plains*, part 1 (Washington, DC: Government Printing Office, 2001), 104–105; Edwin James, comp., *Account of an Expedition from Pittsburgh to the Rocky Mountains Performed in the Years 1819 and '20 . . . under the Command of Major Stephen H. Long*, 2 vols. (Philadelphia: H. C. Carey and I. Lea, 1823), 1:338–340; Thomas L. McKenney and James Hall, *History of the Indian Tribes of North America, with Biographical Sketches and Anecdotes of the Principal Chiefs*, 2 vols. (Philadelphia: D. Rice, 1872), 2:178; Maximilian, Prince of Wied, *Travels in the Interior of North America*, trans. H. Evans Lloyd (London: Ackermann, 1843), [507], appendix 1.

17. Esarey and Conrad, "Bold Counselor Phase," 38–61; Hollinger, "Conflict and Culture Change," 151–163; Jodie A. O'Gorman and Michael D. Conner, "Negotiating Migration and Violence in the Pre-Columbian Mid-continent: A View from the Village," poster presented at the annual meeting of the Society for American Archaeology, April 15–19, 2015.

18. O'Gorman and Conner, "Negotiating Migration and Violence"; Conrad, "Middle Mississippian Cultures," 153–154.

19. Esarey and Conrad, "Bold Counselor Phase," 41–50, 53–54; Sharron K. Santure and Duane Esarey, "Analysis of Artifacts from the Oneota Mortuary Component," in *Archaeological Investigations at the Morton Village and Norris Farms 36 Cemetery*, ed. Sharron K. Santure, Alan D. Harn, and Duane Esarey, Reports of Investigations 45 (Springfield: Illinois State Museum, 1990), 75–110; Conrad, "Middle Mississippian Cultures," 153; Alan D. Harn and Nicholas W. Klobuchar, "Inside Morton House 7: An Oneota Structure from the Central Illinois River Valley," in *Mounds, Modoc, and Mesoamerica: Papers in Honor of Melvin L. Fowler*, ed. Steven R. Ahler (Springfield: Illinois State Museum, 2000), 315–317; Michael Strezewski, "Mississippian Period Mortuary Practices in the Central Illinois River Valley: A Region-Wide Survey and Analysis" (Ph.D. diss., Indiana University, 2003), 338–339.

20. George R. Milner, Eve Anderson, and Virginia G. Smith, "Warfare in Late Prehistoric West-Central Illinois," *American Antiquity* 56 (October 1991): 581–603; George R. Milner and Rebecca J. Ferrell, "Conflict and Death in a Late Prehistoric Community in the American Midwest," *Anthropologischer Anzeiger* 68 (September 2011): 415–436.

21. Wilson, "Modeling Life through Death," 495–509; Ryan Maureen Tubbs, "Ethnic Identity and Diet in the Central Illinois River Valley" (Ph.D. diss., Michigan State University, 2013), 45–51, 80–81, 101–111, 219–225; Sharron K. Santure, "Social Conflict," in Santure, Harn, and Esarey,

Archaeological Investigations, 158; Bonnie W. Styles and Frances B. King, "Faunal and Floral Remains from the Bold Counselor Phase Village," in Santure, Harn, and Esarey, *Archaeological Investigations,* 57–65; Bonnie W. Styles and Frances B. King, "Faunal and Floral Remains from Oneota Contexts at Norris Farms 36," in Santure, Harn, and Esarey, *Archaeological Investigations,* 149–153; Milner, Anderson, and Smith, "Warfare in Late Prehistoric West-Central Illinois," 590–592.

22. Conrad, "Middle Mississippian Cultures," 146–154; Hollinger, "Conflict and Culture Change," 161–162.

23. Esarey and Conrad, "Bold Counselor Phase," 52–53; Hollinger, "Conflict and Culture Change," 162; David Pollack, *Caborn-Welborn: Constructing a New Society after the Angel Chiefdom Collapse* (Tuscaloosa: University of Alabama Press, 2004), 192–196.

24. Hollinger, "Conflict and Culture Change," 132–233. On the Little Ice Age, see Brian Fagan, *The Little Ice Age: How Climate Made History, 1300–1850* (New York: Basic Books, 2000); Sam White, *A Cold Welcome: The Little Ice Age and Europe's Encounter with North America* (Cambridge, MA: Harvard University Press, 2017), especially 19–23.

25. Lauren W. Ritterbush, "Drawn by the Bison: Late Prehistoric Native Migration into the Central Plains," *Great Plains Quarterly* 22 (Fall 2002): 259–270; Ritterbush, "Oneota Interaction and Impact in the Central Plains," in *Plains Village Archaeology: Bison-Hunting Farmers in the Central and Northern Plains,* ed. Stanley A. Ahler and Marvin Kay (Salt Lake City: University of Utah Press, 2007), 181–192.

26. Donald J. Blakeslee, "The Origin and Spread of the Calumet Ceremony," *American Antiquity* 46 (October 1981): 763; Hollinger, "Conflict and Culture Change," 270–271; Alice C. Fletcher and Francis La Flesche, "The Omaha Tribe," in *The Twenty-Seventh Annual Report of the Bureau of American Ethnology* (Washington, DC: Government Printing Office, 1911), 376; Nicolas Perrot, *Memoir on the Manners, Customs, and Religion of the Savages of North America,* in *The Indian Tribes of the Upper Mississippi Valley and Region of the Great Lakes,* ed. Emma Helen Blair, 2 vols. (Cleveland: Arthur H. Clark, 1911), 1:186 ("crime").

27. Perrot, *Memoir,* 1:182–186; Blakeslee, "Origin and Spread of the Calumet Ceremony," 759–768; Ian W. Brown, "The Calumet Ceremony in the Southeast and Its Archaeological Manifestations," *American Antiquity* 54 (April 1989): 311–331; James Novotny Gundersen, "'Catlinite' and the Spread of the Calumet Ceremony," *American Antiquity* 85 (July 1993): 560–562; Robert L. Hall, *The Archaeology of the Soul: North American Indian Belief and Ritual* (Urbana: University of Illinois Press, 1997), 1–4, 48–58; Penelope Ballard Drooker, *The View from Madisonville: Protohistoric Western Fort Ancient Interaction Patterns,* Memoirs of the Museum of Anthropology, University of Michigan 31 (Ann Arbor: University of Michigan Museum of Anthropology, 1997), 311.

28. Hollinger, "Conflict and Culture Change," 72–109, 234–283; James M. Collins, "The Des Moines Rapids and Western Oneota Social-Political Patterns," *Journal of the Steward Anthropological Society* 18 (Fall–Spring 1988–1989): 165–186; Joseph A. Tiffany, "Preliminary Report on Excavations at the McKinney Oneota Village Site (13LA1), Louisa County, Iowa," *Wisconsin Archeologist* 69 (December 1988): 231; Dale R. Henning, "The Oneota Tradition," in *Archaeology on the Great Plains*, ed. W. Raymond Wood (Lawrence: University Press of Kansas, 1998), 399; Douglas Kullen, "The Comstock Trace: A Huber Phase Earthwork and Habitation Site Near Joliet, Will County, Illinois," *Midcontinental Journal of Archaeology* 19 (1994): 3–38; W. Raymond Wood, "Culture Sequence at the Old Fort, Saline County, Missouri," *American Antiquity* 38 (January 1973): 101–111.

29. Michael J. O'Brien and W. Raymond Wood, *The Prehistory of Missouri* (Columbia: University of Missouri Press, 1998), 353; Dale R. Henning, "Continuity and Change in the Eastern Plains, A.D. 800–1700: An Examination of Exchange Patterns," in Ahler and Kay, *Plains Village Archaeology*, 67–82; Henning, "The Oneota Tradition," 375, 384–385, 388; Henning, "The Oneota Tradition," 375; Hollinger, "Conflict and Culture Change," 93–94; Tiffany, "Preliminary Report," 296.

30. R. Eric Hollinger, "Residence Patterns and Oneota Cultural Dynamics," in *Oneota Archaeology: Past, Present, and Future*, ed. William Green (Iowa City: University of Iowa, 1995), 141–174; Jodie A. O'Gorman, "Exploring the Longhouse and Community in Tribal Society," *American Antiquity* 75 (July 2010): 571–597; Hollinger, "Conflict and Culture Change," 267–269.

31. James Warren Springer and Stanley R. Witkowski, "Siouan Historical Linguistics and Oneota Archaeology," in *Oneota Studies*, ed. Guy E. Gibbon (Minneapolis: University of Minnesota, 1982), 74; Michael K. Foster, "Language and the Culture History of North America," in *HNAI*, vol. 17, *Languages*, 102; Lynn Marie Alex, *Iowa's Archaeological Past* (Iowa City: University of Iowa Press, 2000), 214–216; Robert L. Rankin, "Siouan Tribal Contacts and Dispersions Evidenced in the Terminology for Maize and Other Cultigens," in *History of Maize: Multidisciplinary Approaches to the Prehistory, Linguistics, Biogeography, Domestication, and Evolution of Maize*, ed. John Staller, Robert Tykot, and Bruce Benz (Walnut Creek, CA: Left Coast Press, 2006), 573; John H. House, "Native American Material Culture from the Wallace Bottom Site, Southeastern Arkansas," *Southeast Archaeology* 32 (Summer 2013): 54–69; Susan C. Vehik, "Dhegiha Origins and Plains Archaeology," *Plains Anthropologist* 38 (November 1993): 231–252; Dale R. Henning, "The Adaptive Patterning of the Dhegiha Sioux," *Plains Anthropologist* 38 (November 1993): 253–264; Timothy R. Pauketat and Thomas E. Emerson, "Introduction: Domination and Ideology in the Mississippian World," in Pauketat and Emerson, *Cahokia*, 24–26; Alice Beck Kehoe, "Osage Texts and Cahokia Data," in *Ancient Objects and Sacred Realms: Interpretations of Mississippian Iconography*, ed. F. Kent Reilly III and James F.

Garber (Austin: University of Texas Press, 2007), 246–261; Michael P. Hoffman, "The Terminal Mississippian Period in the Arkansas River Valley and Quapaw Ethnogenesis," in *Towns and Temples Along the Mississippi*, ed. David H. Dye and Cheryl Anne Cox (Tuscaloosa: University of Alabama Press, 1990), 208–226; Marvin D. Jeter, "From Prehistory through Protohistory to Ethnohistory in and near the Northern Lower Mississippi Valley," in *The Transformation of the Southeastern Indians*, ed. Robbie Ethridge and Charles Hudson (Jackson: University Press of Mississippi, 2002), 214–219.

32. Fletcher and La Flesche, "Omaha Tribe," 35–36; J. Owen Dorsey, "Migrations of Siouan Tribes," *American Naturalist* 20 (March 1886): 211–222; John Evans and James Mackey, "Indian Tribes," [ca. 1804], Box 11, folder 9, Clark Family Collection, Missouri History Museum, St. Louis, MO; Kathleen Duval, *The Native Ground: Indians and Colonists in the Heart of the Continent* (Philadelphia: University of Pennsylvania Press, 2006), 67–68, 104; Dale R. Henning, "Oneota: The Western Manifestations," *Wisconsin Archeologist* 79 (July–December 1998): 243; Henning, "Continuity and Change in the Eastern Plains," 75; House, "Native American Material Culture," 54–69; Vehik, "Dhegiha Origins and Plains Archaeology," 231–252; Henning, "Adaptive Patterning of the Dhegiha Sioux," 253–264; O'Brien and Wood, *Prehistory of Missouri*, 356.

33. Henning, "Adaptive Patterning of the Dhegiha Sioux," 253–264; Henning, "Continuity and Change in the Eastern Plains," 81; J. Owen Dorsey, "Omaha Sociology," in *Third Annual Report of the Bureau of American Ethnology* (Washington, DC: Government Printing Office, 1884), 211 ("one people"); Jeffrey K. Yelton, "A Different View of Oneota Taxonomy and Origins in the Lower Missouri Valley," *Wisconsin Archeologist* 79 (July–December 1998): 268–283; House, "Native American Material Culture," 54–69.

34. Hollinger, "Conflict and Culture Change," 271; Drooker, *View from Madisonville*, 311; Blakeslee, "Origin and Spread of the Calumet Ceremony," 759–761; Brown, "Calumet Ceremony in the Southeast," 311–331.

35. Marquette, "Of the first Voyage," in *JR*, 59:137.

36. Marquette, "Of the first Voyage," in *JR*, 59:121, 133 ("diversion"); Richard White, *The Middle Ground: Indians, Empires and Republics in the Great Lakes Region, 1650–1815* (Cambridge: Cambridge University Press, 1991), 1–49; Daniel K. Richter, *The Ordeal of the Longhouse: The Peoples of the Iroquois League in the Era of European Colonization* (Chapel Hill: University of North Carolina Press for the Omohundro Institute of Early American History and Culture, 1992), 50–74; José António Brandão, *"Your Fyre Shall Burn No More": Iroquois Policy toward New France and Its Native Allies to 1701* (Lincoln: University of Nebraska Press, 1997); Tracy Neal Leavelle, *The Catholic Calumet: Colonial Conversions in French and Indian North America* (Philadelphia: University of Pennsylvania Press, 2012), 35–37, 42–44.

37. Robert Mazrim and Duane Esarey, "Rethinking the Dawn of History: The Schedule, Signature, and Agency of European Goods in Protohistoric

Illinois," *Midcontinental Journal of Archaeology* 32 (Fall 2007): 161–162; Alan G. Shackelford, "The Illinois Indians in the Confluence Region: Adaptation in a Changing World," in *Enduring Nations: Native Americans in the Midwest,* ed. R. David Edmunds (Urbana: University of Illinois Press, 2008), 23–26; Kathleen L. Ehrhardt, "Problems and Progress in Protohistoric Period Archaeology in the Illinois Country since *Calumet and Fleur-de-Lys,*" *Illinois Archaeology* 22 (2010): 266–267; Edward R. Cook, Richard Seager, Mark A. Cane, and David W. Stable, "North American Drought: Reconstructions, Causes, and Consequences," *Earth-Science Reviews* 81 (2007): 110–113.

38. Drooker, *View from Madisonville,* 283–337; Robert G. McCullough, "Cultural Interaction along the West Fort of the White River during the Late Prehistoric Period," in *Facing the Final Millennium: Studies in the Late Prehistory of Indiana, A.D. 700–1700,* ed. Brian G. Redmond and James R. Jones III (Indianapolis: Indiana Department of Natural Resources, Division of Historic Preservation and Archaeology, 2003), 141–171. The proto-Ho-Chunks also seem to have fallen out of contact with groups to the south around the same time; Elaine A. Bluhm and Allen Liss, "The Anker Site," in *Chicago Area Archaeology,* ed. Elaine A. Bluhm, Illinois Archaeological Survey Bulletin, no. 3 (Urbana: University of Illinois, 1961), 89–137.

39. Richter, *Before the Revolution,* 122–123, 128–130; Drooker, *View from Madisonville,* 283–294; Thomas E. Emerson and James A. Brown, "The Late Prehistory and Protohistory of Illinois," in *Calumet and Fleur-de-Lys: Archaeology of Indian and French Contact in the Midcontinent,* ed. John A. Walthall and Thomas E. Emerson (Urbana: University of Illinois Press, 1992), 99; *Relation of 1669–1670,* in *JR,* 54:161; Marquette, "Of the first Voyage," in *JR,* 59:127.

40. Robert Michael Morrissey, "The Power of the Ecotone: Bison, Slavery, and the Rise and Fall of the Grand Village of the Kaskaskia," *Journal of American History* 102 (December 2015): 667–692.

41. Robert L. Hall, "Relating the Big Fish and the Big Stone: Reconsidering the Archaeological Identity and Habitat of the Winnebago in 1634," in Green, *Oneota Archaeology,* 19–30; Hall, "Rethinking Jean Nicolet's Route to the Ho-Chunks in 1634," in *Theory, Method, and Practice in Modern Archaeology,* ed. Robert J. Jeske and Douglas K. Charles (Westport, CT: Praeger, 2003), 238–251; Mazrim and Esarey, "Rethinking the Dawn of History," 165–85; *Relation of 1642–1643,* in *JR,* 23:277–279; Claude Charles Le Roy, Sieur de Bacqueville de La Potherie, *History of the Savage Peoples who are allies of New France,* in Blair, *Indian Tribes of the Upper Mississippi Valley,* 1:293.

42. La Potherie, *History,* 1:293–299 ("massacred" on 296); Daniel K. Richter, "War and Culture: The Iroquois Experience," *WMQ* 40 (Oct. 1983): 528–559; Thomas S. Abler, "Scalping, Torture, Cannibalism and Rape: An Ethnohistorical Analysis of Conflicting Cultural Values in War," *Anthropologica* 34 (1992): 9–13; Snyder, *Slavery in Indian Country,* 80–100; Radin, "Winnebago Tribe," 57 ("bad luck").

43. La Potherie, *History*, 1:300 ("all the nations"); Radin, "Winnebago Tribe," 58 ("yellow"); *Relation of 1669–1670*, in *JR*, 54:237.

44. Colin M. Betts, "Pots and Pox: The Identification of Protohistoric Epidemics in the Upper Mississippi Valley," *American Antiquity* 71 (April 2006): 233–259; David W. Stahle, Edward R. Cook, Malcolm K. Cleaveland, Matthew D. Therrell, David M. Meko, Henri D. Grissino-Mayer, Emma Watson, and Brian H. Luckman, "Tree-Ring Data Document 16th Century Megadrought over North America," *Eos: Transactions of the American Geophysical Union* 81 (March 2000): 121, 125; Cook et al., "North American Drought," 110–113; Seth Eastman, "Map of the Country formerly occupied by the Ioway Tribe of Indians from a map made by Waw-Non-Que-Skoon-A an Ioway Brave," in *Historical And Statistical Information respecting the History, Condition, and Prospects of the Indian Tribes of the United States*, by Henry Rowe Schoolcraft, 6 vols. (Washington, DC: Government Printing Office, 1851–1857), 3, plate 30; Betts, "Oneota Mound Construction: An Early Revitalization Movement," *Plains Anthropologist* 55 (May 2010): 97–110.

45. The precise nature of the relationship between these divisions is unclear. Scholars have often referred to the Illinois as a "confederacy," but Illinois groups seem to have operated more like bands or villages of a single nation. For a discussion of the subgroups reported by French colonists, see Kathleen L. Ehrhardt, *European Metals in Native Hands: Rethinking Technological Change, 1640–1683* (University: University of Alabama Press, 2005), 84–85.

46. Raymond E. Hauser, "An Ethnohistory of the Illinois Indian Tribe, 1673–1832" (Ph.D. diss., Northern Illinois University, 1973), 18–26, 247–250, 419–425; Margaret Kimball Brown, *Cultural Transformations among the Illinois: The Application of a System Model*, Publications of the Museum, Michigan State Anthropological Series, vol. 1, no. 3 (East Lansing: Michigan State University, 1979), 227, 234–236; Charles Callender, "Illinois," in *HNAI*, vol. 15, *Northeast*, 676; Charles Callender, *Social Organization of the Central Algonkian Indians*, Milwaukee Public Museum Publications in Anthropology 7 (Milwaukee: Milwaukee Public Museum, 1962), 40–41; Deliette, "Memoir," in *IHC*, 23:363, 378–379; "Enumeration of the Indian Tribes Connected with the Government of Canada," 1736, in *NYCD*, 9:1057.

47. Brown, *Cultural Transformations among the Illinois*, 234–236, 262; Hauser, "Ethnohistory of the Illinois Indian Tribe," 275–280.

48. James A. Brown, ed., *The Zimmerman Site: A Report on Excavations at the Grand Village of Kaskaskia, La Salle County, Illinois*, Report of Investigations 9 (Springfield: Illinois State Museum, 1961); Margaret Kimball Brown, *The Zimmerman Site: Further Excavations at the Grand Village of the Kaskaskia*, Reports of Investigations 32 (Springfield: Illinois State Museum, 1975); Charles L. Rohrbaugh et al., *The Archaeology of the Grand Village of the Illinois: Report of the Grand Village Research Project, 1991–1996; Grand Village of the Illinois State Historic Site (11LS13), LaSalle County, Illinois*, Research Reports 60 (Urbana: Illinois Transportation Archaeological Research Program, 1998);

Brown, *Cultural Transformations among the Illinois*, 235; "The Marquette Map of 1673–1674," in *Indian Villages of the Illinois Country*, comp. Sara Jones Tucker, part 1, *Atlas*, Illinois State Museum Scientific Papers 2 (Springfield: Illinois State Museum, 1942), plate 5; Nicolas de La Salle, journal, 11 February 1682, in *The La Salle Expedition on the Mississippi River: A Lost Manuscript of Nicolas de La Salle, 1682*, trans. and ed. William C. Foster (Austin: Texas Historical Commission, 2003), 91; Marquette, "Of the first Voyage," in *JR*, 59:113–125, 151–155; J. Joseph Bauxar, "Historic Period," in *Illinois Archaeology*, Illinois Archaeological Survey Bulletin 1 (Urbana: Illinois Archaeological Survey, 1959), 47; Dan F. Morse, "The Seventeenth-Century Michigamea Village Location in Arkansas," in Walthall and Emerson, *Calumet and Fleur-de-Lys*, 55–75; Jeter, "From Prehistory through Protohistory to Ethnohistory," 191–193; Larry Grantham, "The Illini Village of the Marquette and Jolliet Voyage of 1673," *Missouri Archaeologist* 54 (December 1993): 1–20; J. Joseph Bauxar, "History of the Illinois Area," in *HNAI*, vol. 15, *Northeast*, 596; René-Robert Cavelier, Sieur de La Salle, *Relation of the Discoveries and Voyages of Cavelier de La Salle from 1679 to 1681: The Official Narrative*, trans. Melville B. Anderson (Chicago: Caxton Club, 1901), 215; Daniel Coxe, *A Description of the English Province of Carolana* (London: B. Cowse, 1722), 11; Mazrim and Esarey, "Rethinking the Dawn of History," 156–176, 186.

49. Marquette, "Of the first Voyage," in *JR*, 59:139–141; David J. Costa, "Culture-Hero and Trickster Stories," in *Algonquian Spirit*, ed. Brian Swann (Lincoln: University of Nebraska Press, 2005), 297; George Finley, "Wiihsakacaakwa Aalhsoohkaakana," trans. David J. Costa, in Swann, *Algonquian Spirit*, 303–307; William James Newbigging, "The History of the French-Ottawa Alliance" (Ph.D. diss, University of Toronto, 1995), 72–73; Theresa S. Smith, *The Island of the Anishinaabeg: Thunderers and Water Monsters in the Traditional Ojibwe Life-World* (Moscow: University of Idaho Press, 1995), 95–125; Charles M. Hudson, *The Southeastern Indians* (Knoxville: University of Tennessee Press, 1976), 130–131, 145–146; Francis La Flesche, *A Dictionary of the Osage Language* (Washington, DC: Government Printing Office, 1932), 106–107.

50. Le Boullenger Dictionary, svv. "Barre," "Passage," JCB.

51. Michael McCafferty, *Native American Place Names of Indiana* (Urbana: University of Illinois Press, 2008), 24–26; David J. Costa, *The Miami-Illinois Language* (Lincoln: University of Nebraska Press, 2003), 12–14; Brett Rushforth, *Bonds of Alliance: Indigenous and Atlantic Slaveries in New France* (Chapel Hill: University of North Carolina Press for the Omohundro Institute of Early American History and Culture, 2012), 4n2.

52. Marquette, "Of the first Voyage," in *JR*, 59:131, 137; Perrot, *Memoir*, 1:185 ("render").

53. Callender, "Illinois," 15:676; Charles Callender, "Miami," in *HNAI*, vol. 15, *Northeast*, 684; Heidi Bohaker, "'*Nindoodemag*': The Significance of Algonquian

Kinship Networks in the Eastern Great Lakes Region, 1600–1701," WMQ (January 2006): 34–35 (Ottawas); Marjorie M. Schweitzer, "Otoe and Missouria," in *HNAI*, vol. 13, *Plains*, 1:449–450; Garrick A. Bailey, *Changes in Osage Social Organization, 1673–1906*, University of Oregon Anthropological Papers 5 (Eugene: University of Oregon, 1973), 10–17; DuVal, *Native Ground*, 84–85 (Quapaws); Jacques Gravier to Jean de Lamberville, 16 February 1701, in *JR*, 65:119; Jacques-Pierre de Taffanel de la Jonquière, Marquis de la Jonquière to Antoine-Louis Rouillé, 25 September 1751, in *IHC*, 29:366–367; Jean-Jacques Macarty Mactigue to Pierre Pierre de Rigaud de Vaudreuil de Cavagnial, 2 September 1752, in *IHC*, 29:687; Brown, *Cultural Transformations among the Illinois*, 259–260; Reponse de Pondiac a une Parole et un Collier envoyé par Monsr. Hay . . . , 10 May 1768, in George Turnbull to Thomas Gage, 14 June 1768, vol. 77, TGP.

54. André Pénicaut, *Fleur de Lys and Calumet: Being the Pénicaut Narrative of French Adventure in Louisiana*, trans. and ed. Richebourg Gaillard McWilliams (Tuscaloosa: University of Alabama Press, 1981), 139–140; Deliette, "Memoir," in *IHC*, 23:331 ("five or six"). Another French observer, André Pénicaut, stated that the present was "in keeping with his [the suitor's] means"; Pénicaut, *Fleur de Lys and Calumet*, 140.

55. Pénicaut wrote "ses parents," which could mean either "his parents" or "his relatives"; Pénicaut, *Fleur de Lys and Calumet*, 140n6.

56. Some historians have argued that the Illinois maintained a patrilineal and matrilocal household—that is, lineage followed the father, but the couple lived with the mother's family. However, most evidence from early French accounts states that women lived with their husbands or their husbands' families. Linguistic evidence is less clear, as words and phrases reference both men and women at least at the homes of, if not explicitly living with, their in-laws. See "nahanganac8a," translated as "she is at the home of her husband's parents," and "nahanganapi8o," translated as "he lives at the home of his wife's parents"; Le Boullenger Dictionary, svv. "Femme," "Parent," JCB; Susan Sleeper-Smith, *Indian Women and French Men: Rethinking Cultural Encounter in the Western Great Lakes* (Amherst: University of Massachusetts Press, 2001), 5, 30–33; Robert Michael Morrissey, "Kaskaskia Social Network: Kinship and Assimilation in the French-Illinois Borderlands, 1673–1735," *WMQ* 70 (January 2013): 114–115.

57. Hall, *Archaeology of the Soul*, 50; Hauser, "Ethnohistory of the Illinois Indian Tribe," 226; Brown, *Cultural Transformations among the Illinois*, 238.

58. Marquette, "Of the first Voyage," in *JR*, 59:121, 155; Rushforth, *Bonds of Alliance*, 61–65, 142–144; *Relation of 1669–1670*, in *JR*, 54:177, 187.

59. Deliette, "Memoir," in *IHC*, 23:318, 339–340; Rale to "Monsieur and Very Dear Brother," 12 October 1723, in *JR*, 67:169; Baron de Lahontan, *New Voyages to North America*, 2 vols. (London: H. Bonwicke, 1703), 1:129, 130, 133.

60. Mazrim and Esarey, "Rethinking the Dawn of History," 166–174.

61. M. Catherine Bird, "Temporal, Spatial, and Social Trends: Late Prehistoric and Protohistoric Group Interaction," in Jeske and Charles, *Theory, Method, and Practice in Modern Archaeology*, 222; Ehrhardt, "Problems and Progress," 273–274; Perrot, *Memoir*, 1:173–174 ("old knives"); La Potherie, *History*, 1:307 ("worn-out").

62. For differing accounts of the Iroquois wars of the mid-1600s, see White, *Middle Ground*, 1–49; Richter, *Ordeal of the Longhouse*, 50–74; Brandão, *"Your Fyre Shall Burn No More."* For effects on Ottawas and Wendats, see Michael A. McDonnell, *Masters of Empire: Great Lakes Indians and the Making of America* (New York: Hill and Wang, 2015), 30–36; Kathryn Magee Labelle, *Dispersed but Not Destroyed: A History of the Seventeenth-Century Wendat People* (Vancouver: University of British Columbia Press, 2013).

63. Perrot, *Memoir*, 1:153–157 (quotes on 154, 157). For lack of Iroquois attacks on the Illinois during this era, see George T. Hunt, *The Wars of the Iroquois: A Study in Intertribal Relations* (1940; repr., Madison: University of Wisconsin Press, 1978), 145–164; Brandão, *"Your Fyre Shall Burn No More,"* appendix D, 169–278.

64. *Relation of 1653–1654*, in *JR*, 41:77–79; Bruce G. Trigger, *The Children of Aataentsic: A History of the Huron People to 1660* (1976; repr., Montreal and Kingston: McQill-Queen's University Press, 1987), 820–824; McDonnell, *Masters of Empire*, 36.

65. C.C. Trowbridge, "Traditions, Manners and Customs of the Twaatwaa or Miami Indians," 4–5, 21, Box 15, vol. 1, C.C. Trowbridge Papers, Burton Historical Collection, Detroit Public Library, Detroit, MI; Bert Anson, *The Miami Indians* (1970; repr., Norman: University of Oklahoma Press, 1999), 11–12; Callender, "Illinois," in *HNAI*, 15:673–674; David J. Costa, *The Miami-Illinois Language* (Lincoln: University of Nebraska Press, 2003), 1–7; *Relation of 1657–1658*, in *JR*, 44:249–251, 324n21; Pierre-Esprit Radisson, *The Collected Writings*, vol. 1, *The Voyages*, ed. Germaine Warkentin (Toronto and Montreal: Champlain Society and McGill-Queen's University Press, 2012), 219–225; *Relation of 1672–1673*, in *JR*, 58:23, 41–43 ("twenty").

66. Le Boullenger Dictionary, s.v. "Nom," JCB; *Relation of 1666–1667*, in *JR*, 51:49–51; *Relation of 1669–1670*, in *JR*, 54:161 ("hatchets"), 191.

67. Rushforth, *Bonds of Alliance*, 163–174; Cécile Vidal, "Les implantations françaises au pays des Illinois au XVIIIe siècle (1699–1765)" (Ph.D. diss., École des Haute Études en Sciences Sociales, 1995), 504–506; Eric Hinderaker, *Elusive Empires: Constructing Colonialism in the Ohio Valley, 1673–1800* (Cambridge: Cambridge University Press, 1997), 16–17; Marquette, "Of the first Voyage," in *JR*, 59:127 ("inspire"); Mildred Mott Wedel, "The Identity of La Salle's Pana Slave," *Plains Anthropologist* 18 (August 1973): 203–205; Pierre Le Moyne d'Iberville, *Iberville's Gulf Journals*, ed. and trans. Richebourg Gaillard McWilliams (Tuscaloosa: University of Alabama Press, 1981), 171–177.

68. Pierre Margry, ed., *Découvertes et établissements des Français dans l'ouest et dans le sud de l'Amérique Septentrionale (1614–1754): Mémoires et documents*

originaux, 6 vols. (Paris: D. Jouaust, 1876–1886), 2:324; Wedel, "Identity of La Salle's Pana Slave," 203–217.

69. Robert T. Bray, "The Utz Site: An Oneota Village in Central Missouri," *Missouri Archaeologist* (December 1991): 69–77, 133–135; O'Brien and Wood, *Prehistory of Missouri*, 352–353; Drooker, *View from Madisonville*, 315, 332; Brown, "The Calumet Ceremony in the Southeast," 318; Bray, "European Trade Goods at Utz and the Search for Fort Orleans," *Missouri Archaeologist* 39 (December 1978): 1–75; Grantham, "Illini Village," 5; Collins, "Des Moines Rapids," 169–170.

70. Margry, *Découvertes et établissements*, 2:324; Wedel, "Identity of La Salle's Pana Slave," 203–217; Henri de Tonty, "Memoir sent in 1693, on the Discovery of the Mississippi and the Neighboring Nations by M. D. La Salle, from the Year 1678 to the Time of His Death, and by the Sieur de Tonty to the Year 1691," in *IHC*, 1:154–156; Gravier to "My Reverend Father," 15 February 1694, in *JR*, 64:161, 169; Deliette, "Memoir," in *IHC*, 23:387–389; Carl H. Chapman, *The Origin of the Osage Indian Tribe* (New York: Garland, 1974), 146–150; Zenobius Membré, "Narrative of the Adventures of La Salle's Party at Fort Crevecoeur, in Illinois, from February, 1680, to June, 1681," in *The Journeys of Rene Robert Cavelier, Sieur de La Salle*, ed. Isaac Joslin Cox, 2 vols. (1905–1906; repr., New York: Allerton, 1922), 1:129.

71. Louis Hennepin, *Description de la Louisiane, Nouvellement Decouverte au Sud'Oüest de la Nouvelle France, par Ordre du Roy* (Paris: Veuve Sebastien Huré, 1683), 150; Charles M. Hudson, *Knights of Spain, Warriors of the Sun: Hernando de Soto and the South's Ancient Chiefdoms* (Athens: University of Georgia Press, 1997), 287–303, 320–329; Hoffman, "Terminal Mississippian Period," 208–210; DuVal, *Native Ground*, 67–68, 78; Jeter, "From Prehistory through Protohistory to Ethnohistory," 192; Joni L. Manson, "Trans-Mississippi Trade and Travel: The Buffalo Plains and Beyond," *Plains Anthropologist* 43 (November 1998): 392; Morse, "Seventeenth-Century Michigamea Village," 57, 62; Pénicaut, *Fleur de Lys and Calumet*, 138; John A. Walthall, "Aboriginal Pottery and the Eighteenth Century Illini," in Walthall and Emerson, *Calumet and Fleur-de-Lys*, 169–170; St. Cosme to "My Lord," 2 January 1699, in *Early Narratives of the Northwest*, ed. and trans. Louise Phelps Kellogg (New York: Charles Scribner's Sons, 1917), 356; Gravier to Lamberville, 16 February 1701, in *JR*, 65:103–105; La Salle on the Illinois Country, 1680, in *IHC*, 23:5.

72. Marquette, "Of the first Voyage," in *JR*, 59:89 ("courage" and "dangers"), 155, 161; La Potherie, *History*, 1:348; Hamilton, *Marquette's Explorations*, 184.

73. Marquette, "Of the first Voyage," in *JR*, 59:147–149; "Marquette Map of 1673–1674"; Jean Delanglez, "Marquette's Autograph Map of the Mississippi River," *Mid-America* 27 (January 1945): 50–51; Snyder, *Slavery in Indian Country*, 46–47; Robbie Ethridge, *From Chicaza to Chickasaw: The European Invasion and the Transformation of the Mississippian World, 1540–1715* (Chapel Hill: University of North Carolina Press, 2010), 123–124, 277n26.

2. Conversions

1. Jacques Gravier to "My Reverend Father," 15 February 1694, in *JR*, 64:197 ("ornaments" and "covered"); René-Robert Cavelier de la Salle to "Monsieur," 22 August 1682, in *Découvertes et établissements des Français dans l'ouest et dans le sud de l'Amérique Septentrionale (1614–1754): Mémoires et documents originaux*, ed. Pierre Margry, 6 vols. (Paris: D. Jouaust, 1876–1886), 2:246 ("educated" and "knew"); "La Forest Sells Half-Interest to Accault," 19 April 1693, in *IHC*, 23:264–266.
2. Gravier to "My Reverend Father," 15 February 1694, in *JR*, 64:213.
3. Gravier to "My Reverend Father," 15 February 1694, in *JR*, 64:195, 197, 205–207, 211.
4. Gravier to "My Reverend Father," 15 February 1694, in *JR*, 64:181, 213–215, 221–223.
5. Historians have also divided into two camps, mirroring the two sides of the debate in New France. Jacqueline Peterson and Susan Sleeper-Smith, among others, have emphasized the incorporation of French men into Native communities or development of métis communities as part of the fur trade. Others, such as Carl Ekberg, Robert Morrissey, and Sophie White, have argued that French culture dominated in these marriages. Jacqueline Peterson, "Prelude to Red River: A Portrait of the Great Lakes Metis," *Ethnohistory* 25 (Winter 1978): 41–67; Peterson, "The People In Between: Indian-White Marriage and the Genesis of a Métis Society and Culture in the Great Lakes Region, 1680–1830" (Ph.D. diss., University of Illinois at Chicago Circle, 1981); Susan Sleeper-Smith, *Indian Women and French Men: Rethinking Cultural Encounter in the Western Great Lakes* (Amherst: University of Massachusetts Press, 2001); Carl J. Ekberg with Anton J. Pregaldin, "Marie Rouensa-8cate8a and the Foundations of French Illinois," *Illinois Historical Journal* 84 (Autumn 1991): 146–160; Ekberg, *French Roots in the Illinois Country* (Urbana: University of Illinois Press, 1998); Robert Michael Morrissey, "Kaskaskia Social Network: Kinship and Assimilation in the French-Illinois Borderlands, 1673–1735," *WMQ* 70 (January 2013): 103–146; Sophie White, *Wild Frenchmen and Frenchified Indians: Material Culture and Race in Colonial Louisiana* (Philadelphia: University of Pennsylvania Press, 2012). For varying nature of intermarriage in Louisiana, see Kathleen DuVal, "Indian Intermarriage and Métissage in Colonial Louisiana," *WMQ* 65 (April 2008): 267–304.
6. Jean-Baptiste Colbert to Louis de Buade de Frontenac, 17 May 1674, in *NYCD*, 9:115; Louis XIV to Count de Frontenac, 15 April 1676, in *NYCD*, 9:126; Colbert to Jacques Duchesneau, 28 April 1677, B, 7:79–79v.
7. Marquis de Denonville to the Minister, 25 August 1687, C11a, 9:75; Instructions of the King to Denonville, 10 March 1685, in *IHC*, 23:75; W. J. Eccles, *The Canadian Frontier, 1534–1760*, rev. ed. (Albuquerque: University of New Mexico Press, 1983), 103–131; Gilles Havard, *Empire et métissages: Indiens et*

Français dans le Pays d'en Haut, 1660–1715 (Sillery, QC: Septentrion, 2003), 68–72, 75–77, 325–351.

8. Frontenac to Colbert, 2 November 1672, C11a, 3:239. For example, see the case of Pierre Moreau *dit* La Taupine, whom Frontenac ordered released after he was arrested for trading illegally with Illinois and Ottawas in 1679; "Unfinished Journal of Father Jacques Marquette . . . ," 26 October 1674–6 April 1675, in *JR*, 59:175, 183; Jacques Duchesneau to the Minister, 10 November 1679, in *NYCD*, 9:132; W. J. Eccles, *Frontenac, the Courtier Governor* (1959; repr., Toronto: McClelland and Stewart, 1968), 85–86; Louis XIV, Ordonnance qui defend la chasse hors l'étendüe des terres défrichées et habitées en Canada et une lieue à la ronde, 12 May 1678, C11a, 4:183v; Louis XIV to Frontenac, 29 April 1680, C11a, 5:202.

9. Frontenac to Colbert, 14 November 1674, in *RAPQ*, vol. *1926–1927*, 65–67, 78 (quote on 78); Eccles, *Frontenac*, 43–44, 79–83.

10. License to Sieur de La Salle to Discover the Western part of New France, 12 May 1678, in *NYCD*, 9:127.

11. Louis Dechêne, "Dauphin de La Forest, François," in *DCB;* Extrait de la Revue faite au fort de Frontenac par Monseigneur le Gouverneur, 7 September 1677, in Margry, *Découvertes et établissements,* 1:296; Mémoire pour représenter à Monseigneur [Jean-Baptiste Antoine Colbert] le marquis de Seignelay la nécessité d'envoyer la sieur de La Forest en diligence par la Nouvelle-France, n.d., in Margry, *Découvertes et établissements,* 2:370–373; Ordonnance de M. Duchesneau . . . , 14 July 1682, in Margry, *Découvertes et établissements,* 2:193; Lettre de Cavelier de La Salle, 22 August 1682, in Margry, *Découvertes et établissements,* 2:221; Henri de Tonty, "Memoir Sent in 1693 . . . ," in *Early Narratives of the Northwest, 1634–1699,* ed. Louise Phelps Kellogg (New York: Charles Scribner's Sons, 1917), 286 ("eight years"); Paul du Ru, *Journal of Paul du Ru [February 1 to May 8, 1700] Missionary Priest to Louisiana,* ed. and trans. Ruth Lapham Butler (Chicago: Caxton Club, 1934), 12; Edmund Robert Murphy, *Henry de Tonty: Fur Trader of the Mississippi* (Baltimore: Johns Hopkins University Press, 1941), 7–12; fragment of a letter of La Salle, 31 October 1678, in Récit d'un ami de l'Abbé de Gallinée, in Margry, *Découvertes et établissements,* 1:393.

12. Louis Hennepin, *Description de la Louisiane, Nouvellement Decouverte au Sud'Oüest de la Nouvelle France, par Ordre du Roy* (Paris: Veuve Sebastien Huré, 1683), 145–153.

13. Nicolas Perrot, *Memoir on the Manners, Customs, and Religion of the Savages of North America,* in *The Indian Tribes of the Upper Mississippi Valley and Region of the Great Lakes,* ed. Emma Helen Blair, 2 vols. (Cleveland: Arthur H. Clark, 1911), 1:157 ("utterly"); "La Salle on the Illinois Country," 1680, in *IHC,* 23:13; Tonty, "Memoir Sent in 1693," 289, 291; "Relation des decouvertes et des voyages du sieur de La Salle . . . ," in Margry, *Découvertes et établissements,* 1:440, 443 ("better price").

14. *Relation of 1670–1671,* in *JR*, 54:265.

15. "Relation des decouvertes et des voyages du sieur de La Salle," 1:469, 507 (quotes on 469). For value of a *livre*, see Harold A. Innis, *The Fur Trade in Canada: An Introduction to Canadian Economic History* (1930; paperback ed., New Haven, CT: Yale University Press, 1962), 66; Statement of Account for Illinois Trade, 1689, in *IHC*, 23:162–176.

16. Robert Michael Morrissey, *Empire by Collaboration: Indians, Colonists, and Governments in Colonial Illinois Country* (Philadelphia: University of Pennsylvania Press, 2015), 52–54, 56; "Feuille détachée . . . de la main de La Salle," in Margry, *Découvertes et établissements*, 2:201; "La Salle on the Illinois Country, 1680," in *IHC*, 23:5; "Narrative of a 3rd voyage to the Ilinois, made by Father Claude Allois," in *JR*, 60:158 (quote); Hennepin, *Description de la Louisiane*, 137; Charles L. Rohrbaugh et al., *The Archaeology of the Grand Village of the Illinois: Report of the Grand Village Research Project, 1991–1996: Grand Village of the Illinois State Historic Site (11LS13), La Salle County, Illinois*, Research Reports 60 (Urbana: Illinois Transportation Archaeological Research Program, 1998), 15.

17. Tonty, "Memoir Sent in 1693," 290.

18. Tonty, "Memoir Sent in 1693," 291–294 ("dependent" on 291); Henri de Tonty, *Relation of Henri de Tonty Concerning the Explorations of La Salle from 1678 to 1683*, trans. Melville B. Anderson (Chicago: Caxton Club, 1898), 35–45 ("young men" on 37, "severing" on 39, "devour" on 45); "Relation des decouvertes et des voyages du sieur de La Salle," 1:506–511, 513 ("seven hundred" on 513).

19. Morrissey, *Empire by Collaboration*, 58; "Relation des Decouvertes et des voyages du sieur de La Salle," 1:528 (quotes).

20. "Assembly held at Québec, at the house of the Reverend Jesuit Fathers," 10 October 1682, in *JR*, 62:161; Tonty, "Memoir Sent in 1693," 304–305 ("no pleasure" on 304); Baron de Lahontan, *New Voyages to North America*, 2 vols. (London: H. Bonwicke, 1703), 1:41 ("Trees of Peace"); Conference between Count de Frontenac and the Ottawas, 13–20 August 1682, in *NYCD*, 9:176–177.

21. Jacques de Lamberville to Frontenac, 20 September 1682, in *JR*, 62:151 ("brunt" and "thunderbolt"); Morrissey, *Empire by Collaboration*, 58; Tonty, "Memoir Sent in 1693," 302 ("not a year"); Procés Verbal de Henri de Tonty, 11 April 1694, C13a, 1:27.

22. Conference between Count de Frontenac and a Deputy from the Five Nations, 11 September 1682, in *NYCD*, 9:181, 182, 187.

23. Lahontan, *New Voyages*, 1:37, 70–78 ("strip'd" on 37); Joseph-Antoine Le Febvre de La Barre to the Minister, 5 June 1684, C11a, 6:273–273v; La Barre to Colonel Dongan, 15 June 1684, C11A, 6:265; José António Brandão, *"Your Fyre Shall Burn No More": Iroquois Policy toward New France and Its Native Allies to 1701* (Lincoln: University of Nebraska Press, 1997), table D.1; Eccles, *Frontenac*, 161–185, 192–194; Richard White, *The Middle Ground: Indians, Empires and Republics in the Great Lakes Region, 1650–1815* (Cambridge:

Cambridge University Press, 1991), 31–32; Instructions of the King to Denonville, 10 March 1685, in *IHC*, 23:70 ("humble" and "assistance"); Letter of Callières de Chasteuvilain, 12 October 1687, in *IHC*, 23:133; Claiborne A. Skinner, *The Upper Country: French Enterprise in the Colonial Great Lakes* (Baltimore: Johns Hopkins University Press, 2008), 66–71; Pierre Deliette, "Memoir," in *IHC*, 23:323–324; Tonty to his brother, 28 February 1700, in Delanglez, ed., "Tonti Letters," 219.

24. Daniel K. Richter, *The Ordeal of the Longhouse: The Peoples of the Iroquois League in the Era of European Colonization* (Chapel Hill: University of North Carolina Press for the Omohundro Institute of Early American History and Culture, 1992), 214–235; Brandão, *"Your Fyre Shall Burn No More,"* 127–128; Gilles Havard, *The Great Peace of Montreal of 1701: French-Native Diplomacy in the Seventeenth-Century*, trans. Phyllis Aronoff and Howard Scott (Montreal and Kingston: McGill-Queen's University Press, 2001), 173–178; Brett Rushforth, *Bonds of Alliance: Indigenous and Atlantic Slaveries in New France* (Chapel Hill: University of North Carolina Press for the Omohundro Institute of Early American History and Culture, 2012), 155–161; Michael A. McDonnell, *Masters of Empire: Great Lakes Indians and the Making of America* (New York: Hill and Wang, 2015), 73–78.

25. "Relation des decouvertes et des voyages du sieur de La Salle," 1:520 ("nous sommes"); Olive A. Dickason, *The Myth of the Savage and the Beginnings of French Colonialism in the Americas* (Edmonton: University of Alberta Press, 1984), 63–84; John DuVal and Kathleen DuVal, "Are *Sauvages* Savages, Wild People, or Indians in a Colonial American Reader?," *Translation Review* 79 (Winter 2010): 1–16; Gordon M. Sayre, *Les sauvages Américains: Representations of Native Americans in French and English Colonial Literature* (Chapel Hill: University of North Carolina Press, 1997), xv–xvii; Recensement de La Nouvelle-France, 1681, in *Statistics of Canada*, vol. 4, *Censuses of Canada, 1665–1871* (Ottawa: I. B. Taylor, 1876), 11; S. White, *Wild Frenchmen and Frenchified Indians*, 208–228.

26. Tonty, "Memoir Sent in 1693," 317; Jean Delanglez, "The Voyages of Tonti in North America, 1678–1704," *Mid-America* 26 (October 1944): 256.

27. Pierre-Georges Roy, *La Famille Juchereau Duchesnay* (n.p.: Lévis, 1903), 136; Jay Gitlin, "On the Boundaries of Empire: Connecting the West to Its Imperial Past," in *Under an Open Sky: Rethinking America's Western Past*, ed. William Cronon, George A. Miles, and Jay Gitlin (New York: Norton, 1992), 76–77; Nellis M. Crouse, *Lemoyne d'Iberville: Soldier of New France* (1954; repr., Baton Rouge: Louisiana State University Press, 2001), 87, 155–158.

28. Peter N. Moogk, *La Nouvelle France: The Making of French Canada—A Cultural History* (East Lansing: Michigan State University Press, 2000), 177–233, especially 215–217; John Bosher, "The Family in New France," in *In Search of the Visible Past: History Lectures at Wilfrid Laurier University, 1973–1974*, ed. Barry Gough (Waterloo, ON: Wilfrid Laurier University

Press, 1975), 1–13. On patronage in old-regime France, see Peter Campbell, *Power and Politics in Old Regime France, 1720–1745* (New York: Routledge, 1996), 16–21, 129–155; Peter R. Campbell, "Absolute Monarchy," in *Oxford Handbook of the Ancien Régime*, ed. William Doyle (New York: Oxford University Press, 2011), 26–28; Sharon Kettering, *Patronage in Sixteenth- and Seventeenth-Century France* (Aldershot, UK: Ashgate, 2002); Sara E. Chapman, *Private Ambition and Political Alliances: The Phélypeaux de Pontchartrain Family and Louis XIV's Government, 1650–1715* (Rochester, NY: University of Rochester Press, 2004).

29. Philippe de Rigaud de Vaudreuil to the Minister, 15 May 1713, C11a, 34:37v (quotes); Abstract of letters of the Company of the Indies to the Council of Louisiana, 1719–1729, in *MPA:FD*, 2:253, 255, 258.

30. "Relation des decouvertes et des voyages du sieur de La Salle," 1:449, 519–520; Tonty, "Memoir Sent in 1693," 289, 290 (quote on 290); Tonty, *Relation of Henri de Tonty*, 33; Tonty to his brother, 4 March 1700, in Delanglez, "Tonti Letters," 234; Hennepin, *Description de la Louisiane*, 187, 213, 261–262, 280–281; Morrissey, *Empire by Collaboration*, 48.

31. Tonty, "Memoir Sent in 1693," 317–318; Anastasius Douay, "Narrative of La Salle's Attempt to Ascend the Mississippi in 1687," in *The Journeys of Rene Robert Cavelier, Sieur de La Salle*, ed. Isaac Joslin Cox, 2 vols. (1905–1906; repr., New York: Allerton, 1922), 1:222–247 ("jealousy" on 246); Henri Joutel, *The La Salle Expedition to Texas: The Journal of Henri Joutel, 1684–1687*, ed. William C. Foster (Austin: Texas State Historical Association, 1998), 23–24, 191–202, 217–224, 288.

32. Guillaume Aubert, "'The Blood of France': Race and Purity of Blood in the French Atlantic World," *WMQ* 61 (July 2004): 442–450.

33. Aubert, "Blood of France," 450–453; Paul Le Jeune, *Relation of 1633*, in *JR*, 5:211 (quote); Saliha Belmessous, "Assimilation and Racialism in Seventeenth- and Eighteenth-Century French Colonial Policy," *American Historical Review* 110 (April 2005): 327–333; Robert Michael Morrissey, "Kaskaskia Social Network: Kinship and Assimilation in the French-Illinois Borderlands, 1673–1735," *WMQ* 70 (January 2013): 109–110.

34. It is worth noting that the differences in gender roles between French society and Native societies were much greater in other regions of North America, notably among Wendats, Iroquois, and the matrilineal nations of the South, where women enjoyed greater freedom in choosing marriage and sex partners and, in the cases of the Iroquois and the Cherokees in particular, increased power within their communities. See Elisabeth Tooker, "Women in Iroquois Society," in *Extending the Rafters: Interdisciplinary Approaches to Iroquoian Studies*, ed. Michael K. Foster, Jack Campisi, and Marianne Mithun (Albany: State University of New York Press, 1984), 109–124; Karen L. Anderson, *Chain Her by One Foot: The Subjugation of Women in Seventeenth-Century New France* (New York: Routledge, 1991); Richter, *Ordeal of the Longhouse*, 22–23, 42–48, 63–65; Richard A. Sattler, "Women's Status among the Muskogee

and Cherokee," in *Women and Power in Native North America*, ed. Laura F. Klein and Lillian A. Ackerman (Norman: University of Oklahoma Press, 1995), 214–229; Theda Perdue, *Cherokee Women: Gender and Culture Change, 1700–1835* (Lincoln: University of Nebraska Press, 1998).

35. Moogk, *La Nouvelle France*, 215–33; Sarah Hanley, "Engendering the State: Family Formation and State Building in Early Modern France," *French Historical Studies* 16 (Spring 1989): 4–27; Julie Hardwick, *The Practice of Patriarchy: Gender and the Politics of Household Authority in Early Modern France* (University Park: Penn State University Press, 1998), 159–193; Daniel K. Richter, *Before the Revolution: America's Ancient Pasts* (Cambridge, MA: Harvard University Press, 2011), 46; Vernon W. Kinietz, *Indians of the Western Great Lakes, 1615–1760* (1940; paperback ed., Ann Arbor: University of Michigan Press, 1965), 204–207; Margaret Kimball Brown, *Cultural Transformations among the Illinois: The Application of a System Model*, Publications of the Museum, Michigan State Anthropological Series, vol. 1, no. 3 (East Lansing: Michigan State University, 1979), 234–239.

36. Le Boullenger Dictionary, s.vv. "Neveu," "Oncle," "Parent," "Tante," JCB. For a fuller discussion of Illinois kin terms and relations, see David J. Costa, "The Kinship Terminology of the Miami-Illinois Language," *Anthropological Linguistics* 41 (Spring 1999): 28–53.

37. Deliette, "Memoir," 363–364 (quotes); Floyd G. Lounsbury, "A Formal Account of the Crow- and Omaha-Type Kinship Terminology," in *Explorations in Cultural Anthropology: Essays in Honor of Peter Murdock*, ed. Ward H. Goodenough (New York: McGraw-Hill, 1964), 351–393; Thomas R. Trautmann and Peter M. Whiteley, eds., *Crow-Omaha: New Light on a Classic Problem of Kinship Analysis* (Tucson: University of Arizona Press, 2012); Costa, "Kinship Terminology," 31–32.

38. Merry Wiesner-Hanks, *Christianity and Sexuality in the Early Modern World: Regulating Desire, Reforming Practice* (New York: Routledge, 2000), 114–115; Moogk, *La Nouvelle France*, 180–181, 220–222 (quote on 180). The Illinois phrase *tacamapicat8a a8enti8ni* translates to "He allies himself, marries into this family." "Tacamapicat8a a8enti8ni," in *Kaskaskia Illinois-to-French Dictionary*, ed. Carl Masthay (St. Louis: printed by author, 2002), 304. For Illinois courtship, see Deliette, "Memoir," 330–333; André Pénicaut, *Fleur de Lys and Calumet: Being the Pénicaut Narrative of French Adventure in Louisiana*, trans. and ed. Richebourg Gaillard McWilliams (Tuscaloosa: University of Alabama Press, 1981), 139–141.

39. Wiesner-Hanks, *Christianity and Sexuality*, 123; Suzanne Desan, "Making and Breaking Marriage: An Overview of Old Regime Marriage as Social Practice," in *Family, Gender, and Law in Early Modern France*, ed. Suzanne Desan and Jeffrey Merrick (University Park: Pennsylvania State University Press, 2010), 14–15; Sarah Hanley, "Engendering the State: Family Formation and State Building in Early Modern France," *French Historical Studies* 16 (Spring 1989): 13; Stuart Carroll, *Blood and Violence in Early Modern France*

(New York: Oxford University Press, 2006), 237–238; Moogk, *La Nouvelle France*, 231; Julie Hardwick, "Seeking Separations: Gender, Marriages, and Household in Early Modern France," *French Historical Studies* 21 (Winter 1998): 160; Deliette, "Memoir," 334–337 ("thirty" on 335); Rushforth, *Bonds of Alliance*, 69. Le Boullenger translated "kikiteherimeg8si8o" as "woman who leaves her husband and goes to another so that her angry husband threatens to cut off her nose."; Le Boullenger Dictionary, s.v. "Femme," JCB. Among the Illinois, if the wife's lover died, the husband would have to pay restitution to his family.

40. Morrissey, *Empire by Collaboration*, 58; Deliette, "Memoir," 329, 355; "La Salle on the Illinois Country, 1680," in *IHC*, 23:10; Morrissey, "Kaskaskia Social Network," 115–116; Costa, "Kinship Terminology," 37. Historians of Illinois Indians have also condemned polygamy as exploitive and abusive to Illinois women, rarely acknowledging the potential benefits identified by anthropologists and historians of nations elsewhere in North America. For Illinois, see Sleeper-Smith, *Indian Women and French Men*, 23–24, 26; Morrissey, "Kaskaskia Social Network," 115. For an exception, see Peterson, "People In Between," 73–74. For elsewhere, see Perdue, *Cherokee Women*, 44, 174–176; John D'Emilio and Estelle B. Freeman, *Intimate Matters: A History of Sexuality in America*, 3rd ed. (Chicago: University of Chicago Press, 2012), 88; Tai S. Edwards, *Osage Women and Empire: Gender and Power* (Lawrence: University Press of Kansas, 2018), 54.

41. "Pimit8a," in Masthay, *Kaskaskia Illinois-to-French Dictionary*, 272; "Kissa-bamig8ta," in Masthay, 147; Jennifer M. Spear, *Race, Sex, and Social Order in Early New Orleans* (Baltimore: Johns Hopkins University Press, 2009), 28–30; Hardwick, "Seeking Separations," 157–180 ("extreme wrongdoing" on 160). See also Hanley, "Engendering the State," 13–14; Julie Hardwick, "Early Modern Perspectives on the Long History of Domestic Violence: The Case of Seventeenth-Century France," *Journal of Modern History* 78 (March 2006): 1–36; Carroll, *Blood and Violence*, 239–240; Moogk, *La Nouvelle France*, 229–232.

42. Eccles, *Frontenac*, 76–77, 85–87; Skinner, *Upper Country*, 36; Louis XIV to Count de Frontenac, 25 April 1679, in *NYCD*, 9:128; Extract of Memoir of Duchesneau to du Seignelay, 10 November 1679, in *NYCD*, 9:131; Extracts of a memoir of Duchesneau to the minister, 13 November 1680, in *NYCD*, 9:142.

43. Eccles, *Canadian Frontier*, 109–113, 124–125; Skinner, *Upper Country*, 27–28, 36.

44. Concession des terres du Fort Saint-Louis des Illinois . . . , 14 juillet 1690, in Margry, *Découvertes et établissements*, 5:51–53; Clarence Walworth Alvord, *The Illinois Country, 1673–1818* (Springfield: Illinois Centennial Commission, 1920), 100–102; Deliette, "Memoir," 326–327 (quote on 327); Sebastien Rale to "Monsieur and Very Dear Brother," 12 October 1723, in *JR*, 67:163; Deliette, "Memoir," 327; Joseph Zitomersky, *French Americans–Native*

Americans in Eighteenth-Century French Colonial Louisiana: The Population Geography of the Illinois Indians, 1670s–1760s (Lund, Sweden: Lund University Press, 1994), 167–194.

45. Engagement of De Broyeux to La Forest, 19 August 1687, in *IHC,* 23:123–125; Engagement of Dumay to La Forest, 18 August 1687, in *IHC,* 23:126–128; Engagement of Barette to La Forest, 19 August 1687, in *IHC,* 23:129–132; E.-Z. Masicotte, "Répertoire des Engagements pour l'Ouest Conservés dans les Archives Judiciaires de Montréal," in *RAPQ,* vol. *1929–1930,* 196–199, 201; Lahontan, *New Voyages,* 1:135; Gravier to "My Reverend Father," 15 February 1694, in *JR,* 64:161; Delanglez, "Voyages of Tonti," 287–288.

46. Extrait des lettres de Denonville, 20 August, 3 September, and 12 November 1685, C11a, 7:69v. Pilette's great-grandson Hypolite Pilette relayed this story to the Illinois historian Nehemiah Matson in the nineteenth century; Matson, *Pioneers of Illinois, Containing a Series of Sketches Relating to Events That Occurred Previous to 1813* (Chicago: Knight and Leonard, 1882), 93–96; Skinner, *Upper Country,* 64–65.

47. Eccles, *Frontenac,* 291–292; Jean Bochart de Champigny to the Minister, 13 October 1697, C11a, 15:129–129v (quote).

48. Marquis de Denonville to the Minister, 25 August 1687, C11a, 9:75–75v ("every week"); Gravier to "My Reverend Father," 15 February 1694, in *JR,* 64:213; Gabriel Marest to Father Germon, 9 November 1712, in *JR,* 66:293; Spear, *Race, Sex, and Social Order,* 36–37; Louis XIV to Antoine Laumet *dit* de Lamothe Cadillac, 13 May 1710, in *MPA:FD,* 3:147 ("extreme"); "Extract from a Letter of M. Tonti to His Brother . . . February 28, 1700," in Delanglez, "Tonti Letters," 216–217; Gravier to Sieur de Villermont, 17 March 1694, Manuscrits Français, vol. 22804, fol. 59–60v, Bibliothèque nationale de France, Paris, France, copy in Illinois Historical Survey, Illinois History and Lincoln Collections, University of Illinois, Urbana-Champaign ("scandalous"); Jean-François Buisson de St. Cosme to "My Lord," 2 January 1699, in Kellogg, *Early Narratives of the Northwest,* 353. On fur-trade marriages more generally, see Sylvia Van Kirk, *Many Tender Ties: Women in Fur-Trade Society, 1670–1870* (1980; paperback ed., Winnipeg: Watson and Dwyer, 1999); Jennifer S. H. Brown, *Strangers in Blood: Fur Trade Companies in Indian Country* (Vancouver: University of British Columbia Press, 1980), especially 51–110; Peterson, "People In Between"; Tanis C. Thorne, *The Many Hands of My Relations: French and Indians on the Lower Missouri* (Columbia: University of Missouri Press, 1996); Sleeper-Smith, *Indian Women and French Men.*

49. Rushforth, *Bonds of Alliance,* 19, 68–70; Duval, "Indian Intermarriage and Métissage," 271–280; Juliana Barr, "From Captives to Slaves: Commodifying Indian Women in the Borderlands," *Journal of American History* 92 (June 2005): 22, 29–30; Sleeper-Smith, *Indian Women and French Men,* 40.

50. Sleeper-Smith, *Indian Women and French Men,* 20, 32–33, 75–76; Van Kirk, *Many Tender Ties,* 56–72; Peterson, "People In Between," 61, 66–67;

Bruce M. White, "The Woman Who Married a Beaver: Trade Patterns and Gender Roles in the Ojibwa Fur Trade," *Ethnohistory* 46 (Winter 1999): 109–147.

51. Memoir of the King to Frontenac and Champigny, 26 May 1696, in *NYCD*, 9:637; Jérôme Pontchartrain to Frontenac, 21 May 1698, in *NYCD*, 9:678; Innis, *Fur Trade in Canada*, 70–78; Eccles, *Canadian Frontier*, 125–128; Champigny to the Minister, 13 October 1697, C11a, 15:128v–129 (quote, emphasis in the original); Frontenac and Champigny to the Minister, 15 October 1698, C11a, 16:7v, 8v–9; Memoir of the King to Callières and Champigny, [ca. 1699], in *NYCD*, 9:700; Alvord, *Illinois Country*, 109; Marcel Giraud, *A History of French Louisiana*, vol. 1, *The Reign of Louis XIV, 1698–1715*, trans. Joseph C. Lambert (Baton Rouge: Louisiana State University Press, 1974), 7–8.

52. Extrait d'une lettre de M. de Champigny au Ministre, 6 November 1695, in Margry, *Découvertes et établissements*, 5:66; Delanglez, "Voyages of Tonti," 287–288; Tonty to his brother, 28 February 1700, in Delanglez, "Tonti Letters," 216; Henri de Tonty demande la concession du Pays des Akansas et le government d'un poste a Ouabache, [1700], in Margry, *Découvertes et établissements*, 5:349 ("Akansas" and "Ouabache"); Extrait des lettres du Canada de l'année 1699 avec observations dans la marge, C11a, 120:85 ("New Biscay"); Pontchartrain to Callières and Champigny, 4 June 1701, in Margry, *Découvertes et établissements*, 5:350–351; Concession accordée au Sieur Juchereau . . . , 4 June 1701, in Margry, *Découvertes et établissements*, 5:351–352.

53. Alvord, *Illinois Country*, 98–102, 109; Extrait des lettres particulières et des placets particuliers, [1698–1699], C11a, 120:51–51v ("carrying on"); Callières and Beauharnois to the Minister, 3 November 1702, in *MPHC*, 33:157; Extrait d'une lettre de M. le chevalier de Callières et M. Champigny au ministre, 5 October 1701, in Margry, *Découvertes et établissements*, 5:358–359 ("learned" on 359); Innis, *Fur Trade in Canada*, 78–81; Résumé d'une lettre de La Forest avec commentaires, 20 August 1706, C11a, 24:206v; Memorandum of M. de la Mothe Cadillac Concerning the Establishment of Detroit, 19 November 1704, in *MPHC*, 33:234; Jean Mermet to the Jesuits of Canada, 2 March 1706, in *JR*, 66:51; Jan Noel, *Along a River: The First French Canadian Women* (Toronto: University of Toronto Press, 2011), 103, 276n71; [Regnard Duplessis?] to the Minister, 10 November 1703, C11a, 21:180v.

54. Louise Dechêne, *Habitants and Merchants in Seventeenth-Century Montreal*, trans. Liana Vardi (Montreal: McGill-Queen's University Press, 1992), 92–95; Verner W. Crane, "The Tennessee River as the Road to Carolina: The Beginnings of Exploration and Trade," *Mississippi Valley Historical Review* 3 (June 1916): 5–14.

55. Aubert, "Blood of France," 455–460; Belmessous, "Assimilation and Racialism," 332, 334–339; Moogk, *La Nouvelle France*, 45–46; Havard, *Empire et métissages*, 534–545, 646–651. French-Indian marriages constituted less than 1 percent of all marriages recorded during the French colonial period

(1608–1763) in New France. Aubert, "Blood of France," 456n37; André Lachance and Sylvie Savoie, "Les Amérindiens sous le Régime Français," in *Les marginaux, les exclus et l'autre au Canada aux 17e et 18e siècles,* ed. André Lachance (Quebec: Éditions Fides, 1996), 190.

56. Marquis de Denonville to the Minister, 25 August 1687, C11a, 9:75v ("independent"); Declaration du Roy qui defend la Traitte des Castors avec Les Sauvages, 23 May 1696, B, 19:90v ("abandoned"); Extrait d'une lettre de M. le chevalier de Callières et de M. Champigny au ministre, 5 October 1701, in Margry, *Découvertes et établissements,* 5:356–357; Vaudreuil and Jacques Raudot to the Minister, 14 November 1709, C11a, 30:9v ("never"); Projet du mémoire du Roy au Sr. de l'Espinay gouverneur, et Hubert commissaire ordonnateur a la Louisiane, 1716, C13a, 4:977–978 ("mixing" and "mulattos"); Spear, *Race, Sex, and Social Order,* 36–38.

57. Spear, *Race, Sex, and Social Order,* 18, 24–26; Morrissey, *Empire by Collaboration,* 96–100.

58. Gravier to "My Reverend Father," 15 February 1694, in *JR,* 64:219.

59. Gravier to "My Reverend Father," 15 February 1694, in *JR,* 64:177 ("little"), 185 ("bird"), 191 ("slaves"), 221 ("massacred").

60. Claude Dablon, "Account of the Second Voyage and the death of . . . Marquette," [1677?], in *JR,* 59:189; Tracy Neal Leavelle, *The Catholic Calumet: Colonial Conversions in French and Indian North America* (Philadelphia: University of Pennsylvania Press, 2012), 118–122 (quotes from Hail Mary on 118). For the appeal of Catholicism to Native women, see Nancy Shoemaker, "Kateri Tekakwitha's Tortuous Path to Sainthood," in *Negotiators of Change: Historical Perspectives on Native American Women,* ed. Nancy Shoemaker (New York: Routledge, 1995), 49–71; Sleeper-Smith, *Indian Women and French Men,* 23–37; Tracy Neal Leavelle, "The Catholic Rosary, Gendered Practice, and Female Power in French-Indian Spiritual Encounters," in *Native Americans, Christianity, and the Reshaping of the American Religious Landscape,* ed. Joel W. Martin and Mark A. Nicholas (Chapel Hill: University of North Carolina, 2010), 168–173.

61. [Jacques de Lamberville], "Canadian Affairs in 1696," in *JR,* 65:33; Gravier to Michelangelo Tamburini, 6 March 1707, in *JR,* 66:123.

62. Carole Blackburn, *Harvest of Souls: The Jesuit Missions and Colonialism in North America, 1632–1650* (Montreal: McGill-Queen's University Press, 2000), 42–55; Ekberg, *French Roots;* Julien Binneteau to "My Reverend Father," January 1699, in *JR,* 65:73–75; Gabriel Marest to Father Germon, 9 November 1712, in *JR,* 66:253–255.

63. Pénicaut, *Fleur de Lys and Calumet,* 137–138 (quote); Jacques-Charles de Sabrevois, "Memoir on the Savages of Canada . . . ," 1718, in *WHC,* 16:374; Jean-Baptiste Le Moyne de Bienville, Memoir on Louisiana, [1726], in *MPA:FD,* 3:533; Census of 1726, G1, vol. 464, no folio, ANOM; Ekberg, *French Roots,* 138–170; Robert Michael Morrissey, "Bottomlands and Borderlands: Empires and Identities in the Illinois Country, 1673–1785,"

(Ph.D. diss., Yale University, 2006), 313–314; Gabriel Marest to Father Germon, 9 November 1712, in *JR*, 66:253–255.

64. S. White, *Wild Frenchmen and Frenchified Indians*, 21–142, especially 33–36.

65. Julien Binneteau to "My Reverend Father," January 1699, in *JR*, 65:69.

66. Michael McCafferty, "Peoria," *Society for the Study of the Indigenous Languages of the Americas Newsletter* 25 (January 2007): 13–14; Gravier to "My Reverend Father," 15 February 1694, in *JR*, 64:173 (quote); Tonty to Bishop St. Vallier, 14 July 1699, in *Old Cahokia: A Narrative and Documents Illustrating the First Century of Its History*, ed. and trans. John Francis McDermott et al. (St. Louis: St. Louis Historical Documents Foundation, 1949), 59.

67. Jean Mermet to the Jesuits of Canada, 2 March 1706, in *JR*, 66:53–55; Charles E. O'Neill, "Gravier, Jacques," in *DCB*. For a discussion of the varied meanings and uses of trade goods, see R. White, *Middle Ground*, 99–104, 180–182.

68. N. M. Miller Surrey, *The Commerce of Louisiana during the French Régime, 1699–1763* (New York: Columbia University Press, 1916), 342, 345.

69. Pénicaut, *Fleur de Lys and Calumet*, 40; Claude de Ramezay and Claude Michel Bégon to the Minister, 7 November 1715, in *WHC*, 16:331–332; Memoire concernant le pays des Illinois, 1724, C13a, vol. 8, fol. 226v; Census of 1732, G1, vol. 464, no fol., ANOM.

70. St. Cosme to "My Lord," 2 January 1699, in Kellogg, *Early Narratives of the Northwest*, 355; Giraud, *History of French Louisiana*, 1:338–339; Robert Michael Morrissey, "The Terms of Encounter: Language and Contested Visions of French Colonization in the Illinois Country, 1673–1702," in *French and Indians in the Heart of North America, 1613–1815*, ed. Robert Englebert and Guillaume Teasdale (East Lansing: Michigan State University Press, 2013), 43–49, 57–62; Zitomersky, *French Americans–Native Americans*, 204; Gabriel Marest to Father Germon, 9 November 1712, in *JR*, 66: 263–265 (quote on 265).

71. Tonty to his brother, 4 March 1700, in Delanglez, "Tonty Letters," 222; Iberville to the Minister of the Marine, 26 February 1700, in Margry, *Découvertes et établissements*, 4:364–365; Pierre Le Moyne d'Iberville, *Iberville's Gulf Journals*, ed. and trans. Richebourg Gaillard McWilliams (Tuscaloosa: University of Alabama Press, 1981), 106–109, 117–118; Pénicaut, *Fleur de Lys and Calumet*, 30, 35; Mémoire donné par le sieur d'Iberville des costes, qu'occupe l'Angleterre dans l'Amérique septentrionale, [ca. 1701], in Margry, *Découvertes et établissements*, 4:549–550, 545; Tonty to Cabart de Villermont, 11 September 1694, in Margry, *Découvertes et établissements*, 4:4 (quote); Extrait d'une lettre des directeurs de la Compagnie du Canada, 10 November 1701, in Margry, *Découvertes et établissements*, 5:360–362.

72. Extrait des lettres particulières et des placets particuliers, [1698–1699], C11a, 120:51.

73. Tonty to his brother, 4 March 1700, 223–234; St. Cosme to "My Lord," 2 January 1699, 360; Iberville to the Minister, 26 February 1700, in Margry,

Découvertes et établissements, 4:365 (quote); Giraud, *History of French Louisiana,* 1:14–25.

74. Callières to Pontchartrain, 16 October 1700 (extract), in *WHC,* 16:201; Iberville, *Iberville's Gulf Journals,* 165–166 ("promises"); Jean-Baptiste Le Moyne de Bienville to Pontchartrain, 6 September 1704, in *MPA:FD,* 3:23–24; Memoir of the King [Louis XIV] to Sieur de Muy, 30 June 1707, in *MPA:FD,* 3:56 ("only").

75. Tonty to his brother, 28 February 1700, and Tonty to his brother, 4 March 1700, in Delanglez, "Tonti Letters," 217, 219, 222–223 (quotes); Deliette, "Memoir," 327; Memorandum of M. de la Mothe Cadillac Concerning the Establishment of Detroit, 19 November 1704, in *MPHC,* 33:234; Jean Mermet to the Jesuits of Canada, 2 March 1706, in *JR,* 66:51.

76. Iberville, *Iberville's Gulf Journals,* 119 ("great" and "lure"), 133 ("settled"), 163, 170–177; du Ru, *Journal of Paul du Ru,* 22, 43; Patricia K. Galloway, "Henri de Tonti du Village des Chacta, 1701: The Beginning of the French Alliance," in *La Salle and His Legacy: Frenchmen and Indians in the Lower Mississippi Valley,* ed. Patricia K. Galloway (Jackson: University of Mississippi Press, 1982), 146–175.

77. Bienville to Pontchartrain, 6 September 1704, in *MPA:FD,* 3:29.

78. Pénicaut, *Fleur de Lys and Calumet,* 122–123.

79. Claude de Ramezay to the Minister, 18 September 1714, in *WHC,* 16:303; Ramezay and Bégon to the Minister, 13, 16 September 1715 (extract), in *WHC,* 16:318–319; Ramezay to the Minister, 3 November 1715, in *WHC,* 16:325; Ramezay and Bégon to the Minister, 7 November 1715, in *WHC,* 16:331–332 (quote on 332); Ramezay and Bégon to the Minister, 7 November 1715, in *WHC,* 16:331–332 (quote on 332); Eccles, *Canadian Frontier,* 132–142. For accounts of the battle at Detroit, see Jacques-Charles Renaud Dubuisson to Vaudreuil, 15 June 1712, in *WHC,* 16:267–287; Joseph J. Marest to Vaudreuil, 21 June and 2 July 1712, in *WHC,* 16:288–292; Memoir of [M. de Léry?], 1712, in *WHC,* 16:293–295. For the battle in context, see R. White, *Middle Ground,* 149–175; R. David Edmunds and Joseph L. Peyser, *The Fox Wars: The Mesquakie Challenge to New France* (Norman: University of Oklahoma Press, 1993); Rushforth, *Bonds of Alliance,* 193–221; Richard Weyhing, "'Gascon Exaggerations': The Rise of Antoine Laumet dit de Lamothe, Sieur de Cadillac, the Foundation of Colonial Detroit, and the Origins of the Fox Wars," in Englebert and Teasdale, *French and Indians in the Heart of North America,* 77–112. On the Compagnie d'Occident and Compagnie des Indies, see Gilles Havard and Cécile Vidal, *Histoire de l'Amérique Française,* rev. ed. ([Paris]: Champs histoire, 2014), 129–133; Marcel Giraud, *Histoire de la Louisiane Française,* 5 vols. (Paris: Presses Universitaires de Paris, 1958–1987), vols. 2–4; Cécile Vidal, "French Louisiana in the Age of the Companies, 1712–1731," in *Constructing Early Modern Empires: Proprietary Ventures in the Atlantic World, 1500–1750,* ed. Louis H. Roper and Bertrand Van Ruymbeke (Boston: Brill, 2007), 133–161.

80. Parolles de Chachagouesse ou autrement Nicanapé chef Illinois, 20 August 1712, C11a, 33:91v–93 (Chachagouesse quotes); Réponse de Vaudreuil aux paroles de Chachagouesse, [August 1712], C11a, 33:101–102; Vaudreuil to the Minister, 16 November 1704, in *RAPQ*, vol. *1938–1939*, 44–45; Vaudreuil and Charles de Beauharnois de la Boische to the Minister, 17 November 1704, in *RAPQ*, vol. *1938–1939*, 56, 59–60; Rushforth, *Bonds of Alliance*, 162–163; Pontchartrain to Vaudreuil, 9 June 1706, in *WHC*, 16:228, 231–232; Vaudreuil to the Minister, 6 November 1712, in *RAPQ*, vol. *1947–1948*, 164 ("only"), 166, 168; Vaudreuil and Bégon to the Minister, 20 September 1714, in *RAPQ*, vol. *1947–1948*, 279–280; Ramezay and Bégon to the Minister, 7 November 1715, in *WHC*, 16:333; Morrissey, *Empire by Collaboration*, 107–109, 128.

81. Ramezay to the Minister, 18 September 1714, in *WHC*, 16:302 (quote); Alvord, *Illinois Country*, 158; Morrissey, *Empire by Collaboration*, 107–109; Ekberg, *French Roots*, 35–36.

82. Spear, *Race, Sex, and Social Order*, 26; Morrissey, *Empire by Collaboration*, 106–107. Despite the ban, Jesuits in the Illinois Country continued to perform French-Illinois marriages, and secular officials felt compelled to reiterate the ban at least until the 1730s; Aubert, "Blood of France," 469–472; Spear, *Race, Sex, and Social Order*, 31–32, 37.

83. Richard N. Ellis and Charlie R. Steen, "An Indian Delegation in France, 1725," *Journal of the Illinois State Historical Society* 67 (September 1974): 394 (quotes); Robert Groston de St. Ange to Bienville, 1733, C13a, 17:250–250v; J. Le Boullenger to Bienville, 28 April 1733, C13a, 17: no fol.; J. P. Mercier to Bienville, 25 April 1733, C13a, 17:287–288v; Bienville to the Minister, 22 April 1734, C13a, 18:144–145; M. J. Morgan, *Land of Big Rivers: French & Indian Illinois, 1699–1778* (Carbondale: Southern Illinois University Press, 2010), 65–67.

84. Morrissey, "Kaskaskia Social Network," 122, 144; Census of 1726, G1, vol. 464, no fol.; Sleeper-Smith, *Indian Women and French Men*, 31; Aubert, "Blood of France," 471; Spear, *Race, Sex, and Social Order*, 30–32; Vidal, "Les Implantations Françaises au Pays Des Illinois au XVIIIe Siècle," 488–489; Zitomersky, *French Americans–Native Americans*, 260–261; Morrissey, *Empire by Collaboration*, 127–128. For Franchomme and Marguerite Onaquamoquona, see Declaration regarding marriage contract of Nicolas Pelletier de Franchomme and Marguerite Onaquamoquona, 16 February 1725, Black Book #5, Records of the Louisiana Superior Council, Louisiana State Museum, New Orleans, LA, available at www.crt.state.la.us/louisiana-state-museum/collections/historical-center/colonial-documents/black-books/index; Inventory of the estate of Jacques Bourdon, KM 23:7:1:1; Morrissey, *Empire by Collaboration*, 140–141; S. White, *Wild Frenchmen and Frenchified Indians*, 43–47, 180. In other sources, Marguerite's last name is spelled "8assicani8e"; *PFFA*, 2:152. The numbering system used in the Kaskaskia Manuscripts refers to the year:month:day:document. See Lawrie Cena Dean

and Margaret Kimball Brown, *The Kaskaskia Manuscripts, 1708–1816: A Calendar of Civil Documents in Colonial Illinois* (n.p.: by the authors, 2014), available at www.isas.illinois.edu/office_of_the_illinois_state_archaeologist /public_engagement/public_partnerships/colonial_heritage_project /kaskaskia_manuscripts/. For other Illinois widows marrying in French Kaskaskia, see *PFFA*, 2:88, 101; S. White, *Wild Frenchmen and Frenchified Indians*, 44, 47, 48; Morrissey, *Empire by Collaboration*, 154–155.

85. *PFFA*, 2:81, 94; Ekberg and Pregaldin, "Marie Rouensa-8cate8a," 157.
86. *PFFA*, 2:234; José Iguarta, "de Couagne, René," in *DCB*; Jane E. Graham, "de Couagne, Jean-Baptiste," in *DCB;* S. White, *Wild Frenchmen and Frenchified Indians*, 232; Ekberg and Pregaldin, "Marie Rouensa-8cate8a," 157; Robert M. Owens, "Jean Baptiste Ducoigne, the Kaskaskias, and the Limits of Thomas Jefferson's Friendship," *Journal of Illinois History* 5 (Summer 2002): 112–113; "Répertoire des Engagements pour l'Ouest Conservés dans les Archives Judiciaires de Montréal," *RAPQ*, vol. *1930–1931*, 358, 359, 360, 361, 362, 365, 366, 367, 381; Sleeper-Smith, *Indian Women and French Men*, 119–120, 138–139.
87. Bienville to Pontchartrain, 10 October 1706, C13b, 1:13–14v; Jean-Baptiste du Bois Duclos to Pontchartrain, 25 December 1715, C13a, 3:820–821; [Marc-Antoine Hubert] to the Council of Marine, [1717?], in *MPA:FD*, 2:232 (quotes); Bienville, Memoir on Louisiana, in *MPA:FD*, 3:522–523. See also Jennifer M. Spear, "Colonial Intimacies: Legislating Sex in French Louisiana," *WMQ* 60 (January 2003): 75–98.
88. Raymond J. DeMallie, "Kinship: The Foundation for Native American Society," in *Studying Native America: Problems and Prospects*, ed. Russell Thornton (Madison: University of Wisconsin Press, 1998), 307.

3. Alliances and Fractures

1. Mingo Ouma, "Nations Amies et Ennemies des Tchicachas" (copy), September 1737, C13a, 22:67. For an analysis, see Gregory A. Waselkov, "Indian Maps of the Colonial Southeast," in *Powhatan's Mantle: Indians in the Colonial Southeast*, ed. Gregory A. Waselkov, Peter H. Wood, and Tom Hatley (1989; rev. ed., Lincoln: Nebraska University Press, 2006), 481–484.
2. For discussion of those stereotypes, see Gregory Evans Dowd, "Wag the Imperial Dog: Indians and Overseas Empires in North America, 1650–1776," in *A Companion to American Indian History*, ed. Philip J. Deloria and Neal Salisbury (Oxford, UK: Blackwell, 2002), 55–56; Gilles Havard and Cécile Vidal, *Histoire de l'Amérique Française*, rev. ed. ([Paris]: Champs histoire, 2014), 249–253, 309–310.
3. For the cost of these alliances and the imperial conversations about it, see Catherine M. Desbarats, "The Cost of Early Canada's Native Alliances: Reality and Scarcity's Rhetoric," *WMQ* 52 (October 1995): 609–630.

4. On French ideology behind mediation and their intention to create a *Pax Gallica* throughout the Great Lakes, see Gilles Havard, *The Great Peace of Montreal of 1701: French-Native Diplomacy in the Seventeenth-Century*, trans. Phyllis Aronoff and Howard Scott (Montreal and Kingston: McGill-Queen's University Press, 2001), 155–158; Havard, *Empire et métissages: Indiens et Français dans le Pays d'en Haut, 1660–1715* (Sillery, QC: Septentrion, 2003); Havard, "'Protection' and 'Unequal Alliance': The French Conception of Sovereignty over Indians in New France," in *French and Indians in the Heart of North America, 1613–1815*, ed. Robert Englebert and Guillaume Teasdale (East Lansing: Michigan State University Press, 2013), especially 123–125. For a critique of Havard and his notion of *Pax Gallica*, see Michael Witgen, *An Infinity of Nations: How the Native New World Shaped Early North America* (Philadelphia: University of Pennsylvania Press, 2012), 415n28. For decades, historians have debated the nature of French-Indian diplomacy in the Great Lakes and have increasingly recognized the complexity of relations among diverse populations of Native peoples and the French empire. For competing views, see Richard White, *The Middle Ground: Indians, Empires and Republics in the Great Lakes Region, 1650–1815* (Cambridge: Cambridge University Press, 1991), 50–93, 142–185; William James Newbigging, "The History of the French-Ottawa Alliance" (Ph.D. diss., University of Toronto, 1995); Havard, *Empire et métissages*, especially 205–239, 359–490; Heidi Bohaker, "'Nindoodemag': The Significance of Algonquian Kinship Networks in the Eastern Great Lakes Region, 1600–1701," *WMQ* (January 2006): 23–52; Andrew K. Sturtevant, "Jealous Neighbors: Rivalry and Alliance among the Native Communities of Detroit, 1701–1766 (Ph.D. diss., College of William and Mary, 2011); Brett Rushforth, *Bonds of Alliance: Indigenous and Atlantic Slaveries in New France* (Chapel Hill: University of North Carolina Press for the Omohundro Institute of Early American History and Culture, 2012), especially 193–252; Havard and Vidal, *Histoire de l'Amérique Française*, 249–384; Christian Ayne Crouch, *Nobility Lost: French and Canadian Martial Cultures, Indians, and the End of New France* (Ithaca, NY: Cornell University Press, 2014); Michael A. McDonnell, *Masters of Empire: Great Lakes Indians and the Making of America* (New York: Hill and Wang, 2015).
5. Jacques-Charles de Sabrevois, "Memoir on the Savages of Canada . . . ," 1718, in *WHC*, 16: 364–365, 375; [John Pattin?], "Routes to the Upper Country," 1754, in *WHC*, 18:147. For early French maps of the region showing waterways and portages, see Louis Jolliet, "Nouvelle Decouverte de plusieurs Nations Dans la Nouvelle France en l'année 1673 et 1674," JCB; "Carte de l'Amerique Septentrionale Depuis l'embouchûre de la Riviere St. Laurens jusques au Sein Mexique," ca. 1675–1682, JCB; P. Coronelli, *Partie Occidentale du Canada ou de la Nouvelle France . . .* (Paris: Chez J. B. Nolin, 1688).
6. Vernon W. Kinietz, *Indians of the Western Great Lakes, 1615–1760* (1940; paperback ed., Ann Arbor: University of Michigan Press, 1965), 161–225.

7. "Unfinished Journal of Father Jacques Marquette . . . ," 14 December 1674, in *JR*, 59:173; [Pattin?], "Routes to the Upper Country," in *WHC*, 18:146.

8. Abstract of Letters of the Company of the Indies to the Council of Louisiana, 20 May 1722, in *MPA:FD*, 2:255.

9. Alan Gallay, *The Indian Slave Trade: The Rise of the English Empire in the American South, 1670–1717* (New Haven, CT: Yale University Press, 2002), 14–15; Robbie Ethridge, *From Chicaza to Chickasaw: The European Invasion and the Transformation of the Mississippian World, 1540–1715* (Chapel Hill: University of North Carolina Press, 2010), 149, 153. Both Gallay and Ethridge omit the routes that linked the Chickasaws to the Illinois Country, only highlighting their connections to Carolina and lower Louisiana. For Chickasaws threatening French access to the Mississippi, see Norman W. Caldwell, "The Chickasaw Threat to French Control of the Mississippi in the 1740's," *Chronicles of Oklahoma* 16 (December 1938): 465–492; Vidal, "Les implantations françaises au pays Des Illinois au XVIIIe siècle (1699–1763)," (Ph.D. diss., Écoles des hautes etudes en sciences sociales, 1995), 528–532; Claiborne A. Skinner, *The Upper Country: French Enterprise in the Colonial Great Lakes* (Baltimore: Johns Hopkins University Press, 2008), 124–127.

10. Helen Hornbeck Tanner, ed., *Atlas of Great Lakes Indian History* (Norman: University of Oklahoma Press, 1987), 40–41.

11. Jean-Baptiste Le Moyne de Bienville to Jérôme Pontchartrain, 1 September 1715, in *MPA:FD*, 3:185; Bienville to Pontchartrain, 2 January 1716, in *MPA:FD*, 3:192–193; Marc-Antoine Hubert to the Council, 26 October 1717, in *MPA:FD*, 2:257. For the need for a fort, see Extrait d'une lettre des directeurs de la Compagnie du Canada, 10 November 1701, in *Découvertes et établissements des Français dans l'ouest et dans le sud de l'Amérique Septentrionale (1614–1754): Mémoires et documents originaux*, ed. Pierre Margry, 6 vols. (Paris: D. Jouaust, 1876–1886), 5:361; Bienville, Memoir on Louisiana, [1726], in *MPA:FD*, 3:513–514; Étienne Périer to the Minister, 15 November 1727, C13a, 10:234–234v; Bienville to Jean-Frédéric Phélypeaux, Comte de Maurepas, 28 March 1742, in *MPA:FD*, 3:768.

12. Bienville to Pontchartrain, 20 January 1707, in *MPA:FD*, 3:38–39; Bienville to Maurepas, 30 September 1734, in *MPA:FD*, 1:243; Bienville to Maurepas, 9 September 1735, in *MPA:FD*, 1:273; Louis XV to Bienville, 2 February 1732, in *MPA:FD*, 3:548–549; Bienville to Maurepas, 30 September 1734, in *MPA:FD*, 1:243; Analyse des lettres de Bienville, May–August 1733, in *MPA:FD*, 1:202; Pierre de Rigaud de Vaudreuil de Cavagnial to Antoine-Louis Rouillé, 15 May 1751, in *IHC*, 29:264; Bienville, Memoir on Louisiana, in *MPA:FD*, 3:514; Philippe de Rigaud de Vaudreuil to [Pontchartrain?], 12 December 1717, in *Ouiatanon Documents*, ed. and trans. France Krauskopf, Indiana Historical Society Publications 18, no. 2 (Indianapolis: Indiana Historical Society, 1955), 160; Périer and Jacques de la Chaise to the Directors of the Company of the Indies, 31 July 1728, in

Krauskopf, *Ouiatanon Documents,* 177; Pierre-Joseph Céloron de Blainville to Vaudreuil de Cavagnial, 4 August 1751, in *IHC,* 29:292.

13. Jennifer M. Spear, *Race, Sex, and Social Order in Early New Orleans* (Baltimore: Johns Hopkins University Press, 2009), 42–50; Marcel Giraud, *A History of French Louisiana,* vol. 2, *Years of Transition, 1715–1717,* trans. Brian Pearce (Baton Rouge: Louisiana State University Press, 1993), 33, 101–106; Bienville to Pontchartrain, 2 January 1716, in *MPA:FD,* 3:194; Bienville to Maurepas, 28 June 1736, in *MPA:FD,* 1:310 ("wretched" and "compromise"); Bienville to Pontchartrain, 20 February 1707, in *MPA:FD,* 3:38–39; Bienville to Pontchartrain, 2 January 1716, in *MPA:FD,* 3:196; Edmé Gatien Salmon to the Minister, 22 June 1737, in *The Mission to the Ouabache,* ed. and trans. Jacob Piatt Dunn, Indiana Historical Society Publications 3, no. 4 (Indianapolis: Bowen-Merrill, 1902), 312–313; Charles de Beauharnois de la Boische to the Minister, 12 October 1739, in *WHC,* 17:317; Bienville to Maurepas, 5 September 1746, in *MPA:FD,* 1:329; Maurepas to Beauharnois, 28 April 1745, in *WHC,* 18:6; Vaudreuil de Cavagnial to Maurepas, 28 October 1745, in *MPA:FD,* 4:246; Vaudreuil de Cavagnial to Maurepas, 15 March 1747, in *MPA:FD,* 4:306; Bienville to Maurepas, 9 September 1735, in *MPA:FD,* 1:273.

14. For discussions of alliance-building rituals and gift exchanges, see White, *The Middle Ground,* 1023; Havard, *Empire et métissages,* 169–173, 235–236, 393–395, 410–414; Brett Rushforth, "'A Little Flesh We Offer You': The Origins of Indian Slavery in New France," *WMQ* 60 (Oct. 2003): 777–808.

15. Pierre-Georges Roy, *Sieur de Vincennes Identified,* Indiana Historical Society Publications 7, no. 1 (Indianapolis: C. E. Pauley, 1918), 31–75; Yves F. Zoltvany, "Bissot de Vinsenne, Jean-Baptiste," in *DCB;* Jacques-Charles Renaud Dubuisson to Vaudreuil, 15 June 1712, in *WHC,* 16:271, 286–287; Vaudreuil to the Council, 28 October 1719, in *WHC,* 16:382; Périer and de la Chaise to the Directors of the Company of the Indies, 25 March 1729, in *MPA:FD,* 2:634. See also Roy, *Sieur de Vincennes Identified,* 75.

16. Walter B. Douglas, "The Sieurs de St. Ange," in *Transactions of the Illinois Historical Society for the Year 1909* (Springfield: Illinois State Historical Library, 1910), 135–142; John Francis McDermott, "Saint-Ange, Robert Groston de," in *DCB;* "Victory over the Foxes," after 9 September 1730, in *WHC,* 17:109–113; Nicolas Coulon de Villiers to Beauharnois, 23 September 1730, in *WHC,* 17:113–118; Bienville to the Minister, 25 October 1732, C13a, 14:91v ("wise" and "perfectly").

17. Vaudreuil to Pierre Dugué de Boisbriand, 17 August 1724, in *WHC,* 16:443; Douglas, "Sieurs de St. Ange," 142–143; "Account of the Battle Fought by d'Artaguiette with the Chickasaws, March 25, 1736," in *Indiana's First War,* ed. and trans. Caroline Dunn and Eleanor Dunn, Indiana Historical Society Publications 8, no. 2 (Indianapolis: Wm. B. Burford, 1924), 107, 115; Drouet de Richardville, "Report of Richardville on d'Artaguiette's Expedition against the Chickasaws," in Dunn and Dunn, *Indiana's First War,* 135;

Bienville and Salmon to Maurepas, 29 June 1736, in *MPA:FD*, 3:687; Bienville to Maurepas, 5 September 1736, in *MPA:FD*, 1:328–329 ("very").

18. Patricia Galloway, "'The Chief Who Is Your Father': Choctaw and French Views of the Diplomatic Relation," in Waselkov, Wood, and Hatley, *Powhatan's Mantle*, 345–370; White, *Middle Ground*, 36–40, 84–90, 104–119; Rushforth, *Bonds of Alliance*, 196–221.

19. Speech of the Illinois Indians . . . , 14 January 1725, in *WHC*, 16:456–463 ("Great Ononthyo" on 461). For other instances of Indians in the midcontinent referring to the French as their brothers, see Jacques Marquette, "Of the first Voyage made by Father Marquette toward new Mexico . . . ," [1674], in *JR*, 59:119; Conference between Frontenac and the Ottawas, 15 August 1682, in *NYCD*, 9:178; Claude-Thomas Dupuy, Memoir respecting the English (abstract), 1 November 1727, in *NYCD*, 9:986; Relation of the adventures of Boucherville . . . , 1729, in *WHC*, 17:38, 42; Relation of the Journey of the Sieur de Noyelle . . . , [1735] (copy), in *WHC*, 17:225; George Le Hunte to Thomas Gage, 24 July 1763, vol. 9, TGP; "Loftus Attempts to Ascend the River," in *IHC*, 10:235–236; Havard, *Empire et métissages*, 219; Bohaker, "*Nindoodemag*," 47; Pierre Deliette, "Memoir," in *IHC*, 23:377. Such distinctions fit into the language of fictive kinship employed in Native diplomacy, in which Native peoples referred to other groups as their grandfathers, fathers, uncles, brothers, nephews, or cousins, each signifying a specific relationship; C. C. Trowbridge, *Shawnese Traditions*, ed. Vernon Kinietz and Erminie W. Voegelin (Ann Arbor: Museum of Anthropology of the University of Michigan, 1939), 9, 55; Jane T. Merritt, *At a Crossroads: Indians and Colonists on a Mid-Atlantic Frontier* (Chapel Hill: University of North Carolina Press for the Omohundro Institute of Early American History and Culture, 2003), 214–216; Stephen Warren, *The Shawnees and Their Neighbors, 1795–1840* (Urbana: University of Illinois Press, 2005), 74; Amy C. Schutt, *People of the River Valleys: The Odyssey of the Delaware Indians* (Philadelphia: University of Pennsylvania Press, 2007), 142–143, 227nn33, 36; Sturtevant, "Jealous Neighbors," 283–284.

20. Tanner, *Atlas of Great Lakes Indian History*, 40–41. Richard White provides an excellent depiction of French perceptions of the alliance; White, *Middle Ground*, 142–185.

21. R. David Edmunds, *The Potawatomis: Keepers of the Fire* (Norman: University of Oklahoma Press, 1978), 3–74; Newbigging, "History of the French-Ottawa Alliance"; Bohaker, "*Nindoodemag*," 23–52; Phil Belfry, *Three Fires Unity: The Anishinaabeg of the Lake Huron Borderlands* (Lincoln: University of Nebraska Press, 2011), 1–36; Witgen, *Infinity of Nations*; Pierre Le Moyne d'Iberville, Mémoire sur l'établissement de la Mobile et du Mississipi, n.d., in Margry, *Découvertes et établissements*, 4:587. For the Fox Indians and their allies, see R. David Edmunds and Joseph L. Peyser, *The Fox Wars: The Mesquakie Challenge to New France* (Norman: University of Oklahoma Press, 1993), especially 3–54.

22. On Choctaws, see Patricia Galloway, *Choctaw Genesis, 1500–1700* (Lincoln: University of Nebraska Press, 1995); James Taylor Carson, *Searching for the Bright Path: The Mississippi Choctaws from Prehistory to Removal* (Lincoln: University of Nebraska Press, 1999), 8–69. For Chickasaws, see James Atkinson, *Splendid Land, Splendid People: The Chickasaw Indians to Removal* (Tuscaloosa: University of Alabama Press, 2004), 1–87; Ethridge, *From Chicaza to Chickasaw*. For slave trade, see Gallay, *Indian Slave Trade;* Christina Snyder, *Slavery in Indian Country: The Changing Face of Captivity in Early America* (Cambridge, MA: Harvard University Press, 2010), 46–79 (Choctaw casualties on 61); Ethridge, *From Chicaza to Chickasaw*, 149–254. On Quapaws, see Kathleen DuVal, *The Native Ground: Indians and Colonists in the Heart of the Continent* (Philadelphia: University of Pennsylvania Press, 2006), 62–102; Gallay, *Indian Slave Trade*, 296–297, 299.

23. Richard White has argued that Native peoples sought French mediation, but more often, France's Indian allies wanted the empire to intercede on their behalf against their enemies. When a nation did request mediation, they had almost always suffered the most devastation in the conflict they wanted to end; White, *Middle Ground*, 30–36, 142–185; Newbigging, "History of the French-Ottawa Alliance," 311; Rushforth, *Bonds of Alliance*, 12, 200–206; Havard, "'Protection' and 'Unequal Alliance,'" especially 123–125.

24. Bert Anson, *The Miami Indians* (1970; repr., Norman: University of Oklahoma Press, 1999), 11–12; Charles Callender, "Illinois," in *HNAI*, vol. 15, *Northeast*, 673–674; C. C. Trowbridge, "Account of Some of the Traditions, Manners and Customs of the Twaatwaa or Miami Indians," 4–5, 21, Box 15, vol. 1, C. C. Trowbridge Papers, Burton Historical Collection, Detroit Public Library, Detroit, MI; La Salle on the Illinois Country, 1680, in *IHC*, 23:11, 14; "The Nicolas de La Salle Journal," in *The La Salle Expedition on the Mississippi River: A Lost Manuscript of Nicolas de La Salle, 1682*, ed. and trans. William C. Foster (Austin: Texas Historical Commission, 2003), 125; Claude de Ramezay to the Minister, 18 September 1714, in *WHC*, 16:302–303; Vaudreuil and Claude Michel Bégon to the Minister, 20 September 1714, in *WHC*, 16:303–304 ("two nations" on 304); Ramezay and Bégon to the Minister, 13, 16 September 1715, in *WHC*, 16:313, 318.

25. Pierre de Charlevoix, *Histoire et description generale de la Nouvelle France*, 4 vols. (Paris: Rolin Fils, 1744), 2:368–373; Dubuisson to Vaudreuil, 15 June 1712, in *WHC*, 16:277–283. For more on this council and its context, see Rushforth, *Bonds of Alliance*, 202–204; Dubuisson to Vaudreuil, 15 June 1712, in *WHC*, 16:267–287; Joseph J. Marest to Vaudreuil, 21 June and 2 July 1712, in *WHC*, 16:288–292; Memoir of [M. de Léry?], 1712, in *WHC*, 16:293–295; Memoir de [M. de Léry], [1712], in *WHC*, 16:294–295 ("granted" on 294); Vaudreuil to the Council of Marine, 14 October 1716, in *WHC*, 16:342–344; Vaudreuil to the Council of the Marine, 28 October 1719, in *WHC*, 16:381; Vaudreuil to the Minister, 2 October 1723, in *WHC*, 16:428–430; Extract from a letter from Beauharnois to the minister, 6 September 1741, in *WHC*,

17:362–363, 365–366. Some scholars have argued that France increased the level of destruction in the Fox Wars and, in some cases, have asserted that that violence led Illinois and other nations to grow wary of French military power and push the empire to rely on mediation rather than force. It is true that Anishinaabeg stopped fighting in the early 1730s and even released Fox captives, but Illinois, in particular, continued to encourage war against Foxes. Additionally, the sources used to support the claim about a new desire for mediation in the Illinois Country are rooted not in the Fox Wars but in local disputes in the Illinois Country between French and Illinois at Cahokia, especially over land and agriculture. Kaskaskias wanted no part of these disputes. They tried to soothe tensions, which abated after Peorias and Cahokias moved to Pimiteoui. For Fox Wars, see White, *Middle Ground*, 149–175 (Indian reaction to increased violence on 169, 175); Edmunds and Peyser, *Fox Wars*; Vidal, "Les implantations françaises," 521–528; Havard and Vidal, *Histoire de l'Amérique Française*, 294–297, 382. For dispute at Cahokia, see Robert Groston de St. Ange to Bienville, 1733, C13a, 17:250–250v; J. Le Boullenger to Bienville, 28 April 1733, C13a, 17: no fol.; J. P. Mercier to Bienville, 25 April 1733, C13a, 17:287–288v; Bienville to the Minister, 22 April 1734, C13a, 18:144–145; M. J. Morgan, *Land of Big Rivers: French & Indian Illinois, 1699–1778* (Carbondale: Southern Illinois University Press, 2010), 65–67.

26. Gallay, *Indian Slave Trade*, 171 ("scourge"); "The Voyage of St. Cosme, 1698–1699," in *Early Narratives of the Northwest, 1634–1699*, ed. and trans. Louise Phelps Kellogg (New York: Scribner's, 1917), 351.

27. Patricia K. Galloway, "Henri de Tonti du Village des Chacta, 1701: The Beginning of the French Alliance," in *La Salle and His Legacy: Frenchmen and Indians in the Lower Mississippi Valley*, ed. Patricia K. Galloway (Jackson: University of Mississippi Press, 1982), 146–175; Pierre Le Moyne d'Iberville, *Iberville's Gulf Journals*, ed. and trans. Richebourg Gaillard McWilliams (Tuscaloosa: University of Alabama Press, 1981), 171–173 (all quotes).

28. Iberville, *Iberville's Gulf Journals*, 173–177.

29. Iberville, *Iberville's Gulf Journals*, 175 ("notify"); Thomas Nairne, *Nairne's Muskhogean Journals: The 1708 Expedition to the Mississippi River*, ed. Alexander Moore (Jackson: University Press of Mississippi, 1988), 37 ("slyest").

30. Bienville to Pontchartrain, 2 January 1716, in *MPA:FD*, 3:191–197 ("warriors" on 192); Charlevoix, *Histoire et description generale*, 3:408–409 ("two men" on 408).

31. Périer to Maurepas, 27 March 1731, in *MPA:FD*, 4:75; Périer to Maurepas, 10 December 1731, in *MPA:FD*, 4:108; Diron d'Artaguette to Maurepas, 21 February 1737, in *MPA:FD*, 4:142; Périer and Salmon to Maurepas, 5 December 1731, in *MPA:FD*, 4:91.

32. Joseph Zitomersky, *French Americans–Native Americans in Eighteenth-Century French Colonial Louisiana: The Population Geography of the Illinois Indians, 1670s–1760s* (Lund, Sweden: Lund University Press, 1994), 260–261.

33. *Nairne's Muskhogean Journals*, 38–41; Ethridge, *From Chicaza to Chickasaw*, 222–231; Extract of a letter from M. Chassin to Father Bobe, July 1722, in *MPA:FD*, 2:275; Gallay, *Indian Slave Trade*, 143; Ethridge, *From Chicaza to Chickasaw*, 194–216.

34. On the Natchez War, see numerous documents in *MPA:FD*, vol. 1; Antoine Simon Le Page du Pratz, *Histoire de La Louisiane*, 3 vols. (Paris: Chez de Bure, l'Aîné, Chez la Veuve Delaguette, Chez Lambert, 1758), 3:230–303; Jean-François-Benjamin Dumont de Montigny, *The Memoir of Lieutenant Dumont, 1715–1747: A Sojourner in the French Atlantic*, ed. Sayre and Carla Zecher, trans. Gordon M. Sayre (Chapel Hill: University of North Carolina Press for the Omohundro Institute of Early American History and Culture, 2012), 227–255; Daniel H. Usner, Jr., *Indians, Settlers, and Slaves in a Frontier Exchange Economy: The Lower Mississippi Valley before 1783* (Chapel Hill: University of North Carolina Press for the Institute of Early American History and Culture, 1992), 65–76; Arnaud Balvay, *La révolte des Natchez* (Paris: Le Félin, 2008); George Edward Milne, *Natchez Country: Indians, Colonists, and the Landscapes of Race in French Louisiana* (Athens: University of Georgia Press, 2015).

35. Bienville to Maurepas, 14 April 1735, in *MPA:FD*, 1:257; Atkinson, *Splendid Land, Splendid People*, 38–42.

36. Bienville to Maurepas, 20 August 1735, in *MPA:FD*, 1:266–67; Salmon to Maurepas, 27 August 1735, C13a, 20:238–239v; Bienville and Salmon to Maurepas, 16 May 1735, C13a, 20:89–89v; Bienville to Maurepas, 20 August 1735, in *MPA:FD*, 1:266; Diron d'Artaguiette to Maurepas, 21 February 1737, in *MPA:FD*, 4:147.

37. Bienville to Maurepas, 28 June 1736, in *MPA:FD*, 1:298.

38. Analyse des lettres de Bienville, May–August 1733, in *MPA:FD*, 1:199; Bienville to Maurepas, 28 June 1736, in *MPA:FD*, 1:310 ("slowness"); Bienville to Maurepas, 10 February 1736, in *MPA:FD*, 1:293–294; "Account of the Battle Fought by d'Artaguiette with the Chickasaws," 108–109.

39. Bienville to Maurepas, 20 August 1735, in *MPA:FD*, 1:265; Bienville to Maurepas, 10 February 1736, in *MPA:FD*, 1:294–295; Bienville to Maurepas, 15 February 1737, in *MPA:FD*, 1:330; "Account of the Battle Fought by d'Artaguiette with the Chickasaws," 109.

40. Bienville to Maurepas, 28 June 1736, in *MPA:FD*, 311; "Account of the Battle Fought by d'Artaguiette with the Chickasaws," 107–113; "Account of the March and the Defeat of d'Artaguiette, by Parisien," n.d., in Dunn and Dunn, *Indiana's First War*, 129. For descriptions of the fortified Chickasaw towns, see "Report of Richardville on d'Artaguiette's Expedition against the Chickasaws," in Dunn and Dunn, *Indiana's First War*, 139; Diron d'Artaguiette to Maurepas, 21 February 1737, in *MPA:FD*, 4:150.

41. "Account of the Battle Fought by d'Artaguiette with the Chickasaws," 113, 118–121; Bienville to Maurepas, 28 June 1736, in *MPA:FD*, 1:313; Crémont to Maurepas, 21 February 1737, in *MPA:FD*, 4:141. On killing captives and

blood vengeance, see James Adair, *The History of the American Indians*, ed. Kathryn E. Holland Braund (Tuscaloosa: University of Alabama Press, 2005), 188–191, 384–391; Snyder, *Slavery in Indian Country*, 80–100.

42. "An Incident of the French Chickasaw War of 1736," microfilm roll 3001, folder 65-E, Henry Sale Halbert Papers, Mississippi Department of Archives and History, Jackson, MS ("war prophet"); Crémont to Maurepas, 21 February 1737, in *MPA:FD*, 4:141; "Report of Richardville on d'Artaguiette's Expedition against the Chickasaws," in Dunn and Dunn, *Indiana's First War*, 134–135; Sam Eveleigh to Herman Verelst, 29 June 1736, in *Colonial Records of the State of Georgia*, vol. 21, *Original Papers: Correspondence, Trustees, General Oglethorpe and Others, 1735–1737*, ed. Allen D. Candler (Atlanta: Charles P. Byrd, 1910), 176. On singing, see Bienville to Maurepas, 20 December 1737, in *MPA:FD*, 3:708; Diron d'Artaguiette to Maurepas, 21 February 1737, in *MPA:FD*, 4:149; Crémont to Maurepas, 21 February 1737, in *MPA:FD*, 4:141; Eveleigh to Verelst, 29 June 1736, 21:178; Atkinson, *Splendid Land, Splendid People*, 47–48. For some of the different casualty totals for the French and allied Indians, see "Account of the March and the Defeat of d'Artaguiette," 129–131; Eveleigh to Verelst, 29 June 1736, in *CRSG*, 21:177; Atkinson, *Splendid Land, Splendid People*, 47–48.

43. Bienville to Maurepas, 2 May 1736, in *MPA:FD*, 1:295; Bienville to Maurepas, 28 June 1736, in *MPA:FD*, 1:311 ("circumstances"). For the battle of Ackia, see Bienville to Maurepas, 28 June 1736, in *MPA:FD*, 1:304–309; "Narrative of the War against the Chickasaws," ca. June 1736, in *MPA:FD*, 1:316–320; Henri de Louboey to Maurepas, 7 May 1738, in *MPA:FD*, 1:366; Atkinson, *Splendid Land, Splendid People*, 51–60.

44. "An Incident of the French Chickasaw War of 1736"; Bill Anoatubby, 2017 State of the Nation Address, 7 October 2017, available at https://governor.chickasaw.net/News/Speeches/2017-State-of-the-Nation-Address.aspx ("defense" and "powerful"); Bienville to Maurepas, 5 September 1736, in *MPA:FD*, 1:327.

45. Mingo Ouma specifically named Tamaroas and Piankashaws, which seem to be the names that he used to identify all Illinois and Miamis, respectively; Diron d'Artaguiette to Maurepas, 21 February 1737, in *MPA:FD*, 4:147, 148; Mingo Ouma, "Nations amies et ennemies des Tchicachas" (copy), September 1737, C13a, vol. 22, fol. 67.

46. Bienville to Maurepas, 15 February 1737, in *MPA:FD*, 1:331; Bienville to Maurepas, 5 September 1736, in *MPA:FD*, 1:328 ("avoid").

47. Deliette, "Memoir," 381–332; Wayne E. Lee, "Peace Chiefs and Blood Revenge: Patterns of Restraint in Native American Warfare, 1500–1800," *Journal of Military History* 71 (July 2007): 722–728; Liste des partis sauvages du Canada qui ont passé au poste de Peanquishas pour aller sur les Chicachas, 24 April–8 September 1737, C11a, 67:212–213; Paul-Joseph Le Moyne de Longueuil to Rouillé, 21 April 1752, in *WHC*, 18:104–117; Ange Duquesne de Menneville to Rouillé, 31 October 1753, in *IHC*, 29:844–845.

48. "Account of the Battle Fought by D'Artaguiette with the Chickasaws," 118–121; Drouet de Richardville, "Report of Richardville on d'Artaguiette's Expedition against the Chickasaws," in Dunn and Dunn, *Indiana's First War*, 132–135; Beauharnois to the Minister, 16 October 1737 (extract), in *WHC*, 17:276.

49. Salmon to Maurepas, 4 May 1740, in *MPA:FD*, 1:442 ("leveling"); Bienville to Maurepas, 6 May 1740, in *MPA:FD*, 1:458 ("restrain").

50. Louboey to Maurepas, 10 May 1740, in *MPA:FD*, 1:462 ("irritated"); Jean-Paul Mercier to [Beauharnois?], 27 May 1741, C11a, 75:214v ("failure"). For examples of Chickasaw and Cherokee attacks, see Louboey to Maurepas, 23 June 1740, in *MPA:FD*, 4:168–169; Jadart de Beauchamp to Maurepas, 25 April 1741, in *MPA:FD*, 4:182–183; Louboey to Maurepas, 18 July 1741, in *MPA:FD*, 4:188; Résumé d'une lettre de Hocquart datée du 3 octobre 1741, C11a, 78:375; Salmon to Maurepas, 4 October 1741, in *MPA:FD*, 4:192; "Journal of Antoine Bonnefoy, 1741–1742," trans. J. Franklin Jameson, in *Travels in the American Colonies*, ed. Newton D. Mereness (New York: Macmillan, 1916), 241–255.

51. Jean-Jacques Macarty Mactigue to Vaudreuil de Cavagnial, 2 September 1752, in *IHC*, 29:654–655, 663–665; Vaudreuil de Cavagnial to Rouillé, 28 September 1752, in *IHC*, 29:726–727; Jean-Bernard Bossu, *Travels in the Interior of North America, 1751–1762*, ed. and trans. Seymour Feller (Norman: University of Oklahoma Press, 1962), 78–80; Raymond E. Hauser, "The Fox Raid of 1752: Defensive Warfare and the Decline of the Illinois Indian Tribe," *Illinois Historical Journal* 86 (Winter 1993): 216–218. The clearest statement of Macarty's complicity in the Fox-led attack is from a 1758 report by Governor Louis Billouart, chevalier de Kerlerec; Kerlerec, Memoir on Indians, 12 December 1758, in *MPA:FD*, 5:204. For other indirect or suggestive evidence, see Michel Baudouin to Abbé de l'Isle Dieu, 28 June 1754, in *IHC*, 29:874; Macarty to Vaudreuil de Cavagnial, 2 September 1752, in *IHC*, 29:680, 685; Duquesne to Rouillé, 13 October 1754 (extract), in *NYCD*, 10:263; Hauser, "Fox Raid of 1752," 220–222; James A. Clifton, *The Prairie People: Continuity and Change in Potawatomi Indian Culture, 1665–1965* (1977; exp. ed., Iowa City: University of Iowa Press, 1998), 97. A decade earlier, Canadian governor Beauharnois had also proposed encouraging Sauks, Foxes, and other nations to attack the Illinois if they continued to warm up to the British; Beauharnois to the minister, 12 October 1742, in *WHC*, 17:430.

52. Longueuil to Rouillé, 18 August 1752, in *IHC*, 29:652–653; Macarty to Vaudreuil de Cavagnial, 2 September 1752, in *IHC*, 29:680–681; François-Marie le Marchand de Ligneris to Vaudreuil de Cavagnial, 3 October 1752, in *IHC*, 29:733; Duquesne to Jean-Baptiste Machault d'Arnouville, 10 September 1754, in *IHC*, 29:904–905; "A Journal of Captain William Trent to the Twightwee [Miami] Indians, 1752," 6 July 1752, in *Journal of William Trent from Logstown to Pickawillany, A.D. 1752*, ed. Alfred T. Goodma

(Cincinnati: Robert Clarke, 1871), 86–88; R. David Edmunds, "Pickawillany: French Military Power versus British Economics," *Western Pennsylvania Historical Magazine* 58 (April 1975): 181–183; White, *Middle Ground,* 230–231; Crouch, *Nobility Lost,* 41–46.

53. Vaudreuil de Cavagnial to Maurepas, 28 October 1745, in *MPA:FD,* 4:245 ("acts" and "might"); Beauharnois to the Minister, 12 October 1742, in *WHC,* 17:429; Newbigging, "History of the French-Ottawa Alliance," 351–354; "Paroles de M. le marquis de Beauharnois . . . ," 8 July 1740, C11a, 74:23v; Résumé des lettres de Beauharnois . . . , January 1739, C11a, 72:291v–293; Message of Beauharnois to the Hurons of Detroit, 12 June 1741, in *WHC,* 17:344–345; Beauharnois to Father de la Richardie, 14 June 1741 (copy), in *WHC,* 17:350; Beauharnois to the Minister, 15 September 1742, in *WHC,* 17:414; "Memorandum of what occurred in the Affair of the hurons of Detroit . . . 12th of August, 1738, to the 12th of June, 1741," in *WHC,* 17:279–288; Sturtevant, "Jealous Neighbors," 138–143, 175–245; Richard White, *The Roots of Dependency: Subsistence, Environment, and Social Change among the Choctaws, Pawnees, and Navajos* (Lincoln: University of Nebraska Press, 1983), 54–63; Patricia Galloway, "Choctaw Factionalism and Civil War, 1746–1750," in *Pre-removal Choctaw History: Exploring New Paths,* ed. Greg O'Brien (Norman: University of Oklahoma Press, 2008), 70–102; Carson, *Searching for the Bright Path,* 30–33; Greg O'Brien, "Quieting the Ghosts: How the Choctaws and Chickasaws Stopped Fighting," in *The Native South: New Histories and Enduring Legacies,* ed. Tim Alan Garrison and Greg O'Brien (Norman: University of Oklahoma Press, 2017), 47–69.

54. Caldwell, "Chickasaw Threat," 478–479 ("Frenchman is a dog"); "Occurrences in Canada during the year 1747–1748," in *NYCD,* 10:143 ("his poverty"), 156; Vaudreuil de Cavagnial to Maurepas, 28 December 1744, in *MPA:FD,* 4:230 ("indigence"); Vaudreuil de Cavagnial to Maurepas, 22 March 1747, in *IHC,* 29:15; D. Peter MacLeod, "Une conspiration générale: The Exercise of Power by the Amerindians of the Great Lakes during the War of the Austrian Secession, 1747–1748" (Ph.D. diss., University of Ottawa, 1992), 57–67; Galloway, "Choctaw Factionalism and Civil War," 78–79.

55. Vaudreuil de Cavagnial to Maurepas, 19 September 1747, in *IHC,* 29: 33–34; Vaudreuil de Cavagnial to Maurepas, 20 March 1748, in *MPA:FD,* 4:315–16; Maurepas to Vaudreuil de Cavagnial, 4 November 1748, in *IHC,* 29:76; Maurepas to Claude de Bertet, 23 December 1748, in *IHC,* 29:81; Roland Michel Barrin de La Galisonnière to Rouillé, 26 June 1749, in *IHC,* 29:99 ("excellent"); Bienville to Maurepas, 29 June 1736, in *MPA:FD,* 3:688 ("brave"); Jacques-Pierre de Taffanel de La Jonquière to Rouillé, 25 September 1751, in *IHC,* 29:365.

56. Macarty Mactigue to Rouillé, 1 June 1752, in *IHC,* 29:644 (quote); Duquesne to Rouillé, 31 October 1753, in *IHC,* 29:846.

57. Macarty to Vaudreuil de Cavagnial, 20 January 1752, in *IHC,* 29:433–436, 455–459; Alexis F. X. de Guyenne to Vaudreuil de Cavagnial, 10

September 1752, in *IHC*, 29:713; Louis St. Ange de Bellerive to Vaudreuil de Cavagnial, 28 February 1752, in *IHC*, 484–485; Longueuil to Rouillé, 21 April 1752, in *NYCD*, 10:247 (quote); Robert Michael Morrissey, *Empire by Collaboration: Indians, Colonists, and Governments in Colonial Illinois Country* (Philadelphia: University of Pennsylvania Press, 2015), 190–192.

58. Yves Zoltvany, *Philippe de Rigaud de Vaudreuil: Governor of New France, 1703–1725* (Toronto: McClelland and Stewart, 1974); S. Dale Standen, "Beauharnois de la Boische, Charles de, Marquis de Beauharnois," in *DCB*; White, *Middle Ground*, 202–203. Louisiana fared better in this period, with Philippe de Rigaud de Vaudreuil's son serving as governor for a decade from 1743 to 1753, following the decade-long fourth term of Bienville.

59. White, *Middle Ground*, 203–206; Journal of Conrad Weiser, 8 September 1748, in *CRP*, 5:350.

60. Anson, *Miami Indians*, 40–43; R. David Edmunds, "Old Briton," in *American Indian Leaders: Studies in Diversity*, ed. R. David Edmunds (Lincoln: University of Nebraska Press, 1980), 2–5; "Occurrences in Canada during the year 1747–1748," in *NYCD*, 10:140; Edmunds, "Pickawillany," 171.

61. Nicholas B. Wainwright, *George Croghan, Wilderness Diplomat* (Chapel Hill: University of North Carolina Press for the Institute of Early American History and Culture, 1959), 29–31; Edmunds, "Pickawillany," 175–179; Fred Anderson, *Crucible of War: The Seven Years' War and the Fate of Empire in British North America, 1754–1766* (New York: Vintage, 2001), 25–30; Albert T. Volwiler, *George Croghan and the Westward Movement, 1741–1782* (Cleveland: Arthur H. Clark, 1926), 17–80; Examinations of Morris Turner and Ralph Kilgore, [1750], in *CRP*, 5:483.

62. Maurepas to Vaudreuil de Cavagnial, 23 February 1748, in *IHC*, 29:49 ("occasion"); Maurepas to Roland-Michel Barrin de La Galissonière, 23 February 1748, in *WHC*, 18:12; Vaudreuil to Maurepas, 30 August 1744, LO 9, vol. 1, fol. 33v–34, VP; Vaudreuil de Cavagnial to Maurepas, 4 November 1745, LO 9, vol. 1, fol. 67v–68v, VP; Vaudreuil de Cavagnial to Maurepas, 10 November 1745, LO 9, vol. 1, fol. 70v–71, VP; Vaudreuil de Cavagnial to the Court, 8 April 1747, LO 9, vol. 2, fol. 30–31, VP; Vaudreuil de Cavagnial to Maurepas, 22 March 1747, in *IHC*, 29:15–16; Vaudreuil de Cavagnial to Maurepas, 8 April 1747, in *IHC*, 29:21; Vaudreuil de Cavagnial to Maurepas, 24 May 1748, in *IHC*, 29:71; Vaudreuil de Cavagnial to Rouillé, 28 September 1752, in *IHC*, 29:726; M. le Bailly Mesnager, "Memoir on Louisiana," in *IHC*, 29:133 ("living among them").

63. Tanner, *Atlas of Great Lakes Indian History*, 40–41; Reports to Raymond, March–April 1750, in *IHC*, 29:176–177; La Jonquière to Rouillé, 25 September 1751, in *IHC*, 29:366–367; De Guyenne to Vaudreuil de Cavagnial, 10 September 1752, in *IHC*, 29:719; Jean-Baptiste Benoist de St. Clair to Raymond, 11 February 1750, in *IHC*, 29:164–165; Longueuil to Rouillé, 21 April 1752, in *NYCD*, 10:248.

64. Longueuil to Rouillé, 21 April 1752, in *NYCD*, 10:248; La Jonquière to Rouillé, 17 September 1751, in *IHC*, 29:349; Macarty to Vaudreuil de Cavagnial, 18 March 1752, in *IHC*, 29:518 (quote).

65. All reports from Longueuil to Rouillé, 21 April 1752, in *NYCD*, 10:246–248.

66. Kerlerec, Memoir on Indians, in *MPA:FD*, 5:204. For Langlade, see Michael A. McDonnell, "Charles-Michel Mouet de Langlade: Warrior, Soldier, and Intercultural 'Window' on the Sixty Years' War for the Great Lakes," in *The Sixty Years War for the Great Lakes, 1754–1814*, ed. David Curtis Skaggs and Larry L. Nelson (East Lansing: Michigan State University Press, 2001), 79–103; McDonnell, *Masters of Empire*, 3–7, 149–194; Paul Trap, "Mouet de Langlade, Charles-Michel," in *DCB*; Rushforth, *Bonds of Alliance*, 287–290.

67. White, *Middle Ground*, 234–236, 242.

68. Rouillé to Duquesne, 15 May 1752, in *WHC*, 18:118–122; Memorandum from the King to . . . Sieur de Vaudreuil de Cavagnal, 22 March 1755, in *WHC*, 18:151–153; White, *Middle Ground*, 204–208; Eric Hinderaker, *Elusive Empires: Constructing Colonialism in the Ohio Valley, 1673–1800* (Cambridge: Cambridge University Press, 1997), 43–44, 139; Anderson, *Crucible of War*, 25–26, 31–32; W. J. Eccles, *The Canadian Frontier, 1534–1760*, rev. ed. (Albuquerque: University of New Mexico Press, 1983), 160–163.

69. Anderson, *Crucible of War*, 5–73 (Tanaghrisson quote on 6). Who killed Jumonville and how has been a matter of dispute since 1754; Francis Jennings, *Empire of Fortune: Crowns, Colonies, and Tribes in the Seven Years War in America* (New York: Norton, 1988), 68–70.

70. Paul E. Kopperman, *Braddock at the Monongahela* (Pittsburgh: University of Pittsburgh Press, 1977), 25–27; Anderson, *Crucible of War*, 97, 99; Ian Steele, *Betrayals: Fort William Henry and the Massacre* (New York: Oxford University Press, 1990), 78–80; White, *Middle Ground*, 236–246; Michael N. McConnell, *A Country Between: The Upper Ohio Valley and Its Peoples, 1724–1774* (Lincoln: University of Nebraska Press, 1992), 120–121; Ian K. Steele, "The Shawnees and the English: Captives and War, 1753–1765," in *The Boundaries between Us: Natives and Newcomers along the Frontiers of the Old Northwest Territory, 1750–1850*, ed. Daniel P. Barr (Kent, OH: Kent State University Press, 2006), 1–13; Daniel P. Barr, "'This Land Is Ours and Not Yours,'" in Barr, *Boundaries between Us*, 25–40; Abstract of Despatches from Canada, [1756], in *NYCD*, 10:423–424 ("avenge"); Vaudreuil de Cavagnial to Machault, 8 August 1756, in *NYCD*, 10:437; John Armstrong to Robert Hunter Morris, 20 August 1756, in *CRP*, 7:232; Kerlerec to the Minister, 23 January 1758 [*sic*: 1757], C13a, 40:24–25v; David L. Preston, *The Texture of Contact: European and Settler Communities on the Frontiers of Iroquoia, 1667–1783* (Lincoln: University of Nebraska Press, 2009), 173–174; Anderson, *Crucible of War*, 162–163; Abstract of Despatches from America, [1756], in *NYCD*, 10:486. An undated letter, ca. 1757, seems to garble the details of the Miami attacks on South Carolina and the Shawnee-Delaware-Illinois

capture of Fort Granville; Reverend Claude Godfroy Cocquard to his brother, n.d., in *NYCD*, 10:530, 533. I have found only one instance in which Illinois warriors joined French military expeditions between 1740 and 1756. In July 1746 during King George's War, ten Illinois visited Montreal as France prepared a campaign to Lake Champlain and seem to have spent the winter in Canada; Extrait des différens mouvements qui se sont faite à Montréal à L'occasion de la guerre depuis le mois de Décembre 1745, jusques au mois d'Aoust 1746, C11a, 86:305v–306; Journal of Occurrences in Canada, 1746, 1747, in *NYCD*, 10:91. Some secondary sources claim that Miamis were present at Braddock's Defeat, but I have found no primary sources to support that assertion. For example, see Louise Phelps Kellogg, *The French Régime in Wisconsin and the Northwest* (Madison: State Historical Society of Wisconsin, 1925), 425; Anson, *Miami Indians*, 54; David Preston, *Braddock's Defeat: The Battle of the Monongahela and the Road to Revolution* (New York: Oxford University Press, 2015), 150. Some of this confusion seems to stem from a document from 1756 in which French officials at Fort Duquesne reported that their Indian allies "on the continent" included "a number of Illinois" and "about 250 Miamis and Outaganons [Weas]." This report dates from after Shawnees called their allies to join them in attacking the British and more than eight months after Braddock's Defeat; Abstract of Despatches from Canada, [1756], in *NYCD*, 10:424.

71. "Tableau des sauvages qui se trouvent à l'armée du marquis de Montcalm, le 28 juillet 1757 . . . ," in *Collection des manuscrits du maréchal de Lévis*, ed. H. R. Casgrain, 12 vols. (Montreal: L.-J. Demers and Frère, 1889–1895), 7:264–266; "Detail of the Campaign of 1757," *NYCD*, 10:629–630; "Journal de Niagara du mois de Juin au mois d'Aout 1757," in Casgrain, *Collection des manuscrits du maréchal de Lévis*, 11:98–99; D. Peter MacLeod, "Microbes and Muskets: Smallpox and the Participation of the Amerindian Allies of New France in the Seven Years' War," *Ethnohistory* 39 (Winter 1992): 45, 52, 63n5; Mémoire du Canada, in *RAPQ*, vol. *1924–1925*, 154–155; McConnell, *Country Between*, 126–138; Sami Lakomäki, *Gathering Together: The Shawnee People through Diaspora and Nationhood, 1600–1870* (New Haven, CT: Yale University Press, 2014), 72–95; Nicholas B. Wainwright, ed., "George Croghan's Journal, April 3, 1759 to April [30] 1763," *Pennsylvania Magazine of History and Biography* 71 (October 1947): 335–340, 343 ("remain").

72. Macarty to Kerlerec, 30 August 1759 (copy), C13a, 41:103v ("spectators"); Charles-Philippe Aubry, Account of the Illinois Country, 1763, in *IHC*, 10:4 ("idle"); Vaudreuil de Cavagnial to Berryer, 30 March 1759, in *NYCD*, 10:948 ("neither"). In 1759, Aubry had traveled from the Illinois Country to Fort Duquesne, arriving with 600 Indians whom he "had engaged along the route to follow him." It seems that no Illinois Indians accompanied him; [Pierre] Pouchot, *Mémoires sur la derniere guerre de l'Amérique septentrionale, entre la France et l'Angleterre*, 3 vols. (Yverdon, [Switzerland], 1781), 1:170–171, 2:91. Although many scholars have identified the recurring outbreaks of smallpox

as a key factor in discouraging Native peoples from backing France, especially after the defeat of Fort William Henry in 1757, many Indians continued to fight alongside French troops until 1760, a sharp contrast with the largely absent Illinois and Wabash River Miamis. On smallpox and its effects, see White, *Middle Ground*, 246; Anderson, *Crucible of War*, 199, 236; Susan Sleeper-Smith, *Indian Women and French Men: Rethinking Cultural Encounter in the Western Great Lakes* (Amherst: University of Massachusetts Press, 2001), 55–56; McDonnell, *Masters of Empire*, 188–191, 195–199; Gregory Evans Dowd, *Groundless: Rumors, Legends, and Hoaxes on the Early American Frontier* (Baltimore: Johns Hopkins University Press, 2015), 47–57; MacLeod, "Microbes and Muskets," 42–64.

73. "Tableau des sauvages qui se trouvent à l'armée du marquis de Montcalm, le 28 juillet 1757 . . . ," in Casgrain, *Collection des manuscrits du maréchal de Lévis*, 7:264–266; MacLeod, "Microbes and Muskets," 45, 52, 63 n.75; McDonnell, *Masters of Empire*, 195–199; Conseil tenu le 28 Novembre 1760 au Detroit . . . , C11a, 105:358–358v; Journal du Marquis de Montcalm, 28 July 1757, in Casgrain, *Collection des manuscrits de maréchal de Lévis*, 7:263 ("warning"), 267 ("contagious").

74. Paul W. Mapp, *The Elusive West and the Contest for Empire, 1713–1763* (Chapel Hill: University of North Carolina Press for the Institute of Early American History and Culture, 2011), 359–427; Anderson, *Crucible of War*, 503–506; Colin G. Calloway, *The Scratch of a Pen: 1763 and the Transformation of North America* (New York: Oxford University Press, 2006); Crouch, *Nobility Lost*, 126–177.

4. A New World?

1. A Council held at the House of Mons. de Neyon de Villiers . . . by Pondiack, 15 and 17 April 1764 (translated copy), in Robert Farmar to Thomas Gage, 21 December 1764, vol. 28, TGP. I follow the work of Gregory Evans Dowd in using the terms "nativists" and "nativism" to refer to the movements and ideologies of Native peoples who promoted pan-Indian resistance against colonialism; Dowd, *A Spirited Resistance: The North American Indian Struggle for Unity, 1745–1815* (Baltimore: Johns Hopkins University Press, 1992), especially xvii–xxii.

2. [William Franklin], Reasons for Establishing a Colony in the Illinois, 1766, in *IHC*, 11:248–257 (quotes on 248, 249, 256); Articles of Agreement of the Illinois Company, 29 March 1766, in *IHC*, 11:203–204.

3. Plan of Forts and Garrisons proposed for the Security of North America, 1763, in *IHC*, 10:5–11; Charles Wyndham, Earl of Egremont's Memoir, 26 June 1762, in *IHC*, 27:435–437; Egremont to Comte de Choiseul, 10 July 1762, in *IHC*, 27:450–451; Max Savelle, *George Morgan: Colony Builder* (New York: Columbia University Press, 1932), 18–20. For the Illinois

Company, see Savelle, *George Morgan*, 57–62, 64; Jack M. Sosin, *Whitehall and the Wilderness: The Middle West in British Colonial Policy, 1760–1775* (Lincoln: University of Nebraska Press, 1961), 140–145; Eric Hinderaker, *Elusive Empires: Constructing Colonialism in the Ohio Valley, 1673–1800* (Cambridge: Cambridge University Press, 1997), 166–167; Patrick Griffin, *American Leviathan: Empire, Nation, and Revolutionary Frontier* (New York: Hill and Wang, 2007), 53–56.

4. Sir William Johnson to Sir Jeffery Amherst, 14 August 1762, in *PSWJ*, 3:859; Richard White, *The Middle Ground: Indians, Empires and Republics in the Great Lakes Region, 1650–1815* (Cambridge: Cambridge University Press, 1991), 112, 180–182; Gregory Evans Dowd, *War under Heaven: Pontiac, the Indian Nations, and the British Empire* (Baltimore: Johns Hopkins University Press, 2002), 54–89; Wilbur R. Jacobs, *Wilderness Politics and Indian Gifts: The Northern Colonial Frontier, 1748–1763* (1950; paperback ed., Lincoln: Bison Books, 1966).

5. Fred Anderson, *Crucible of War: The Seven Years' War and the Fate of Empire in British North America, 1754–1766* (New York: Vintage, 2001), 275–279.

6. Paul Kelton, "The British and Indian War: Cherokee Power and the Fate of Empire in North America," *WMQ* 69 (October 2012): 763–792 (quote on 789).

7. George Croghan to Johnson, 12 October 1761, in *PSWJ*, 3:551; Alan Taylor, *The Divided Ground: Indians, Settlers, and the Northern Borderland of the American Revolution* (New York: Knopf, 2006), 47–48; James Taylor Carson, "Molly Brant: From Clan Mother to Loyalist Chief," in *Sifters: Native American Women's Lives*, ed. Theda Perdue (New York: Oxford University Press, 2001), 48–59; Barbara Graymont, "Konwatsitsiaienni," in *DCB*; Daniel Claus to Frederick Haldimand, 30 August 1779, in *Indian Affairs Papers: American Revolution*, ed. Maryly B. Penrose (Franklin Park, NJ: Liberty Bell Associates, 1981), 233 ("one word").

8. Colin G. Calloway, *White People, Indians, and Highlanders: Tribal Peoples and Colonial Encounters in Scotland and America* (New York: Oxford University Press, 2008), 151–152; Theda Perdue, *Cherokee Women: Gender and Culture Change, 1700–1835* (Lincoln: University of Nebraska Press, 1998), 82; James Grant to Amherst, 19 October 1760, Box 32, folder 2, James Grant of Ballindalloch Papers, LC ("protected & Delivered"); *South Carolina Gazette*, 23 September 1761, quoted in Grace Steele Woodward, *The Cherokees* (Norman: University of Oklahoma Press, 1963), 79 ("All the Indians").

9. Larry L. Nelson, *A Man of Distinction among Them: Alexander McKee and the Ohio Country Frontier, 1754–1799* (Kent, OH: Kent State University Press, 1999), 24–28, 31–47; Johnson to Alexander McKee, 1 December 1763, in *PSWJ*, 4:256.

10. Calloway, *White People, Indians, and Highlanders*, 152–154; Henry Stuart to John Stuart, 25 August 1776, in *Colonial Records of North Carolina*, ed. William Saunders, 10 vols. (Raleigh, NC: P. M. Hale, 1886–1890), 10:767 ("lived so long"); Perdue, *Cherokee Women*, 81–85.

11. Amherst to Johnson, 12 December 1761, in *PSWJ*, 3:594; Amherst to Johnson, 11 June 1761, in *PSWJ*, 10:284; Amherst to Johnson, 26 December 1761, in *PSWJ*, 10:348.
12. Croghan to Johnson, 22 December 1759, in *PSWJ*, 10:132; Croghan to Johnson, 25 January 1760, *PSWJ*, 10:134.
13. Journal and Report of Thomas Hutchins, 4 April–24 September 1762, in *PSWJ*, 10:523–524, 526–528.
14. Amherst to Johnson, 9 August 1761, in *PSWJ*, 3:515; Amherst to Johnson, 9 August 1761, in *PSWJ*, 3:520; Amherst to Johnson, 11 July 1761, in *PSWJ*, 3:506–507; Johnson to Amherst, 24 September 1762, in *PSWJ*, 3:884; Croghan to Johnson, 10 December 1762, in *PSWJ*, 3:964.
15. George Washington, "Journey to the French Commander: Narrative," in *The Papers of George Washington Digital Edition* (Charlottesville: University of Virginia Press, Rotunda, 2008), available at http://rotunda.upress.virginia .edu.proxyiub.uits.iu.edu/founders/GEWN-01-01-02-0003-0002 (accessed 21 December 2016); Charles Frederick Post, "From Philadelphia to the Ohio . . . , July 15–September 22, 1758," in *Early Western Travels, 1748–1846*, ed. Reuben G. Thwaites, 32 vols. (Cleveland: Arthur H. Clark, 1904–1906), 1:216 (quote, emphasis in the original). For examples of British assurances about land, see William Johnson, Niagara and Detroit Proceedings, July–September 1761, in *PSWJ*, 3:429, 478; Amherst to Johnson, 11 July 1761, in *PSWJ*, 3:506; Amherst to Johnson, 9 August 1761, in *PSWJ*, 3:515; William Johnson, Indian Proceedings, 21–28 April 1762, in *PSWJ*, 3:701–702; Johnson to Earl of Egremont, [May] 1762, in *PSWJ*, 10:462.
16. Croghan to Johnson, 24 April 1763 (extract), in *PSWJ*, 10:660; Dowd, *War under Heaven*, 36–37; Sami Lakomäki, *Gathering Together: The Shawnee People through Diaspora and Nationhood, 1600–1870* (New Haven, CT: Yale University Press, 2014), 88–92; Johnson to Croghan, 15 May 1762, in *PSWJ*, 3:741; Johnson to Amherst, 19 May 1762, in *PSWJ*, 3:743; Amherst to Johnson, 17 October 1762, in *PSWJ*, 3:904.
17. Johnson to Lords of Trade, 1 August 1762, in *PSWJ*, 3:851 ("Colonies"); Croghan to Johnson, 10 December 1762, in *PSWJ*, 3:964 ("Intensions").
18. Gregory Evans Dowd provides the best account of the war; Dowd, *War under Heaven*, 114–173. See also Howard H. Peckham, *Pontiac and the Indian Uprising* (Princeton, NJ: Princeton University Press, 1947), 92–264; Francis Jennings, *Empire of Fortune: Crowns, Colonies, and Tribes in the Seven Years' War in America* (New York: Norton, 1988), 438–453; White, *Middle Ground*, 269–314; Anderson, *Crucible of War*, 535–553, 617–632; David Dixon, *Never Come to Peace Again: Pontiac's Uprising and the Fate of the British Empire in North America* (Norman: University of Oklahoma Press, 2005); Colin G. Calloway, *The Scratch of a Pen: 1763 and the Transformation of North America* (New York: Oxford University Press, 2006), 66–91. For maps of the events, see Helen Hornbeck Tanner, ed., *Atlas of Great Lakes Indian History* (Norman: University of Oklahoma Press, 1987), 48–49.

19. Dowd, *A Spirited Resistance*, 27–33; James Kenny Journal, 15 October 1762, in "Journal of James Kenny, 1761–1763 (continued)," ed. John W. Jordan, *Pennsylvania Magazine of History and Biography* 37 (1913): 171 (quotes); Pierre Joseph Neyon de Villiers to Jean-Jacques Blaise d'Abbadie, 1 December 1763, in *IHC*, 10:51.

20. Gage to Lord Halifax, 14 April 1764, in *IHC*, 10:241; Gage to Johnson, 2 July 1764 (copy), vol. 21, TGP; Gage to Henry Gladwin, 23 April 1764 (copy), vol. 17, TGP (quote); Dowd, *War Under Heaven*, 8–9.

21. Dowd, *War under Heaven*, 22–53; "Journals of the Travels of Jonathan Carver," 26 June 1766, in *The Journals of Jonathan Carver and Related Document, 1766–1770*, ed. John Parker (St. Paul: Minnesota Historical Society, 1976), 66; Peckham, *Pontiac and the Indian Uprising*, 15–18.

22. Susan Sleeper-Smith, *Indian Women and French Men: Rethinking Cultural Encounter in the Western Great Lakes* (Amherst: University of Massachusetts Press, 2001), 23–37; Tracy Neal Leavelle, *The Catholic Calumet: Colonial Conversions in French and Indian North America* (Philadelphia: University of Pennsylvania Press, 2012); Dowd, *War under Heaven*, 109–112.

23. Gage to Gladwin, 10 June 1764 (copy), vol. 19, TGP; Edward Jenkins to Gladwin, 29 July 1763, in *IHC*, 10:13; Journal of d'Abbadie, [late February] 1764, in *IHC*, 10:175; Neyon de Villiers to d'Abbadie, 1 December 1763, in *IHC*, 10:50–52, 54–56 (quotes on 51 and 56).

24. Reponse de Pondiac a une Parole et un Collier envoyé par Monsr. Hay . . . , 10 May 1768, in George Turnbull to Gage, 14 June 1768, vol. 77, TGP.

25. Council held at the House of Mons. de Neyon de Villiers (quotes); Intelligence from Detroit, 9 June 1764, in Gladwin to Gage, 11 June 1764, vol. 20, TGP; Neyon de Villiers to Arthur Loftus, 20 April 1764, in *IHC*, 10:244.

26. Copy of a Council held at Illinois, 7 April 1765, in Farmar to Gage, 1 June 1765, vol. 37, TGP, transcript in Illinois Indians, 1765, OV-GLEA. In the summer of 1764, the Quapaws killed one British soldier, probably a deserter from a British convoy that spring. James Campbell to Gage, 20 August 1764, vol. 23, TGP. See also Gage to Campbell, 16 November 1764 (copy), vol. 26, TGP; Gage to Henry Bouquet, 20 December 1764 (copy), vol. 28, TGP; Thomas Gage, Instructions for Alexander Frazer, 30 December 1764 (copy), vol. 29, TGP.

27. Anderson, *Crucible of War*, 618–619; Loftus to Gage, 26 February 1764, vol. 14, TGP ("few"); Journal of d'Abbadie, 1763–1764, in *IHC*, 10:162–204 ("difficulties" on 172); "Loftus Attempts to Ascend the River," in *IHC*, 10:229–230, 234–235; Loftus to Gage, 19 April 1764, vol. 17, TGP; Gage to Haldimand, 27 May 1764, in *IHC*, 10:250. According to French reports, the British did fire their swivel guns at the Tunica village during their return to New Orleans.

28. Address of d'Abbadie to the Tunica Indians, 14 July 1764, in *IHC*, 10: 285–287 ("when I learned" on 285); "Loftus Attempts to Ascend the River," in *IHC*, 10:236.

29. James Stanley Goddard, "Journal of a Voyage, 1766–1767," in Parker, *Journals of Jonathan Carver and Related Document*, 185 ("perpetual war"); An Indian Conference, [9–11 August 1763], in *PSWJ*, 10:781 ("resolved"); Gage to Lord Halifax, 21 May 1764, in *IHC*, 10:238–249; Gage to Johnson, 24 June 1764, in *IHC*, 10:268; John Stuart to Gage, 29 April 1764, vol. 25, TGP; Alexander Fraser to Gage, 27 April 1765, vol. 35, TGP, transcript in Illinois Indians, 1765, OV-GLEA. On Fox conflicts with Anishinaabeg and others, see White, *Middle Ground*, 149–175; R. David Edmunds and Joseph L. Peyser, *The Fox Wars: The Mesquakie Challenge to New France* (Norman: University of Oklahoma Press, 1993); Brett Rushforth, *Bonds of Alliance: Indigenous and Atlantic Slaveries in New France* (Chapel Hill: University of North Carolina Press for the Omohundro Institute of Early American History and Culture, 2012), 199–205, 214–221; Michael Witgen, *Infinity of Nations: How the Native New World Shaped Early North America* (Philadelphia: University of Pennsylvania Press, 2012), 280–283.

30. Dowd, *War under Heaven*, 153–168; Peckham, *Pontiac and the Indian Uprising*, 244–264; White, *Middle Ground*, 291–295; Dixon, *Never Come to Peace Again*, 227–243; "Loftus Attempts to Ascend the River," in *IHC*, 10:230–231.

31. Gage, Instructions for Alexander Frazer; Gage, Instructions for George Croghan, 30 December 1764 (copy), vol. 29, TGP.

32. Calloway, *White People, Indians, and Highlanders*, 151–152; John Stuart, Instructions to Charles Stuart, 1 November 1764 (copy), in Stuart to Gage, 19 November 1764, vol. 27, TGP.

33. George Croghan, Journal, 1765, in Thwaites, *Early Western Travels*, 1:138–146; Croghan to McKee, 13 July 1765, in John Reed to Gage, 2 August 1765, vol. 40, TGP, transcript in Illinois Indians, 1765, OV-GLEA (quote); Minutes of a council with the Ouiatanons, Kecopoes, Mascoutens, and Ottawas, 13 July 1765, in Croghan to McKee, 13 July 1765, vol. 40, TGP, transcript in Illinois Indians, 1765, OV-GLEA; Croghan to Gage, 17 August 1765, vol. 41, TGP, transcript in Illinois Indians, 1765, OV-GLEA.

34. Copy of a Council held at Illinois, 7 April 1765, in Farmar to Gage, 1 June 1765, vol. 37, TGP, transcript in Illinois Indians, 1765, OV-GLEA. On declining Illinois population, see Emily J. Blasingham, "The Depopulation of the Illinois Indians, Part 2, Concluded," *Ethnohistory* 3 (Autumn 1956): 361–412; Rushforth, *Bonds of Alliance*, 89. Emily J. Blasingham estimates Illinois population as 6,250 people around 1700 and 1,900 in 1763. Joseph Zitomersky estimates a similar decline but a larger population (8,300 Illinois in 1701; 2,400 in 1765); Blasingham, "Depopulation of the Illinois Indians, Part 2," 367, 370; Zitomersky, *French Americans–Native Americans in Eighteenth-Century French Colonial Louisiana: The Population Geography of the Illinois Indians, 1670s–1760s* (Lund, Sweden: Lund University Press, 1994), 261, 321.

35. Calloway, *Scratch of a Pen*, 92–98.

36. Calloway, *Scratch of a Pen*, 97–100; John Borrows, "Wampum at Niagara: The Royal Proclamation, Canadian Legal History, and Self-Government," in *Aboriginal and Treaty Rights in Canada*, ed. Michael Asche (Vancouver: University of British Columbia, 1997), 155–172, 262; Croghan to McKee, 3 August 1765, in Reed to Gage, 24 August 1765, vol. 41, TGP, transcript, Kickapoo Indians, 1761–1765, OV-GLEA ("Success").

37. Address of D'Abbadie to the Tunica Indians, 14 July 1764, in *IHC*, 10: 285–287 ("ungrateful" on 286); Campbell to Gage, 10 December 1764, vol. 28, TGP; Campbell to George Johnstone, 12 December 1764, in *MPA:ED*, 267; Gage to Campbell, 16 November 1764 (copy), vol. 26, TGP; John Oliphant, *Peace and War on the Anglo-Cherokee Frontier* (Baton Rouge: Louisiana State University Press, 2001), 201–205; Calloway, *Scratch of a Pen*, 100–108; "Chactaw Council," in Johnstone and John Stuart to "My Lord," 12 June 1765, in *MPA:ED*, 215–255.

38. Philip Pittman, *The Present State of the European Settlements on the Mississippi; with a Geographical Description of that River* (London: J. Nourse, 1770), 7; Charles-Philippe Aubry, Account of the Illinois Country, 1763, in *IHC*, 10:1; Louis Billouart, Chevalier de Kerlerec to Farmar, 2 October 1763, in *MPA:ED*, 54–58; Farmar to Gage, 16 December 1765, vol. 46, TGP, transcript in Illinois Indians, 1765, OV-GLEA; John Stuart to Henry Seymour Conway, 9 August 1766, Colonial Office Records, Series 5, National Archives, Kew, United Kingdom, transcript in Foreign Copying Program, LC; Clarence Edwin Carter, *Great Britain and the Illinois Country, 1763–1774* (Washington, DC: American Historical Association, 1910), 43–45.

39. Gage to Johnson, 23 January 1764 (copy), vol. 12, TGP; Pittman, *Present State of the European Settlements*, 45–46; Jane F. Babson, "The Architecture of Early Illinois Forts," *Journal of the Illinois State Historical Society* 61 (Spring 1968): 22–24; Fraser to Gage, 27 April 1765, vol. 35, TGP, transcript in Illinois Indians, 1765, OV-GLEA; Farmar to Gage, 18 March 1766, vol. 49, TGP, transcript in Illinois Indians, 1766–1767, OV-GLEA; Gordon Forbes to Gage, 15 April 1768, vol. 76, TGP; Pittman, *Present State of the European Settlements*, 51. See also Aubry's Account of the Illinois Country, 1763, in *IHC*, 10:5; d'Abbadie to the Minister, 10 January 1764, in *IHC*, 10:209.

40. Fraser to Gage, 19 December 1765, vol. 46, TGP, transcript in Illinois Indians, 1765, OV-GLEA; Farmar to Gage, 18 March 1766, vol. 49, TGP, transcript in Illinois Indians, 1766–1767, OV-GLEA; Farmar to Gage, 16 December 1765, vol. 46, TGP, transcript in Illinois Indians, 1765, OV-GLEA; Gordon Forbes to Gage, 23 June 1768, vol. 78, TGP, transcript in Illinois Indians, 1768–1769, OV-GLEA; Forbes to Gage, 18 July 1768, vol. 79, TGP, transcript in Illinois Indians, 1768–1769, OV-GLEA; Report of Philip Pittman, in Pittman to Gage, 17 December 1765, vol. 46, TGP.

41. George Le Hunte to Gage, 24 July 1763, vol. 9, TGP; Jenkins to Gladwin, 29 July 1763, in *IHC*, 10:13–14. For British suspicions and accusations, see Loftus to Gage, 17 August 1764, vol. 23, TGP; Loftus to Gage, 6 De-

cember 1764, vol. 28, TGP; Farmar to Gage, 27 December 1764, vol. 29, TGP; John Stuart to Gage, 19 March 1765, vol. 32, TGP; Fraser to Gage, 21 March 1765, vol. 32, TGP, transcript in Illinois Indians, 1765, OV-GLEA; Farmar to Gage, 24 March 1765, vol. 32, TGP. For French efforts to obtain peace, see Neyon de Villiers to d'Abbadie, 1 December 1763, in *IHC*, 10:50, 54–55; Journal of d'Abbadie, 1763–1764, in *IHC*, 19:162–204; Address of d'Abbadie to the Tunica Indians, 14 July 1764, in *IHC*, 10:285–287; Louis St. Ange to [Fraser?], 7 April 1765, vol. 37, TGP, transcript in Illinois Indians, 1765, OV-GLEA; Copy of a Council held at Illinois, 7 April 1765, in Farmar to Gage, 1 June 1765, vol. 37, TGP, transcript in Illinois Indians, 1765, OV-GLEA.

42. Johnson to Gage, 12 January 1764, vol. 12, TGP; Gage to Gladwin, 10 June 1764, vol. 19, TGP; Gage to John Bradstreet, 15 July 1764, in *IHC*, 10:288; Bradstreet to Gage, 4 November 1764, vol. 26, TGP; John Stuart to Gage, 19 March 1765, vol. 32, TGP; Fraser to Gage, 21 March 1765, vol. 32, TGP; St. Ange to [Bradstreet?], 5 January 1765, vol. 34, TGP, transcript in Illinois Indians, 1765, OV-GLEA.

43. Gage, Instructions to Captain Sterling of the 42nd Regiment, 20 May 1765, vol. 36, TGP, transcript in Illinois Indians, 1765, OV-GLEA.

44. Aubry to the Minister, 27 January 1766, in *IHC*, 11:140; Forbes to Gage, 15 April 1768, vol. 76, TGP; Forbes to Gage, 23 June 1768, vol. 78, TGP; Alejandro O'Reilly, Instructions to Pedro Piernas, 17 February 1770, in *Spanish Regime in Missouri*, ed. Louis Houck, 2 vols. (Chicago: R. R. Donnelley, 1909), 1:76–83.

45. Fraser to Gage, 15 May 1765, vol. 36, TGP, transcript in Illinois Indians, 1765, OV-GLEA ("look upon"); Fraser to Gage, 26 May 1765, vol. 36, TGP, transcript in Illinois Indians, 1765, OV-GLEA ("cutting"); Pittman, *Present State of the European Settlements*, 48–49 ("poor families" on 48); Fraser to Gage, 16 December 1765, vol. 46, TGP; Auguste Chouteau, "Narrative of the Settlement of St. Louis," n.d., Auguste Chouteau Papers, SLML ("boards"). Gordon Forbes reported that some French had become fed up with the Spanish government in Louisiana, and he hoped they would return to British Illinois; but this seems to have been more wish than reality; Forbes to Gage, 23 June 1768, vol. 78, TGP; Gage to John Wilkins, 19 June 1768 (copy), vol. 78, TGP.

46. Fraser to Gage, 16 December 1765, vol. 46, TGP, transcript in Illinois Indians, 1765, OV-GLEA.

47. John Stuart to Payamataha, 3 November 1764 (copy), in John Stuart to Gage, 19 November 1764, vol. 27, TGP ("most favoured"); Helen Hornbeck Tanner, "The Land and Water Communication Systems of the Southeastern Indians," in *Powhatan's Mantle: Indians in the Colonial Southeast*, ed. Gregory A. Waselkov, Peter H. Wood, and Tom Hatley (1989; rev. ed., Lincoln: Nebraska University Press, 2006), 31–32; Farmar to Gage, 16 and 19 December 1765, vol. 46, TGP; Gage to Farmar, 12 March 1766, vol. 49, TGP, transcript in

Illinois Indians, 1766–1767, OV-GLEA ("introduce"); Fraser to Gage, 16 December 1765, vol. 46, TGP, transcript in Illinois Indians, 1765, OV-GLEA.

48. Farmar to Gage, 16, 19 December 1765, vol. 46, TGP; Farmar to Gage, 9 May 1766, vol. 51, TGP, transcript in Illinois Indians, 1766–1767, OV-GLEA; Gage to Farmar, 22 August 1766, vol. 56, TGP, transcript in Illinois Indians, 1766–1767, OV-GLEA; Farmar to Gage, 16 and 19 December 1765, vol. 46, TGP; Extract of Letter of François Desmazellières, 4 June 1770, legajo 107, PC, translation in Folder 1, Box 9, APNDC (quote).

49. Entries for 22 April 1769, 10 May 1769, 7 July 1769, 19, 20, 21, 22–25 April 1771, in "Journal of Transactions and Presents Given to Indians," in Wilkins to Gage, 1 June 1772, vol. 138, TGP, transcript, in Illinois Indians, 1768–1769, OV-GLEA; William Conolly to Wilkins, 12 January 1772, in Wilkins to Gage, 18 January 1772, vol. 109, TGP; Isaac Hamilton to Gage, 8 August 1772, vol. 113, TGP; Alexander Maisonville to Johnson, 23 December 1772, in *PSWJ*, 8:667. For Illinois working as British scouts and informants, see entries for 5 September 1770, 8 April 1771, 18 April 1771, in "Journal of Transactions and Presents Given to Indians." For Chickasaw population decline, see Peter H. Wood, "The Changing Population of the Colonial South: An Overview by Race and Region, 1687–1790," in Waselkov, Wood, and Hatley, *Powhatan's Mantle*, 95. For Chickasaw diplomacy in this era, see Kathleen A. DuVal, *Independence Lost: Lives on the Edge of the American Revolution* (New York: Random House, 2015), 16–22. Blasingham estimates the Illinois population east of the Mississippi in 1766 as 560 individuals and as 970 individuals "ca. 1772–1775"; Blasingham, "Depopulation of the Illinois Indians, Part 2," 370.

50. Stephen Warren, *The Worlds the Shawnees Made: Migration and Violence in Early America* (Chapel Hill: University of North Carolina Press, 2014), 180–207; Liste des partis sauvages du Canada qui ont passé au poste de Peanquishas pour aller sur les Chicachas, 24 April–8 September 1737, C11a, 67:212–213; Reply of Beauharnois to the Ouyatanons, Petikokias, Kikapoux, and Maskoutins, 12 July 1742, in *WHC*, 18:387; entries for 8 March, 26 July 1769, 19, 20, 21, 22–25 April 1771, 11 June 1771, 20 June 1771, in "Journal of Transactions and Presents Given to Indians," in Wilkins to Gage, 1 June 1772, vol. 138, TGP, transcript, in Illinois Indians, 1768–1769, OV-GLEA; Gordon Forbes to Gage 18 July 1768, vol. 79, TGP, transcript in Illinois Indians, 1768–1769, OV-GLEA; Edward Cole to Johnson, 13 June 1769, in *PSWJ*, 7:16; George Butricke to Captain Barnsley, 27 June 1769, in *IHC*, 16:566; Gage to Johnson, 14 August 1771, in *PSWJ*, 8:225; George Morgan to Daniel Blouin, 25 August 1771, George Morgan Letterbook, 1769–1772, Reel 1, f. 477, microfilm, BWM; Gage to Johnson, 24 September 1771, in *PSWJ*, 8:279; Johnson to Gage, 23 April 1772, in *PSWJ*, 8:453. Woody Holton links the anti-British sentiments of the Wabash River nations to the 1768 Treaty of Fort Stanwix, by which Iroquois diplomats

ceded other nations' territory to the British, but at least some of those nations began attacking Anglo-Americans before 1768; Holton, *Forced Founders: Indians, Debtors, Slaves, and the Making of the American Revolution in Virginia* (Chapel Hill: University of North Carolina Press for the Omohundro Institute of Early American History and Culture, 1999), 15–26.

51. Sleeper-Smith, *Indian Women and French Men*, 38–53; R. David Edmunds, *The Potawatomis: Keepers of the Fire* (Norman: University of Oklahoma Press, 1979), 48, 96, 98 ("suffer"); Reed to Gage, 3 April 1767, vol. 63, TGP, transcript in Illinois Indians, 1766–1767, OV-GLEA; Turnbull to Croghan, 1 March 1768, in Croghan to Gage, 14 April 1768, vol. 76, TGP; Gage to Turnbull, 2 May 1768 (copy), vol. 76, TGP; Edward Stuard and his Wife to Turnbull, 28 May 1768, in Turnbull to Gage, 14 June 1768, vol. 77, TGP; Forbes to Gage, 23 June 1768, vol. 78, TGP, transcript in Illinois Indians, 1768–1769, OV-GLEA; Forbes to Gage, 18 July 1768, vol. 78, TGP, transcript in Illinois Indians, 1768–1769, OV-GLEA; entry for 28 March 1771, in "Journal of Transactions and Presents Given to Indians," in Wilkins to Gage, 1 June 1772, vol. 138, TGP, transcript, in Illinois Indians, 1768–1769, OV-GLEA ; Gage to John Stuart, 20 January 1772 (copy), vol. 109, TGP; Henry Basset to Gage, 20 December 1772, vol. 116, TGP.

52. Turnbull to Gage, 23 May 1768, vol. 77, TGP; Speech of Hananaa, Chief of war and of the village, to Wilkins, ca. August 1769, in *PSWJ*, 7:139. Hananaa's nation is not identified.

53. Wilkins to Gage, 7 April 1772, vol. 110, TGP; Dowd, *Spirited Resistance*, 40–46; Hugh Lord to Gage, 11 September 1772, vol. 114, TGP; Gage to John Stuart, 20 December 1772 (copy), vol. 116, TGP; Gage to Lord, 20 February 1773 (copy), vol. 117, TGP; John McIntosh to John Stuart, 3 September 1772 (copy), in Haldimand to Gage, 27 December 1772, vol. 116, TGP; McIntosh to John Stuart, 3 September 1772 (copy), in Haldimand to Gage, 27 December 1772, vol. 116, TGP; Dowd, *Spirited Resistance*, 40–46; White, *Middle Ground*, 351–365. For changing opinions of southern Indians, see Christina Snyder, *Slavery in Indian Country: The Changing Face of Captivity in Early America* (Cambridge, MA: Harvard University Press, 2010), 156–172.

54. Savelle, *George Morgan*, 18–20.

55. Gage to John Penn, 7 December 1764, in *IHC*, 10: 370–371; Baynton, Wharton & Morgan to Johnson, 7 July 1765, in *PSWJ*, 5:787–88; Articles of Agreement of the Illinois Company, 29 March 1766, in *IHC*, 11:203–204; Croghan to Johnson, 30 March 1766, in *IHC*, 11:205; Thomas Wharton et al. to Johnson, 6 June 1766, in *IHC*, 11:247–248; Johnson to "Messrs Wharton &ca", 20 June 1766, in *IHC*, 11:319; Benjamin Franklin to William Franklin, 27 September 1766, in *IHC*, 11:394–395; Benjamin Franklin to William Franklin, 30 September 1766, in *IHC*, 11:395; Benjamin Franklin to William Franklin, 8 November 1766, in *IHC*, 11:422; Benjamin Franklin to William Franklin, 28 August 1767, in *IHC*, 16:1–3.

56. Gage to Johnson, 15 April 1765, in *PSWJ*, 4:717–719; Savelle, *George Morgan*, 19, 22–24.
57. Savelle, *George Morgan*, 11–12. See for example, Invoices of Goods Bought at Philadelphia, 1768, George Morgan Letterbook, 1768–1770, Reel 1, microfilm, BWM; Morgan to John and Peter Chevalier, 15 May 1770, George Morgan Letterbook, 1769–1772, Reel 1, f. 419–420, microfilm, BWM.
58. Morgan to Wilkins, 11 May 1770, George Morgan Letterbook, 1769–1772, Reel 1, f. 414–415, microfilm, BWM; Morgan to Thomas Lawrence, Jr., 29 October 1770, George Morgan Letterbook, 1769–1772, Reel 1, f. 441, microfilm, BWM; Morgan to John Baynton, November 1770, George Morgan Letterbook, 1769–1772, Reel 1, f. 449, microfilm, BWM; Morgan to Baynton and Samuel Wharton, 24 December 1767, Reel 5, f. 796, microfilm, BWM; Walter S. Dunn, Jr., *Frontier Profit and Loss: The British Army and the Fur Traders, 1760–1764* (Westport, CT: Greenwood, 1998), 134. On the extent of French trade networks in the late eighteenth century, see Jay Gitlin, *The Bourgeois Frontier: French Towns, French Traders, and American Expansion* (New Haven, CT: Yale University Press, 2010), especially 26–45; Robert Englebert, "Beyond Borders: Mental Mapping and the French River World in North America, 1763–1805" (Ph.D. diss., University of Ottawa, 2010).
59. Morgan to Baynton and Samuel Wharton, 10 December 1767, in *IHC*, 16:129.
60. For complaints of smugglers and illegal French traders and efforts to stop them, see Gage to Forbes, 2 April 1768 (copy), vol. 75, TGP; Croghan to Gage, 14 April 1768, vol. 76, TGP; Gage to Antonio de Ulloa, 26 April 1768 (copy), vol. 76, TGP; Gage to Turnbull, 2 May 1768 (copy), vol. 76, TGP; Forbes to Gage, 18 July 1768, vol. 79, TGP, transcript in Illinois Indians, 1768–1769, OV-GLEA.
61. The figure of £30,000 is based on supplies on hand and outstanding debts receivable in November 1766; Account with the Crown (Croghan and Cole), Reel 7, f. 419–425, microfilm, BWM. Exchange rate figured from livres to pounds New York currency in Indian Department commissary Edward Cole's accounts with Baynton, Wharton & Morgan and the historian John Mc-Cusker's exchange rate of New York pounds to pounds sterling; Account with the Crown (Croghan and Cole), Reel 7, f. 388–389, microfilm, BWM; Cole to "Dear Sir," 11 November 1766, Reel 7, f. 390, microfilm, BWM; John J. McCusker, *Money and Exchange in Europe and America, 1600–1775: A Handbook* (Chapel Hill: University of North Carolina Press for the Institute of Early American History and Culture, 1978), 158. For purchases, see Journal A, 1766–1767 (Kaskaskia), Reel 8, f. 293–321, microfilm, BWM; Crown account with Baynton, Wharton & Morgan, 6 September 1766, Account with the Crown (Croghan and Cole), Reel 7, f. 398, microfilm, BWM; Crown account with Baynton, Wharton & Morgan, 25 September 1766, Account with the Crown (Croghan and Cole), Reel 7, f. 388–389, microfilm, BWM.

62. Bouquet to Gage, 27 May 1764, in *IHC*, 10:252–253; Reed to Gage, 3 April 1767, vol. 63, TGP, transcript in Illinois Indians, 1766–1767, OV-GLEA; George Morgan's Journal, 30 September 1767–1 November 1767, in *IHC*, 16:67–71; Morgan to Baynton and Samuel Wharton, 2 December 1767, in *IHC*, 16:125–128; George Morgan to Molly Morgan, 16 July 1769, in *IHC*, 16:570–571; George Morgan to James Rumsey, 19 September 1769, in *IHC*, 16:601–605; George Morgan to Lewis Wynn, 6 April 1770, George Morgan Letterbook, 1769–1772, Reel 1, f. 410, microfilm, BWM; George Morgan to Thomas Lawrence, Jr., 3 July 1770, George Morgan Letterbook, 1769–1772, Reel 1, f. 437, microfilm, BWM; George Morgan to Wilkins, 16 September 1770, George Morgan Letterbook, 1769–1772, Reel 1, f. 432–433, microfilm, BWM; George Morgan to Baynton and Samuel Wharton, 24 December 1767, Reel 5, f. 796, microfilm, BWM; George Morgan to Baynton and Samuel Wharton, 14 May 1770, George Morgan Letterbook, 1769–1772, Reel 1, f. 417, microfilm, BWM ("loss"); Baynton, Wharton & Morgan to William Franklin, 10 December 1766, in *IHC*, 11:447–448.
63. Robert Michael Morrissey, *Empire by Collaboration: Indians, Colonists, and Governments in Colonial Illinois Country* (Philadelphia: University of Pennsylvania Press, 2015), 207; George Morgan to Baynton and Samuel Wharton, February 1768, in *IHC*, 16:162.
64. Proposals of Baynton, Wharton & Morgan to Gage, 5 January 1767, in *IHC*, 11:471–472; Baynton, Wharton & Morgan to Lauchlin Macleane, 9 January 1767, in *IHC*, 11:473–576; Baynton, Wharton & Morgan to the Lords of the Treasury, 9 January 1767, in *IHC*, 11:477–478; Macleane to William Petty, Lord Shelburne, 1767, in *IHC*, 11:478.
65. Morrissey, *Empire by Collaboration*, 209–211; Savelle, *George Morgan*, 39, 59–62, 66; George Morgan to Alexander Williamson, 24 November 1768, George Morgan Letterbook, 1768–1770, Reel 1, microfilm, BWM. Baynton, Wharton, and Morgan seem to have maintained a similar relationship with Indian Department commissary Edward Cole; Morgan to Baynton and Samuel Wharton, February 1768, in *IHC*, 16:162–163.
66. Carter, *Great Britain and the Illinois Country*, 145–155; Morrissey, *Empire by Collaboration*, 214–223; Butricke to Barnsley, 12 February 1769, in *IHC*, 16:497 (quote); George Morgan to Baynton and Samuel Wharton, 14 May 1770, George Morgan Letterbook, 1769–1772, Reel 1, f. 416, microfilm, BWM; George Morgan to Baynton and Samuel Wharton, 14 June 1770, George Morgan Letterbook, 1769–1772, Reel 1, f. 417, microfilm, BWM; George Morgan to Wilkins, 11 May 1770, George Morgan Letterbook, 1769–1772, Reel 1, f. 415, microfilm, BWM.
67. George Morgan to Wilkins, 11 May 1770, George Morgan Letterbook, 1769–1772, Reel 1, f. 415, microfilm, BWM (quote); Savelle, *George Morgan*, 37; George Morgan to Baynton and Samuel Wharton, 24 March 1770, George Morgan Letterbook, 1769–1772, Reel 1, microfilm, BWM; George Morgan to Joseph Shelton, 28 October 1769, George Morgan Letterbook,

1769–1772, Reel 1, f. 400, microfilm, BWM; Morgan to Baynton and
Samuel Wharton, 14 June 1770, George Morgan Letterbook, 1769–1772,
Reel 1, f. 417, microfilm, BWM; George Morgan to Wilkins, 16 September 1770, George Morgan Letterbook, 1769–1772, Reel 1, f. 432,
microfilm, BWM; George Morgan to Baynton, November 1770, George
Morgan Letterbook, 1769–1772, Reel 1, f. 458, microfilm, BWM; George
Morgan to Hutchins, 19 December 1770, George Morgan Letterbook,
1769–1772, Reel 1, f. 470–471, microfilm, BWM. For a synopsis of the
Morgan-Wilkins dispute, see Savelle, *George Morgan*, 63–72; Robert M.
Sutton, "George Morgan, Early Illinois Businessman: A Case of Premature
Enterprise," *Journal of the Illinois State Historical Society* 69 (August 1976):
182–185. For some of the court proceedings related to these litigations, see
John Moses, "Court of Enquiry at Ft. Chartres," in *Early Chicago and Illinois*
ed. Edward G. Mason (Chicago: Fergus, 1890), 420–485.
68. Samuel Wharton to William Franklin, [1767], in *IHC*, 11:468; Sosin,
Whitehall and the Wilderness, 181–210; Griffin, *American Leviathan*, 87–88;
Hinderaker, *Elusive Empires*, 172–175, 187–225; Holton, *Forced Founders*,
3–38; Griffin, *American Leviathan*, 97–151.
69. George Morgan to John Morgan, 10 November 1770, George Morgan
Letterbook, 1769–1772, Reel 1, f. 447, microfilm, BWM; George Morgan to
John Morgan, 8 June 1770, George Morgan Letterbook, 1769–1772, Reel 1,
f. 423, microfilm, BWM.
70. Gage to Wilkins, 5 May 1768 (copy), vol. 76, TGP ("sensible"); Gage to
Wilkins, 5 August 1772 (copy), vol. 113, TGP ("many Enemies"). For
correspondence to and from Gage regarding Wilkins and his actions, see
Memorial and Remonstrances of George Morgan in behalf of himself and
John Baynton and Samuel Wharton his partners, 14 October 1771, vol. 107,
TGP; Wilkins to Gage, 25 December 1771, vol. 108, TGP; Wilkins to Gage,
18 January 1772, vol. 109, TGP; Wilkins to Gage, 7 April 1772, vol. 110,
TGP; Wilkins' Reply or Observation on Mr. Blouin's Memorial, 4
April 1772, in Wilkins to Gage, 7 April 1772, vol. 110, TGP; Gage to
Wilkins, 9 April 1772 (copy), vol. 110, TGP; Wilkins to Gage, 1 June 1772,
vol. 111, TGP; Robert Leake to Gage, 29 July 1772, vol. 113, TGP; Gage to
Wilkins, 5 August 1772 (copy), vol. 113, TGP.
71. Gage to Johnson, 9 March 1772, in *PSWJ*, 8:416; Gage to Charles
Edmonstone, 20 October 1772 (copy), vol. 115, TGP; Hamilton to Gage, 8
August 1772, vol. 113, TGP. See also Gage to Johnson, 7 September 1772,
in *PSWJ*, 8:593; White, *Middle Ground*, 353; Carter, *Great Britain and the
Illinois Country*, 155–163; Edward G. Mason, "Philippe-François de
Rastel, Chevalier de Rocheblave," in Mason, *Early Chicago and Illinois*,
360–381.
72. A Council held at the House of Mons. de Neyon de Villiers . . . by Pondiack,
15 and 17 April 1764 (translated copy), in Farmar to Gage, 21 December 1764,
vol. 28, TGP.

73. Jehu Hay to Croghan, 22 Aug. 1767, in *PSWJ*, 5:638 ("sensible"); Benjamin Roberts to Johnson, 23 June 1766, *PSWJ*, 5:279; Trumbull to Gage, 14 June 1768, vol. 77, TGP ("severall").

74. Cole to Johnson, 23 June 1766, in *PSWJ*, 5:278–279; Reponse de Pondiac a une Parole et un Collier envoyé par Monsr. Hay . . . , 10 May 1768, in Turnbull to Gage, 14 June 1768, vol. 77, TGP ("brothers"); entries for 29 March 1769 ("Cutt off"), 30 March 1769, 20 April 1769, in "Journal of Transactions and Presents Given to Indians." in Wilkins to Gage, 1 June 1772, vol. 138, TGP, transcript, in Illinois Indians, 1768–1769, OV-GLEA; White, *Middle Ground*, 313; Cole to Johnson, 13 June 1769, in *PSWJ*, 7:16.

75. George Morgan to Baynton and Samuel Wharton, 14 May 1770, George Morgan Letterbook, 1769–1772, Reel 1, f. 416, microfilm, BWM; George Morgan to John Morgan, 8 June 1770, George Morgan Letterbook, 1769–1772, Reel 1, f. 424, microfilm, BWM; entry for 7 May 1770, in "Journal of Transactions and Presents Given to Indians," in Wilkins to Gage, 1 June 1772, vol. 138, TGP, transcript, in Illinois Indians, 1768–1769, OV-GLEA.

76. Gage to Forbes, 2 April 1768 (copy), vol. 75, TGP.

5. An Empire of Kin

1. Auguste Chouteau, "Narrative of the Settlement of St. Louis," n.d., Chouteau Papers, SLML. The 1804 date is from Jay Gitlin, *The Bourgeois Frontier: French Towns, French Traders, and American Expansion* (New Haven, CT: Yale University Press, 2010), 195n3.

2. Carl J. Ekberg and Sharon Person, "The 1767 Dufossat Maps of St. Louis: Who Was 'the Joyful One'?," *Gateway* 32 (2012): 9–25.

3. Auguste Chouteau, "Narrative."

4. J. Frederick Fausz, *Founding St. Louis: First City of the New West* (Charleston, SC: History Press, 2011), 44–47; James Julian Coleman, *Gilbert Antoine de St. Maxent: The Spanish Frenchman of New Orleans* (New Orleans: Pelican, 1968); Shannon Lee Dawdy, *Building the Devil's Empire: French Colonial New Orleans* (Chicago: University of Chicago Press, 2008), 179; John Francis McDermott, "The Exclusive Trade Privilege of Maxent, Laclède, & Company," *Missouri Historical Review* 29 (July 1935): 272–278. Historians usually refer to Maxent as "St. Maxent," which probably stems from a transcription error from documents in which he was called "Sr. Maxent." He always signed his named "Maxent," with no "St." Thanks to Alexandre Dubé for pointing this out to me.

5. William E. Foley and C. David Rice, *The First Chouteaus: River Barons of Early St. Louis* (Urbana: University of Illinois Press, 1983), 2–3; Fausz, *Founding St. Louis*, 45–46; Procès verbal of Tropé Ricard, Jean Baptiste Sarpy, Joseph Labussiere, Fernando de Leyba, 19 July 1778 (transcript), Pierre Laclède Collection, MHS.

6. Marc de Villiers du Terrage, *The Last Years of French Louisiana*, ed. Carl A. Brasseaux and Glenn R. Conrad, trans. Hosea Phillips (Lafayette: Center for Louisiana Studies, 1982), 98–156; Fausz, *Founding St. Louis*, 48–66; Lawrence N. Powell, *The Accidental City: Improvising New Orleans* (Cambridge, MA: Harvard University Press, 2012), 142; Memoire of the Merchants to Kerlerec, 25 June 1759, in *Commerce and Contraband in New Orleans during the French and Indian War: A Documentary Study of the* Texel *and* Three Brothers *Affairs*, ed. Abraham P. Nasatir and James R. Mills (Cincinnati: American Jewish Archives, 1968), 116–117; Petition to the Minister of Marine, 29 April 1763, in Villiers du Terrage, *Last Years of French Louisiana*, 150–151; Michel Baudouin to de l'Isle Dieu, 28 June 1754, *IHC*, 29:869–878. On Fort de Cavagnial and its closing, see Order of Vaudreuil, 8 August 1744, C13a, 28:224–232; Jean-Jacques Macarty Mactigue to Pierre de Rigaud de Vaudreuil de Cavagnial, 27 March 1752, *IHC*, 29:548–549; Willard H. Rollings, *The Osage: An Ethnohistorical Study of Hegemony on the Prairie-Plains* (Columbia: University of Missouri Press, 1995), 91; Auguste Chouteau, "Narrative."

7. David J. Weber, *The Spanish Frontier in North America* (New Haven, CT: Yale University Press, 1992), 198–199; Paul W. Mapp, *The Elusive West and the Contest for Empire, 1713–1763* (Chapel Hill: University of North Carolina Press for the Institute of Early American History and Culture, 2011), 387–412; Alejandro O'Reilly to Marqués de Grimaldi, 30 September 1770, no. 41, in *SMV*, 1:183–186.

8. Auguste Chouteau, "Narrative"; Sebastian Louis Meurin to Bishop Briand, 23 March 1767, in *IHC*, 11:523; Robert Farmar to Thomas Gage, 16 December 1765, vol. 46, TGP, transcript in Illinois Indians, 1765, OV-GLEA (quotes).

9. Carl J. Ekberg and Sharon K. Person, *St. Louis Rising: The French Regime of Louis St. Ange de Bellerive* (Urbana: University of Illinois Press, 2015), 97–105; Patricia Cleary, *The World, the Flesh, and the Devil: A History of Colonial St. Louis* (Columbia: University of Missouri Press, 2011), 53–57; Eric Sandweiss, *St. Louis: The Evolution of an American Urban Landscape* (Philadelphia: Temple University Press, 2001), 28–33; Louis St. Ange de Bellerive to [Antonio de Ulloa], 16 June 1766, Legajo 2357, fol. 18–18v, PC (quotes).

10. Charles-Philippe Aubry to St. Ange, 4 April 1767 (copy), Legajo 187A, fol. 83v, 86, PC ("department" on 83v, "merits" on 86); St. Ange to [Francisco Ríu], 27 June 1767 (copy), Legajo 187A, fol. 391, PC ("state").

11. John Preston Moore, "Antonio de Ulloa: A Profile of the First Spanish Governor of Louisiana," *Louisiana History* 8 (Summer 1967): 201–202; Moore, *Revolt in Louisiana: The Spanish Occupation, 1766–1770* (Baton Rouge: Louisiana State University Press, 1976), 49. For example, the first three "Spanish" commandants at Arkansas Post were French; Kathleen DuVal, *The Native Ground: Indians and Colonists in the Heart of the Continent* (Philadelphia: University of Pennsylvania Press, 2006), 131.

12. Aubry to St. Ange, 6 April 1767 (copy), Legajo 187A, fol. 85, PC ("two nations"); Alejandro O'Reilly to Julian de Arriaga, no. 3, 17 October 1769, in *SMV,* 1:101–103 ("close bonds" on 102); Ulloa, Instructions to Ríu, [January 1767], in *SRM,* 1:10–13. On Spanish understandings of French practices, see DuVal, *Native Ground,* 147–148.

13. Esteban Miró to Josef Antonio Rengel, 12 December 1785, in *BLC,* 1:119; Ulloa, Secret Instructions to Ríu, 7 January 1767, in *SRM,* 1:22.

14. Alejandro O'Reilly, Instructions to Pedro Piernas, 17 February 1770, in *SRM,* 1:77–78; Pedro Piernas, Inventory and report of the papers, instructions, orders, and other documents . . . , 19 May 1775, in *SRM,* 1:128; Extrait des lettres de M. de St. Ange, 15 November 1769, Legajo 2357, fol. 17, PC; Ríu to Ulloa, 2 May 1768, Legajo 109, fol. 1116v, PC; Frederic L. Billon, comp., *Annals of St. Louis in Its Early Days under the French and Spanish Dominations* (St. Louis: by the author, 1886), 150; Will of Louis St. Ange, 26 December 1774, in Billon, *Annals of St. Louis,* 125–127.

15. Aubry to the Minister, 27 January 1766, in *IHC,* 11:147; Auguste Chouteau, "Narrative."

16. Aubry to the Minister, 27 January 1766, in *IHC,* 11:146. Accounts from the early nineteenth century offer the best descriptions of the fickle nature of the Missouri. For example, see Journal of Titian Ramsay Peale, entries for 22 June, 24 June, 6 July 1819, vol. 1, Titian Ramsay Peale Journals, 1819–1842, Manuscript Division, LC; J. M. Peck, *A Guide for Emigrants, Containing Sketches of Illinois, Missouri, and the Adjacent Parts* (Boston: Lincoln and Edmands, 1831), 16–21. See also Robert Kelley Schneiders, *Unruly River: Two Centuries of Change along the Missouri* (Lawrence: University Press of Kansas, 1999), 23–37.

17. Auguste Chouteau, "Narrative."

18. The best contemporary account of the location and territorial borders of most of these nations is Miró to Rengel, 12 December 1785, in *BLC,* 1:119–127.

19. Louis Billouart, Chevalier de Kerlerec, "Indian Nations of Louisiana," 12 December 1758, in *MPA:FD,* 5:206; Pedro Piernas to Luis de Unzaga y Amezaga, 4 July 1772, in *SMV,* 1:205; "Nations of the Missouri," 19 May 1775, in *SMV,* 1:228. Initially, the Missouria Indians lived closer to St. Louis than did the Osages, but the Missourias suffered rapid depopulation in the eighteenth century and allied with the Little Osages for protection. By the 1780s, they lived west of the Little Osages, possibly relying on the Osages to shield them from attacks by the Sauks and Foxes. For a discussion of the Missouria Indians in this era, see Michael E. Dickey, *People of the River's Mouth: In Search of the Missouria Indians* (Columbia: University of Missouri Press, 2011), 85–111.

20. John Joseph Mathews, *The Osages: Children of the Middle Waters* (Norman: University of Oklahoma Press, 1961), 141–148; Rollings, *Osage,* 28, 46–47.

21. "Extrait de la Relation de Bénard de La Harpe," in *Découvertes et établissements des Français dans l'ouest et dans le sud de l'Amérique Septentrionale*

(1614–1754): Mémoires et documents originaux, ed. Pierre Margry, 6 vols. (Paris: D. Jouaust, 1876–1886), 6:310 ("jealous"); Charles Claude du Tisné to Jean-Baptiste Le Moyne de Bienville, 22 November 1719, in Margry, *Découvertes et établissements,* 6:313–315.

22. Inventory of the late Jean Rivet, KM 24:9:2:1; Statement of Jean Baptiste Sarasin, KM 26:8:22:1; Statement of Jean Jacques Desmanets, KM 26:9:2:1; Contract of Joseph Quenel, KM 37:2:25:2; Contract of Jean Baptiste Emond, KM 37:3:7:2; Contract of Jean Baptiste Emond, KM 37:3:9:1; Contract of Alphonse Mercier, KM 37:9:23:1; Contract of Louis La Vallee, KM 37:9:23:2; Contract of Jean Francois Mauricette, KM 37:11:17:1.

23. Ekberg and Person, *St. Louis Rising,* 24; Bienville to Jean-Frédéric Phélypeaux, Comte de Maurepas, 29 June 1736, in *MPA:FD,* 3:688; Vaudreuil orders, 8 August 1744, C13a, vol. 28, fol. 224.

24. Vaudreuil orders, 8 August 1744, C13a, vol. 28, fol. 224–232; Memoir of Louis Antoine Bougainville, 1757, in *WHC,* 18:175–178.

25. DuVal, *Native Ground,* 109–110, 122–125; Rollings, *Osage,* 135–136.

26. Rollings, *Osage,* 47–51, 163; Francis La Flesche, "The Osage Tribe: Rite of the Chiefs; Sayings of the Old Men," in *The Thirty-Sixth Annual Report of the Bureau of American Ethnology* (Washington, DC: Government Printing Office, 1921), 53; Ríu to Ulloa, 25 June 1768, Legajo 109, fol. 1186v, PC; Clermont to Piernas, 14 June 1772, in *SMV,* 1:203. Willard Rollings and John Joseph Mathews state that the Osages had a peace chief and a war chief, with the war chief coming from the Earth moiety and the peace chief coming from the Sky moiety. However, Francis La Flesche indicated in his study of Osage chiefs that the responsibilities were not so clearly divided between peace and war and that most chiefly duties revolved around settling internal, not external, matters. Garrick A. Bailey asserts in his account of Osage politics, based on La Flesche's research, that chiefs presided over internal matters, while priests "controlled the relationship between the Osages and the external world, both visible and invisible. In matters of peace and war, they were the ultimate authority"; Rollings, *Osage,* 47–49; Mathews, *Osages,* 56; La Flesche, "Osage Tribe: Rite of the Chiefs," 66–67; Garrick A. Bailey, *The Osage and the Invisible World: From the Works of Francis La Flesche* (Norman: University of Oklahoma Press, 1995), 42–45 (quote on 44). See also Garrick A. Bailey, *Changes in Osage Social Organization, 1673–1906,* University of Oregon Anthropological Papers 5 (Eugene: University of Oregon, 1973), 19, 22–23.

27. Francis La Flesche, "The Osage Tribe: Rite of the Vigil," in *Thirty-Ninth Annual Report of the Bureau of American Ethnology* (Washington, DC: Government Printing Office, 1925), 238 (quote); Tai S. Edwards, *Osage Women and Empire: Gender and Power* (Lawrence: University Press of Kansas, 2018), 14–37; Francis La Flesche, *Traditions of the Osage: Stories Collected and Translated by Francis La Flesche,* ed. Garrick Bailey (Albuquerque: University of New Mexico Press, 2010), 30.

28. Saucy Calf, "Instructions to the Wife of a Priest," in La Flesche, *Traditions of the Osage*, 67–68; La Flesche, "Osage Tribe: Rite of the Vigil," 238–242; La Flesche, *Traditions of the Osage*, 34. Willard Rollings suggests that the advent of female priests is a later development, but given the other contemporaneous changes in Osage society, especially the presence of polygamy and the switch to matrilocality, that indicate a decreasing number of men, it seems likely that this was present in the eighteenth century as well; Rollings, *Osage*, 31.

29. La Flesche, *Traditions of the Osage*, 22, 26–27. 30–32; La Flesche, "Osage Tribe: Rite of the Vigil," 238 (quote); Shun-kah-mo-lah, "Counting the *O'don*," in La Flesche, *Traditions of the Osage*, 70–72; Rollings, *Osage*, 34–36.

30. Rollings, *Osage*, 79–81; Tanis C. Thorne, *The Many Hands of My Relations: French and Indians on the Lower Missouri* (Columbia: University of Missouri Press, 1996), 53–63, 95; Mathews, *Osages*, 285; Pierre Chouteau to unknown, 3 September 1825, in "Indians of North America," *North American Review* 22 (January 1826): 106.

31. La Flesche, "Osage Tribe: Rite of the Chiefs," 51; Betty R. Nett, "Historical Changes in the Osage Kinship System," *Southwestern Journal of Anthropology* 8 (Summer 1952): 178, 181; Bailey, *Changes in Osage Social Organization*, 16; John Dunn Hunter, *Manners and Customs of Several Tribes Located West of the Mississippi* (Philadelphia: J. Maxwell, 1823), 243; Francis La Flesche, "Osage Marriage Customs," *American Anthropologist*, n.s., 14 (January–March 1912): 127–130; Bailey, *Changes in Osage Social Organization*, 16–17; Rollings, *Osage*, 27–28; Louis F. Burns, *A History of the Osage People*, 2nd ed. (Tuscaloosa: University of Alabama Press, 2004), 54, 99; Thorne, *Many Hands of My Relations*, 95; Rollings, *Osage*, 27–28; Edwards, *Osage Women and Empire*, 56.

32. Victor Tixier, *Tixier's Travels on the Osage Prairies*, ed. John Francis McDermott, trans. Albert J. Salvan (Norman: University of Oklahoma Press, 1940), 182 (quote); Hunter, *Manners and Customs of Several Tribes*, 244–245; La Flesche, "Osage Marriage Customs," 127–128, 130; Francis La Flesche, *A Dictionary of the Osage Language* (Washington, DC: Government Printing Office, 1932), 38–39; Edwards, *Osage Women and Empire*, 10, 56; Michael Lansing, "Plains Indian Women and Interracial Marriage in the Upper Missouri Trade, 1804–1868," *Western Historical Quarterly* 31 (Winter 2000): 423–424. For a composite courtship and wedding, see Mathews, *Osages*, 312–326.

33. Rollings, *Osage*, 28; Edwards, *Osage Women and Empire*, 53–54; Tixier, *Tixier's Travels on the Osage Prairies*, 184 (quote); Burns, *History of the Osage People*, 210; Edwards, *Osage Women and Empire*, 55–56. Along with other evidence, this quote also suggests that men still wielded substantial authority over the household, but even if that complicated division of power worked within Osage marriages, it would likely matter less in Osage women's marriages to French men, who also lived in St. Louis part of the year; Nett, "Historical Changes in the Osage Kinship System," 180; Bailey, *Changes in Osage Social Organization*, 13, 16; DuVal, *Native Ground*, 115. For matrilocality

and external relations in an earlier context, see R. Eric Hollinger, "Residence Patterns and Oneota Cultural Dynamics," in *Oneota Archaeology: Past, Present, and Future*, ed. William Green (Iowa City: University of Iowa, 1995), 141–174; Jodie A. O'Gorman, "Exploring the Longhouse and Community in Tribal Society," *American Antiquity* 75 (July 2010): 571–597; Hollinger, "Conflict and Culture Change in the Late Prehistoric and Early Historic American Midcontinent" (Ph.D. diss., University of Illinois at Urbana-Champaign, 2005), 267–269.

34. La Flesche, "Osage Marriage Customs," 129–130; Edwards, *Osage Women and Empire*, 56, 57–58; Thorne, *Many Hands of My Relations*, 94–95; Mathews, *Osages*, 308; Burns, *History of the Osage People*, 326. The presence of Chouteaus as members of the Osage Nation in later years reveals that they followed these practices, as the children of illegitimate marriages were not considered members of the nation. Adoption probably occurred through the calumet ceremony and a subsequent naming ceremony; Alice C. Fletcher and Francis La Flesche, "The Omaha Tribe," in *The Twenty-Seventh Annual Report of the Bureau of American Ethnology* (Washington, DC: Government Printing Office, 1911), 377; La Flesche, "The Osage Tribe: Two Versions of the Child-Naming Rite," in *Forty-Third Annual Report of the Bureau of American Ethnology* (Washington, DC: Government Printing Office, 1928); Burns, *History of the Osage People*, 501n56; James R. Duncan, "The Cosmology of the Osage: The Star People and Their Universe," in *Visualizing the Sacred: Cosmic Visions, Regionalism, and the Art of the Mississippian World*, ed. George E. Lankford, F. Kent Reilly III, and James F. Garber (Austin: University of Texas Press, 2011), 20.

35. Alexandra Harmon, *Rich Indians: Native People and the Problem of Wealth in American History* (Chapel Hill: University of North Carolina Press, 2010), 63–67.

36. William Johnson to the Lords of Trade, 16 November 1765, in *IHC*, 11:120 (quote); Harry Gordon Journal, 31 August 1766, in *IHC*, 11:299–300; Coleman, *Gilbert Antoine de St. Maxent*, 24–25; Contract of termination for Maxent, Laclède & Co., 8 May 1769, in *BLC*, 1:68–69.

37. Coleman, *Gilbert Antoine de St. Maxent*, 29–30; *BLC*, 1:63; Aubry to Monseigneur, 10 July 1765, C13a, 45:66 ("honest"); Billon, *Annals of St. Louis*, 50–51 ("employees" on 50); Gilbert Antoine de Maxent to Ulloa, 8 May 1769, Legajo 188A, document 8–3, PC. Datchurut's last name is sometimes spelled Datcherut.

38. St. Ange to [Ulloa?], 16 May 1769, Legajo 187A, fol. 397–397v, PC ("accustomed"); Ríu to Ulloa, 25 June 1768, Legajo 109, fol. 1184, 1186v, PC ("happy" and "disgusted"): Petition of the Merchants of St. Louis to Captain Ríu, 15 January 1769, in *SRM*, 1:38; Estado, que manifiesta los nombres de los Sujetos, a quienes he permitido, passen a tratan en el Rio Missury . . . , 17 June 1768, in Ríu to Ulloa, 25 June 1768, Legajo 109, fol. 1188–1188v, PC; Orders of Francisco Ríu, 1769, in *SRM*, 1:35.

39. Estado, que manifiesta los nombres de los Sujetos, a quienes he permitido, passen a tratan en el Rio Missury . . . , 17 June 1768, in Ríu to Ulloa, 25 June 1768, Legajo 109, fol. 1188, PC; Maxent to Ulloa, 8 May 1769, Legajo 188A, document 8-3, PC; Contract of termination for Maxent, Laclède & Co., 8 May 1769, in *BLC*, 1:68-69; Petition of the Merchants of St. Louis to Captain Ríu, 15 January 1769, in *SRM*, 1:38.

40. Contract with Thomas Blondeau, 3 June 1767, Instrument 1502, St. Louis Archives, MHS; Contract with Jacques Chauvin, 22 August 1770, Instrument 1548, St. Louis Archives, MHS; Piernas to Louis Villars, 14 July 1770, Legajo 188A, document 4-3, PC; Ekberg and Person, *St. Louis Rising*, 124-125, 201; Cleary, *World, the Flesh, and the Devil*, 114; Relacion de la Carga de los Tres Batoes q. vataron de Ilinoeses, 4 September 1770, Legajo 188A, document 4-7, PC.

41. Estado, que manifiesta los nombres de los Sujetos; Report of Indian Traders Given Passports by Francisco Cruzat, 28 November 1777, in *SRM*, 1:139; Jean Baptiste Martigny to [Bernardo de Gálvez?], 30 October 1779, Legajo 113, fol. 993, PC (quote). Chouteau also traded under his own name in the mid-1770s and sent a shipment of furs to New Orleans in 1775, but it is unclear whether this was before or after he, Laclède, and Labbadie formed their partnership; Foley and Rice, *First Chouteaus*, 21.

42. Mary B. Cunningham and Jeanne C. Blythe, *The Founding Family of St. Louis* (St. Louis: Midwest Technical Publications, 1977), 145, 192; Marriage Contract of Silvestre Labbadie and Pelagie Chouteau, 27 July 1776, Instrument 2039, St. Louis Archives, MHS; Marriage Contract of Joseph Marie Papin and Marie Louise Chouteau, 19 January 1779, Instrument 2049, St. Louis Archives, MHS; Susan C. Boyle, "Did She Generally Decide? Women in Ste. Genevieve, 1750-1805," *WMQ* 44 (October 1987): 775-789; Ekberg and Person, *St. Louis Rising*, 127-146; Amos Stoddard, *Sketches, Historical and Descriptive, of Louisiana* (Philadelphia: Matthew Carey, 1812), 323, 328 (quote); Foley and Rice, *First Chouteaus*, 3, 22-23, 24-25, 43; Billion, *Annals of St. Louis*, 233-243. Pelagie and Marie Louise appear as owners, landlords, and sellers of real estate in St. Louis following the deaths of their husbands in the 1790s. As other historians have suggested, the ability of widows to capably manage their property suggests that they performed similar duties while their husbands were still alive. For example, see Instrument 729; vol. 1, book 1, 35-36, 99-100; all in St. Louis Archives, MHS.

43. Gonzalo M. Quintero Saravia, *Bernardo de Gálvez: Spanish Hero of the American Revolution* (Chapel Hill: University of North Carolina Press, 2018), 80, 130-134, 347; Coleman, *Gilbert Antoine de St. Maxent*, 52-53; Fausz, *Founding St. Louis*, 159-160; Ramón Ezquerra, "Un Patricio Colonial: Gilberto de Saint-Maxent, Teniente Gobernador de Luisiana," *Revista de Indias* 10 (1950): 112-113, 119, 124-136; Charles Gratiot to William Kay, 22 March 1778, in "The Letterbooks of Charles Gratiot, Fur Trader: The Nomadic Years, 1769-1797," ed. Warren L. Barnhart (Ph.D. diss., St. Louis

University, 1972), 191. As in francophone communities in former New France, arranged marriages were common in colonial Latin America; Susan Migden Socolow, *The Women of Colonial Latin America*, 2nd ed. (Cambridge: Cambridge University Press, 2015), 66–68.

44. Ellen Hartigan-O'Connor, *The Ties That Buy: Women and Commerce in Revolutionary America* (Philadelphia: University of Pennsylvania Press, 2009), 61; Auguste Chouteau account with Maxent, 9 February 1780, *The Papers of the St. Louis Fur Trade*, part 1, *The Chouteau Collection, 1752–1925*, ed. William R. Swagerty, 40 microfilm reels (Bethesda, MD: University Publications of America, 1991), 1:233 (Hereafter cited as *Chouteau Collection*); Power of Attorney Document, 26 July 1780, vol. 1, book 1, 143–144, St. Louis Archives, MHS.

45. Receipt from Auguste Chouteau to George Rogers Clark, 19 November 1778, Box 3, folder 6, Clark Family Collection, MHS; List of claims owed Charles Gratiot, 27 September 1781, in Billon, *Annals of St. Louis*, 215; Receipt from Gabriel Cerré to George Rogers Clark, 25 July 1778, Box 3, folder 2, Clark Family Collection, MHS; Receipt from Gabriel Cerré to George Rogers Clark, 22 November 1778, Box 3, folder 6, Clark Family Collection, MHS; Account of George Rogers Clark with Gabriel Cerré, 10 July 1779, Box 3, folder 10, Clark Family Collection, MHS.

46. Charles Gratiot to John Kay, 26 April 1779, in Barnhart, "Letterbooks of Charles Gratiot," 207 (quote); Charles Gratiot to William Kay, 14 June 1779, in Barnhart, "Letterbooks of Charles Gratiot," 213–214. Virginia then lost Clark's receipts and refused to compensate him. His papers were discovered in 1913 in the attic of the Virginia capitol building. For a discussion of some of these debts and the lingering problems they caused for both Clark and his creditors, see James Alton James, *The Life of George Rogers Clark* (1928; repr., New York: Greenwood, 1969), 125–126, 288–298.

47. George Rogers Clark to John Brown, [1791?], in *IHC*, 8:236 ("conserned"); Clark to Brown, [1791?], in *IHC*, 8:228–229 ("inveterate" on 228); Walter B. Douglas, "Jean Gabriel Cerré—A Sketch," *Transactions of the Illinois State Historical Society for the Year 1903* (Springfield, IL: Phillips Brothers, 1904), 283; Clarence Walworth Alvord, *The Illinois Country, 1673–1818* (Springfield: Illinois Centennial Commission, 1920), 346.

48. Barnhart, "Letterbooks of Charles Gratiot," 42–46; Charles Gratiot to David Gratiot, 1778, in Barnhart, "Letterbooks of Charles Gratiot," 202–204; Memorial of John Kay and David M'Crea to Frederick Haldimand, 12 November 1780, in *WHC*, 12:54–55; Documents related to Lafleur, et al. v. Charles Gratiot, in Billon, *Annals of St. Louis*, 210–214; Barnhart, "Letterbooks of Charles Gratiot," 84–86.

49. Charles Gratiot to Richard McCarty, 9 November 1779, in Barnhart, "Letterbooks of Charles Gratiot," 239–240; Charles Gratiot to John Montgomery, 15 November 1779, in Barnhart, "Letterbooks of Charles Gratiot," 240–242; Charles Gratiot to Montgomery, December 1779, in Barnhart,

"Letterbooks of Charles Gratiot," 249–250 ("obliged" on 250); List of claims owed Charles Gratiot, 27 September 1781, in Billon, *Annals of St. Louis*, 215; Charles Gratiot to Clark, 6 May 1780, Box 3, folder 16, Clark Family Collection, MHS ("cannot help"); Montgomery to Clark, 7 May 1780, Box 3, folder 16, Clark Family Collection, MHS.

50. For Chouteau dealings with Gratiot, see Charles Gratiot to John Kay, 26 April 1779, in Barnhart, "Letterbooks of Charles Gratiot," 207–208; Charles Gratiot to Joseph-Marie Papin, 23 October 1779, in Barnhart, "Letterbooks of Charles Gratiot," 238. For Cerré, see Jean Baptiste Martigny to [Bernardo de Gálvez?], 30 October 1779, Legajo 113, fol. 993, PC. In March 1778, Charles Gratiot recognized the advantages of dealing in both New Orleans and Montreal, but he lacked the personal ties and the financial backing to extend his reach; Charles Gratiot to William Kay, 22 March 1778, in Barnhart, "Letterbooks of Charles Gratiot," 190–192.

51. Marriage contract of Charles Gratiot and Victoire Chouteau, 25 June 1781, Instrument 2057, St. Louis Archives, MHS; Marriage contract of Auguste Chouteau and Marie Thérèse Cerré, *Chouteau Collection*, 1:430–444. For Cerré business and family connections in Canada, see Robert Englebert, "Beyond Borders: Mental Mapping and the French River World in North America, 1763–1805" (Ph.D. diss., University of Ottawa, 2010), 107–122. For Papin business at Montreal, see Charles Gratiot to "Mr. Bernard," 15 June 1779, in Barnhart, "Letterbooks of Charles Gratiot," 222.

52. Miró to Gálvez, 1 August 1786, in *SMV*, 2:184. For Osage attacks on hunters on the Arkansas River, see Manuel Perez to Miró, no. 100, 8 October 1789, in *SMV*, 2:285–286; Miró to Perez, 10 May 1790, Legajo 7, PC, translation in Box 9, folder 4, APNDC; Miró to [Conde del Campo de] Alange, 7 August 1792, in *BLC*, 1:158–159; Zenon Trudeau to Francisco Luis Héctor de Carondelet, no. 50, 10 April 1793, in *BLC*, 1:173; Trudeau to Ygnacio Delinó, 20 May 1793, Legajo 124, PC, translation in Box 9, folder 5, APNDC. For theft of horses from Ste. Genevieve and the Meramec River settlements, see Perez to Miró, no. 129, 24 March 1790, Legajo 16, fol. 285, PC; Peyroux de la Coudrenière to Miró, 7 April 1790, Legajo 203, PC, translation in Box 9, folder 4, APNDC; Perez to Miró, no. 211, 29 March 1792, Legajo 17, PC, translation in Box 9, folder 4, APNDC; Trudeau to Carondelet, no. 48, 2 March 1793, in *BLC*, 1:167–168. For Osage commerce in horses, see Rollings, *Osage*, 92, 115, 131, 137.

53. Stephen Aron, *American Confluence: The Missouri Frontier from Borderland to Border State* (Bloomington: Indiana University Press, 2006), 77–84; Alan Taylor, "Remaking Americans: Louisiana, Upper Canada, and Texas," in *Contested Spaces of Early America*, ed. Juliana Barr and Edward Countryman (Philadelphia: University of Pennsylvania Press, 2014), 211–214; Trudeau to Carondelet, 28 September 1793, in *BLC*, 1:199 (quote); Pedro Foucher to Miró, 11 December 1789, Legajo 15A, PC, translation in Box 9, folder 1, APNDC; Trudeau to Carondelet, no. 50, 10 April 1793, in *BLC*, 1:172–173.

54. David J. Weber, *Bárbaros: Spaniards and Their Savages in the Age of Enlightenment* (New Haven, CT: Yale University Press, 2005), 179–186; "Literary News," 1 August 1790, in *BLC,* 1:133–134.

55. DuVal, *Native Ground,* 124–126; Declaration of Juan Joffre, 24 March 1791, in Ygnacio Delinó to Carondelet, no. 38, 24 March 1791, Legajo 17, PC, translation in Box 9, folder 4, APNDC; Declaration of Luis Daragua, 24 March 1791, in Delinó to Carondelet, no. 38, 24 March 1791, Legajo 17, PC, translation in Box 9, folder 4, APNDC; Delinó to Carondelet, no. 77, 27 April 1792, Legajo 25A, PC, translation in Box 9, folder 4, APNDC; Delinó to Carondelet, no. 96, 30 December 1792, Legajo 25A, PC, translation in Box 9, folder 5, APNDC; Log of His Majesty's Galiot, *La Fleche,* entry for 9 February 1793, in *SMV,* 3:119.

56. Trudeau to Carondelet, no. 63, 16 May 1793, Legajo 26, fol. 934, PC ("avoided"); Draft of Carondelet to Trudeau, n.d., in Trudeau to Carondelet, 21 May 1793, Legajo 26, fol. 985v, PC ("example"). Trudeau claimed that he had not yet publicized Carondelet's ban on the trade in order to protect the traders already operating in Osage Country; Trudeau to Carondelet, no. 50, 10 April 1793, in *BLC,* 1:171.

57. Carondelet to Tomas Portell, 22 December 1792, Legajo 18, PC, translation in Box 9, folder 4, APNDC (quote); Carondelet to Trudeau, 22 December 1792, Legajo 18, PC, translation in Box 9, folder 4, APNDC; Gilbert C. Din and A. P. Nasatir, *The Imperial Osages: Spanish-Indian Diplomacy in the Mississippi Valley* (Norman: University of Oklahoma Press, 1983) 177–216; DuVal, *Native Ground,* 165. In particular, Trudeau warned Carondelet and others of the limitations of Spanish presence in Upper Louisiana and cautioned against war; Trudeau to Carondelet, no. 48, 2 March 1793, in *BLC,* 1:169; Trudeau to Carondelet, no. 81, 21 May 1793, Legajo 26, fol. 985–986, PC; Trudeau to Portell, 18 September 1793, Legajo 2363, fol. 226–227, PC; Trudeau to Carondelet, 28 September 1793, in *BLC,* 1:197–203. Esteban Miró had also supplied Osage enemies with weapons; Din and Nasatir, *Imperial Osages,* 199–200.

58. Agreement of the Arkansas Traders to Fight the Osages, 8 April 1793, in *SMV,* 3:145–146 ("humanity" on 146); Carondelet to Delinó, 5 May 1793, Legajo 19, PC, translation in Box 9, folder 5, APNDC; Trudeau to Carondelet, 28 September 1793, in *SMV,* 3:206 ("single").

59. Census of St. Louis and Its Districts, 1791 (copy), Census Collection, MHS; Trudeau to Carondelet, 28 September 1793, in *SMV,* 3:206. In 1794, Carondelet estimated that the Osages had about 1,200 warriors, who probably made up at least a quarter of the total population; Carondelet to Luis de Las Casas, 31 May 1794, in *SRM,* 2:100.

60. Miró to Rengel, 12 December 1785, in *BLC,* 1:120 (distance via Arkansas River), 122 (distance via Missouri); Trudeau to Carondelet, 28 September 1793, in *BLC,* 1:197–203 (quote on 198).

61. Clark to Citizen Genêt, 28 April 1794, in "George Rogers Clark to Genet, 1794," *American Historical Review* 18 (July 1913): 781; Trudeau to Carondelet,

8 June 1794, in *BLC*, 1:231 ("already"); Ernest R. Liljegren, "Jacobinism in Spanish Louisiana (1791–1797)," *Louisiana Historical Quarterly* 22 (January 1939): 62–63; Carondelet to Miguel José de Asansa, 1 December 1796, in *SRM*, 2:134 ("audacity").

62. Trudeau to Carondelet, 28 September 1793, in *BLC*, 1:198–199; Perez to Miró, no. 194, 8 November 1791, in *BLC*, 1:150; Carondelet to Las Casas, 31 May 1794, in *SRM*, 2:100–101. Spanish officials repeatedly requested, and were denied, permission and funds to build a fort at the mouth of the Des Moines River, in order to combat this illicit trade; Leyba to Gálvez, 16 November 1778, in *SMV*, 1:310–312; Gálvez to Leyba, 13 July 1779, in *SMV*, 1:320; Perez to Miró, 5 April 1791, in *BLC*, 1:145.

63. Auguste Chouteau to Carondelet, 19 May 1794, in *SRM*, 2:106 (quote); Carondelet to Las Casas, 31 May 1794, in *SRM*, 2:101; Distribution of Missouri Trading Posts, 1–3 May 1794, in *BLC*, 1:209.

64. C. H. Haring, *The Spanish Empire in America* (1947; repr., New York: Harcourt, Brace and World, 1963), 126; Foley and Rice, *First Chouteaus*, 40–41.

65. Auguste Chouteau to Carondelet, 10 November 1793, Legajo 207B, PC, translation in Box 9, folder 5, APNDC; Trudeau to Carondelet, no. 170, 24 April 1794, Legajo 126, PC, translation in Box 9, folder 6, APNDC (quote); Trudeau to Carondelet, 27 April 1794, Legajo 189A, PC, translation in Box 9, folder 6, APNDC. Carondelet, in writing to his superiors, repeated much of the information and many of the opinions offered by Trudeau; Carondelet to Las Casas, 31 May 1794, in *SRM*, 2:101.

66. Carondelet to Trudeau, 15 April 1794, Legajo 21, PC, translation in Box 9, folder 5, APNDC; Carondelet to Las Casas, 31 May 1794, in *SRM*, 2:101 ("rich man"); Carondelet to Duke of Alcudia, 31 May 1794, in *SRM*, 2:104; Carondelet to Trudeau, 21 May 1794 (draft), Legajo 126, PC, translation in Box 9, folder 6, APNDC; Carondelet, Secret Orders to Carlos Howard, 26 November 1795, in *SRM*, 2:131 ("deserve").

67. Foley and Rice, *First Chouteaus*, 55; DuVal, *Native Ground*, 171–172; Trudeau to [Carondelet], 18 April 1795, in *BLC*, 1:320 (quotes).

68. Carondelet to Las Casas, 31 May 1794, in *SRM*, 2:101; Carondelet to Francisco Rendon, 27 October 1794, Legajo 618, PC, translation in Box 9, folder 6, APNDC; Carl Chapman, "The Indomitable Osage in the Spanish Illinois, 1763–1804," in *The Spanish in the Mississippi Valley, 1762–1804*, ed. John Francis McDermott (Urbana: University of Illinois Press, 1974), 303; Trudeau to [Carondelet], 12 March 1795, in *BLC*, 1:320–321; Trudeau to [Carondelet], 30 August 1795, in *BLC*, 1:345; Carondelet to Carlos Howard, 26 November 1795, in *SRM*, 2:131.

69. Rollings, *Osage*, 163; Bailey, *Changes in Osage Social Organization*, 22, 59. Spanish sources refer to Pawhuska as Clermont's "uncle," which is probably a European understanding of the relation of "father's brother," which patrilineal Osages would have called "father"; Nett, "Historical Changes in the Osage Kinship System," 180; Burns, *History of the Osage People*, 53–55.

70. Trudeau to Carondelet, no. 170, 24 April 1794, Legajo 126, PC, translation in Box 9, folder 6, APNDC. Rollings argues that Clermont refused to attend the council because he resented Chouteau interference in Osage politics. His resentment of the Chouteaus seems clear—and grew in subsequent years—but if that was his motivation to skip the meeting with Carondelet, Clermont took a shortsighted view of Osage relations with Spain. Rollings, *Osage*, 175.

71. La Flesche, "Osage: Rite of the Chiefs," 68; Rollings, *Osage*, 50; Trudeau to Carondelet, no. 170, 24 April 1794, Legajo 126, PC, translation in Box 9, folder 6, APNDC ("related"); La Flesche, *Traditions of the Osage*, 34 ("symbolically"); Bailey, *Osage and the Invisible World*, 44–45; Thorne, *Many Hands of My Relations*, 94–95.

72. Trudeau to Carondelet, no. 170, 24 April 1794, Legajo 126, PC, translation in Box 9, folder 6, APNDC (quote); [Carondelet] to Trudeau, 21 May 1794, Legajo 126, PC, translation in Box 9, folder 6, APNDC.

73. John C. Ewers, "Symbols of Chiefly Authority in Spanish Louisiana," in McDermott, *Spanish in the Mississippi Valley*, 272–286; DuVal, *Native Ground*, 90.

74. Auguste Chouteau to Carondelet, 1 June 1794, Legajo 209, PC, translation in Box 9, folder 6, APNDC; Carondelet to Manuel Gayoso de Lemos, 3 June 1794, Legajo 21, PC, translation in Box 9, folder 6, APNDC ; Trudeau to Carondelet, 15 September 1794, Legajo 126, PC, translation in Box 9, folder 6, APNDC; Auguste Chouteau to Carondelet, 19 September 1794, Legajo 209, PC, translation in Box 9, folder 6, APNDC (quote).

75. Trudeau to Carondelet, 30 May 1795, in *BLC*, 1:326; Rollings, *Osage*, 200–201, 207; Charles Dehault Delassus to Marquis de Casa Calvo, 25 September 1800, in *SRM*, 2:301.

76. DuVal, *Native Ground*, 188; Trudeau to Gayoso de Lemos, 15 January 1798, in *BLC*, 2:539; Thorne, *Many Hands of My Relations*, 105; Rollings, *Osage*, 210–211; Perly Wallis to Frederick Bates, 18 December 1808, in *The Life and Papers of Frederick Bates*, ed. Thomas Maitland Marshall, 2 vols. (St. Louis: Missouri Historical Society, 1926), 2:46 (quote).

77. Henry Payet to Howard, 6 April 1797, Legajo 35, PC, translation, Box 9, folder 8, APNDC; François Vallé to Gayoso de Lemos, 13 March 1797, Legajo 204, PC, translation, Box 9, folder 8, APNDC (quotes).

78. Louis Lorimier to Delassus, 11 December 1797, Legajo 2365, PC, translation in Box 9, folder 8, APNDC; Lorimier to Delassus, 13 April 1798, Legajo 2365, PC, translation in Box 9, folder 8, APNDC; Trudeau to Gayoso de Lemos, no. 325, 23 April 1798, Legajo 49, PC, translation in Box 9, folder 8, APNDC.

79. Trudeau to Howard, 19 September 1797, Legajo 131, PC, translation in Box 9, folder 8, APNDC; Carondelet to Pierre Chouteau, 26 January 1797 (draft), Legajo 131A, PC, translation in Box 9, folder 7, APNDC ("annul"); Rollings, *Osage*, 33–34, 65; Trudeau to Gayoso de Lemos, no. 325, 23 April 1798,

Legajo 49, PC, translation in Box 9, folder 8, APNDC ("complete"); Gayoso de Lemos to Trudeau, 10 July 1798, Legajo 44, PC, translation in Box 9, folder 8, APNDC ("doubt"); Auguste Chouteau to Gayoso de Lemos, 29 November 1798, Legajo 215A, PC, translation in Box 9, folder 8, APNDC ("everything").

80. Juan Ventura Morales to Gayoso de Lemos, 29 March 1798, Legajo 91, PC, translation in Box 9, folder 8, APNDC ("useful"); Gayoso de Lemos to Mr. Chouteau, 25 April 1798 (draft), Legajo 215A, PC, translation in Box 9, folder 8, APNDC; Gayoso de Lemos to Auguste Chouteau, 4 April 1797, Chouteau Papers, SLML; [Auguste Chouteau] to [Gayoso de Lemos], 24 June 1797, *Chouteau Collection*, 2:61–62; Gayoso de Lemos to Mr. Chouteau, 25 April 1798 (draft), Legajo 215A, PC, translation in Box 9, folder 8, APNDC ("continue"); Trudeau to Gayoso de Lemos, no. 13, 17 July 1798, Legajo 49, PC, translation in Box 9, folder 8, APNDC; Gayoso de Lemos to Auguste Chouteau, 14 August 1798, Chouteau Papers, SLML; Auguste Chouteau to Gayoso de Lemos, 29 May 1799, Legajo 216, PC, translation in Box 9, folder 8, APNDC.

81. Carl J. Ekberg, *A French Aristocrat in the American West: The Shattered Dreams of De Lassus de Luzières* (Columbia: University of Missouri Press, 2010), 101.

82. Din and Nasatir, *Imperial Osages*, 314–319 (first quote on 317); DuVal, *Native Ground*, 173–174; Delassus to Casa Calvo, 25 September 1800, in *SRM*, 2:301–307; Casa Calvo to Ramón de Lopez y Angulo, 8 May 1801, in *SRM*, 2:310 (second quote); Relation of the presents given to the tribe of the Big Osages . . . , 6 September 1800, in *SRM*, 2:310–311.

83. Trudeau to Howard, 19 September 1797, Legajo 131, PC, translation in Box 9, folder 8, APNDC; DuVal, *Native Ground*, 174.

84. Delassus to Casa Calvo, 29 November 1800, in *BLC*, 2:623–624 (quotes); Casa Calvo to Delassus, 30 December 1800, in *BLC*, 2:628.

85. Memorial of Manuel Lisa, et al., to the Governor, 8 October 1801, in *BLC*, 2:646–651; Manuel Lisa, Charles Sanguinet, and Gregoire Sarpy to Juan Manuel de Salcedo, 4 June 1802, in *BLC*, 2:677–680; Delassus to Casa Calvo, 7 October 1801, in *BLC*, 2:642 ("few"). For Lisa, see Richard Edward Oglesby, *Manuel Lisa and the Opening of the Missouri Fur Trade* (Norman: University of Oklahoma Press, 1963).

86. Delassus to Casa Calvo, 7 October 1801, in *BLC*, 2:643 ("inconsistency"); Petition of Charles Sanguinet, 14 March 1801, in *BLC*, 2:631; Oglesby, *Manuel Lisa*, 19; Delassus to Salcedo, 13 May 1802, in *BLC*, 2:674–675 ("imprudent" on 674); Concession of Salcedo to Lisa, et al., 2:687–689 ("honorable" on 688). François Benoît married Marie Anne Catherine Sanguinet, the daughter of Charles. Both Benoît and Charles Sanguinet joined Lisa's Osage trading monopoly. Marriage Contract of François Benoît and Marie Anne Catherine Sanguinet, 22 November 1798, vol. 1, book 1, 33, St. Louis Archives, MHS; Concession of Salcedo to Lisa, et al., 12 June 1802, in *BLC*, 2:687–689.

87. Oglesby, *Manuel Lisa*, 24–25; Foley and Rice, *First Chouteaus*, 62–63; documents in Billion, *Annals of St. Louis*, 335–338 (quote on 338).
88. Auguste Chouteau, "Narrative."

6. Conquest

1. Charles Dehault Delassus to Marques de Casa Calvo, August 1804 (copy); James Bruff to Delassus, 25 September 1804; Delassus to Bruff, 27 September 1804; Delassus to Casa Calvo, 3 October 1804 (copy), all in Box 2, folder 7, Delassus-St. Vrain Collection, MHS; Diary of Charles Dehault Delassus, entry for 17 November 1804, Box 2, folder 8, Delassus-St. Vrain Collection, MHS ("current"); William Henry Harrison to Delassus, 2 August 1803, in *The Papers of William Henry Harrison, 1800–1815*, ed. Douglas E. Clanin, 10 microfilm reels (Indianapolis: Indiana Historical Society, 1993–1999), 1:616 ("opportunity"); hereafter cited as *Papers of WHH*. See also Delassus, untitled list, 6 March 1804, Box 2, folder 6, Delassus-St. Vrain Collection, MHS.
2. Document of Transfer of Upper Louisiana, 9 March 1804, Louisiana Purchase Transfer Collection, MHS; Amos Stoddard to William C. C. Claiborne and James Wilkinson, 26 March 1804, in "Transfer of Upper Louisiana: Papers of Captain Amos Stoddard," ed. Stella M. Drumm, *Glimpses of the Past* 2 (May–September 1935): 96 ("federal"); Stoddard to Phoebe Reade Benham, 16 June 1804, in Drumm, "Papers of Captain Amos Stoddard," 113. In Lower Louisiana, similar patterns unfolded, with U.S. officials relying on the advice and aid of francophone New Orleanians and attempting to smooth over disputes between Louisianans and Anglo-Americans; Peter J. Kastor, *The Nation's Crucible: The Louisiana Purchase and the Creation of America* (New Haven, CT: Yale University Press, 2004), 92–108; Ari Kelman, *A River and Its City: The Nature of Landscape in New Orleans* (Berkeley: University of California Press, 2003), 19–49.
3. Thomas Jefferson, *Notes on the State of Virginia* (London: John Stockdale, 1787), 274–275; Anthony F. C. Wallace, *Jefferson and the Indians: The Tragic Fate of the First Americans* (Cambridge, MA: Harvard University Press, 1999), 241–275; Nicholas Guyatt, *Bind Us Apart: How Enlightened Americans Invented Racial Segregation* (New York: Basic Books, 2016), 231–233; Robert Lee, "Accounting for Conquest: The Price of the Louisiana Purchase of Indian Country," *Journal of American History* 103 (March 2017): 921–942.
4. Thomas Jefferson to Chiefs and Warriors of the Osage Nation of Indians, 18 July 1804, microfilm M15, 2:13, Letters Sent, 1800–1824, Records of the Secretary of War Relating to Indian Affairs, Records of the Bureau of Indian Affairs, RG 75, NARA; Jefferson to Benjamin Hawkins, 18 February 1803, *Founders Online*, National Archives, last modified April 12, 2018, http://

founders.archives.gov/documents/Jefferson/01-39-02-0456; Guyatt, *Bind Us Apart,* 93–96.

5. Amos Stoddard, Address to the People of Upper Louisiana, 10 March 1804, in *Seeking St. Louis: Voices of a River City, 1670–2000,* ed. Lee Ann Sandweiss (St. Louis: Missouri Historical Society Press, 2000), 36–40 (quote on 36).

6. D. W. Meinig, *The Shaping of America: A Geographical Perspective on 500 Years of History,* 4 vols. (New Haven, CT: Yale University Press, 1986–2004), 2:15; Jay Gitlin, *The Bourgeois Frontier: French Towns, French Traders, and American Expansion* (New Haven, CT: Yale University Press, 2010), 49–52 ("people" on 49). See also Kastor, *Nation's Crucible,* 55–108.

7. Andrew R. L. Cayton, *Frontier Indiana* (Bloomington: Indiana University Press, 1996), 178–179; Hattie M. Anderson, "Missouri, 1804–1828: Peopling a Frontier State," *Missouri Historical Review* 31 (January 1937): 150.

8. Sidney H. Aronson, *Status and Kinship in the Higher Civil Service: Standards of Selection in the Administrations of John Adams, Thomas Jefferson, and Andrew Jackson* (Cambridge, MA: Harvard University Press, 1964), especially 7–14; Peter J. Kastor, *William Clark's World: Describing America in an Age of Unknowns* (New Haven, CT: Yale University Press, 2011), 132. Howard was the first cousin of Clark's brother-in-law, William Preston. For Clark-Preston-Howard connection, see Benjamin Howard to Major William Preston, 11 April 1810, folder 20, Preston Family Papers—Joyes Collection, FHS; W. P. Anderson to Major William Preston, 28 January 1811, folder 21, Preston Family Papers—Joyes Collection, FHS; James J. Holmberg, ed., *Dear Brother: Letters of William Clark to Jonathan Clark* (New Haven, CT: Yale University Press, 2002), 250n6.

9. For Harrison's early career, see Robert M. Owens, *Mr. Jefferson's Hammer: William Henry Harrison and the Origins of American Indian Policy* (Norman: University of Oklahoma Press, 2007), 3–66; Adam Jortner, *The Gods of Prophetstown: The Battle of Tippecanoe and the Holy War for the American Frontier* (New York: Oxford University Press, 2011), 38–49, 73–79.

10. William Henry Harrison to Auguste Chouteau, 20 July 1805, Chouteau Papers, SLML ("youth"); Owens, *Mr. Jefferson's Hammer,* 23; Meriwether Lewis to William Clark, 19 June 1803, in *Letters of the Lewis and Clark Expedition, with Related Documents, 1783–1854,* ed. Donald Jackson, 2nd ed., 2 vols. (Urbana: University of Illinois Press, 1978), 1:57 ("long"; spelling as in original); William Clark to Meriwether Lewis, 18 July 1803, in Jackson, *Letters of the Lewis and Clark Expedition,* 1:110–111 ("no man"; spelling as in original). Few scholars have emphasized the significance of Harrison and Clark's friendship, although Peter Kastor repeatedly notes their long-standing relationship; Kastor, *William Clark's World,* 105, 126, 138, 201, 248. For Clark and Lewis in the 1790s, see William E. Foley, *Wilderness Journey: The Life of William Clark* (Columbia: University of Missouri Press, 2004), 39–40, 46. For skepticism about the closeness of their friendship during that era, see Kastor, *William Clark's World,* 80–81.

11. Owens, *Mr. Jefferson's Hammer,* 67–98; Jortner, *Gods of Prophetstown,* 85–86; Cayton, *Frontier Indiana,* 228–35.
12. Harrison to Delassus, 2 August 1803, in Clanin, *Papers of WHH,* 1:616 (quote; emphasis in original). In March 1804, Delassus sent to Amos Stoddard a list of prominent citizens of Upper Louisiana in which he highlighted Pierre Chouteau's skill in dealing with Osage Indians; Delassus, untitled list, 6 March 1804, Box 2, folder 6, Delassus-St. Vrain Collection, MHS.
13. Harrison to Jonathan Dayton, 29 May 1804, in Clanin, *Papers of WHH,* 1:806 ("strictest"); Harrison to Jefferson, 28 May 1804, in Clanin, *Papers of WHH,* 1:1804; Harrison to Harrison Gray Otis, 29 May 1804, in Clanin, *Papers of WHH,* 1:807; Harrison to Dayton, 29 October 1804, in Clanin, *Papers of WHH,* 1:955 ("most respectable"); Harrison to Jefferson, 9 November 1804, in Clanin, *Papers of WHH,* 2:33–34 ("first citizen").
14. Delassus to Manuel de Salcedo and Marqués de Casa Calvo, 9 December 1803, in *BLC,* 2:719–720; Jefferson to Henri Peyroux, 3 July 1803, in *BLC,* 2:721. Further revealing American lack of knowledge about goings-on in Upper Louisiana, Jefferson erroneously believed that Peyroux commanded the colony.
15. Foley, *Wilderness Journey,* 42.
16. William Clark to Jonathan Clark, 25 February 1804, in Holmberg, *Dear Brother,* 77; William Clark to William Croghan, 2 May 1804, in Jackson, *Letters of the Lewis and Clark Expedition,* 1:178; William Clark to Jonathan Clark, 3 May 1804, in Holmberg, *Dear Brother,* 81; Meriwether Lewis to William Preston, 3 May 1804, in Jackson, *Letters of the Lewis and Clark Expedition,* 1:179; Meriwether Lewis, entry for 20 May 1804, in *Journals of the Lewis and Clark Expedition,* ed. Gary E. Moulton, 13 vols. (Lincoln: University of Nebraska Press), 2:240; Meriwether Lewis to Auguste Chouteau, 4 January 1804, in Jackson, *Letters of the Lewis and Clark Expedition,* 1:161–162; William Clark to Meriwether Lewis, [April 1804], in Jackson, *Letters of the Lewis and Clark Expedition,* 1:175; Meriwether Lewis to William Clark, 2 May 1804, in Jackson, *Letters of the Lewis and Clark Expedition,* 1:178; Meriwether Lewis to Jefferson, 26 March 1804, in Jackson, *Letters of the Lewis and Clark Expedition,* 1:170–171; Meriwether Lewis to Jefferson, 18 May 1804, in Jackson, *Letters of the Lewis and Clark Expedition,* 1:192–194; Meriwether Lewis to Stoddard, 16 May 1804, in Jackson, *Letters of the Lewis and Clark Expedition,* 1:189–191. The most detailed list of Indian goods that Lewis and Clark purchased from the Chouteaus contained the items given as gifts to an Osage delegation to Washington, DC, but circumstantial evidence indicates that Lewis and Clark acquired similar items for their expedition; Final Summation of Lewis's Account, 5 August 1807, in Jackson, *Letters of the Lewis and Clark Expedition,* 2:424–425. For a full account of the Chouteaus' relationship to the Corps of Discovery, see William E. Foley, "The Lewis and Clark Expedition's Silent Partners: The

Chouteau Brothers of St. Louis," *Missouri Historical Review* 77 (January 1983): 131–146.

17. Wallace, *Jefferson and the Indians,* 248–251; Treaty with the Sacs and Foxes, 3 November 1804, in *ASPIA,* 1:693–694; Appointment of Auguste Chouteau, 1 October 1804, in Clanin, *Papers of WHH,* 1:937 (Court of Common Pleas); Appointment of Auguste Chouteau, 1 October 1804, in Clanin, *Papers of WHH,* 1:938 (justice of the peace); Appointment of Charles Gratiot, et al., 1 October 1804, in Clanin, *Papers of WHH,* 1:932.

18. Harrison to Auguste Chouteau, 20 July 1805, Chouteau Papers, SLML; Harrison to Wilkinson, 7 June 1805 (extract), in *TPUS,* 13:134 (quote); William E. Foley and C. David Rice, *The First Chouteaus: River Barons of Early St. Louis* (Urbana: University of Illinois Press, 1983), 115; Wilkinson to Henry Dearborn 27 June 1805, in *TPUS,* 13:144; Wilkinson to Dearborn, 31 December 1805, in *TPUS,* 13:370.

19. William E. Foley, *The Genesis of Missouri: From Wilderness Outpost to Statehood* (Columbia: University of Missouri Press, 1989), 143.

20. Antoine Soulard to the Board of Land Commissioners, 2 May 1806, in *TPUS,* 13:533–534; Foley, *Genesis of Missouri,* 171; Stoddard to Dearborn, 10 January 1804, in *ASPPL,* 1:177; Amos Stoddard, *Sketches, Historical and Descriptive, of Louisiana* (Philadelphia: Matthew Carey, 1812), 253–258 (quote on 253); Stephen Aron, *American Confluence: The Missouri Frontier from Borderland to Border State* (Bloomington: Indiana University Press, 2006), 123–124.

21. Thomas Jefferson, Draft of Constitutional Amendment Incorporating Louisiana Territory into the United States, 1803, Series 1: General Correspondence, 1651–1827, Thomas Jefferson Papers, LC (Hereafter cited as Jefferson Papers, LC). Available at http://hdl.loc.gov/loc.mss/mtj .mtjbib000856; Meriwether Lewis to Jefferson, 28 December 1803, in Jackson, *Letters of the Lewis and Clark Expedition,* 1:148; Foley, *Genesis of Missouri,* 170–172.

22. Foley, *Genesis of Missouri,* 172–173; William C. Carr to John Breckinridge, 24 December 1805, in *TPUS,* 13:323 ("abominable"); Albert Gallatin to Jefferson, 12 February 1806, Jefferson Papers, LC, available at http://hdl.loc .gov/loc.mss/mtj.mtjbib015861 ("united"); Jefferson to Gallatin, 22 March 1806, Jefferson Papers, LC, available at http://hdl.loc.gov/loc.mss/mtj .mtjbib016009 ("improper" and "error"); Gallatin to Jefferson, 15 March 1806, Jefferson Papers, LC, available at http://hdl.loc.gov/loc.mss/mtj .mtjbib015979; Breckinridge to Jefferson, 22 March 1806, Jefferson Papers, LC, available at http://hdl.loc.gov/loc.mss/mtj.mtjbib016007; Harrison to Jared Mansfield, 19 April 1806, in *TPUS,* 13:492; Mansfield to Gallatin, 15 June 1806, in *TPUS,* 13:519.

23. Foley, *Genesis of Missouri,* 179; Gallatin to the Board of Land Commissioners, 13 February 1807, in *TPUS,* 14:97; Carr to Breckinridge, 24 December 1805, in *TPUS,* 13:324 ("land"); John B. C. Lucas to Gallatin, 22 December 1806,

in *TPUS*, 14:53 ("speculators"); Eric Sandweiss, *St. Louis: The Evolution of an American Urban Landscape* (Philadelphia: Temple University Press, 2001), 34–35; Auguste Chouteau to Wilkinson, n.d. [1806], vol. 3, James Wilkinson Papers, Chicago History Museum, Chicago, IL ("benefits" and "guardian").

24. Meriwether Lewis to William Clark, 18 February 1804, in Jackson, *Letters of the Lewis and Clark Expedition*, 1:168; Final Summation of Lewis's Account, 5 August 1807, in Jackson, *Letters of the Lewis and Clark Expedition*, 2:424–425; Lewis's Account through 1805, [1807], in Jackson, *Letters of the Lewis and Clark Expedition*, 2:419–424; Auguste Chouteau to Jefferson, 19 November 1804, Jefferson Papers, LC, available at http://hdl.loc.gov/loc.mss/mtj.mtjbib014018; Pierre Chouteau to Jefferson, 2 mars 1805, Jefferson Papers, LC, available at http://hdl.loc.gov/loc.mss/mtj.mtjbib014422; Pierre Chouteau to Jefferson, 1 December 1805, Jefferson Papers, LC, available at http://hdl.loc.gov/loc.mss/mtj.mtjbib015348; Jefferson to James Madison, 17 May 1814, *Founders Online*, National Archives, last modified 1 February 2018, http://founders.archives.gov/documents/Madison/03-07-02-0439 (quotes).

25. Gallatin to Jefferson, 20 August 1804, Jefferson Papers, LC, available at http://hdl.loc.gov/loc.mss/mtj.mtjbib013746 (quotes); Dearborn to Pierre Chouteau, 17 July 1804, in *TPUS*, 13:31–33.

26. Foley, *Genesis of Missouri*, 165, 179–181; William Clark, entry for 23 September 1806, in Moulton, *Journals of the Lewis and Clark Expedition*, 8:371 (quote).

27. Thomas Jefferson, Notes on Speech of White Hair, Great Chief of the Osages, 12 July 1804, Jefferson Papers, LC, available at http://hdl.loc.gov/loc.mss/mtj.mtjbib013623. See also Jefferson to William Dunbar, 17 July 1804, Jefferson Papers, LC, available at http://hdl.loc.gov/loc.mss/mtj.mtjbib013639; Jefferson to Chiefs and Warriors of the Osage Nation of Indians, 18 July 1804, 2:14.

28. Report of James B. Wilkinson to James Wilkinson, 6 April 1807, in *The Journals of Zebulon Montgomery Pike, with Letters and Related Documents*, ed. Donald Jackson, 2 vols. (Norman: University of Oklahoma Press, 1966), 2:12. "Tuttasuggy" and "Nezuma" are Anglicizations of the Osage names, Ta-Des-K'o-E and Ni-Zhiu-Mo'n-I'n. Nezuma also sometimes appears as "Nichu Malli" in American documents; John Joseph Mathews, *The Osages: Children of the Middle Waters* (Norman: University of Oklahoma Press, 1961), 360, 391; Treaty with the Osage, 1808, in *Indian Affairs: Laws and Treaties*, comp. Charles G. Kappler, 5 vols. (Washington, DC: Government Printing Office, 1904–1941), 2:97.

29. Dearborn to Pierre Chouteau, 12 May 1806, in *TPUS*, 13:510; Dearborn to Pierre Chouteau, 7 March 1807, in *TPUS*, 14:107–108 (quote).

30. David Andrew Nichols, *Engines of Diplomacy; Indian Trading Factories and the Negotiation of American Empire* (Chapel Hill: University of North Carolina Press, 2016), especially 1–11, 97. This account of the Missouri Fur Company

draws primarily on Richard Edward Oglesby, *Manuel Lisa and the Opening of the Missouri Fur Trade* (Norman: University of Oklahoma Press, 1963), 65–149; Foley and Rice, *First Chouteaus,* 144–146; Foley, *Wilderness Journey,* 177–181; Wallace, *Jefferson and the Indians,* 264–268.

31. Dearborn to William Clark, 9 March 1807, in *TPUS,* 14:108–109; William Clark to Dearborn, 1 June 1807, in *TPUS,* 14:126–127; Nathaniel Pryor to William Clark, 16 October 1807, in Jackson, *Letters of the Lewis and Clark Expedition,* 2:432–438; William Clark to Dearborn, 3 December 1807, in *TPUS,* 14:153; Agreement for Return of the Mandan Chief, 24 February 1809, in Jackson, *Letters of the Lewis and Clark Expedition,* 2:446–450; Meriwether Lewis to Dearborn, 7 March 1809, in *TPUS,* 2:450–451.

32. William Clark to Jonathan Clark, 22, 24 November 1808, in Holmberg, *Dear Brother,* 167–168. In 1808, Manuel Lisa traded buffalo robes to Fitzhugh, and in 1811, Clark called on his Louisville relatives to supply trade goods; Account of Manuel Lisa, November 1808–April 1809, Fitzhugh & Rose Ledger, 1807–1810, Charles Thruston Collection, FHS; entry for Manuel Lisa, 1 November 1808, Fitzhugh & Rose Journal, 1808–1813, Charles Thruston Collection, FHS; William Clark to Edmund Clark and John Hite Clark, 1 March 1811, in Holmberg, *Dear Brother,* 291–293.

33. Meriwether Lewis to Pierre Chouteau, 8 June 1809, in Pierre Chouteau to William Eustis, 14 December 1809, in *TPUS,* 14:348–351; Meriwether Lewis to Eustis, 18 August 1809, in *TPUS,* 14:292; Pierre Chouteau to Eustis, 14 December 1809, in *TPUS,* 14:344–346; Reuben Lewis to Meriwether Lewis, 21 April 1810, Meriwether Lewis Collection, MHS; Tanis C. Thorne, *The Many Hands of My Relations: French and Indians on the Lower Missouri* (Columbia: University of Missouri Press, 1996), 107–108; Pierre Chouteau to Eustis, 12 April 1810, Pierre Chouteau Letterbook, in *The Papers of the St. Louis Fur Trade,* part 2, *Fur Company Ledgers and Account Books,* ed. William R. Swagerty, 23 microfilm reels (Bethesda, MD: University Publications of America, 1991), 22: no frame (quote); Meriwether Lewis to Eustis, 13 May 1809, in Jackson, *Letters of the Lewis and Clark Expedition,* 2:451; Meriwether Lewis to Eustis, 18 August 1809, in *TPUS,* 14:291–292.

34. Oglesby, *Manuel Lisa,* 85–98; Manuel Lisa to Pierre Chouteau, 14 February 1810, Reel 7, f. 63, *The Papers of the St. Louis Fur Trade,* part 1, *The Chouteau Collection, 1752–1925,* ed. William R. Swagerty, 40 microfilm reels (Bethesda, MD: University Publications of America, 1991), 7–63 (quote; hereafter cited as *Chouteau Collection*); Reuben Lewis to Meriwether Lewis, 21 April 1810, Meriwether Lewis Collection, MHS.

35. William Clark to Pierre Chouteau, 20 February 1810, in *Chouteau Collection,* 7:71; Meriwether Lewis to Eustis, 18 August 1809, in *TPUS,* 14:291 (quote).

36. Meriwether Lewis to Eustis, 18 August 1809, in *TPUS,* 14: 292–293; Pierre Chouteau, Jr., to Eustis, 1 September 1809, in *TPUS,* 14:318 (quote). In June 1810, William Eustis apologized for "any inconvenience" Chouteau suffered due to the controversy over the Missouri Fur Company and its

expenses; Eustis to Pierre Chouteau, 16 June 1810, microfilm M15, 3:32, Letters Sent, 1800–1824, Records of the Secretary of War Relating to Indian Affairs, Records of the Bureau of Indian Affairs, RG 75, NARA.

37. Foley and Rice, *First Chouteaus*, 174–181; Gitlin, *Bourgeois Frontier*, 68–138.

38. Jefferson to Chiefs and Warriors of the Osage Nation of Indians, 18 July 1804, 2:13–14 ("one family" on 13); Dearborn to Pierre Chouteau, 17 July 1804, in *TPUS*, 13:31–33; Jefferson to Claiborne, 7 July 1804, Jefferson Papers, LC, available at http://hdl.loc.gov/loc.mss/mtj.mtjbib013610 ("plan").

39. Richard White, *The Middle Ground: Indians, Empires and Republics in the Great Lakes Region, 1650–1815* (Cambridge: Cambridge University Press, 1991), 413–468; Gregory Evans Dowd, *A Spirited Resistance: The North American Indian Struggle for Unity, 1745–1815* (Baltimore: Johns Hopkins University Press, 1992), 90–115; David Andrew Nichols, *Red Gentlemen and White Savages: Indians, Federalists, and the Search for Order on the American Frontier* (Charlottesville: University of Virginia Press, 2008), 128–189; Jortner, *Gods of Prophetstown*, 51–71; Guyatt, *Bind Us Apart*, 45.

40. Henry Knox to George Washington, 7 July 1789, in *ASPIA*, 1:53–54 (quotes on 53). For a recent overview of the ideology behind "civilization" policy, see Guyatt, *Bind Us Apart*, 43–50.

41. Bernard W. Sheehan, *Seeds of Extinction: Jeffersonian Philanthropy and the American Indian* (Chapel Hill: University of North Carolina Press, 1973), 15–44, 89–116; Wallace, *Jefferson and the Indians*, 161–205.

42. Knox to Washington, 7 July 1789, in *ASPIA*, 1:53 ("obligations" and "considerations"); Jefferson to James Jackson, 16 February 1803, in *The Papers of Thomas Jefferson*, ed. Julian P. Boyd et al., 43 vols. (Princeton, NJ: Princeton University Press, 1950–), 39:541 ("preservation").

43. The historiography on Native responses to "civilization" policy is best developed for the nations of the South. For example, see Theda Perdue, *Cherokee Women: Gender and Culture Change, 1700–1835* (Lincoln: University of Nebraska Press, 1998); Claudio Saunt, *A New Order of Things: Property, Power, and the Transformation of the Creek Indians, 1733–1816* (Cambridge: Cambridge University Press, 1999); Perdue, *"Mixed-Blood" Indians: Racial Construction in the Early South* (Athens: University of Georgia Press, 2003); Alexandra Harmon, *Rich Indians: Native People and the Problem of Wealth in American History* (Chapel Hill: University of North Carolina Press, 2010), 92–132. For nations in the midcontinent, see Dowd, *Spirited Resistance*, 114–122, 148–166; Jortner, *Gods of Prophetstown*, 87–91; Stephen Warren, *The Shawnees and Their Neighbors, 1795–1870* (Urbana: University of Illinois Press, 2005), 43–68; Willard Hughes Rollings, *Unaffected by the Gospel: Osage Resistance to the Christian Invasion, 1673–1906: A Cultural Victory* (Albuquerque: University of New Mexico Press, 2004), 1–20, 45–113.

44. Wallace, *Jefferson and the Indians*, 206–240; Jefferson to Harrison, 27 February 1803, in *Messages and Letters of William Henry Harrison*, ed. Logan Esarey, 2 vols. (Indianapolis: Indiana Historical Commission, 1922), 1:70–71,

73 ("incorporate" and "glad" on 71); Thomas Jefferson, "Hints on the subject of Indian boundaries, suggested for consideration," 29 December 1802, in Boyd et al., *Papers of Thomas Jefferson*, 39:231–233.

45. Wilkinson to Jefferson, 6 November 1805, in *TPUS*, 13:266.

46. Zebulon M. Pike, "A dissertation on . . . Louisiana," January 1808, in Jackson, *Journals of Zebulon Montgomery Pike*, 2:32–33.

47. Report of James B. Wilkinson to James Wilkinson, 6 April 1807, 2:13; Bruff to Wilkinson, 12 March 1805, in *TPUS*, 13:102; Speech of Jean Baptiste Ducoigne to Gomo, 2 March 1805, in Bruff to Wilkinson, 12 March 1805, in *TPUS*, 13:103–104; Speech of Jean Baptiste Ducoigne to Sagueenawk, 2 March 1805, in Bruff to Wilkinson, 12 March 1805, in *TPUS*, 13:104; Pike, "A dissertation on . . . Louisiana," 2:33; William Clark to Dearborn, 3 December 1807, in *TPUS*, 14:154; Jefferson to Harrison, 16 January 1806, in Esarey, *Messages and Letters of William Henry Harrison*, 1:186 ("river").

48. Anderson, "Missouri, 1804–1828," 150–151; Bruff to Wilkinson, 29 September 1804 (copy), in Wilkinson to Dearborn, 2 November 1804, in *TPUS*, 13:60; Frederick L. Bates to Meriwether Lewis, [28] April 1807, in *The Life and Papers of Frederick Bates*, ed. Thomas Maitland Marshall, 2 vols. (St. Louis: Missouri Historical Society, 1926), 1:105–106; Frederick Bates to Richard Bates, 24 March 1808, in Marshall, *Life and Papers of Frederick Bates*, 1:316–317; Meriwether Lewis to Dearborn, 1 July 1808, in *TPUS*, 14:196–97; Willard H. Rollings, *The Osage: An Ethnohistorical Study of Hegemony on the Prairie-Plains* (Columbia: University of Missouri Press, 1995), 222; Kathleen DuVal, *The Native Ground: Indians and Colonists in the Heart of the Continent* (Philadelphia: University of Pennsylvania Press, 2006), 200–201; Pike, "A dissertation on . . . Louisiana," 2:32–33. See also Aron, *American Confluence*, 111; John Mack Faragher, "'More Motley than Mackinaw': From Ethnic Mixing to Ethnic Cleansing on the Frontier of the Lower Missouri, 1783–1833," in *Contact Points: American Frontiers from the Mohawk Valley to the Mississippi, 1750–1830*, ed. Andrew R. L. Cayton and Fredrika J. Teute (Chapel Hill: University of North Carolina Press, 1998), 316.

49. DuVal, *Native Ground*, 200–201; Meriwether Lewis to Dearborn, 1 July 1808, in *TPUS*, 14:197–198.

50. Journal of William Clark, 14 September 1808, in *Westward with Dragoons: The Journal of William Clark on His Expedition to Establish Fort Osage, August 25 to September 22, 1808*, ed. Kate L. Gregg (Fulton, MO: Ovid Bell, 1937), 40–41; William Clark's Treaty with the Osages, 14 September 1808, in Gregg, *Westward with Dragoons*, 64–68; William Clark to Dearborn, 23 September 1808, in *TPUS*, 14:224–28; William Clark to Jonathan Clark, 5 October 1808, in Holmberg, *Dear Brother*, 154.

51. Rollings, *Osage*, 224–25; DuVal, *Native Ground*, 201–204; William Clark to Dearborn, 23 September 1808, in *TPUS*, 14:227 (quote).

52. Meriwether Lewis to Pierre Chouteau, 3 October 1808, in *TPUS*, 14:230.

53. Pierre Chouteau to Delassus, 19 November 1799, in *ASPPL*, 6:838; Statement of Delassus, 20 November 1799, in *ASPPL*, 6:838–39 (quote); Concession of Pierre Chouteau, 19 March 1792, in *ASPPL*, 6:839; William Clark to Dearborn, 2 December 1808, in *TPUS*, 14:243–44; Treaty with the Osages, 1808, in Kappler, *Indian Affairs*, 2:95–98; Meriwether Lewis to Jefferson, 15 December 1808, in *ASPIA*, 1:767. The grant was for 30,000 arpents. An arpent was equal to 0.845 acres in Louisiana surveying; Donald A. Wilson, *Interpreting Land Records*, 2nd ed. (New York: Wiley, 2015), 40.

54. Meriwether Lewis to Dearborn, 1 July 1808, in *TPUS*, 14:196; George C. Sibley to Samuel H. Sibley, 16 September 1808, Box 1, folder 5, George C. Sibley Papers, MHS (quote).

55. Meriwether Lewis to Dearborn, 1 July 1808, in *TPUS*, 14:196 (quote); William Clark to Dearborn, 30 April 1809; E. B. Clemson et al. to Eustis, 16 July 1812, in *TPUS*, 14:587; DuVal, *Native Ground*, 205.

56. George C. Sibley Diary, entries for 4 May, 5 May, 7 May 1811, Box 1, folder 8, George C. Sibley Papers, MHS.

57. Nichols, *Engines of Diplomacy*, 98–99; Clemson et al. to Eustis, 16 July 1812, in *TPUS*, 14:588 (quote).

58. Clemson et al. to Eustis, 16 July 1812, in *TPUS*, 14:588 ("continually" and "object"; spellings as in original); George Sibley to William Clark, 28 November 1813, in *TPUS*, 14:712–714 ("bones" and Big Soldier quotes on 714; emphasis in original).

59. Anthony F. C. Wallace notes that the United States focused on pushing Indians away from rivers in treaty negotiations, but he emphasizes it as a military strategy to encircle eastern Indians; Wallace, *Jefferson and the Indians*, 239.

60. James Monroe to Auguste Chouteau, 11 March 1815, Chouteau Papers, SLML; Monroe to William Clark, 11 March 1815, Box 12, folder 7, Clark Family Collection, MHS; *Missouri Gazette*, 23 November 1816; Monroe to William Clark, 25 March 1815, in *ASPIA*, 2:6; Monroe to John Mason, 27 March 1815, in *ASPIA*, 2:7; Stan Hoig, *The Chouteaus: First Family of the Fur Trade* (Albuquerque: University of New Mexico Press, 2008), appendix C, 261–263.

61. Guyatt, *Bind Us Apart*, especially 281–305 (Morse quote on 283); Reginald Horsman, *Race and Manifest Destiny: The Origins of American Racial Anglo-Saxonism* (Cambridge, MA: Harvard University Press, 1981), especially 103–138, 189–207 (Clay quote on 198).

62. Anderson, "Missouri, 1804–1828," 151; Rufus Babcock, *Forty Years of Pioneer Life: Memoir of John Mason Peck, D.D.* (Philadelphia: American Baptist Publication Society, 1864), 146; Proclamation of Meriwether Lewis, 6 April 1809, in *TPUS*, 14:261; Eustis to William Clark, 31 May 1811, in *TPUS*, 14:452; Howard to Eustis, 14 June 1812, in *TPUS*, 14:568; William H. Crawford to William Clark, 5 February 1816, in *TPUS*, 15:113–114; James McFarlane to Meriwether Lewis, 11 December 1808, in *TPUS*, 14:267 ("white people").

63. William Clark to Crawford, 30 September 1816, in *TPUS*, 15:177 ("little value"); David Musick and William Parker to William Clark, 1 August 1816, in Clark to Crawford, 30 September 1816, in *TPUS*, 15:180–182; Petition of Inhabitants of Missouri Territory, n.d., in Clark to Crawford, 30 September 1816, in *TPUS*, 15:182–183; William Rector to Josiah Meigs, 25 November 1816, in *TPUS*, 15:210 ("precedents"); Meigs to Crawford, 14 May 1821, in *TPUS*, 15:726; Z. to Joseph Charless, in *Missouri Gazette*, 10 February 1816 ("settlements" and "wrongfully," emphasis in the original).

64. Warren, *Shawnees and Their Neighbors*, 78–79, 81–82; Nicolas de Finiels, *An Account of Upper Louisiana*, ed. Carl J. Ekberg and William E. Foley, trans. Ekberg (Columbia: University of Missouri Press, 1989), 34; John P. Bowes, *Exiles and Pioneers: Eastern Indians in the Trans-Mississippi West* (New York: Cambridge University Press, 2007), 32; Faragher, "More Motley than Mackinaw," 321–322; Resolutions of the Missouri Territorial Assembly, 24 January 1817, in *TPUS*, 15:235 ("persuits"). For an example of the United States continuing to offer farming implements, see Treaty with the Osage, 1825, in Kappler, *Indian Affairs*, 2:218.

65. Warren, *Shawnees and Their Neighbors*, 81–82 ("behavior" on 82); Faragher, "More Motley than Mackinaw," 321–322 ("good cabin" on 321).

66. Treaty with the Kickapoo, 1819, in Kappler, *Indian Affairs*, 2:183 (quote); Pascal Cerré to Auguste Chouteau and Benjamin Stephenson, 6 December 1819 (transcript), Gabriel Cerré Papers, MHS; Abstract of expenditures by William Clark . . . , 1 January–31 December 1820, in *ASPIA*, 2:290; Treaty with the Osage, 2 June 1825, in Kappler, *Indian Affairs*, 2:217–221. This treaty ceded all lands between the Kansas and Red Rivers and west to "a line to be drawn from the head sources of the Kansas, Southwardly through the Rock Saline." Two other nations, Quapaws and Kaws, signed treaties surrendering claims to portions of this land; Charles C. Royce, comp., *Indian Land Cessions in the United States*, in *Eighteenth Annual Report of the Bureau of American Ethnology*, part 2 (Washington, DC: Government Printing Office, 1899), 688, 708, plate 21, plate 26. Between 1810 and 1820, the population of Missouri jumped from 19,783 to 66,586, with about 41,000 Americans moving to the territory between 1814 and 1820. By 1830, the state's population exceeded 140,000; Anderson, "Missouri, 1804–1828," 150–151, 180.

67. William Clark Account with B. Pratte & Co., 5 July 1825; Box 13, folder 12, Clark Family Collection, MHS; William Clark Account with B. Pratte & Co., 1 January–30 May 1826, Box 13, folder 13, Clark Family Collection, MHS; William Clark Account with B. Pratte & Co., 4 August 1827, Box 13, folder 15, Clark Family Collection, MHS. On Bernard Pratte & Co., see Gitlin, *Bourgeois Frontier*, 129–130. James and George Hancock Kennerly, Clark's relatives through his wife, provided another $3,600 worth of goods. Abstract of expenditures by William Clark . . . , 1 January–31 December 1820, in *ASPIA*, 2:294–297. These numbers only concern the transactions listed as "Presents." Probably reflecting immediate need, Clark relied on a more diverse group of businessmen to supply food to deported Indians and

to render services such as ferrying, blacksmithing, and gun repair, although
the Chouteaus and their kin frequently appear in those accounts as well;
Abstract of expenditures, 1 January–31 December 1820, in *ASPIA*, 2:289–
294. See also William Clark to George Graham, 18 December 1822, in
ASPIA, 2:536.

68. Babcock, *Forty Years of Pioneer Life*, 146. For an example of Chouteau land
claims, see "No. 13—Auguste Chouteau, claiming 7,056 arpents," in *ASPPL*,
6:738–739; *Choteau [sic] et al. vs. The United States*, 21 February 1835, in
ASPPL, 7:730–731; *The Devisees of Auguste Choteau [sic] vs. The United States*,
21 February 1835, in *ASPPL*, 7:731–732. For immigration up Missouri River,
see Foley, *Genesis of Missouri*, 238–259; R. Douglas Hurt, *Agriculture and
Slavery in Missouri's Little Dixie* (Columbia: University of Missouri Press,
1992), 1–81; Diane Mutti Burke, *On Slavery's Border: Missouri's Small-
Slaveholding Households, 1815–1865* (Athens: University of Georgia Press,
2010), 17–51.

69. Foley, *Genesis of Missouri*, 247–253; "No. 83—Peter Chouteau, Sr., claiming
30,000 arpents," in *ASPPL*, 6:838–839; Foley and Rice, *First Chouteaus*, 180;
Richard M. Clokey, *William H. Ashley: Enterprise and Politics in the Trans-
Mississippi West* (Norman: University of Oklahoma Press, 1980), 37–38,
247–248, 270–272; Foley and Rice, *First Chouteaus*, 201.

70. Treaty with the Osage, 1825, in Kappler, *Indian Affairs*, 2:218–219 ("reserva-
tions" on 218); Thorne, *Many Hands of My Relations*, 141–143; William Least
Heat-Moon and James K. Wallace, introduction to *An Osage Journey to
Europe, 1827–1830: Three French Accounts* (Norman: University of Oklahoma
Press, 2013), 9; William Clark to James Barbour, 11 June 1825, in Ratified
Treaty No. 126, microfilm T494, microfilm reel 1, no frame, Documents
Relating to the Negotiation of Ratified and Unratified Treaties with Various
Indian Tribes, 1801–1869, Records of the Bureau of Indian Affairs, RG 75,
NARA ("good effect"). Two daughters of an Osage woman and William
Sherley "Old Bill" Williams, an American missionary-turned-trader among
the Osages, also received plots of land in the 1825 treaty. As that case indicates,
American fur traders and trappers continued to marry Indian women well into
the nineteenth century, but their numbers were dwarfed by the number of
Americans who moved west to farm and who married other colonists; Treaty
with the Osage, 1825, in Kappler, *Indian Affairs*, 2:219; Alpheus H. Favour, *Old
Bill Williams, Mountain Man* (1936; repr., Norman: University of Oklahoma
Press, 1962), 44–45; Mathews, *The Osages*, 526; William R. Swagerty, "Mar-
riage and Settlement Patterns of Rocky Mountain Trappers and Traders,"
Western Histoical Quarterly 11 (April 1980): 164–168.

71. William Clark to Barbour, 11 June 1825, in Ratified Treaty No. 126; Theda
Perdue and Michael D. Green, *The Cherokee Nation and the Trail of Tears* (New
York: Penguin, 2007); Christina Snyder, *Great Crossings: Indians, Settlers, and
Slaves in the Age of Jackson* (New York: Oxford University Press, 2017), 154–155;
John Bowes, *Land Too Good for Indians: Northern Indian Removal* (Norman:

University of Oklahoma Press, 2016), 170; Meinig, *Shaping of America,* 2:93, 99; Ethan Allen Hitchcock, *A Traveler in Indian Territory: The Journal of Ethan Allen Hitchcock, late Major-General in the United States Army,* ed. Grant Foreman (1930; paperback ed., Norman: University of Oklahoma Press, 1996), 56 (quote). Foreman and others following his lead have believed that this statement referred to the Treaty of 1808, but Hitchcock's description of the provisions more closely resembles those of the Treaty of 1825. Likewise, the land Foreman says was ceded in the Treaty of 1808 was actually sold in 1825.
72. Anderson, "Missouri, 1804–1828," 150, 180.
73. Foley and Rice, *First Chouteaus,* 196–197; Gitlin, *Bourgeois Frontier,* 48, 69–70; Nichols, *Engines of Diplomacy,* 160–166.
74. For development of the idea of Indian Territory, see James P. Ronda, "'We Have a Country': Race, Geography, and the Invention of Indian Territory," *Journal of the Early Republic* 19 (Winter 1999): 739–755.

Conclusion

1. Edmund Flagg, *The Far West; or, A Tour beyond the Mountains,* 2 vols. (New York: Harper and Brothers, 1838), 1:125, 128, 159, 165–167.
2. Flagg, *Far West,* 1:161.
3. For narratives that erase Native peoples, see Jean M. O'Brien, *Firsting and Lasting: Writing Indians Out of Existence in New England* (Minneapolis: University of Minnesota Press, 2010). For American theories on mounds, see Randall H. McGuire, "Archaeology and the First Americans," *American Anthropologist* 94 (December 1992): especially 820–821; Anthony F. C. Wallace, *Jefferson and the Indians: The Tragic Fate of the First Americans* (Cambridge, MA: Harvard University Press, 1999), 130–160; Matthew Denis, "Patriotic Remains: Bones of Contention in the Early Republic," in *Mortal Remains: Death in Early America,* ed. Nancy Isenberg and Andrew Burstein (Philadelphia: University of Pennsylvania Press, 2003), 137–141; Steven Conn, *History's Shadow: Native Americans and Historical Consciousness in the Nineteenth Century* (Chicago: University of Chicago Press, 2004), 116–153; "Correspondence between Noah Webster, esq., and the rev. Ezra Stiles . . . , respecting the fortifications in the western country," *American Museum* 6 (July 1790): 27–30; Noah Webster to Ezra Stiles, 15 December 1787, *American Museum* 6 (August 1790): 136–141; "Correspondence between Noah Webster, esq., and the rev. Ezra Stiles . . . , respecting the fortifications in the western country," *American Museum* 6 (September 1790): 232–234; "Letter from mr. Noah Webster, esq., to the rev. dr. Stiles . . . , on the remains of the fortifications in the western country," *American Museum* 7 (June 1790): 323–328; Noah Webster to Matthew Carey, 3 September 1789, *American Museum* 8 (July 1790): 11–12. George Rogers Clark read Webster's hypotheses and responded with a lengthy letter based on his conversations

with Kaskaskia Indians and credited the mounds to the ancestors of the Illinois Indians. Matthew Carey, the editor of the *American Museum*, did not publish it. Clark to Matthew Carey, [ca. 1790], in *The Life of George Rogers Clark*, by James Alton James (1928; repr., New York: Greenwood, 1969), 495–499. For Prince Madoc, see John Evans and James Mackey, "Indian Tribes," [ca. 1804], Box 11, folder 9, Clark Family Collection, Missouri History Museum Archives, St. Louis, MO. On Madoc, see Amos Stoddard, *Sketches, Historical and Descriptive, of Louisiana* (Philadelphia: Matthew Carey, 1812), 464–488; David Williams, "John Evans' Strange Journey: Part 1. The Welsh Indians," *American Historical Review* 54 (January 1949): 277–295; Gwyn A. Williams, *Madoc: The Making of a Myth* (London: Eyre Methuen, 1979); Derrick Spradlin, "'GOD ne'er Brings to pass Such Things for Nought': Empire and Prince Madoc of Wales in Eighteenth-Century America," *Early American Literature* 44 (2009): 39–70; Elizabeth A. Fenn, *Encounters at the Heart of the World: A History of the Mandan People* (New York: Hill and Wang, 2014), 184–185.

4. Washington Hood, "Field Notes on Eastern Boundaries of Indian Land," entry for 28 July 1839, Series 1, Box 1, folder 6, Washington Hood Papers, Western Americana Collection, Beinecke Rare Book and Manuscript Library, Yale University, New Haven, CT; D. W. Meinig, *The Shaping of America: A Geographical Perspective on 500 Years of History*, 4 vols. (New Haven, CT: Yale University Press, 1986–2004), 2:93, 98; Treaty with the Kaskaskia, etc., 1832, in *Indian Affairs: Laws and Treaties*, comp. Charles G. Kappler, 5 vols. (Washington, DC: Government Printing Office, 1904–1941), 2:376; Treaty with the Kaskaskia, Peoria, etc., 1854, in Kappler, *Indian Affairs*, 2:636–40; C. C. Trowbridge, "Account of Some of the Traditions, Manners and Customs of the Twaatwaa or Miami Indians," 4–5, 21, Box 15, vol. 1, C. C. Trowbridge Papers, Burton Historical Collection, Detroit Public Library, Detroit, MI. Since the 1760s, Peorias lived west of the Mississippi River "separate and apart" from the rest of the Illinois Nation, and in the early nineteenth century, they lived near present-day Arrow Rock, Missouri, where Fort Osage briefly moved during the War of 1812; Treaty with the Peoria, etc., 1818, in Kappler, *Indian Affairs*, 2:165.

5. Jay Gitlin, *The Bourgeois Frontier: French Towns, French Traders, and American Expansion* (New Haven, CT: Yale University Press, 2010), 72, 74–75, 94, 130, 218n32 ("several millions" on 94, "*cher* cousin" on 130); Anne F. Hyde, *Empires, Nations, and Families: A History of the North American West, 1800–1860* (Lincoln: University of Nebraska Press, 2011), 475–476.

6. Hiram Martin Chittenden, *History of Early Steamboat Navigation on the Missouri River*, 2 vols. (New York: Francis P. Harper, 1903), 1:139 (quote); Stan Hoig, *The Chouteaus: First Family of the Fur Trade* (Albuquerque: University of New Mexico Press, 2008), 168–170; Gitlin, *Bourgeois Frontier*, 72, 98.

7. Gitlin, *Bourgeois Frontier*, 114–116; David Lavender, *Bent's Fort* (New York: Doubleday, 1954); Ari Kelman, *A Misplaced Massacre: Struggling over the*

Memory of Sand Creek (Cambridge, MA: Harvard University Press, 2013), 16, 33. On economic ties between St. Louis and New Mexico during this era, see Andrés Reséndez, *Changing National Identities at the Frontier: Texas and New Mexico, 1800–1850* (Cambridge: Cambridge University Press, 2005), 93–123.

8. Barton H. Barbour, *Fort Union and the Upper Missouri Fur Trade* (Norman: University of Oklahoma Press, 2001), 29–34; Hoig, *Chouteaus*, 186–190; Gitlin, *Bourgeois Frontier*, 75–76.

9. Flagg, *Far West*, 1:135; Louis C. Hunter, *Steamboats on the Western Rivers: An Economic and Technological History* (Cambridge, MA: Harvard University Press, 1949); Erik F. Haites, James Mak, and Gary M. Walton, *Western River Transportation: The Era of Early Development, 1810–1860* (Baltimore: Johns Hopkins University Press, 1975); Ari Kelman, *A River and Its City: The Nature of Landscape in New Orleans* (Berkeley: University of California Press, 2003), 50–68; Robert H. Gudmestad, *Steamboats and the Rise of the Cotton Kingdom* (Baton Rouge: Louisiana State University Press, 2011).

ACKNOWLEDGMENTS

I have been fortunate to work with a series of generous mentors. At the University of California, Davis, I had the pleasure of learning from an incredible group of scholars of early America and the American West. Throughout this project, Alan Taylor has offered encouragement and guidance and always pushed me to write and argue more clearly. Ari Kelman offered invaluable advice on all matters related to my scholarship and the profession more broadly. Andrés Reséndez carefully read my work and shared his insights about borderlands. Thanks also to Louis Warren, Lorena Oropeza, Ellen Hartigan-O'Connor, Ian Campbell, and Chuck Walker. When I was an undergraduate at the University of Louisville, Thomas Mackey, Tracy K'Meyer, Glenn Crothers, and Michael Johmann first taught me what it meant to be a historian and a mentor.

I also owe debts to brilliant, generous scholars across the profession. Kathleen Duval, Jay Gitlin, Lucy Murphy, Josh Reid, Brett Rushforth, and Susan Sleeper-Smith offered valuable comments and guidance on early versions of my work at meetings of the American Society for Ethnohistory, the Omohundro Institute for Early American History and Culture, the Organization of American Historians, the Southern Historical Association, and the Western History Association, and at the Filson Historical Society's conference "The Long Struggle for the Ohio Valley, 1750–1815." Members of the Kentucky Early American Seminar, the University of North Carolina's American Indian and Indigenous Studies Seminar, Indiana University's American History Seminar, and the Center for Eighteenth-Century Studies, also at IU, commented on drafts of chapters. I have also been lucky enough to call on friends in the broader community of early American history and archaeology for their insights. Many thanks to John Bowes, Kathryn Braund, Christian Crouch, Alejandra Dubcovsky, Alexandre Dubé, Liz Ellis, Robbie Ethridge, Robb Haberman, Jonathan Hancock, Rob Harper, Scott Heerman, Brian Hosmer, Katie Johnston, Karen Marrero, Darrell Meadows, Bob Morrissey, Theda Perdue, Kelly Ryan, Jennifer Spear, and Sophie White for their generosity and counsel. Jodie O'Gorman was kind enough to share her unpublished research on the Morton Village site. David Costa helped me with Illinois-language sources and, where possible, brought the spellings into conformity with current usage. Michael McDonnell took the time to offer incisive comments on a complete early draft of the manuscript. Two anonymous readers provided thoughtful, valuable feedback.

Support from the History Departments at UC Davis, Indiana University, and Penn State, as well as Penn State's College of Liberal Arts, made this project possible. The Center for French Colonial Studies / Centre pour l'étude du pays des Illinois funded a trip to the Archives Nationales d'Outre-Mer. Fellowships from the Huntington Library, the Newberry Library, the Filson Historical Society, the Bancroft Library at UC Berkeley, the William L. Clements Library at the University of Michigan, and the John Carter Brown Library at Brown University supported my research. I thank the archivists, librarians, and curators at those institutions as well as at the American Antiquarian Society, Archives Nationales d'Outre-Mer, Chicago History Museum Research Center, Historic New Orleans Collection, Illinois History and Lincoln Collections at the University of Illinois at Urbana-Champaign, Illinois State Archaeological Survey, Library of Congress Manuscripts Division, Missouri History Museum Archives, National Anthropological Archives, National Archives in Washington, DC, and St. Louis Mercantile Library. Jim Akerman, Jaime Bourassa, Jennifer Brathovde, Charles Brown, Brian Dunnigan, Paul Erickson, Jeffrey Flannery, Vincent Golden, David Halpin, Lauren Hewes, Bruce Kirby, Adam Minakowksi, Alisa Monheim, Pat Morris, Dennis Northcott, Kim Nusco, Mary Frances Ronan, Neil Safier, Jaeda Snow, Heather Szafran, Robert Ticknor, and Olga Tsapina went out of their way to make sure I found everything I needed. Special thanks to my former colleagues at the Filson Historical Society: Joan Brennan, Jennie Cole, Heather Fox, Jim Holmberg, Sarah-Jane Poindexter, and Robin Wallace. The wonderful interlibrary-loan librarians at UC Davis, IU, and Penn State tracked down materials from across North America.

Thanks also to my editor, Kathleen McDermott, who has been an unflagging champion of this project, and to the whole crew at Harvard University

Press, who turned my manuscript into a book. I could not ask for a better cartographer than Isabelle Lewis.

Along the path from Louisville to State College, I have benefited from communities of exceptional colleagues and friends. For more than a dozen years, Matt Stanley has been a comrade in academia as well as on cemetery-centric road trips. At Davis, I quickly fell in with Chelsea Bell, Mark Dries, Theresa Dries, Mary Mendoza, and Jordan Scavo—an irreplaceable group of friends. In Bloomington, Cara Caddoo, Claire Caffery, Josh Caffery, Brian Gilley, Caroline Gilley, Henry Glassie, Jason McGraw, Michelle Moyd, Dina Okamoto, Ougie Pak, Chris Pelton, Pravina Shukla, Scot Wright, and Ellen Wu made up a wonderful community that emphasized a well-rounded life of brilliance, fun, and pie. In the final stages of this project, I was welcomed to central Pennsylvania by David Atwill, Jade Atwill, Cathleen Cahill, John Eicher, Michael Kulikowski, Zach Morgan, Andrew Sandoval-Strauss, Ellen Stroud, Julia Whicker, and Cynthia Young. Writing sessions with Jyoti Balachandran helped keep me on track during the last months of revision. Many others deserve thanks as well: Tim Baumann, John Bodnar, Kalani Craig, Ray DeMallie, Nancy Gallman, Wendy Gamber, Melissa Gismondi, Amy Greenberg, Peter Guardino, Rajbir Judge, Rita Koryan, Brandon Layton, Pedro Machado, Bryan McDonald, Brenda Medina-Hernandez, Bill Monaghan, A. J. Morgan, Doug Parks, Kaya Şahin, Eric Sandweiss, Jonathan Schlesinger, and David Stenner.

Finally, I dedicate this book to my family. My parents, Dan and Linda, have offered endless encouragement and support and have always pushed me to read, think, and explore. That my earliest memory is walking up Monk's Mound on a family trip reveals, as much as anything, how I ended up a historian. My brother and sister-in-law, Stephen and Kendal, have been great friends. My wife, Christina, deserves more thanks than I can express here. She inspires me as a partner, a friend, and a historian.

CREDITS

Fig. I.1: J. C. Wild, "Northeast View of St. Louis from the Illinois Shore," ca. 1840. Courtesy of the Missouri Historical Society, St. Louis.

Fig. 1.1: Louis Nicolas, "Capitaine de La Nation des Illinois . . . ," in *Codex Canadensis*, 5, ink on paper, overall: 13¼ × 8½ in. (33.7 × 21.6 cm), GM 4726.7, Gilcrease Museum, Tulsa, Oklahoma.

Fig. 1.2: From Baron Lahontan, *New Voyages to North-America*, vol. 2 (London: J. Brindley, 1735). Courtesy of the John Carter Brown Library at Brown University.

Fig. 3.1: Collection Moreau de Saint-Mery, Série F3, vol. 290, fol. 12. Courtesy of the Archives nationales d'outre-mer, Aix-en-Provence, France.

Fig. 3.2: Alexandre de Batz, "Desseins de sauvages de plusieurs nations," 1735. Gift of the Estate of Belle J. Bushnell, 1941. Courtesy the Peabody Museum of Archaeology and Ethnology, Harvard University, PM# 41-72-10/20.

Fig. 5.1: From *Encyclopedia of the History of St. Louis*, vol. 1 (New York: Southern History Company, 1898). Courtesy of the Missouri Historical Society, St. Louis.

Fig. 5.2: "Payouska (Pawhuska)—Chief of the Great Osages," drawing by Charles Balthazar Julien Fevret de Saint-Memin, ca. 1806; black chalk and charcoal with stumping white chalk, pastel, and graphite on pink prepared paper, 23 × 17⅛ inches. Purchase, Elizabeth DeMilt Fund, New-York Historical Society, 1860.92. Photography © New-York Historical Society.

Fig. 6.1:   Courtesy of Independence National Historical Park.

Fig. 6.2:   "Mo-Hon-Go, Osage Woman." From Thomas L. McKenney and
              James Hall, *History of the Indian Tribes of North America,* vol. 1
              (London: Campbell and Burns, 1837–1838). Courtesy of the Library
              of Congress, LC-DIG-pga-07534.

Fig. C.1:   Courtesy of the Missouri Historical Society, St. Louis.

Fig. C.2:   Courtesy of the Missouri Historical Society, St. Louis.

INDEX

Index entries in italics indicate an illustration.

www.ingramcontent.com/pod-product-compliance
Lightning Source LLC
Chambersburg PA
CBHW021829090426

42811CB00032B/2079/J